Anil Shah
The Violence of Financial Inclusion

Political Science | 180

This open access publication has been enabled by the support of Pollux (Fachinformationsdienst Politikwissenschaft

and a collaborative network of academic libraries for the promotion of the Open Access transformation in the Social Sciences and Humanities (transcript Open Library Politikwissenschaft 2025):

Vollsponsoren: Technische Universität Braunschweig | Technische Universität Berlin | Carl von Ossietzky-Universität Oldenburg | Goethe-Universität Frankfurt am Main | Gottfried Wilhelm Leibniz Bibliothek – Niedersächsische Landesbibliothek | TIB – Leibniz-Informationszentrum Technik und Naturwissenschaften und Universitätsbibliothek | Humboldt-Universität zu Berlin | Institut für Auslandsbeziehungen (IfA) | Justus-Liebig-Universität Gießen | Universitätsbibliothek Eichstätt-Ingolstadt | Landesbibliothek Oldenburg | Ludwig-Maximilians-Universität München | Max Planck Digital Library (MPDL) | Ruhr-Universität Bochum | Universitäts- und Landesbibliothek Darmstadt | Universitäts- und Landesbibliothek Düsseldorf | Universitäts- und Landesbibliothek Münster | Universitäts- und Stadtbibliothek Köln | Universitätsbibliothek Bielefeld | Universitätsbibliothek der Bauhaus-Universität Weimar | Universitätsbibliothek Bayreuth | Universitätsbibliothek Duisburg-Essen | Universitätsbibliothek Erfurt | Universitätsbibliothek der FernUniversität in Hagen | Universitätsbibliothek Kassel | Universitätsbibliothek Kiel (CAU) | Universitätsbibliothek Leipzig | Universitätsbibliothek Mannheim | Universitätsbibliothek Osnabrück | Universitätsbibliothek Potsdam | Universitätsbibliothek der RPTU Kaiserslautern-Landau | Universitätsbibliothek St. Gallen | Universitätsbibliothek Tübingen | Universitätsbibliothek Vechta | Zentralbibliothek Zürich ZHAW Zürcher Hochschule für Angewandte Wissenschaften, Hochschulbibliothek
Sponsoring Light: Bundesministerium der Verteidigung | Staatsbibliothek zu Berlin | Freie Universität Berlin – Universitätsbibliothek | Universitätsbibliothek Klagenfurt
Mikrosponsoring: Leibniz-Institut für Europäische Geschichte | Stiftung Wissenschaft und Politik (SWP) – Deutsches Institut für Internationale Politik und Sicherheit | Universitätsbibliothek Regensburg | Pädagogische Hochschule Freiburg

Anil Shah

The Violence of Financial Inclusion

Chronic Indebtedness as Class Oppression in Modern India

[transcript]

This work was submitted as dissertation to the Faculty of Social Sciences at the University of Kassel under the title "Fractured Lives. Regimes of Re/Productive Finance in Modern India". It was reviewed by Prof. Dr. Christoph Scherrer and Prof. Dr. Gargi Bhattarchayya. Date of thesis defence: 23rd April 2024.

Bibliographic information published by the Deutsche Nationalbibliothek
The Deutsche Nationalbibliothek lists this publication in the Deutsche Nationalbibliografie; detailed bibliographic data are available in the Internet at https://dnb.dnb.de

transcript Verlag | Hermannstraße 26 | D-33602 Bielefeld | live@transcript-verlag.de

Cover design: Maria Arndt
Cover image: Anil Shah
Printing: Elanders Waiblingen GmbH, Waiblingen
https://doi.org/10.14361/9783839480649
Print-ISBN: 978-3-8376-8064-5 | PDF-ISBN: 978-3-8394-8064-9
ISSN of series: 2702-9050 | eISSN of series: 2702-9069

Contents

Part II: Foundations for Researching Fractured Lives

Part III: Regimes of Re/Productive Finance in Modern India

Part IV: Beyond India's Silicon Valley: Precarious Migrant Workers and Re/Productive Finance in Bengaluru

Appendix

Abbreviations

AFI	Alliance for Financial Inclusion
ASHA	Accredited Social Health Worker
BBMP	Bruhat Bengaluru Mahangara Palike
BMGF	Bill and Melinda Gates Foundation
BMIC	Bengaluru-Mysuru Infrastructure Corridor
BJP	Bharatiya Janata Party
CGAP	Consultative Group to Assist the Poor
CSR	Corporate Social Responsibility
DFI	Development Finance Institution
EIC	(British) East India Company
EPF	Employees Provident Fund
ESI	Employees State Insurance
FDI	Foreign Direct Investment
GATWU	Garment and Textile Workers Union
GDP	Gross Domestic Product
GLU	Global Labour Union
GoI	Government of India
GPFI	Global Partnership for Financial Inclusion
HYV	High-Yielding Variety
IFC	International Finance Corporation
IMF	International Monetary Fund
INC	Indian National Congress
IPO	Initial Public Offering
IRDP	Integrated Rural Development Programme
JLG	Joint-Liability Group
KSDB	Karnataka Slum Development Board
MFI	Microfinance Institution

MDG	Millennium Development Goals
MFA	Multi Fibre Agreement
NABARD	National Bank for Agriculture and Rural Development
NBFC	Non-Bank Financial Corporation
NDA	National Democratic Alliance
NGO	Non-Governmental Organisation
NIEO	New International Economic Order
NRLM	National Rural Livelihood Mission
NREGA	National Rural Employment Guarantee Scheme
OBC	Other Backward Caste
ODA	Official Development Aid
OOPS	Out-Of-Pocket Spending
PACS	Primary Agricultural Credit Society
PDS	Public Distribution System
PSB	Public Sector Bank
PSL	Priority Sector Lending
PMJDY	Pradhan Mantri Jan Dhan Yoyana
RBI	Reserve Bank of India
SC	Scheduled Caste
SDG	Sustainable Development Goals
SFB	Small Finance Bank
SGSY	Swarnajayanti Grameen Swarojgar Yojana
SHG	Self-Help Group
SHG-BPL	Self-Help Group Bank-Linkage Programme
SIDBI	Small Industries Development Bank India
ST	Scheduled Tribes
SWAN	Stranded Workers Action Network
USAID	United States Agency for International Development
UPA	United Progressive Alliance
WB	World Bank
WTO	World Trade Organisation

Acknowledgements

This research started with a relatively narrow focus on studying the changing dynamics of access to credit in urbanising Bengaluru. Over the years, it evolved into something much bigger. To begin with, I would like to express my gratitude to all those migrant workers and cultivators in and around Bengaluru who shared their life stories and helped me better understand the intricate mechanics of chronic indebtedness amongst subaltern classes. Moreover, I owe many thanks to all the other interviewees from diverse civil society organisations, microfinance institutions, and the Reserve Bank of India.

During my field research, I was hosted by the Institute of Social and Economic Change (ISEC) in Bengaluru, which provided a stimulating academic and social environment to develop this research. Meenakshi Rajeev, Vidya Puttur Sadashiva, Devraj R., Vinaya S., Jina Sharma and Pallav Karmakar supported my fieldwork in various ways, including facilitating contacts, navigating the slums of Bengaluru, translating interviews, and providing valuable exchange and support.

Christoph Scherrer has accompanied me on this journey as main supervisor with great patience, critical feedback on presentations and draft chapters and the faith that this research will be completed eventually. I am grateful for Gargi Bhattacharyya acting as my second reviewer and accompanying me in the final steps of the project. I benefitted greatly from teaching in the M.A. Global Political Economy and Development and working with colleagues at the Faculty of Social Sciences at the University of Kassel. The continuous debates with inspiring colleagues, fellow PhD researchers and students sharpened my critical thinking and broadened my horizons. Despite being a beacon for critical thinking, the university as a workplace is shaped by a toxic mix of feudal and neoliberal logic. Therefore, I am very grateful for having colleagues and comrades who organise and protest against precarious working conditions in German academia in our union-backed campaign *Uni Kassel Unbefristet*. Being part of this struggle has been essential for my motivation to continue working, teaching, and researching at the university.

Without the support, care, and encouragement of many people around me, this work would probably never have been completed. I would like to particularly thank all friends and colleagues who read draft chapters at different stages of the process and provided valuable feedback and encouragement, especially Frauke Banse, Jannis Eicker, Anne Engelhardt, Simone Claar, Jenny Simon, Nina Baghery, Franziska Müller, Christa Wichterich, Pedro Salgado, Jahnavi Rao, Nomaswazi Mthombeni, Pavlos Roufos, and Eleonora Roldán Mendívil. Moreover, Temitope Alarape and Virendra Shah have significantly supported the final manuscript preparation phase. Thank you all!

Finally, I am tremendously thankful for my entire family's indefinite and sustained support. My parents have backed me over the years in many ways. Without my partner Sophia, this work would have never been finished, and I would probably not be sane anymore. And Sammie and Yuna, born along this journey, remind me daily what matters in life.

Introduction: Fractured Lives

> "Financial inclusion has got so many facets, but the basic facet is be counted, be included, be somebody, have the dignity of your identity"
> –*Ajay Banga (Ted 2021)*

> "Clients of microfinance institutions are poor city dwellers housed in slums or squatter settlements, often living in appalling overcrowded settings, lacking access to basic services such as health. [...] Many of them are women, poorly trained and playing dual roles of provider and caregiver. These poor people are more exposed to the threats of contamination, bad sanitation, and disease than the rest of the population. When disaster strikes, in the form of inflation, earthquakes, or other outside forces, they are the most exposed."
> –*Maria Otero (2000)*

In early 2023, US president Joe Biden nominated Ajay Banga as World Bank Group president with much acclaim. The step was an attempt to preserve the institution's legitimacy amidst multiple crises. The Bank's overarching aim to eradicate poverty by 2030 is nowhere near reached, especially after the COVID-19 pandemic and escalating geopolitical tensions (World Bank 2024). Cumulating indebtedness and bankruptcy of governments, firms, and households worldwide are producing a vicious interlocking dynamic which may plunge the world economy into another great recession (World Bank 2022). Climate change is wreaking havoc in many parts of the world, even if the former World Bank president, David Malpass, publicly denied the existence of it (Markotoff 2023). And, the legitimacy of the US-dominated World Bank is increasingly challenged by alternative institutions, mainly promoted by the People's Republic of China.[1] What is more compelling is that the World Bank has received heavy criticism spanning decades for undemocratic governance, investing in large-scale projects fostering fossil fuels, forced displacements, and loss of biodiversity.[2] At such a "critical moment in history" (The White House 2023), a change of face at the top of the World Bank that signals change on the horizon seems urgent.

The Identity of Financial Inclusion

What qualifies Ajay Banga, the Indo-American business tycoon, with a fortune of more than US$ 200 million, to lead the world's largest multilateral development bank? Of course, Banga has a track record of successfully managing large corporations, that is, profitably. He spent his entire career working for some of the largest transnational corporations in the world, including Nestlé, PepsiCo, Citigroup, and Mastercard. During his time as President and Chief Executive Offer (CEO) at Mastercard, from 2010 to 2020, the company's revenue tripled, net income increased sixfold, and the market cap sky-rocketed more than ten times from below US$ 30 billion to more than US$ 300 billion (Harvard Business Review 2021). Banga never tires of emphasising that this success was only possible through broad-based partnerships and alliances within the private sector and across the public-private-divide.[3] Such an approach is akin to the relatively recent paradigm shift in development finance, which the World Bank has heavily promoted.

At a time when reaching the Sustainable Development Goals (SDGs) is a long way off from being achieved, the World Bank must redefine its strategy to tackle both escalating global poverty and climate change. In recent years it has attempted to do so by surpassing the foreign aid model of development finance, where donor countries contributed Official Development Assistance (ODA), to embrace the role of business, venture capital, sovereign wealth funds and other non-state sources to finance the SDGs (World Bank 2017). This shift in development finance seeks to leverage billions of ODA to catalyse trillions of private funds through increased

1 For instance, the Chinese Development Bank (CDB) overtook the World Bank as largest development finance institution in the past decade, and the BRICS (Brazil, Russia, India, China and South Africa) have created the New Development Bank (NDB) to underline their positioning within contemporary global governance, challenging the Western hegemony that has characterised the Bretton Woods institutions since their creation in the 1940s.

2 For a detailed and critical assessment of the World Bank, see Toussaint (2023).

3 One of the key quotes in the mission statement of the Mastercard Center for Inclusive Growth is: "Remember this rule of thumb: If you want to go wide, go with government. If you want to go deep, go with NGOs and academic institutions. If you want to go fast, go with the private sector. And if you want to go far, you must go together" (Mastercard 2023).

blended finance, including debt and equity finance of public-private partnerships (PPPs) and de-risking of investments through state-backed guarantees and other incentives (Bayliss and Van Waeyenberge 2018; Mawdsley 2018; Perry 2021). Consequently, the new development finance paradigm is aligned with the dynamics and accumulation strategies of financial institutions to turn all areas of life (housing, transport, education, health care, pensions etc.) into investable and profitable assets (Bonizzi, Churchill, and Guevara 2021; Hunter and Murray 2019; Langley 2020; Musthaq 2021). The so-called (Post-)Washington Consensus has promoted and entrenched market-based development since the 1980s through disciplinary lending and other mechanisms. Yet, this has become increasingly redefined along the needs and opportunities of financial market actors in the 2010s. Daniela Gabor (2021) has coined the term "Wall Street Consensus" to highlight this shift and the centrality of financial markets for global governance and development.

Financial inclusion, broadly understood as widened access to credit and other financial services to previously unbanked populations, is critical to this agenda (Bateman, Blankenburg, and Kozul-Wright 2019; Mader 2018; Soederberg 2013).[4] After all, the World Bank strives for a world free from poverty, and banking the global poor is presented as the foremost strategy to achieve this ambitious goal (United Nations 2015a; World Bank 2014). During his time at Mastercard, Ajay Banga has pioneered public-private partnerships in financial inclusion, including the Mastercard Center for Inclusive Growth and many high-level international fora associated with the UN and G20. One of the flagship programmes to banking millions of unbanked was rolled out in South Africa. In this case, Mastercard collaborated with the South African government and the transnational corporation Net1, of whom World Bank's International Finance Corporation (IFC) was the single largest shareholder.[5] The aim was to digitise the operations of the South African Social Security Agency (SASSA), using Mastercard debit cards for welfare grant distribution to 10.5 million South Africans, ostensibly making the system cheaper for the state and safer for recipients (Bond et al. 2023; Torkelson 2021).

Mastercard and others portrayed the programme as a significant success in giving underbanked populations an identity. As Banga reasons in an interview during the COVID-19 pandemic, providing people with a (financial) identity is vital to the agenda of financial inclusion:

4 Financial inclusion is usually understood as delivering an array of commercial financial products, including credit, insurance, payments, and others, from mainstream financial players. The role of microloans is paramount to this agenda and throughout the book financial inclusion will be explored primarily through the lens of microcredit.

5 To be precise, Cash Payment Services (CPS), a subsidiary of Net1 UEPS Technologies, was responsible for digitising the grant systems. CPS was eventually liquidated in 2020, and the head company was renamed Lesaka Technologies.

> "Financial inclusion or exclusion is an underlying social problem that dates back to well before this [pandemic]. [..]. Of seven billion people in the world, close to two billion are either underbanked or unbanked in some way [...] Most of these people do not have a formal identity that they had received or got from their government [...] to show that they exist in the system. Their opinions don't count. They don't get counted in census very often, they don't get counted for their opinion of what government should be doing, they get left out, they are locked out" (TED 2021, 1:24-2:57).

Giving people an identity and including them in the digital (financial) economy might seem reasonable. In reality, however, the initiative is an example *par excellence* for the structural violence of financial inclusion (Ansari 2022; Gronbach 2023; Torkelson 2021). Not only did millions of low-income households receive an identity. The private service provider Net1 accessed this identity, that is, the personal and biometric information, including the complete history of income and spending patterns of more than 10 million South Africans, 85 per cent of whom are black and coloured women (Torkelson 2021, 68). While Mastercard issued millions of debit cards, Net1 used its positioning as a monopoly service provider to build a dense network of subsidiary companies that would offer customised financial inclusion products, including loans, insurance, airtime and electricity, and payments for grantees (Bond et al. 2023). Significantly, grantees typically used borrowed money for reproductive needs (food, clothing, rent) to make ends meet and not for entrepreneurial activities (Torkelson 2021, 68). The consequences were disastrous:

> "There was no possibility for grantees to default on their debts because repayments were deducted automatically, and no longer depended on consumer behavior. As repayments to Net1 whittled away the promised value of social entitlements, grantees turned to other formal and informal lenders, many of whom were also repaid automatically through Net1's same debit-order powers" (Bond et al. 2023)

Put differently, social security was collateralised for profit-oriented lending in the name of financial inclusion.[6] In this regard, critical scholars have long highlighted how "poverty finance" is essentially extending the frontiers of financialised capital accumulation to incorporate the masses in the global South, profiting from their misery, rather than providing any structural route to improve their livelihoods (Bernards 2022; Jafri 2019; Kar 2018; Mader 2015; Rankin 2013; Soederberg 2015).

What is striking about this case and the new president of the World Bank is the vast chasm between the rhetoric and practice of development finance, specifically

6 Similar dynamics are also visible in other contexts, like Brazil (Lavinas 2018), or India, as will be discussed in Part IV.

financial inclusion. Of course, buzzwords like empowerment, improvement, recognition, inclusion, and representation, to name but a few, have always been fundamental to gloss over the contradictions between Development (big "D"), understood as an institutional ensemble of interventionist initiatives, and capitalist development (small "d"), understood as a dynamic and highly uneven process of creation and destruction that underpin global capital accumulation (Hart 2010; Mawdsley and Taggart 2022). The span between the benevolent discourse of financial inclusion and the structural violence that respective populations experienced in the case described above is simply outrageous, but not exceptional. We must broaden our understanding of microfinance and financial inclusion to understand why it is not. And I suggest that the chasm between benevolent rhetoric and structural violence is an excellent place to start this. Despite much talk of identity and dignity, financial inclusion policies operate on binary accounts of banked/unbanked, served/underserved and formal/informal with little regard for living realities. It is based on the fantasy of finance as something devoid of power relations and systemic violence, something neutral that can be put to work to do good things in the world.

However, reducing the real-world constraints and challenges of a landless migrant labourer in an Indian metropolis, a subsistence farmer in rural Kenya, or a vegetable cart seller in peri-urban Mexico to the problem of accessing credit from commercial banks, microfinance institutions (MFIs) or fintechs, the discourse of financial inclusion flattens their histories, social embeddedness, and identities into a lucid but superficial binary. This flattening underpins the chasm between benevolent rhetoric and structural violence of financial inclusion. Essentially, the talk of a level-playing field through widening access to financial services primarily levels the lived realities into nothing more than a necessary customer. As Lamia Karim has shown, the development discourse creates specific forms in which people with low incomes are known and represented in particular ways, which make microfinance appear as the only appropriate policy to confront their problems, ultimately silencing the poor in the name of representing them (Karim 2011, 162).

Confronting the idealising and homogenising discourse of financial inclusion, this book investigates the fractured lives of the unbanked in modern India. Fractured lives must be understood as a metaphor highlighting the uneven nature of (financialised) capital accumulation, working through different segmentations and fragmentations that run through the social body, the working class, and individual lives. These fractures result from the structural violence of racial finance capitalism and simultaneously form the condition upon which financial accumulation rests. As such, fractured lives are the antidote to the flattening discourse of financial inclusion. Ultimately, by investigating the governance of access to credit through these fractures, we can comprehend the vast chasm between the benevolent rhetoric and the structural violence of financial inclusion. Before further specifying the research focus, objective and question, the following part will briefly map the academic literature on microfinance and financial inclusion to explain how this work fits into contemporary academic debates.

Mapping Debates on Microfinance and Financial Inclusion

The literature on microfinance and financial inclusion is vast and includes contributions from numerous disciplines, focussing on various scales and aspects of the phenomenon. What this section seeks to do, is to map two opposite poles, outlining critical narratives that frame microfinance in fundamentally different ways. Mapping these debates is important in making sense of how this research's framing fits into the overall academic and public discussion.

Decent Microfinance: From Entrepreneurial Spirits to Existential Safety Nets

Until the mid-2000s, affirmative literature endorsed the entrepreneurial spirits of poor households. The hopes that access to credit would allow those at the "bottom of the pyramid" (Prahalad 2005) to turn their "dead capital" (de Soto 2001) into a powerful lever to escape poverty and profit triggered the first wave of microfinance hype. Hulme and Mosley's (1996) assertion that, compared with other "potential weapons against poverty", like social safety nets, employment-generation programmes or investment in primary health and education, "credit is the only one which places a tangible capital asset in the hands of the poor" (Hulme and Mosley 1996, 203; see also Lopatta and Tchikov 2015) continues to underpin contemporary reasoning, at least in part.

The relevance of women in this regard can hardly be overemphasised. Ever since Muhammad Yunus' group-lending model has shown that poverty lending could be profitable even without demanding collateral if loans are given to women who vouch for one another and who, in case of default, are collectively disciplined (Yunus 2007; Yunus and Jolis 1998), microfinance research became absorbed by the linkages between income-generating microloans and women empowerment. It was argued that borrowing to women empowers them through a better role in household decision-making, independent access to financial resources, increase in freedom of mobility and more flexible household consumption (Ghosh and Vinod 2017; Pitt, Khandker, and Cartwright 2006; Pitt and Khandker 1998; Swamy 2014). The perspective of microfinance as a critical tool to empower poor women remains consensual amongst the international development community and reiterates in most official reports and publications.

However, the discourse on the entrepreneurial spirits of poor women has become fragile. The narrative of employment-generating microloans was debunked by several studies, showing that many microbusinesses were not viable in the medium run and often displaced others, thus not creating any net jobs (Banerjee and Duflo 2011, 343; Bateman 2019; for India see Guérin, Espallier, and Venkatasubramanian 2015). Moreover, a meta-analysis of 32 systematic reviews finds that "[t]he effects of financial services on core economic and social poverty indicators are small and inconsistent" (Duvendack and Mader 2020, 595). Although this review suggests financial inclusion might generally improve women's empowerment positively, it also acknowledges that definitions and measurements of empowerment remain ambiguous (see also Armendáriz and Roome 2006). Moreover, a rich body of studies from various disciplines and regions of the world has emerged in recent years. This has shown that even in cases of specific improvements in women's life, microloans often reinforce gender roles and hierarchies, undermine solidary relations by introducing competitive logic, create a novel form of gendered dependencies, and therefore contribute to deepening gender inequalities (Guérin, Kumar, and Agier 2013; Kabeer 2001; Keating, Rasmussen, and Rishi 2010; Wichterich 2017; Young 2010a; Zulfiqar 2017).

Despite the role of entrepreneurial spirits reappearing in academic contributions to date, the key rationale for financial inclusion has thus moved on to broaden the scope of the power of finance to a realm beyond entrepreneurship: to the world of basic needs.[7] Rupert Scofield, CEO and co-founder of FINCA International, a major impact investor, has argued that in contrast to how the sector envisioned entrepreneurial microfinance in the 1980s today "to adequately address the myriad of challenges the poor face, we need solutions in other sectors that more directly tackle the problems of energy, sanitation, education, health and agriculture" (Scofield 2018). This expansion is necessary to expand the market of poverty finance because a focus on vulnerability "will enable the impact of microfinance to stretch further down the income scale" (Mosley 2001, 130). After all, the livelihoods of poor households are characterised by low and irregular incomes, unpredictable expenses, higher vulnerability to external shocks, and fewer coping strategies (Morduch 1999; Otero 2000; Pitt and Khandker 2002). Both past income (savings) and future income (debt) are crucial to manage basic needs and to cope with existential risks. Since low-income households usually don't have notable savings, extending loans is understood as a purposeful business. The authors of the landmark study *Portfolios of the Poor* have summarised the shift from entrepreneurial to reproductive finance as follows:

7 The UN Secretary-General's Special Advocate for Inclusive Finance for Development (UNSGSA), Queen Máxima of the Netherlands, also advertises financial inclusion in a similar way: "A purpose of financial inclusion is to help people and communities meet basic needs such as nutritious food, clean water, housing, education, healthcare, and more" (UNSGSA n.d.).

> "A fundamental but easily overlooked lesson from the diaries is that the demand for microcredit extends well beyond the need for just microenterprise credit. The poor households in the study seek loans for a multitude of uses besides business investment: to cope with emergencies, acquire household assets, pay schooling and health fees, and, in general, to better manage complicated lives" (Collins et al. 2009, 25)

In economics jargon, this rationale is usually called "consumption smoothing" (Cull and Morduch 2018; Demirgüc-Kunt, Klapper, and Singer 2018). Additionally, there are also numerous other fancy catchphrases, including 'financial risk management', 'vulnerability management', 'mitigating unparticipating shocks', 'financial resilience', and 'financial wellness' (Islam and Maitra 2012; Kuri and Laha 2011; Scofield 2018). The World Bank's *New Microfinance Handbook* (2013) also recognises the fundamental uncertainty that poor households experience throughout different stages of their life:

> "Sons migrate in search of more income; young mothers manage child-birth expenses, health care, and nutrition; parents struggle to educate their children. Widows are threatened with loss of land and other assets to their husbands' relatives. Elderly clients face acute vulnerabilities, including loss of productivity due to deteriorating health, physical immobility, and the loss of family support as children become independent and develop their own financial commitments [...]. These changes result in the need for different financial services at different life-cycle stages." (Ledgerwood and Gibson, 2013, 16ff.)

Notably, endorsing this all-encompassing role of finance for a (poor) people's well-being diminishes any separation between working capital and consumption credit, which has dominated economics for decades (see e.g. Ray 1998, 531). From this perspective, *eliminating* poverty has taken a backseat. Since child-birth expenses, health care, nutrition and other purposes listed above are not income-generating, the broadened notion of financial inclusion does not have a strong vision of eradicating poverty. At best, it emphasises poverty *management* understood as providing further financial means to manage survival. Practically, the extension of commercial financial services is labelled as "democratisation of the financial system", understanding (micro-)credit as a "fundamental human right" (Meyer 2017; Ramesh 2007; Robinson 2001, 25; Yunus 2010). However, this new human right to credit, creepingly dominates or even replaces other human rights, such as the right to food, housing, or decent work. In this context, microfinance represents a "new mode of development intervention, one that displaced governments as central actors and turns to market-mechanisms to deliver services through a range of institutions that integrate social and financial goals" (Cull and Morduch 2018, 550).

In sum, the dominant literature has turned from focusing on entrepreneurial finance as a measure to eradicate poverty to a broadened understanding of financial services for basic (consumption) needs. This change acknowledges that a substantial part of the global population is exposed to a chronic subsistence crisis. Engaging with this problem, the affirmative literature generally suggests that widened access to credit and other financial services is a sensible development intervention. Inclusive finance thus primarily aims at creating and maintaining a "surrogate safety net" (Viola, Shi, and Murthy 2013) for poor households across the globe. However, when reviewing this rationale, many questions are begging for answers: Why exactly do these people need a *surrogate* safety net instead of a regular one? What hinders people from accessing essential services such as health care or education? Why should a loan that has to be continuously paid off, including interest and fees attached, be an adequate *emergency* relief tool?

In engaging with some of these questions, critiques of the decent finance narrative have suggested we must not only ask who gains access to financial services but also ask who accesses gain from expanding financial services into organising daily life (Martin 2002, 162).

Predatory Microfinance: From Local Neoliberalism to the Financialisation of Poverty

The affirmative literature of decent finance takes the necessity of demand for credit for granted. Focusing on supply, it highlights the opportunities for extended financial services, particularly credit, for low-income households. In contrast, the critical literature emphasises the conditions upon which the demand for credit comes into being not because of household decision-making but due to dynamic shifts in the broader political economy. In this context, the overarching common ground of the latter emphasises the contradictory and predatory aspects of financial inclusion.

Milford Bateman's (2010) influential book *Why doesn't microfinance work?* suggests that the depoliticisation of Development occurs through what he dubs 'local neoliberalism'. Instead of discussing, implementing, and researching new avenues for state intervention, or collective organisations in unions, or social movements confronting the unevenness of capitalist development, microfinance maintains that individual entrepreneurship is poor people's only route out of poverty. In effect, microfinance renders policy proposals like land redistribution or tax reforms unintelligible. It promotes financial liberalisation and privatisation and re-organises government departments and other state institutions in line with private sector interests (Bateman 2010, 160ff.).

Likewise, feminist scholars have emphasised how microfinance renders poverty, gender hierarchies and other inequalities as problems that must be overcome *individually* rather than as structural and political issues (Kabeer 2001; Karim 2011; Wichterich 2017). In this process, the notion of women empowerment has become emptied of significance, essentially conflating the term with gender equity in *access* to finance, regardless of the consequences (Young 2010a; Zulfiqar 2017). Rather than a random by-product, this ignorance is promoted and entrenched by "financial literacy" programmes for unbanked populations, which obfuscate "the systemic and structural dimensions of debt, financial hardship, and the patterns of financialisation, thus reaffirming a neoliberal trend to privatise social problems" (Haiven 2017, 348). As such, microfinance may be understood as a political tool of depoliticisation, "dampening and undermining [of] resistance to neoliberal development policies" (see also Bateman and Chang 2012; Weber 2014, 545). Consequently, microfinance shifts collective costs and associated risks to those in need. The emphasis on household's rational behaviour promotes the individualisation of risk and responsibility but renders the irrationality of markets and the material interests of commercialised poverty finance invisible (Lazzarato 2009; Rankin 2013; Wichterich 2012).

Although it might not comprise of large chunks of the international development budget, as compared to infrastructure financing, for example, "microfinance is everywhere; it exists in the sub-terrain of almost everything in development" (Roy 2010, 22). In this regard, the democratisation of capital, as emphasised by microfinance proponents, is deeply entangled with the financialisation of development, as Ananya Roy (2010) elaborates in her widely acclaimed book *Poverty Capital*. Essentially, the globalisation of microfinance, heavily promoted by the World Bank, expresses the "Washington consensus on poverty", ultimately constructing poor households across the globe as a profitable asset class (Roy 2010, 50ff.). This is not meant to be metaphorical. The commercialisation and financialisation of poverty lending have accompanied the mainstreaming of microfinance. In this process, microfinance institutions (MFIs) have frequently transformed from non-profit organisations into powerful corporate entities, listed in major stock exchanges, acquiring capital through securitising their loan portfolios, i.e. turning the flows of microfinance into a tradable asset (Aitken 2015, 67ff.; Mader 2015; Soederberg 2013). For institutions at the centre of global finance, investments into the "fringes" through, for example, Microfinance Investment Vehicles (MIVs) is particularly interesting because repayments are less dependent on macroeconomic cycles and thus allow for risk diversification (Aitken 2015, 76; Kar 2018; Nair 2015).

In this context, the vision of debt-based provisioning of basic needs expresses a specific neoliberal form of governing poverty and the precarity of working-class households, one in which states play a vital role (Lazzarato 2015; Soederberg 2015). Moreover, neoliberal governance is not limited to the state in a narrow sense. As Lamia Karim has shown for the case of Bangladesh, one of the most vibrant regions for modern microfinance and home to the sector's guru Muhammad Yunus, non-government organisations (NGOs) have morphed into a "shadow state in the rural economy" (Karim 2011, 33) with the help of international organisations like the World Bank. In many regions, development NGOs facilitate access to so-called poverty markets by collaborating with transnational corporations, thereby opening a vast untapped consumer segment previously out of the reach of companies providing drinking water, sanitation, consumer items and many other goods and services (Mader 2011; Roberts 2015; Roy 2010, 114ff.).

More recently, the hype around digital financial inclusion, including e-payments (mobile money, remittances, etc.), has gained widespread attention (Guermond 2020; Natile 2020; Santos and Kvangraven 2017). A broad coalition between governments, international development organisations, fintech companies and philanthropic bodies actively promotes it. This "fintech-philanthropy–development complex" (Gabor and Brooks 2016) extends the reach of poverty finance rapidly by using digital (meta-) data to profile underbanked populations, create finance-based identities and customise profitable financial products. The previously discussed case of Mastercard, Net1 and the South African Social Security Agency (SASSA) teaming up to digitise South Africa's grant system demonstrated the predatory aspects of digital financial inclusion (Bond et al. 2023; Torkelson 2021).

Financial inclusion is thus understood as a concomitant of market-based finance at the household level. The privatisation, commodification, and financialisation of social infrastructure, including housing, education, health care, and many more, increases the need for money, which, in times of casualisation of wage work in many parts of the global economy, must be raised through indebtedness (Bayliss, Robertson, and Fine 2018; Jafri 2019; Soederberg 2015). Importantly, critiques have highlighted how the individualisation of risks and the constitution of financially responsible poor are systematically linked to "racialised and gendered forms of difference and the exercise of imperialism and dispossession by financial means" (see also Bernards 2022; Haiven 2020; Rankin 2013, 548). Rather than being neutral, the gendered and racialised accounts of creditworthiness, as defined by the financial service industry allow to siphon off profit through punitive interest rates and exorbitant fees for late payments (McNally 2011a, 123f.). In this sense, financial inclusion primarily legitimises, normalises, and consolidates the claims of powerful, transnational capital interests that benefit from finance-led capitalism by obscuring and concealing the exploitative relations of poverty finance (Soederberg 2013, 593).

Ultimately, microfinance offers a contradictory promise to hundreds of millions of peasants and labourers in the informal economy to improve their socio-economic positioning via indebtedness without providing any substantial argument for how decent finance, decent work and a decent life are connected (Bateman 2019; Bernards 2018; Natarajan et al. 2021). Particularly in agrarian settings, the rise of microfinance may trap farmers in low-productivity economic activities of petty production and trading, exacerbating agrarian distress, entrenching over-indebtedness vis-à-vis multiple creditors, and at times even catalysing suicides (Bateman 2010, 83ff.; Nagaraj et al. 2014; Taylor 2012; Vasavi 2014).

The affirmative literature has moved beyond the narrative of entrepreneurial microfinance, allowing poor women to lift themselves out of poverty. Instead, it has increasingly embraced the relevance of debt and other financial products in managing the chronic precarity of the global poor without any vision of how this management eradicates poverty. In this regard, microfinance fulfils primarily reproductive needs, including decent housing, sanitation, education, health care, etc. Consequently, financial services are understood as a market-based welfare safety net. This is where the critical literature on predatory microfinance comes in. It highlights how neoliberal austerity, privatisation, and commodification policies have downscaled risks and responsibilities to working-class households while corporate capital reaps hefty profits. The twin dynamics of financialisation and digitisation of the world economy have allowed poverty finance to rapidly broaden and deepen its hold over the global poor, operating along gendered and racialised lines. The broader shift towards market-based development finance intensifies this trend further, since the assetisation of public infrastructure is necessarily associated with (increased) fees for public-private services.

The Relevance of Investigating Fractured Lives

The critical political economy literature has convincingly shown why microfinance does *not* work, at least not in the proclaimed way as a panacea for poverty eradication, and *how* it increasingly works through financialisation. Yet, it has engaged insufficiently with a sophisticated explanation of *why* microfinance remains successful in terms of growing clients and expanding portfolios. Focussing on the political economy dynamics that shape microfinance customer's demand for credit is a promising starting point. However, the bulk of critical microfinance and financial inclusion studies has focussed rather narrowly on the neoliberal era. Therefore, the main research question of this research is: why and how could commercial microfinance expand so rapidly in India in recent decades? Engaging with this question, my work expands the critical literature in three significant ways.

First, I propose to understand the recent rise of microfinance and financial inclusion by embedding these into a broader history of the modern world economy, including the formative phase of European colonialism. Doing so is essential because a narrow focus on the neoliberal era amongst critical scholars has produced its own silencing and blind spots, including the erasure of (post-)colonial histories of the unbanked.[8] The dominant financial inclusion discourse operates along a simple

8 For a rare exception focussing on Africa, see Bernards (2022).

formal/informal finance binary. While the former is understood to be decent, safe, and comparatively cheap, the latter, represented most prominently in the figure of the usurious moneylender, is inherently exploitative. The critical literature has convincingly shown how formal finance entails predatory aspects, too. However, it has rarely questioned the formal/informal divide and scrutinised the internal relations between these seemingly distinct spheres.

For instance, Philip Mader's widely acclaimed work *The Political Economy of Microfinance*, amongst few others, recognised the relevance of British colonial rule in creating credit cooperatives in the early twentieth century on the Indian subcontinent as debt-based welfare policy against the power of moneylenders in rural areas (Mader 2015, 44ff.). However, his genealogy of microfinance emphasises that "microfinance and the cooperative movement have very little in common" (Mader 2013, 268) since they differ categorically regarding property relations, governance and product. Ultimately, understanding microfinance in the lineages of credit cooperatives falls prey to a myth and presents a "false history" (Mader 2013). From a historical-institutionalist perspective, separating these indeed different creditor institutions might make sense. However, from the perspective of borrowers, this distinction may be irrelevant. Moreover, this account fails to acknowledge the intricate relationship between British colonial rule and the rise of moneylenders.

In tracing the governance of access to credit in India, I seek to debunk the superficial binary of formal/informal finance to show how from the perspective of subaltern working-class households' multiple creditors, including MFIs, moneylenders, and different types of banks, might not compete but complement one another. In this sense, I claim that microfinance is only the latest incarnation in a series of modern attempts to govern a chronic subsistence crisis of subaltern working-class households which date back to British colonial rule and an imperial political economy of plunder. In other words, the financialisation of daily life and debt-based welfare strategies may not be as novel as the literature suggests. This is not to deny the peculiarities of contemporary financial inclusion policies. Instead, it points to the multivalence of credit-debtor relationships that shape the real world of the global poor. In this context, engaging with the colonial past is necessary for understanding the present inequalities of financial inclusion/exclusion.

The second way I intend to stretch the critical literature is by taking some of the arguments from microfinance proponents more seriously. Specifically, I suggest the notion of microfinance as an existential safety net to access basic needs, like housing, education, health care and others, is a valid entry point to understanding the success of microfinance. For instance, María Otero, former president of ACCION International, one of the leading NGOs that spearheaded the globalisation of microfinance in the 1990s, acknowledged more than twenty years ago that "[c]lients of microfinance institutions are poor city dwellers housed in slums or squatter settlements, often living in appalling overcrowded settings, lacking access to basic services such as health" (Otero 2000, 10). However, if financial vulnerability is core to understanding why financial inclusion a timely development approach is, it would be necessary to scrutinise the political, economic, and social dynamics that shape households' highly irregular income and expenditure patterns. People with low incomes themselves hardly determine these volatilities. Yet, they are a given in parameters by most of the affirmative microfinance literature, as if labelling these households poor already explains the fundamental uncertainty and insecurity that mark their daily lives.

Engaging with their lives as a precarious class of labourers rather than as borrowers or (self-employed) entrepreneurs helps to understand the roots of their financial vulnerability. After all, only a tiny fraction of the global working poor are entrepreneurs, while the share of casual wage labourers is a significant and growing part, particularly in sprawling megacities in the global South (Davis 2006; Roy-Chowdhury 2021). Although some of the largest MFIs in India have emerged from the slums of megacities, banking on these precarious migrant workers, there are hardly any studies that centre the latter's livelihoods to investigate why and how commercial microfinance could expand so rapidly.[9] Researching rural-urban migrants in Bengaluru, one of the fastest growing cities in the world, and a buzzing centre for Indian microfinance, I intend to unearth some of the silenced histories and fractures that underpin the financial vulnerability of these populations, and thus the success of commercial microfinance.

Reframing the discussion on microfinance as one about labouring classes rather than customers also redefines the political implications that critical analysis has. On the one hand, it may highlight the disconnect and contradictions between the global agendas of decent work and financial inclusion (Natarajan et al. 2021). On the other hand, it can show that labour struggles for a living wage or incorporation into social security systems are intimately connected to questions of financial inclusion/exclusion and indebtedness. Inversely, studying precarious labour through the lens of creditor-debtor relationships might provoke important insights into how financial means beyond the workplace shape class formation and class struggle. Ultimately, this reframing may open new avenues to discuss political strategies that challenge predatory (micro-)finance and the financialisation of poverty effectively.

Finally, engaging with these two gaps, the historicisation of the rise of commercial microfinance and its entanglement with questions of class formation and class struggle requires a conceptual framework that allows us to investigate fractured lives empirically. Drawing on Marx's understanding of money and finance, social reproduction feminism, and the notion of racial capitalism, I intend to grasp the multiplicity of fragmentations and segmentations that generally underpin capitalist social formations and the workings of financial exclusion/inclusion more specif-

9 For exceptions, see Natarajan, Brickel and Parsons (2021) and Natarajan (2021).

ically . The ultimate expression of these fractures is the notion of re/productive finance. The term highlights the use of credit for social reproduction (housing, education, health care, etc.). But is also stresses the internal relations between seemingly separate spheres of the productive/reproductive and real/financial economy.

In a nutshell, this book investigates how access to credit produces fractured lives and how the latter is a suitable basis for expanding financial accumulation. The guiding assumption is that substantial parts of India's subaltern working class have historically experienced a chronic subsistence crisis which is managed through several different creditor-debtor relationships in specific contexts. Looking at these regimes of re/productive finance is important to understand how gendered and racialised class oppression, exploitation, and struggle have evolved in modern India. Moreover, such an investigation reframes our understanding of microfinance and financial inclusion. It highlights how financial inclusion is only the latest incarnation of debt regimes subordinating a cheap, fragmented labour force under capital. Furthermore, embedding the rapid rise of microfinance in the broader political economy also points to addressing the root causes rather than engaging with reformist calls to regulate microfinance.

This book consists of four major parts. The first part will explore how Development has become increasingly thought of through the logic and structures of financial markets, and how the transformation from microcredit to financial inclusion has been crucial for this change. Drawing on flagship reports from the UN, World Bank, and others, the chapter also specifies what financial inclusion is, who the unbanked are, and why the distinction between formal and informal lending is crucial for the dominant narrative. Moreover, it substantiates why India is critical for this international development agenda. In doing so, Part I deepens some aspects briefly introduced in this chapter, providing an essential context for the remainder of the book.

Part II will lay the methodological foundations for investigating fractured lives. It outlines the ontological and epistemological premises that have guided this research and develops a theoretical framework in three steps. First, a re-reading of Marx's understanding of money as societal relation of oppression and how borrowing to working-class households is a form of financial expropriation prepares the ground. Second, a shift in perspective through employing social reproduction feminism and particularly the notion of financialisation of social reproduction is necessary to understand the significance of reproductive debt in capitalist social formations. Third, by recognising the relevance of colonialism and racism in the making of the modern world economy, including the pivotal role of finance in this regard, I suggest framing the analysis as one informed by racial finance capitalism. Based on these foundations, the final chapter of this part introduces the notion of a regime analysis in critical political economy and the method of incorporated comparison. Both are combined into what I refer to as regimes of re/productive finance, a notion that helps to systematise and periodise how poverty finance has been governed in India over the past two centuries. Moreover, this chapter also outlines the process of accruing and processing original data through empirical field research in Bengaluru.

Part III applies the regime analysis to the history of modern India, identifying three regimes: First a colonial regime which incrementally emerged since the late eighteenth century and lasted until India's independence in the mid-twentieth century. Second, a developmental regime, following the four decades after independence. Third, a neoliberal regime, which emerged since the early 1990s and continues in the present. Each of these regimes is characterised by a specific political economy, social stratification, and positioning of subaltern classes, including their need for credit, and unique governance of access to credit. Yet, despite their relative coherence, there are important continuities which help understand the contemporary rise of commercialised and financialised microfinance.

Based on this deep history of microfinance in India, Part IV zooms in on the contemporary regime of re/productive finance to investigate how rural-urban migrant labourers in Bengaluru live through debts. It stretches the scope of empirical microfinance research to explore the labour-finance nexus through the perspective of migrant worker's social reproduction. This chapter suggests that the dynamics of expropriation, exploitation, and exclusion are crucial to sustaining the vicious debt distress cycle, in which the labouring classes resort to reproductive debts to manage a chronic subsistence crisis. As such, it engages empirically with the structural violence of financial inclusion and how migrant workers live through and respond to contemporary modes of financial expropriation.

Finally, the conclusion summarises key insights and answers the research question. It returns to the chasm between the benevolent rhetoric and the structural violence of financial inclusion. Moreover, it outlines some political implications that emerge from the analysis. Instead of regulating microfinance or reforming financial inclusion policies, the findings from this research call for the necessity to challenge the roots of regimes of re/productive finance by overcoming subaltern classes' dependency on reproductive debts.

Part I: Thinking Development through Finance

"Our dream is a world free of poverty. [...] And I really think we're not going to eradicate poverty unless we have financial inclusion [...] You have good finance, bad finance, and ugly finance. You need to make sure it serves citizens, the SMEs [small and medium-sized enterprises], and not just the banker, or the wealthy, or the chosen few"
– Ceyla Pazarbasioglu, Vice-President, Equitable Growth, Finance and Institutions (EFI), World Bank Group (Politi 2019)

"Five years ago, we didn't have money, so we never even thought of going to a bank. We still don't have money. So what will we do there now?"
– Mukhne, Adivasi woman, daily wage labourer in agriculture (Abraham 2019)

Chapter 1
Boom and Bust: A Very Brief History of Modern Microfinance

This part summarises the evolution of microfinance as a development policy in the context of the global political economy, explicitly highlighting continuities and changes in the shift towards financial inclusion. It thereby provides an essential context for the following investigation. To engage with the periodisation of microfinance initiatives, I draw on Gillian Hart's (2010) proposition to understand Development ('big D') and capitalist development ('little d') as different though interconnected processes. Development refers to a bundle of interventionist institutions that have begun to work on the growth-poverty nexus in the Third World in the context of a fundamental crisis of Western imperialism in the first half of the twentieth century, most prominently marked by decolonisation struggles and the Cold War (Escobar 1999; see also Esteva 2010; McMichael 2017, 40ff.). In contrast, 'little d' comprises the uneven process of destruction and creation that underpins global capital accumulation, requiring and calling forth ongoing interventions to grapple with the permanent production of contradictions (Hart 2010, 119).

Importantly, from this perspective, the role of Development institutions, like the World Bank or International Monetary Fund (IMF), is not understood as a functionalist necessity to solve the contradictions of global capital accumulation. Rather, Development operates unwillingly on the background conditions of uneven capitalist development, working through its contradictions and reproducing them in new and mutated ways (Taylor 2005, 154). As such, this framing allows an understanding of microfinance's evolution as part of a broader process of thinking and practising D/development through finance since the 1970s.

Talk of financial inclusion as an explicit concept and development strategy has been a relatively recent phenomenon since the late 2000s. However, the notion closely ties with microcredit's international rise and promotion since the 1970s. Thus, the following chapter will briefly review the history of microfinance before discussing the political, economic, and ideational context in which financial inclusion emerged and transformed development policies.

Finance and Development in a Post-Colonial Context

In the aftermath of the third wave of decolonisation in the 1960s, Development was primarily understood as fostering economic growth and mobilising resources for industrialisation. For post-colonial societies dominated by agricultural production, the central challenge was to enhance productivity, most prominently fostered by the Green Revolution, and accumulate capital that could be invested in emerging industries (McMichael 2017, 73ff.). In this regard, the role of a developmental state, coordinating economic activities and allocating credit, was seen as a crucial precondition for successful industrialisation and improving living standards (Kohli 2004; Shah, Rao, and Shankar 2007; Williams 2014). The creation of roughly 550 public development finance institutions (DFI) worldwide in the second half of the twentieth century boosted economic growth through targeted investment in agriculture and other priority sectors (Bruck 1998).

However, criticism of targeted and subsidised access to credit through public banks and DFIs cumulated in the early 1970s. Misallocation, moral hazard problems, enormous costs weighing heavy on government budgets, and crowding-out of private credit suppliers were major arguments from economists calling for a more liberalised, market-oriented credit facilitation structure with a more prominent role for private corporations (Braverman and Guasch 1986; Calomiris and Himmelberg 1994; McGuire and Conroy 2000).[1] In line with a general shift in academia, particularly pronounced in the domain of economics, the central role of governments as economic actors became increasingly controversial, and macroeconomic policies prescribing a significant role to the state lost credibility. Instead, neoliberal thought advocating "free market economics" swept university departments, development institutions and policymakers across the world (Harvey 2005; Milonakis and Fine 2009; Mirowski and Plehwe 2009). Accordingly, many of the development banks and other state-owned enterprises that mushroomed in the context of the nascent post-colonial era were privatised, restructured or liquidated, and public 'divestment' made room for new private actors (Bruck 1998; Cowan 1985).[2]

This ideological shift was paralleled by fundamental changes in the world economy, particularly the international financial system. US president Nixon's decision to unilaterally cancel the direct international convertibility of the US dollar to gold in 1971 ushered in the abrupt end of the Bretton Woods System and signalled the rapid

1 For a critical account of how "moral hazard" has evolved from an economics concept to become "a part of mainstream development thinking, traveling across the world through diverse networks of think tanks, NGOs, and financial institutions", see Young (2010b).

2 Ironically, "the pervasive role of the state in economic development in the Third World stemmed in part from the pre-independence period in which the colonial administrations controlled the direction and rate of economic change" (Cowan 1985, 47). See also Chapter 10.

rise of financial markets, including new products, actors and regulations (Harvey 2005, 12ff.; Helleiner 1994; McNally 2011a, 85ff.). In this context, many newly independent countries in the South were flooded with foreign capital from North Atlantic banks which had accumulated gigantic surpluses during the oil price hikes in the early 1970s (the so-called *Petro-Dollar-Recycling*).[3] External debt of Third World states (particularly of non-OPEC countries) exploded from US$ 47.5 billion in 1968 to US$ 560 billion in 1980 (McNally 2011a, 98). Vijay Prashad argues that loans to these countries were "the international sub-prime market" of the day since credit was given without care for the borrower's solvency (Prashad 2012, 50).

When Paul Volcker, Chairman of the Federal Reserve, raised interest rates to 20 per cent to fight domestic inflation in March 1980, most borrower countries struggled to repay the rising interest rates, despite repaying billions of dollars. Twenty-four of these had to reschedule or refinance their sovereign loans between 1982 and 1984, with large US banks like Chase Manhattan, Bank of America and Citibank as their creditors. Because no formal international solvency mechanism was in place, the International Monetary Fund (IMF), the World Bank, and the US government created an *ad-hoc* regime, famously known as the Washington Consensus: The IMF and World Bank set up a number of short and medium-term loans to refinance the credit owed to large commercial banks based on the conditionality that debtor countries implemented cuts in public budgets, privatised public sector firms, deregulated utilities, desiccated social service provision (health, education, and agricultural subsidies), and introduced financial liberalisation (McMichael 2017, 114ff.; Prashad 2012, 58). In effect, the informal arrangements of transnational debt negotiations[4] helped to augment the power of credit to serve as an effective form of social discipline, allowing donor states and capital "to coerce debtor states into accepting, implementing and internalising neoliberal policies" (see also McNally 2011a, 135ff.; Soederberg 2005, 928).

The bitter irony of this historical context is that access to finance, for governments, not households, in the global South had become one of the most contested

---

3 Chandrashekhar and Ghosh (2002, 12) maintain that OPEC countries had accumulated US$ 475 billion by 1981, of which US$ 400 billion were parked with financial institutions in the global North. Many US and European corporations faced dismal conditions at the time, struggling to revive profitability in a stagnating economic atmosphere, and thus not in demand for such massive credits.

4 This refers to the arrangements of the Paris and London Club as well as the surveillance duties of the International Monetary Fund (IMF) that came into place in 1977. The proposal of the United Nations Conference on Trade and Development (UNCTAD) and the G-77 to create a permanent body called International Debt Commission (IDC), that would deal with the rescheduling and refinancing of Third World debt, was resisted by donor countries because these governments did not want to treat debt as *political* (Prashad 2012, 54; Soederberg 2005, 935).

issues of international politics in the 1980s. As Sarah Bracking notes in her reflection on the structural adjustment programmes (SAPs), "[w]hole countries are seen as unworthy 'too risky' and are then, on the basis of this decision, denied the necessary means with which to build a better future" (Bracking 1999, 208). Moreover, the macro-debts of states and the micro-debts of households were intimately linked. Most SAPs featured the same policies, including the re-structuring of public expenditure priorities (e.g. cutting subsidies for farmers or reducing expenditure for welfare measures), tight fiscal discipline to prevent new public investment programmes, tax reforms to attract foreign direct investment (FDI), privatisation of nationalised industries and services amongst others, and trade liberalisation (e.g. mass imports of food from the West).[5] Consequently, structural adjustment had not only meant a considerable wealth transfer from "so-called developing nations for banks in the North" (McNally 2011a, 132). It also eroded the emerging middle-classes – most notably in Latin America – through the spread of unemployment and poverty (George 1990, 64f.), fostered the destruction of subsistence economies through a new wave of enclosing the commons, and generally increased the market-dependent social reproduction of the masses in the global South (Federici 2012, 101ff.; McMichael 2017, 116ff.).

In a context of a dramatic balance of payments and debt crises of many countries in the Southern Hemisphere, the policy space for governments to tackle surging unemployment and social and economic immiseration was limited. Congruent with the trends of growing beliefs in the power of markets, development thinkers started to emphasise income-generation through self-employment as an alternative. Rather than promoting job creation in the formal sector, the poor might work out of poverty through self-employment (McGuire and Conroy 2000). In the wake of the deteriorating livelihoods of significant shares of populations in structurally adjusted countries, microfinance emerged as a viable strategy pushed by development institutions.

Experimenting with Microcredit

The consequences of the new international financial architecture not only influenced those countries directly affected by the debt crisis of the 1980s. For example, an OPEC member, Indonesia, profited from high oil prices in the 1970s, translating into vibrant economic growth. With declining oil prices and respective effects on the domestic economy in the early 1980s, the country embarked on a path of

5 A survey of IMF loan conditionalities across 130 countries, mostly in Asia, Africa and Latin America, between 1985 and 2014 finds little evidence of transformative changes over time (Kentikelenis, Stubbs, and King 2016).

neoliberal "shock doctrine" under the military dictator Suharto to revive economic growth (Klein 2007, 68f.). As part of this shift, experiments with modern microcredit started in Indonesia. The country's oldest and largest commercial bank was transformed from a loss-producing state-owned financial institution "into the most profitable bank with the largest micro banking network in Indonesia" (Seibel and Ozaki 2009). Since the 1950s, Bank Rakyat Indonesia (BRI) has provided targeted credit, for example, to foster the Green Revolution in agriculture. During the 1980s, the bank's units were re-structured according to profitability, including incentives for management and staff that would perform well, penalties for those who would perform below specific benchmarks, and incentives for customers for timely repayment of loans. Henceforth savings were mobilised in villages nationwide, while loan disbursement was oriented toward profitability. BRI diversified its credit products and now offers a gradual ladder of (micro-)loans to every creditworthy customer for both income-generating activities and consumption loans. The transformation from targeted to market-based credit was a financial success. By the end of the 1980s, BRI had become economically self-sufficient and independent from the government funds (which provided the initial capital) and from further liquidity assistance provided by the World Bank (Seibel and Ozaki 2009). Like many microcredit experiments, BRI's transformation was celebrated as a significant achievement on the road to eliminating poverty. Although the bank reached roughly one-fourth of the country's households, the proliferation of microcredit might not be associated with substantial poverty alleviation. When the bank began its new course in the mid-1980s, the "reported incidence of poverty nationwide had already fallen from 60 to just over 20 per cent" (Henley 2010, 184).

The international political and economic context is also essential for the most potent narrative of the emergence of modern microfinance, namely that of Grameen Bank in Bangladesh. Most microfinance accounts celebrate Muhammad Yunus as the founding father of contemporary microcredit. Driven by his encounters with the poverty ridden villagers of Jobra, close to the campus of the University of Chittagong, where he read economics, Yunus started to advance small amounts of cash to artisans and businesswomen. He was a guarantor for their loans with a local bank branch in the mid-1970s before eventually founding the Grameen Bank (literally: village bank). His mission was to provide an alternative to local moneylenders that demanded absurdly high-interest rates and to ameliorate the immiseration caused by the 1974 Bangladesh famine (Yunus and Jolis 1998). Despite his recognition that poverty is rarely caused by the poor themselves but rather by the circumstances surrounding them, neither Yunus nor microfinance enthusiasts explore the context of the devastating famine.

While the immediate causes of the 'man-made famine' are to be found in the hoarding and speculation of grain producers and traders, as well as a series of bad harvests in the early 1970s, and the consequences of the liberation war and devastating floods in the Monsoon season of 1974, the international political economy also shaped the dramatic episode of the newly independent country in crucial ways. To reverse the trend of rising oil prices in the 1970s, the US government used the dependency of developing countries like Bangladesh on food aid to exercise leverage on OPEC to reduce prices.[6] Eventually, this pressure destabilised Bangladesh's food import regime and the local public distribution system, failing to assist those in need (Sobhan 1979).[7] Under these circumstances, modern microfinance was 'invented' by Yunus as a strategy to alleviate the poverty of the rural population, which had been exacerbated due to the famine. The idea of lending small amounts of money to peasants, small artisans, business people or even labourers was not entirely new (see e.g. Armendáriz and Morduch 2010, 67ff.). But Yunus 'invention' was based on three novel characteristics.

First, his Grameen Bank approach pioneered group lending based on peer pressure. While cooperatives or credit associations are usually also governed by their members, the new microcredit system was controlled by so-called banks for the poor (often non-governmental organisations), which relied on the joint liability of borrowers to ensure repayment on time. Although many initial operations were not premised on profit, the group-lending model showcased how lending to the poor can become financially viable and thus appealed to the international financial community. Second, lending occurred almost exclusively to women, arguing that they have better repayment morale and would generally use credit more beneficially for the household's welfare. This aspect dovetailed with a mainstreaming of gender equality and women's empowerment in international development that already started in the 1980s and became institutionalised in the mid-1990s (Kabeer 2001; Walby 2005; Weber 2014). Third, microcredit was linked to a strong notion of the entrepreneurial spirits of poor women, resonating with the above-described shifts in intellectual currents, building on the omnipresence of self-employment in the informal economy and complementing state-led welfare programmes by engaging the 'social capital' of the poor (Harris 2001; Rankin 2002).

The microcredit approach of Yunus and the Grameen Bank appealed to the international development and business community because it had an essential liberal, pro-business and market-oriented narrative to offer while adding an ethical dimension. Importantly, however, these early experiments with microcredit were still primarily financed through public money, mainly through development departments from OECD countries and respective national and multilateral development banks.

6 This included both pressures on food procurement and on the balance of payments of non-OPEC developing countries in order to divide the ambitions of a new international economic order of Third World countries (Sobhan 1979).

7 For a more detailed popular exploration of the entitlement failure in the Bangladesh famine of 1974, see Sen (1981).

The Grameen Model was not replicated with all its features throughout the world. Nonetheless, it served as a blueprint of how microfinance worked, legitimising different loan programmes targeting 'the poor'. BancoSol is perhaps one of the most prominent examples.[8] The bank had emerged from PRODEM, a Bolivian non-government organisation established by the American organisation ACCION and with substantial financial support from USAID and Bolivian businessman and former Finance Minister Fernando Romero. It adopted the joint liability principle, borrowing to individuals in solidarity groups of up to eight individuals, whilst a group member can only receive a credit if no other member is in default. The microcredit experiment, mainly targeting urban dwellers, many of whom had been struck by the austerity measures from the SAPs, quickly grew and eventually was the first NGO providing microloans that turned into a commercial bank (BancoSol) in 1992 (Mosley 2001).

This brief review may show how microcredit experiments emerged as a Development approach ('big D') to entrenched poverty in the context of a broader crisis of global capital accumulation, particularly the Third World Debt crisis and the consequences of structural adjustments. The latter must be understood as part of the neoliberal counter-revolution against calls to decolonise and democratise the international political and economic order ('small d'). Official development aid (ODA) maintained this first wave's NGOs and government initiatives since the 1970s. In this regard, Hulme and Mosley's widely recognised study *Finance against Poverty* argued that there must not be a trade-off between poverty alleviation and economic growth in the context of structural adjustment since lending to the working poor reduces poverty and has still proven to be financially viable (Hulme and Mosley 1996, 207). NGOs, public development banks and parastatal bodies were encouraged to adopt private-sector management techniques to prove economically sound. However, for neoliberal market radicals, this was not enough.

From Villages to Washington...to Crisis

In the 1990s, the early microcredit experiments were increasingly criticised by radical proponents of financial liberalisation and market efficiency who denounced these approaches as 'poverty lending'. In contrast, the 'financial systems' approach emphasised the need to entangle emerging microcredit with the growth of financial markets (Rhyne and Otero 2006; Robinson 2001). Essentially it aspired to "a level of

8 Other examples include the funding of the Kenya Rural Enterprise Programme (K-REP) through the British Department for International Development (DFID) or the Self-Employed Women's Association (SEWA) in India through the World Bank, International Labour Organisation, and German development bank KfW.

compatibility" between finance and development as two distinct "ways of thinking" by integrating the rise of microfinance as development policy within the logic and structure of financial markets (Otero 2000, 16). Most importantly, informal sources of credit and finance had to be formalised and controlled by private institutions (NGOs or corporations), which could then access capital markets to fund their lending portfolio, dramatically scaling up their businesses (Otero and Ryhne 1994).

The focus on microloans as a primary strategy to tackle the growth-poverty nexus also fitted the Post-Washington Consensus (PWC) and its emphasis on getting institutions right (Johnson 2009, 293). Consequently, donors and multilateral organisations endorsed the slogan "making markets work (better) for poor people" (World Bank, 2001, p. 61ff.). Consistent with this motto, finance and development consultants increasingly pushed the financial systems approach, "making *financial* markets work for the poor" and constructing low-income households across the globe as a new market frontier (Porteous 2004; Robinson 2001). Although the agenda emphasised the role of private actors as more efficient and custom-made service providers, governments were still crucial for providing adequate infrastructure and facilitating access to populations previously out of reach of the financial system (Otero 2000).

The World Bank has been particularly relevant in promoting and disseminating the "microfinance revolution" (Robinson 2001). As Ananya Roy notes in her critically acclaimed work on microfinance:

> "Indeed, it is the World Bank that controls the portals of knowledge, establishing the norms, metrics, rankings, and best practices of microfinance. World Bank training workshops, texts, and reports disseminate such authoritative knowledge, investing some experts with the authority to be microfinance experts and denying others legitimacy and significance. In short, what is at work is a "Washington consensus on poverty." (Roy 2010, 5)

Key to the institutional mainstreaming of microfinance was creating a global platform named the Consultative Group to Assist the Poorest (CGAP), an in-house organisation of the World Bank. Today's 30 members include ministries of foreign affairs and development of most significant OECD countries, development banks such as the African Development Bank and the KfW Bank Group, philanthropic foundations such as the Bill & Melinda Gates Foundation (BMGF), and corporate financial players like Credit Suisse. These agencies have pledged resources to support sustainable microfinance per best practice principles agreed upon by the group. Since its inception, a significant share of the CGAP's donor budget has come from private entities, including the Bill & Melinda Gates Foundation, the Mastercard Foundation, the Omidyar Network and Citi Foundation. The CGAP and its members quickly adopted the financial systems approach as the only reasonable way to promote access to credit for low-income households.

To institutionalise microfinance as a top development policy, the Microcredit Summit Campaign launched a major international conference in February 1997 in Washington, DC. Almost 3,000 delegates from more than 130 countries convened to discuss the potentials and challenges of microcredit, commencing a decade-long campaign with annual summits to boost the new instrument. According to the campaign, the global customer base had grown from 13 million in 1997 to 211 million in 2013 (Reed et al. 2015). Without any doubt, by the turn of the millennium, microcredit had emerged as the "most innovative strategy to address the problems of global poverty", as the editors of the newly founded *Journal of Microfinance* put it in their opening statement to the journal's first volume (Woodworth & Woller 1999).

However, microfinance had fallen into disgrace by the end of the 2000s among many journalists, academics and former practitioners. Influential media outlets in the US and Europe, including *The Washington Post*, *The Atlantic*, *The Guardian*, *Frankfurter Allgemeine*, and many others, all featured lengthy essays and background articles demystifying the microcredit hype, blaming the new development ideology for having fostered indebtedness and further despair amongst the world's poor (Hein and Bernau 2011; Provost 2012; Roodman 2012; Toyama 2011). In a contribution to the *New York Times*, Muhammed Yunus confessed a "mission shift" in which microfinance has essentially become dominated by the profit-motive: "In 1983, I founded Grameen Bank to provide small loans that people, especially poor women, could use to bring themselves out of poverty. At that time, I never imagined that one day microcredit would give rise to its own breed of loan sharks" (Yunus 2011). Like Hugh Sinclair, former microfinance employees started to speak out on the microfinance sector's corrupted, coercive, and ethically questionable sides (Sinclair 2012). Roy (2010) reports from several senior advisors and staff members of the CGAP (between 2004 and 2008) who reflected on microfinance's limits and admitted that only little empirical evidence indicated that microfinance was either sustainable or reducing poverty.

The burgeoning scepticism was not only based on newspaper and insider reports. Increasingly, economists questioned the rigorousness of used methodologies and inadequate data, reviewing impact evaluations and claiming that there was no sound evidence that microfinance worked (Armendáriz and Morduch 2010; Banerjee et al. 2009; Duvendack et al. 2011; Hermes and Lensink 2011). These insights also widened attention to a more fundamental questioning of the kind of development logic microfinance promotes (Bateman 2010; Guérin, Labie, and Servet 2015; Karim 2011). Moreover, several regional crises from Nicaragua and Bosnia-Herzegovina to Morocco and Pakistan hit the microcredit sector in the late 2000s (Mader 2015, 68f.). Shortly after the US subprime crisis and the ensuing global slump, critical scholars referred to the major microcredit crisis in the Indian state of Andhra Pradesh as "the other financial crisis" where about 82 per cent of rural households were indebted in 2010, most of them juggling with three or more loans at a time (Taylor 2012; Wichterich 2012).

Despite microcredit remaining essential to the international development community, the discourse shifted around the recent financial crisis. However, this change has not marginalised microfinance's role but instead exacerbated it as part of a broader strategy. Alok Prasad, former chief executive of India's Microfinance Network, sums up the paradigm shift in a recent interview with the *Financial Times*: "That rosy view we have of microfinance is over [...]. The terminology has [also] moved on from 'microfinance' to 'access to finance'" (Kazim 2018).

Chapter 2
Expanding the Frontiers of Poverty Finance

The shift from microfinance to access to finance, inclusive finance or financial inclusion can be understood as a discursive strategy of involved actors to regain legitimacy against cumulating criticism (Mader and Sabrow 2015). Yet, it must also be understood as the result of a broader struggle over the orientation of development policy in the context of the financialisation of the world economy (Soederberg 2013). This section sheds light on the transformations of global development financing since the millennium. It highlights how the financial systems approach to microfinance became entrenched through the broader notion of financial inclusion. In this regard, creating the 'unbanked' as a new development subject allowed for expanding the frontiers of poverty finance, reaping profits from the bottom of the pyramid.

Leveraging the Financial Systems Approach

Inclusiveness had already been a buzzword in Development since the World Bank and others admitted to the critics of neoliberal policies endorsed by the PWC that "globalisation could be much more effective for poor people, and its adverse effects could be substantially reduced" (Collier and Dollar 2002, 155). Around the millennium, pro-poor growth suggesting that low-income households should benefit from economic growth on absolute terms gained widespread attention. In this framework, distributional corrections are necessary to make ordinary economic growth work for the poor (see e.g. Ravallion 2004). The emphasis on welfare targets and equity should demonstrate that the World Bank has moved beyond the neoliberal Washington Consensus. At the global level, the Millennium Development Goals (MDGs) emphasised the necessity to increase Official Development Aid (ODA) to address the multiple dimensions of poverty (Biswas 2016; Mawdsley and Taggart 2022). However, despite donor states having pledged to spend 0.7 of their Gross National Income (GNI) on ODA in the early 1970s and reaffirming this ambition in the early 2000s, five years after the launch of the MDGs only about a third of the envisioned US$ 200 billion were raised annually (Sachs and McArthur 2005, 348).

While the MDGs were at the centre of public attention, market proponents contested the conventional link between equity and redistribution behind the scenes, arguing for equal opportunities and a call to move from pro-poor to inclusive growth (Saad-Filho 2010, 2013). This reframing combined the merits of finance-led growth and social inclusion, hence financial inclusion. According to a World Bank report, financial inclusion was a necessary corrective to the prevailing notion of redistributive measures in development policy in the 2000s (World Bank 2008, 2). Instead of focusing on redistribution (of public funding, income, wealth, etc.), the growth-development-poverty nexus became increasingly centred around *opportunities* in financial markets. These would go both ways. People with low incomes could profit from access to financial services as novel customers, while financial institutions could expand their market share and diversify underlying risks inherent to financial products. This resonated with the broader euphoria of global finance in the early 2000s (Harvey 2010; McNally 2011a).

In line with the already proposed role of the state in microfinance as an "enabler, not provider" (Roy 2010, 47), governments were challenged to facilitate broad alliances and provide adequate infrastructure extending private sector financial services. For instance, the UN's Second International Conference on Financing for Development in Monterrey, Mexico, 2002 acknowledged that "microfinance and credit for micro-, small and medium enterprises [...] are important for enhancing the social and economic impact of the financial sector. [...] In addition, the promotion of private-sector financial innovations and public-private partnerships can also deepen domestic financial markets and further develop the domestic financial sector" (United Nations 2003, 8). In a follow-up to the Monterrey Consensus, the UN Department of Economic and Social Affairs (DESA) and the UN Capital Development Fund (UNCDF) summarised the outcomes of a multi-stakeholder consultation from 2004 and 2005, with the help of the World Bank, IMF and ILO in a publication titled *Building Inclusive Financial Sectors for Development*. Acknowledging the diverse regional contexts, the so-called UN Blue Book was admittedly not intended as a blueprint for financial inclusion but as a companion that would guide "national dialogues to develop strategies for building inclusive financial sectors, emphasis is placed on the full examination of constraints and opportunities as perceived domestically" (United Nations 2006, 2). Ultimately, these processes should not only result in according policies to foster inclusive financial markets but, more importantly, in *ownership* and a political commitment of governments, donors and other important actors to implement and foster the agenda of financial inclusion.

The UNCDF's role in promoting financial inclusion paid off. Between 2007 and 2017, the organisation's budget doubled through voluntary contributions from transnational corporations (TNCs) and philanthropic think tanks with a vested interest in expanding the poverty finance frontiers. In 2017, UNCDF accepted more than US$ 11 million from Mastercard Worldwide/Foundation, VISA Inc., BMGF, Metlife Foundation, Omidyar Network and PACT Global Microfinance Fund. These private players now covered about one-fifth of the organisation's budget. In 2012, a similar group of organisations[1] started to fund the *Better than Cash Alliance* housed at the UNDFC. The Alliance seeks to create a consensus amongst governments, the private sector, and development organisations to move from cash to electronic payments. As such, the group is but one example of corporative-driven initiatives to facilitate broad coalitions for expanding the frontiers of poverty finance in the name of digital financial inclusion (Gabor and Brooks 2016; Mader 2016; Santos and Kvangraven 2017). The adverse implications of this push were already touched upon in the introduction when discussing the case of how South Africa's social security system was digitised and collateralised for profitable financial services.

Numerous other examples also underscore the importance of public-private partnerships for institutionalising financial inclusion as a premier development strategy. In the wake of the global financial crisis, the G20 emerged as an essential international *ad-hoc* forum to manage the trembling world economy and to create consensus amongst the largest economies on the directions of future financial market reforms (Cammack 2012; Wade 2011). As part of their strategy to strengthen resilience, the G20 endorsed the agenda of financial inclusion as a critical development policy. The *G20 Principles for Innovative Financial Inclusion* were drafted by three key implementing partners, namely the Alliance for Financial Inclusion (AFI), the Consultative Group to Assist the Poor (CGAP), and the World Bank's International Finance Corporation (IFC). AFI is perhaps the best institutional example of how state bodies internalise the ownership of a corporate-driven agenda. The organisation was founded in 2008, essentially financed by the BMGF, and with contributions from the German Federal Ministry for Economic Cooperation and Development[2] and Omidyar Network. It originated as a grant-making facility but quickly developed into a vital network that would drive policies of central banks and governments in so-called developing and emerging economies. At annual Global Policy Forums, central bankers, government officials and private-sector providers discuss common approaches and instruments to fostering financial inclusion, each time reaffirming their commitment by a declaration. The first such statement was the Maya Declaration in 2011,[3] which sought to complement the G20 Principles of strengthening and expanding financial inclusion (Soederberg 2013, 598f.). Since

1 The Bill & Melinda Gates Foundation, Citi, Ford Foundation, MasterCard, Omidyar Network, USAID, and Visa Inc.

2 As well as knowledge and logistics support from the German Development Corporation GIZ.

3 The following declarations included new commitments (or old commitments with new, fashionable titles), including the Maputo Accord 2015 on SME Financing, the Denarau Action Plan on Gender and Women's Financial Inclusion, the Sharm El Sheikh Accord 2017 on Financial

2016 the AFI has been owned by members, who comprise the central banks of most countries in the global South.[4]

Furthermore, the G20 created the Global Partnership for Financial Inclusion (GPFI) in 2010 as a platform for all G20 countries, plus interested non-G20 countries and 'relevant stakeholders' to follow up on the commitments and Action Plan made at the G20 Summit in Seoul. The implementing partners read like a summary of all other initiatives and include AFI, Better Than Cash Alliance, CGAP, IFC, International Fund for Agricultural Development (IFAD), OECD, SME Finance Forum, and the World Bank Group. On top of these high-level networks and institutions, the financial inclusion agenda also receives royal support. Her Majesty Queen Máxima of the Netherlands was appointed UN Secretary-General Special Advocate for Financial Inclusion (UNSGSA) in 2009, seeking to boost financial inclusion amongst governments in the global South and to sell the agenda to the public.[5]

The importance of broad public-private alliances seeks to manifest a global discourse and entrench the notion of inclusive financial markets in domestic policymaking. Ultimately, it aims to expand the market for financial services through Development. The case of the Sustainable Development Goals (SDGs), adopted in 2015, demonstrates this well. Financial inclusion is central to achieving at least seven out of 17 goals, including poverty reduction, zero hunger, good health and well-being, gender equality, decent work and economic growth, industry, innovation and infrastructure, and reduced inequalities (United Nations 2015b). In contrast to the MDG's emphasis on ODA, financing the SDGs is premised on private investment. The UN's Third International Conference on Financing for Development in Addis Ababa adopted a framework that emphasised the need to "unlock[ing] the transformative potential of [...] the private sector" (United Nations 2015a). Likewise, the Multilateral Development Banks (MDBs), spearheaded by the World Bank, have emphasised that financing the SDGs is possible only by leveraging billions of public funding (ODA) to unlock trillions of financial means through extension and closer integration with financial markets (African Development Bank et al. 2015; World Bank 2017).

The massive re-direction of financial development flows parallels this shift in rhetoric. In 2020, international funders invested US$ 58 billion in financial inclusion projects worldwide. While private investments have slowly but steadily

---

Inclusion, Climate Change and Green Finance, and the Sochi Accord 2018 on FinTech for Financial Inclusion.

4 In March 2019, the alliance had 84 principle and 17 associate members. According to the organisation, 85 percent of the world's 'unbanked' live in a country with an AFI member.

5 Her advisory reference group includes the who is who of institutions aggressively pushing financial inclusion: AFI, Better than Cash Alliance, The Bill & Melinda Gates Foundation, CGAP, IFC, IMF, Omidyar Network, UNCDF, UNDP, UNDESA and the World Bank.

increased over the past years, they still account for only US$ 14 billion of the total investment (Tolzmann 2022). The larger share stems from public sources: Development Finance Institutions (DFIs), Bilateral and Multilateral Development Banks.[6] The case of South Asia, arguably the most vibrant region for financial inclusion, demonstrates how most of this public funding is diverted towards private financial service providers, primarily as debt, equity, and grants. In 2014, two-thirds of the international financing for financial inclusion in the region was allocated to governments (67%), while financial service providers received about 18 per cent. In 2020, the share had inverted, with financial service providers receiving 62 per cent and governments only a mere 9 per cent of the US$ 4.7 billion invested (CGAP 2022).

This section has highlighted how the crisis of microfinance towards the end of the 2000s was essentially resolved by embracing broad public-private coalitions for inclusive financial markets. The new financial inclusion agenda has entrenched the 'financial systems approach' to commercialised and financialised microfinance. Thereby, it has also expanded the frontiers of poverty finance. Against this backdrop, the following section will explore the contradictions of financial inclusion more thoroughly, focusing on the new development subject: the unbanked.

Developing A New Market Segment: The Unbanked

Critiques have emphasised that Development is inherently ambiguous, malleable and contradictory and has shaky normative and methodological foundations (Escobar 1995; Sachs 2010; Ziai 2016). For instance, Arturo Escobar has suggested that Development proceeds by producing abnormalities, such as 'underdevelopment', to define problems in ways that allow specific interventions to appear as reasonable treatments (Escobar 1999, 384). In this sense, the 'unbanked', 'underbanked' or 'underserved' have already become a powerful new development subject of the twenty-first century, creating the urgent need to treat them with the only rational solution that is thinkable: access to financial services. The power of Development apparatuses lies in quantifying such random categories, turning them into something sensible that can be investigated scientifically and acted upon (Escobar 1999, 386). Moreover, beyond justifying interventions, the value of measuring also lies in countries becoming part of a competitive race on which the economy is 'more inclusive' in terms of inclusive financial markets, as Kaushik Basu, former Chief Economist of the World Bank, knows (Basu, 2018).

6 The CGAP 2020 Funder Survey included FCDO (UK), SIDA (Sweden), USAID (US), AFD Group (France), CDC (UK), DFC (US), EBRD and EIB (EU), FMO (Netherlands), IDB Invest, IFC (WB), KfW (Germany), African and Asian Development Bank, European Commission, IFAD, World Bank. Moreover, the Bill & Melinda Gates Foundation.

According to the World Bank, significant progress has been made toward universal financial inclusion in recent years. The percentage of unbanked in so-called developing countries has dropped from 58 per cent in 2011 to 37 per cent in 2017 (Demirgüc-Kunt et al. 2018). At the 10th anniversary of the Alliance for Financial Inclusion (AFI) in September 2018, the international development community celebrated that its policies had resulted in 634 million adults being integrated into the global financial system over the past decade (AFI 2018). At first sight, these numbers may indicate substantial progress. However, a closer look reveals that the success story tells us next to nothing about the actual living realities of either the 'banked' or the 'unbanked'. Instead, as Aram Ziai has argued for the Development discourse more generally, the construction of the unbanked as new development subjects has Eurocentric, depoliticising and authoritarian implications (Ziai 2016, 59). Drawing on this categorisation, the following addresses some fundamental contradictions of the financial inclusion discourse.

Firstly, the financial inclusion discourse reproduces the Eurocentric assumption that European societies, including many former European settler colonies, are the ideal models to be followed by the rest of the world. The civilising mission is clear from how the benchmark of the unbanked is constructed. According to the World Bank's Global Findex database, 96% of adults were financially included in the UK and 93 per cent in the US (Demirgüc-Kunt et al. 2018). Naturally, neither the World Bank nor other development organisations would explore the lived realities behind these numbers for high-income countries. The near-to-100-percent figure simply fulfils the function of a benchmark for the new 'underdeveloped'. The notion of financial inclusion assumes that widened access to financial services is *per se* desirable, without providing robust evidence for this.

However, many studies have shown how in the context of neoliberal austerity and declining real wages in recent decades, working-class households in the US and UK had to increasingly rely on predatory financial services, including mortgages, payday loans, credit card debts, and others to organise their daily lives (Crouch 2009; Montgomerie 2013; Roberts 2016; Soederberg 2015). In other words, the financial inclusion of these households is fostered by distress and, in many cases, contributes to the eroding living standards rather than improving them (Dymski, Hernandez, and Mohanty 2013; McNally 2011a; Wang 2018). Moreover, beyond obscuring and idealising the lived realities of the presumed standards, the Eurocentric character of financial inclusion is also witnessed by its disregard for the history of unbanked people. Flattening their stories and lives into a binary consumer choice in the present eclipses the entire history of financial inclusion/exclusion these populations have experienced until now. This silencing, including the vast colonial and racial violence, is not limited to financial inclusion but incorporates the broader relation between D/development (Haiven 2020; Hart 2006; McNally 2020).

Secondly, the financial inclusion discourse has authoritarian implications because it prescribes interventions into people's lives that people may themselves disapprove of (Ziai 2016, 62). It assumes that exclusion from (global) financial circuits is always involuntary without providing evidence for it. However, the 'unbanked' may consciously decide not to engage with financial services for various reasons. All too often, these reasons are simply silenced with reference to a lack of financial literacy or awareness. However, the World Bank's data suggest that exclusion from financial services is primarily caused by insufficient incomes and the realistic assessment that financial services are too expensive (see Figure 1).

Figure 1: Reasons for Not Having a Financial Institution Account in 2017

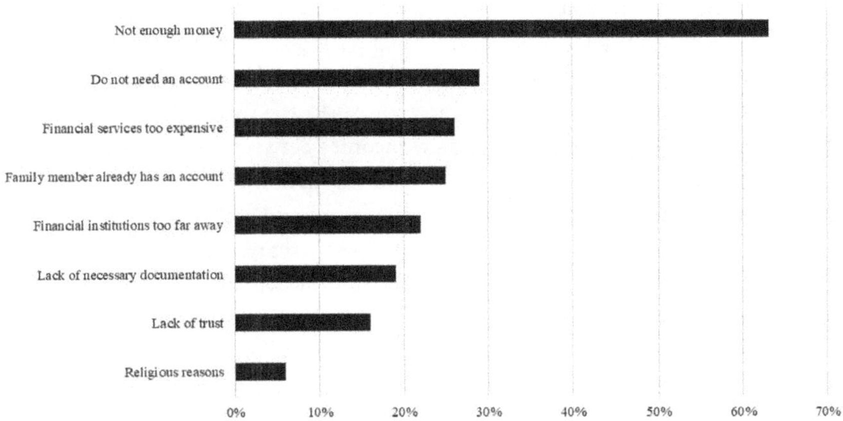

Source: Global Findex Database. Note: Adults without account, age 15+, in developing economies. Multiple answers are possible.

Rather than a general disregard for financial services (or a lack of awareness), these numbers suggest that unbanked households consciously decide against financial inclusion because of their precarious livelihoods. These results are even more pressing considering that nearly half of all the unbanked adults live in just seven countries, including China, India, Pakistan, Indonesia, Nigeria, Bangladesh and Mexico (Demirgüc-Kunt et al. 2018). Except for China and Mexico, the principal home countries of the unbanked are all among the regions in the world where the state of hunger is either serious or alarming, according to the *Global Hunger Index 2018*. More than one in six, or 290 million of the 1.7 billion 'unbanked' worldwide, live in just India and Pakistan together, which despite vibrant economic growth and a surge of microfinance in recent decades, are ranked 103 and 106 respectively out of

119 countries in terms of hunger and undernourishment (von Grebmer et al. 2018).[7] In a context where the contemporary corporate food regime excludes hundreds of millions of people from basic food security (McMichael 2009; Patel and Moore 2017; Patnaik 2007), lecturing people without a bank account about financial literacy is indeed authoritarian.

Thirdly, talk of the unbanked as a development subject obscures inequalities and conflicts (Ziai 2016, 60), including how the financial inclusion discourse facilitates the creation of a new market segment for global finance. The pioneers of the 'financial systems approach' had a more concrete vision of their target population than the opaque notion of the unbanked.[8] The World Bank's *International Finance Corporation* (IFC) defines the "working poor" earning less than US$ 2 a day, who make up the bulk of the labour force in developing countries, as the "*key target market segment* for expanding financial inclusion" (Stein, Randhawa, and Bilandzic 2011, 2 own emphasis). Under neoliberal globalisation, this "market segment" has experienced rapid growth. While the Development community has praised the impressive progress made in terms of reducing extreme poverty since 1990, the World Bank data suggests that the number of people living on daily incomes between the US$ 1.25 extreme poverty line and the US$ 2 per day poverty line has doubled between 1981 and 2008 (Phillips 2017b, 429).[9] Of the 1.6 billion adults "working poor", who largely overlap with the 1.7 billion unbanked, just 200 million are entrepreneurs. The vast majority are "small-holder farmers, casual labourers, and low wage salaried workers", as the World Bank's *New Microfinance Handbook* knows (Ledgerwood and Gibson 2013, 20).

Despite the centrality of the working poor in the new development agenda, there is a staunch silencing of systemic relations between financial inclusion and decent work (Bernards 2018; Natarajan et al. 2021). Tackling this silence requires unravelling the intimate and contradictory relationship between Development and capitalist development. After all, the generalisation of market-based finance in the name of sustainable development institutionalises imperatives of bankability into the social infrastructures of societies – from housing, energy and water provisioning to education, health care and others (Bayliss and Van Waeyenberge 2018; Elsner et al. 2022; Gabor 2021; Perry 2021). In doing so, it also increases pressures to privatise

7 The GHI tracks hunger annually and worldwide, measuring the combined the share of the population that is undernourished (insufficient calorie intake), the share of children under the age of five who are waster and stunted, and the mortality rate of children under the age of five (von Grebmer et al. 2018, 7f.)

8 At the turn of the millennium Robinson (2001) already maintained in a World Bank publication that 1.8 billion people could benefit from access to commercial microfinance.

9 Moreover, many critiques have highlighted how the international poverty line (IPL) is ridiculously low and tends to significantly underreport the actual number of working poor (Hickel 2016; Prashad 2012; Selwyn 2017).

and commodify social provisioning, leading to the monetisation of accessing basic needs. If substantial parts of the labour force in the global South earn poverty wages, the expansion of market-based finance may create a bottleneck in terms of lagging (aggregate) demand.[10] Access to credit for working-class households is thus a powerful strategy to deal with the contradictions of financial capital accumulation (see also Chapter 5). Importantly, this solution is not merely an ameliorative welfare project. Rather, it opens a new market for financial capital to serve respective households with credit and other financial services necessary to access basic needs.

The previous chapter briefly explored the shift in reasoning for financial inclusion towards microfinance as an existential safety net. A glance at the operations of commercial microfinance can substantiate this reasoning. According to industry estimates, MFIs have doubled their gross loan portfolio to just below US$ 80 billion in the past decade (Finch et al. 2022). Profit-oriented financial service providers give more than two-thirds of these loans. While the share of loans for income-generating activities has only marginally increased, the bulk of this expansion is based on "credit for daily living expenses, consumer goods, home improvements and loans to pay off other loans" (Finch et al. 2022). This is where we come full circle. The unbanked are not only a depoliticised object of development bureaucracy (Escobar 1999). They are also a profitable business case for global investors who can simultaneously invest money profitably and regain recognition for ostensibly making an 'impact', promoting sustainable development, and contributing to the fight against poverty.

Profits at the Bottom of the Pyramid

One could argue that account ownership is crucial for financial inclusion because customers can save money and thus build financial cushions that come in handy in cases of income fluctuations or emergencies. However, the World Bank data suggests that only 20 – 30 per cent of account holders have saved money in formal accounts in many countries, including India, Kenya, Brazil and South Africa (Demirgüc-Kunt et al. 2018). Moreover, as the previous section has shown, the unbanked may hardly have enough income to survive, so regular saving seems rather tricky. Notably, the same dataset suggests that access to credit may not even be an issue for the unbanked. Overall, adults in high-income economies borrow money more frequently (64%) than in so-called developing economies (44%). However, the difference is not very pronounced, particularly when considering borrowing

10 The same mechanism has been discussed in the literature on financialisation in the US and UK (see e.g. Crouch 2009; Harvey 2011; McNally 2011a).

within the category 'high income countries' is quite uneven.[11] So, what drives the meticulous occupation with the unbanked?

The incidence of indebtedness across income-categories becomes more meaningful when differentiating the numbers for various suppliers of credit. Figure 2 shows that most credit in so-called developing economies is supplied by families and friends or other sources like self-help groups, moneylenders, or employers, which are all usually clubbed together in a category of informal sources. In contrast, credit supply in high-income economies is dominated by formal financial institutions, usually commercial banks or other recognised financial service providers.

Figure 2: Sources of Credit in 2017

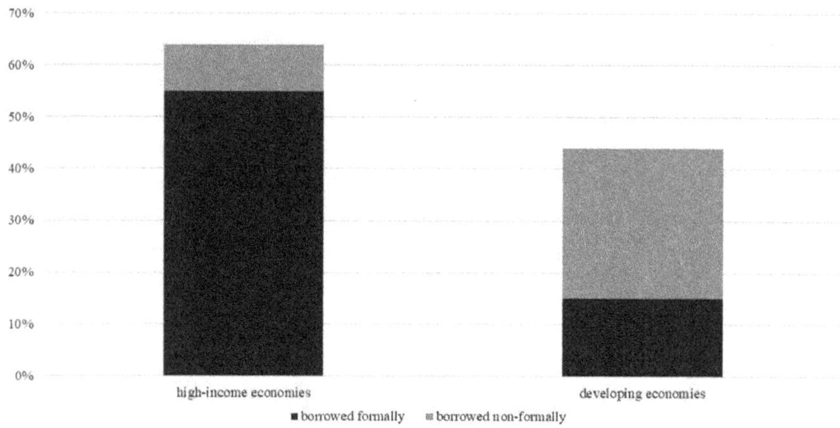

Source: Global Findex database. Note: Adults 15+ who borrowed any money in the past year. Formal borrowing refers to all credit relations with financial institutions like banks, MFIs or credit card debt. Non-formal borrowing refers to all other sources, including for example friends and family. Since multiple borrowing is possible but the categories are created mutually exclusive, the actual number of informal borrowings is likely to be underrepresented.

The graph shows the potential of bringing the 'unbanked' into the formal financial system. Vibrant debt relations already characterise many so-called developing economies. However, most of these are not organised by and integrated into the

11 In 2017, for example, about 77% of adults (age 15+) in the US and 75% in the UK said they had borrowed any money in the past year, while the respective share for the Eurozone was only 55%. Furthermore, the difference could also be justified by acknowledging that generally higher average incomes and entirely different labour markets (in which formalised wage labour predominates) in the former category allow for broader sections of society to borrow money in the first place.

flows of global capitalist finance. The catchphrase of the bottom of the pyramid (BOP) is sometimes misunderstood and often also actively miscommunicated as a charity case. According to commercial microfinance proponents, however, the BOP is primarily a business case, or as business guru C.K. Prahalad put it: "this is not a market to be ignored" (Prahalad 2005, 10). If we think of the unbanked as a strategically constructed development subject of the agenda of financial inclusion, integrating these subjects into debt-based accumulation becomes a pivotal task for proponents. In other words, financial inclusion is primarily a battle over credit supply, with the expansion of formal credit delivered by commercial banks, MFIs or other financial institutions linked to global capital accumulation.

Since the mid-2000s, many of the large MFIs went public or got involved with private equity and the securitisation of microfinance portfolios to secure cheap funding beyond obtaining loans from commercial banks and DFIs. Notably, DFIs were crucial in accompanying this transformation, guaranteeing the securitisation of loan portfolios and demonstrating to global investors that microfinance was a viable asset class. For instance, BRAC was the first MFI to securitise a microfinance portfolio (worth US$ 180) in July 2006, selling one-third to Citigroup, an investment that was double-guaranteed by the Dutch agency FMO and the German KfW (Mader 2015, 66f.). The Citigroup, again, is a significant driver for financial inclusion policies in Development through its foundation. In 2016, Citigroup partnered with the U.S. government's Overseas Private Investment Corporation to provide more than US$ 430 million to 47 MFI in 25 countries (reportedly reaching 1.2 million borrowers) and signed an agreement with the Asian Development Bank (ADB) to facilitate up to US$ 100 million of local currency loans to MFIs in the Asia-Pacific region (Citi 2017, 24).

With the rise of finance-led accumulation, rising inequality, persistent poverty and increasing concern for environmental degradation, the question of socially and environmentally responsible investments has gained momentum in global finance. Often referred to as 'impact investing', money holders invest capital to generate social or environmental impact beyond financial return (Jafri 2019, 525f.; Kar 2018, 43f.).[12] In this context, specialised investment funds turned microfinance into "its own asset class with an image of social responsibility [...] with particular small risk for investors due to high repayment rate and widespread outreach" (Wichterich

12 Drawing on data from the Global Impact Investor Network (GIIN), Jafri (2019) shows that the vast majority (roughly 64%) of more than 4,600 impact investors stem from financial services, with microfinance being the most important asset class (see also Fanconi and Scheurle 2017, 28).

2012, 407).[13] At the end of the 2000s, these funds managed assets worth US$ 1.5 billion and thus represented more than half of the total international funding for the sector (Convergences 2011). By the end of 2016, the total sum had increased almost ten times. According to the Microfinance Barometer 2018, 127 MIVs – juridically mostly based in tax havens of Luxembourg, the Netherlands, and the United States – managed roughly US$ 13.5 billion, with most of the funding stemming from institutional investors (pensions funds, banks, and foundations), and further significant contributions deriving from retail investors and high net worth individuals (28%) as well as public investors (20%) (Convergences 2018, 10). According to a joint publication of CGAP and the 'impact investor' Symbiotics, the number of active borrowers financed by MIVs has increased from more than half a million in 2006 to 24 million at the end of 2015, generating on average stable net returns of 3.3% for investors between 2006 and 2015 (Symbiotics and CGAP 2016).

Figure 3: Profits at the Bottom of the Pyramid

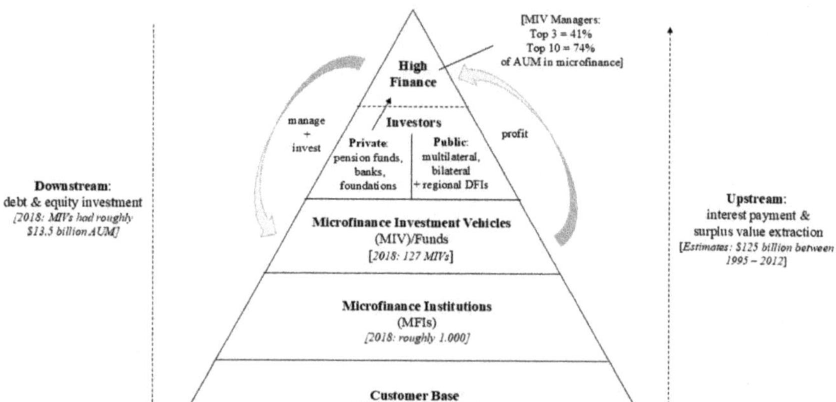

Sources: Own illustration. Data from Convergences (2018); Fanconi and Scheurle (2017), Mader (2015).

13 Moreover, this new asset class was presented as being delinked from capital market trends, making it a perfect investment to diversify the 'portfolios of the rich' (Janda and Svárovksá 2010).

Figure 3 visualises the financial flows in structured microfinance. According to industry estimates, more than a thousand commercial MFIs served approximately 130 million customers in 2018. These are increasingly funded through MIVs managed by a few large financial entities, including investment banks and asset management companies, which reap profits from the bottom of the pyramid through their 'impact investment'. Mader (2015a, 117) estimates that, in the early phase of the financialisation of microfinance between 1995 and 2012, at least US$ 125 billion were extracted from MFI customers. Since 2012, the speed and scope of financialisation have increased many times over, as the above-discussed trends show. In other words, the expansion of poverty finance is far from over.

The affirmative financial inclusion discourse rarely talks about these profits and the uneven financial flows of commercialised and financialised microfinance. Instead, they justify the expansion of global finance as a benevolent mission that liberates the unbanked from "the clutches of high-cost moneylenders" (Mahadeva 2011, 197; Yunus 2007, 46). Ironically, the battle over credit supply is waged through the formal/informal divide. While the former is understood to be safe, cheap, and inherently good, the latter is associated with usurious debt practices of moneylenders. However, the rise of MFIs since the 1990s is essentially associated with expanding shadow banking, a largely non-regulated financial services industry with little transparency and accountability (Finch et al. 2022; Jafri 2019; Mader 2015). Moreover, studies have emphasised striking similarities in business operations between MFIs and moneylenders (Kar 2018, 81ff.), rendering the differentiation between formal and informal finance at least problematic, if not irrelevant. Finally, there is hardly any empirical evidence reflecting that the rise of MFIs has diminished the role of moneylenders, while however counterevidence confirming a complementarity between the two creditor institutions does exist (Agarwal 2021; Guérin et al. 2022). Looking at the case of India, Part III and Part IV will scrutinise these contradictions in more detail. However, before concluding this first part, the following section will briefly explore India's significance for the financial inclusion agenda.

India's Significance for the New Development Agenda

It would not be exaggerated to claim that the rise of microfinance in recent decades, particularly the success story of integrating hundreds of millions of unbanked into the formal financial system, has been primarily backed by the proliferation of financial services in India. Home to more than 1.2 billion people, the rapid rise in the share of account holders rose from 35 per cent in 2011 to 80 per cent in 2017. What is the story behind this impressive growth? Soon after Narendra Modi took office as prime minister of India in May 2014, he launched the Pradhan Mantri Jan Dhan Yojana (PMJDY), a flagship financial inclusion program of the Government of India (GoI) to broaden access to financial services. At the end of August 2014, more than 18 million bank accounts were opened within a week. By August 2019, more than 367 million accounts had been opened, according to the official website.[14] The programme was not only celebrated for its astounding growth rate. The World Bank emphasised how account ownership had increased between 2014 and 2017 "by more than 30% among women as well as among adults in the poorest 40 percent of households" (Demirgüc-Kunt et al. 2018, 19). The incentives to open a PMJDY account were high, since accounts opened under the scheme included an overdraft facility of Rs. 5,000, a debit card of RuPay, and an insurance cover of Rs. 100,000 for accidents and Rs. 30,000 for life. Based on Modi's campaign slogans and speeches on confiscating and returning black money to ordinary people's bank accounts, rumours spread, suggesting account holders would receive between Rs. 5,000 and Rs. 150,000 for free once they had opened an account. The alleged money gifts were also the reason for Mukhne, an Adivasi woman from Maharashtra who works as a daily wage labourer in agriculture and earns up to Rs. 250 a day, to open an account under the scheme. In an interview a few years later, she demonstrated that she was not inclined to use banking facilities: "Five years ago, we didn't have money, so we never even thought of going to a bank [...]. We still don't have money. So what will we do there now?" (Abraham 2019). According to the World Bank Findex database, less than half of all (bank) accounts in India in 2017 were used at least *once* in the past year (Demirgüc-Kunt et al. 2018, 65). The Reserve Bank of India (RBI) estimates that almost 75 per cent of savings accounts lie dormant, and other estimates are even higher (Patel 2016).

Looking at those countries which host nearly half of the world's unbanked today, the vibrant credit-debt relations are striking. Borrowing money in Indonesia is as frequent as it is in the Eurozone. In all the listed economies, the share of formal borrowing (including borrowing from MFIs and credit card debt) is significantly smaller than informal borrowing from family, friends, moneylenders and other sources (see Figure 4).

For South Asia, formal borrowing covers only a tiny share of overall lending, indicating a promising market for commercial microfinance. This is the case, even though the region is already the most populous regarding global microfinance customers. In 1995, the World Bank proclaimed that 12 million microfinance customers worldwide had borrowed a total of US$ 5 billion. Ten years later, the customer base has quadrupled (48.8 million), while the portfolio size has increased at a similar pace (US$ 18.2 billion) (Mader 2015). Another decade later, in 2017, the number of microfinance clients reached a staggering 139 million globally, with outstanding loans of US$ 114 billion. South (East) Asia comprises approximately 60 per cent of the global customer base and a quarter of the total global portfolio. India is by far the largest country for microfinance services worldwide, comprising more than one-third of

14 https://www.pmjdy.gov.in/account [accessed on August 28, 2019]

the global customer base and more than 60 per cent of South Asia's portfolio size (see Table 1).

Figure 4: Sources of Credit in Countries Where Most 'Unbanked' Live, 2017

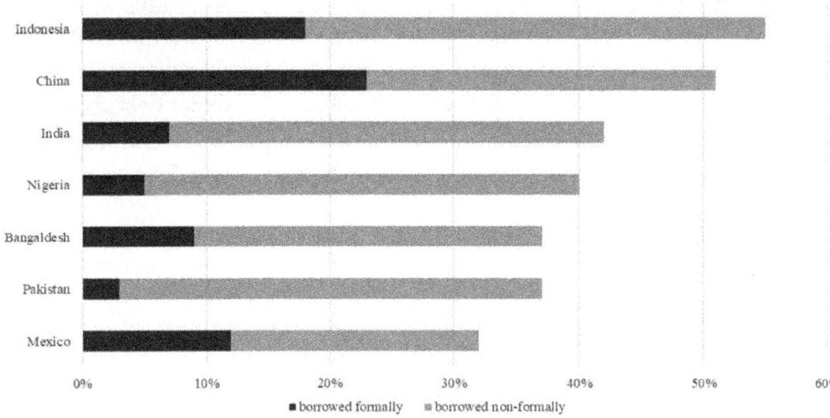

Source: Global Findex database. Note: Adults 15+, borrowing any money in the past year. Formal borrowing refers to all credit relations with financial institutions like banks, MFIs or credit card debt. Non-formal borrowing refers to all other sources, including for example friends and family. Since multiple borrowing is possible but the categories are created mutually exclusive, the actual number of informal borrowings is likely to be underrepresented.

Table 1: Microfinance's Global and Regional Figures in 2017

	Portfolio ($)	% of total	No. of borrowers	% of total
World	114 billion	100	139 million	100
South (East) Asia	27.9 billion	24.5	83.3 million	59.9
India	17.1 billion	14.9	50.9 million	36.6

Source: Microfinance Barometer 2018.

Although the loan portfolio is significantly smaller compared with Latin America and the Caribbean, growth rates in South Asia have been much faster in recent years. Regarding global investments through MIVs, South Asia was the fastest-growing region in the past decade, with a staggering compound annual growth rate (CAGR) of 47 per cent (Convergences 2018). Moreover, profits are the highest on average (with 3.5% on assets) because interest rate yield is similar to other world regions (roughly

21%). At the same time, the operating costs of MFIs are comparatively small thanks to group-based methodologies of lending, which outsource repayment surveillance to peer groups (Convergences 2018).

Proponents of financial inclusion frequently talk about the need to build a financial ecosystem (see e.g. Ehrbeck, Pickens, and Tarazi 2012). As should have become apparent, this refers only to profit-oriented financial services. Looking at Figure 4, it is obvious how leveraging the financial systems approach to microfinance in India engages in a battle over credit supply with already established creditors. To explore the dynamics of expanding commercial microfinance into vibrant debt economies beyond the formal banking system, the distinction between formal and informal financial services is of little help. Instead, one has to trace the foundations of this existing creditor ecosystem.

Chapter 3
Synopsis: Thinking Development through Finance

This first part of the book sought to contextualise the evolution of microfinance in the broader trajectory of international development. It has highlighted the political, economic, and ideological dynamics that have contributed to the rise of commercial microfinance at the global level. In this regard, it stressed how Development thinking and practice is embedded in the broader shifts of capitalist development, how it works through its contradictions, and reproduces them in new and mutated ways (Hart 2010; Taylor 2005). Rather than a straightforward process, the success of microfinance must be understood as a contingent result of multiple intersecting dynamics since the 1970s (see Figure 5). On the one hand, targeted and subsidised public credit programmes were retrenched in the context of the crumbling Bretton Woods System and disciplinary lending from IFIs demanding neoliberal austerity, liberalisation, and privatisation. On the other hand, substantial parts of the global population were immiserated by a new wave of enclosing the commons, cancelled subsidies for agricultural production, and new dependencies on export markets, which pushed ever more people into precarious labour and survival activities in the so-called informal sector (Federici 2012; George 1990; Ghosh 2015).

In this context, experiments with income-generating (group) loans mushroomed across the global South, often driven by civil society organisations and supported by national and international DFIs. When some of these experiments demonstrated that poverty finance could be a profitable business case, especially when borrowing to women's groups who would vouch for one another, corporate capital began to push for the professionalisation and scaling-up of the sector since the 1990s. This process triggered the commercialisation of microfinance and its integration into the expanding domain of global finance. With increased investments from global financial institutions through structured finance, microfinance expanded rapidly in the 2000s, reflecting the broader euphoria of finance-led growth in global capitalism. However, the increased linkages with international finance also exposed microfinance to the volatilities of financial markets. Toward the end of the 2000s, when the sector experienced numerous repayment crises and the myth of entrepreneurial credit as an effective tool for sustained income generation was increasingly debunked, commercial microfinance experienced a profound crisis (Guérin, Labie, and Servet 2015; Mader and Sabrow 2015).

Figure 5: The Evolution of Microfinance in D/development

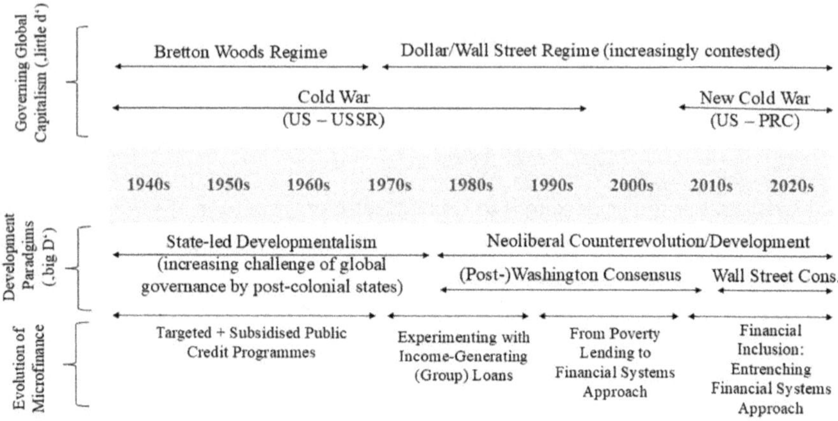

Source: own illustration, adapted and expanded from Hart (2010).

After the global financial crisis, the G20, IMF, World Bank and others defended the broader legitimacy of finance-led economic growth by popularising decent finance and inclusive growth. At the household level, this agenda was framed under financial inclusion, providing access to financial services to previously unbanked populations. Essentially, the new development agenda entrenched commercialised and financialised microfinance in the name of inclusive (finance-led) growth. Broad alliances between financial institutions, philanthropic think tanks, development ministries/agencies of the global North, central banks, and international organisations and fora of Development (UN, World Bank, G20, etc.), such as the AFI or the GPFI, manifested the agenda of inclusive finance as the primary approach to tackling the growth-poverty nexus (Gabor and Brooks 2016; Mader 2018; Soederberg 2013).

Essentially, the shift towards financial inclusion resonates with the broader trend toward market-based finance in the era of sustainable development. As such, it is part of the new Wall Street Consensus, which elaborates on the PWC and is a strategy in the recent rivalry for global hegemony between the United States and the People's Republic of China (Alami, Dixon, and Mawdsley 2021; Gabor 2018; Mawdsley and Taggart 2022). In a context where social infrastructure is increasingly indexed against its bankability, commodification and financialisation lead to monetising access to basic needs. Since the 'unbanked' largely overlap with the working poor, who struggle to make ends meet, access to credit replaces the right to essential entitlements, including housing, education, and health care, amongst others. This reality lies at the ground of the chasm between benevolent rhetoric and structural violence of financial inclusion.

Finally, this chapter demonstrated India's significance in the inclusive finance agenda. The country is one of the most dynamic microfinance markets and hosts the most extensive customer base in the world. As such, the chapter provides a meaningful context and background for further investigation. Most of the developments discussed here are already well-researched. However, in re-narrating the story of microfinance based on the critical literature, there is a danger of reproducing significant blind spots.

First, an analysis of the evolution of microfinance in D/development at the global level is undoubtedly important. However, if exclusively employed, it reproduces a particular top-down perspective, insufficiently attentive to how Development policies respond to concrete problems in specific contexts, and how they might be applied differently from the general rhetoric. In other words, one cannot deduce the workings of microfinance on the ground either from its function to global capital accumulation or the imperatives of the Development paradigm (Taylor 2005). Second, by exclusively focusing on neoliberal development, most of the microfinance literature silences the colonial histories and legacies that matter to understand the rise of commercial microfinance in the present. As such, the periodisation represented in this chapter might obscure the intimate relationship between colonialism, racism, capitalism and Development (Bernards 2022; Wilson 2012). Third, the periodisation presented above has a certain institutional bias. By looking at the evolution of microfinance through the evolution of microfinance institutions, there is a dangerous tendency to flatten the livelihoods of the global poor into a customer base, reifying the affirmative narrative. Doing so underappreciates microfinance as one amongst many other tools for dominating and exploiting working-class households. Put differently, looking at the evolution of access to credit from the perspective of subaltern working-class households might tell us more about the intimate and dynamic relationship between class formation, exploitation, and struggle on the one side and the uneven (financial) capital accumulation on the other side.

So, while this brief review of thinking D/development through finance is an important context which helps understand the rise of commercial microfinance in recent decades, it does not account for the fractured lives that underpin this rise. Before engaging with a deep history of microfinance in India in Part III, the following chapters will discuss the methodological foundations and relevant theoretical concepts necessary to pursue such an investigation.

Part II: Foundations for Researching Fractured Lives

"How to tell a shattered story? By slowly becoming everybody. No. By solely becoming everything"
– *Arundathi Roy (2017)*

"If *money* is the bond binding me to *human* life, binding society to me, connecting me with nature and man, is not money the bond of all *bonds?* Can it not dissolve and bind all ties? Is it not, therefore, also the universal *agent of separation?*"
– *Karl Marx (1988)*

"We surrender our life-strength, and all we have to show for it afterwards is a little money. We have always insisted that the process 'life in exchange for money' is irreversible. Money engenders no new life. Life arises only from life. We must act to reappropriate our lives."
– *Maria Mies (2014)*

Chapter 4
Coming to Terms with A Historical and Materialist Reality

This research attempts to investigate the fractured lives of subaltern class indebtedness in India. It aims to broaden the critical political economy literature on financial inclusion to understand how and why microfinance could proliferate rapidly in recent decades. On the one hand, I intend to reframe the debates on microfinance by looking at the labour-debt nexus: how an increasing share of borrowers becomes indebted not as entrepreneurs but as precarious workers. On the other hand, I want to extend the historical scope for understanding the governance of access to credit for working-class households in the modern era, paying specific attention to the process of British colonialism and its aftermath on the subcontinent. Both dimensions are crucial to understanding the chasm between benevolent rhetoric and structural violence of financial inclusion.

The task at hand is far from straightforward. It is an endeavour that draws on extensive theoretical reflection, historical and empirical field research. The following chapters develop the methodological foundations for investigating fractured lives in five steps. Following Johnna Montgomerie, I understand methodology as "the interface between ontology (how the world is), epistemology (how the world can be known), substantive theory (how the world is understood) and method (how the world is examined)" (Montgomerie 2017, 4). I will first discuss the ontological and epistemological premises of this research. Then I will detail how chronic household indebtedness can be understood as a gendered and racialised form of class rule, drawing on Marx's conceptualisation of money and finance, social reproduction feminism, and contemporary debates on racial capitalism. The final chapter of this part reconstructs the concrete research process and how the notion of regimes of re/productive finance is a valuable frame to understand the historical and spatial broadening of financial inclusion analysis.

To make sense of the philosophy of science that underpins this research, I suggest engaging with the epigraph from Arundathi Roy. The question of how to tell a shattered story is foundational to understanding fractured lives. 'By slowly becoming everybody' could be understood as a metaphor for a research strategy that engages seriously with the worldviews and lived realities of different people. For example, whether the story of the modern world economy is narrated as one of universal progress, rationality and wealth or as contradictory and uneven development marked by colonial violence, extinction, and dispossession, has far-reaching implications. As such, slowly becoming everybody may correspond to the postcolonial criticism which intervenes "in those ideological discourses of modernity that attempt to give a hegemonic normality to the uneven development and the differential, often disadvantaged, histories of nations, races, communities, peoples" (Bhabha 1994, 171).[1] By resurrecting marginalised knowledge, practices, and worldviews, slowly becoming everybody may be understood as a metaphor for the struggle for "epistemic justice" (Santos 2014).

Arundathi Roy considers this perspective, but she rejects it and opts for an alternative. By 'solely becoming everything', she consciously emphasises the relationality of social life. How else can we think that the one telling a story becomes solely everything? With her simple yet complex statement, Roy suggests that all parts of the shattered story already embody the other parts and that this web of relations forms the whole. Only if one already is *potentially* everything, only if the two are internally related and constitute one another, does this option make any sense. For the philosophy of (social) science, then, the most promising way of telling a shattered story lies in understanding *everything* as conditioned relationality. This claim is not limited to understanding the present exclusively through contemporary conditions. As Gurminder Bhambra remarks, "[i]n misidentifying the past as unconnected, there is no way in which they can address the inequalities of the present as consequent of shared historical processes" (Bhambra 2014, 145).

This brings us to a methodological problem. How can a shattered story be told without narrating it as an additive collection of fragments or treating the fragments as mere reflections of a grand narrative? In what follows, I will argue that Critical Realism and Marx's philosophy of internal relations are a fruitful foundation for telling the shattered story of India's indebted subaltern classes. This does not deny the relevance of postcolonial critiques against Eurocentric knowledge production and the silencing of (post-)colonial violence. Instead, I suggest incorporating these into a historical materialist perspective to avoid a critical methodological problem which will be discussed in the following section.

---

1 Postcolonial and Decolonial scholarship are internally heterogeneous and differently applied across regions and disciplines. However, they are used interchangeably in this section because the argument refers to basic ontological and epistemological assumptions and general tendencies which underpin most research in these fields (Bhambra 2014, 117ff.).

The Case for A Realist and Stratified Ontology

Most postcolonial approaches are grounded in poststructuralist/postmodern philosophy of science, eschewing the grand modern narratives of Enlightenment, evolutionism, and utilitarianism, which have been instrumental in European colonial and imperial rule (Bhabha 1994; Mignolo 2002; Ziai 2016). Deconstructing modern discourses is the central task for much of this scholarship. From this perspective, Marxist political economy is inappropriate to account for the shattered story of a (post-)colonial world economy. It is criticised for being Eurocentric and historicist, leaving no room for the agency of colonised and marginalised populations, silencing their diverse histories and livelihoods (Chakrabarty 2000; Grosfoguel 2007). For instance, the eminent postcolonial writer Homi K. Bhabha maintains that "[t]he great connective narratives of capitalism and class drive the engines of social reproduction, but do not, in themselves, provide a foundational frame for those modes of cultural identification and political effect that form around issues of sexuality, race, feminism, the lifeworld of refugees or migrants, or the deathly social destiny of AIDS" (Bhabha 1994, 6). However, treating questions of feminism, racism or migration primarily as cultural problems detached from questions of class or political economy more broadly precludes a relational understanding.

Moreover, the deconstruction of modern discourses is frequently paralleled by a reconstruction of a new grand narrative. Many postcolonial writings summarise the complexity of colonialism, imperialism, capitalism, modernity, Enlightenment and Development all together under a civilisational encounter between the 'West' and the 'Rest' without dissecting the internal relations, contradictions, and contestations within this new grand narrative, and without locating specific configurations of political economy within a historical trajectory (Dirlik 1999; Lazarus 2011; Virdee 2019). This tendency is rooted in a methodological problem. In primarily scrutinising the politics of knowledge (epistemology), social reality (ontology) turns into a derivative condition. As Sabelo Ndlovu-Gatsheni puts it, the inquiry of the "epistemicides", "linguicides", and "culturecides" of "cognitive empire" require a method which acknowledges "the primacy of epistemology as a creator of ontology" (Ndlovu-Gatsheni 2020).

From a critical realist standpoint, the major underlying problem here seems to be what Roy Bhaskar calls "epistemic fallacy" (Bhaskar 2008, 5), the collapse of ontology into epistemology. If the social is understood exclusively or primarily as discursive, it risks turning social reality into a mere thought object or linguistic practice (Bannerji 2020, 10). The ontological level becomes a simple representation of our epistemologies, leading to an unspecified or flat ontology. In contrast to such a flat ontology or flat epistemology that underpins positivist research, critical realists suggest a stratified ontology consisting of different levels (observable, actual, real) with distinct properties, and a reflexive epistemology to investigate the world.[2]

Critical realists distinguish between the transitive and intransitive dimensions of knowledge to highlight that the world as it exists should not be conflated with how we experience it (Sayer 2000, 10). While there are empirically observable phenomena which we can sensually grasp (domain of the observable), there are also events which shape the social world regardless of our perception (domain of the actual) and underlying mechanisms which cannot be grasped in any sensuous way, but which nonetheless maintain, challenge, and transform the appearances on the previous two levels (Bhaskar 2008; Sayer 1992). Importantly, each layer of reality has distinct properties and powers which are related to one another but nonetheless irreducible:

> "Emergent properties are relational, arising out of combination (e.g. the division of labour from which high productivity emerges), where the latter is capable of reacting back on the former (e.g. producing monotonous work), has its own causal powers (e.g. differential wealth of nations), which are causally irreducible to the powers of its components (individual workers). This signals the stratified nature of social reality where different strata possess different emergent properties and powers" (Archer 1995, 9)

What follows is that "knowledge follows existence, in logic and in time" (Bhaskar 2008, 29). This is not only a philosophical debate. After all, science is inherently explanatory and not simply descriptive; explanation "is achieved by reference to enduring mechanisms" (Bhaskar 2008, 177). If these mechanisms are merely a discursive product (of our minds) without having independent properties and powers, explanations risk becoming either arbitrary or self-referential. At the same time, critical realism suggests that knowledge production is far from neutral, straightforward, or absolute. Knowledge is inherently social and produced by human activity, and yet it is irreducible to the acts of humans (Bhaskar 2008, 178). Rather than being 'constructed' from scratch, already existing knowledge is constantly reproduced or transformed (Sayer 1992, 41).

To avoid telling a shattered story as an addition of fragments or treating the fragments as a mere reflection of the main story, the logic of inquiry has to move beyond inductive or deductive reasoning. Critical realists suggest navigating between the foreground, that is, the description of observable phenomena, and the background, i.e. the exploration of possible explanations for such phenomena by suggesting and substantiating specific generative mechanisms. Rather than a straightforward research process, such retroductive analysis is best described as "gentle art", moving

2 For an overview of the basics of critical realism and its implications for social research, see Sayer (1992) and Archer et al. (1998).

back and forth between the empirical (observable phenomena) and theoretical (possible explanations), "making use of both qualitative and quantitative [...] data depending on their 'practical adequacy' for answering particular research questions, while being reflective of the role of the researcher in the process of knowledge production" (Belfrage and Hauf 2017, 255; see also Blaikie and Priest 2017, 175f.). Practising retroductive research is closely related to the complex process of abstraction. Therefore, the following sections will discuss the complexity of abstraction within a philosophy of internal relations, building from Marx's writings.

Marx's Philosophy of Internal Relations

Stuart Hall has claimed that the purpose of (critical) social science is to "undermine the obvious", to neither take common sense pretences nor other scientific explanations for given, but to explain why things that appear to be "just like that" are, in fact, "social and historical processes" (Hall 2021, 127). While a philosophy of external relations operates with discrete entities (things) as the most important unit of analysis, a philosophy of internal relations highlights that all 'things' are nothing but relations and processes, and this relational aspect of social reality is an irreducible minimum from where social research starts (Ollman 2003, 25). The object of the investigation thus becomes "a field of reciprocally-determining transformations" (McNally 2015, 134). The complexity of abstraction is key to understanding this ontological claim and practising research according to it.

When it is claimed that Marx's method was to move from the abstract-simple to the concrete-complex, this process can be easily misunderstood. It could foster the delusion that this is a linear, straightforward process which starts from abstract concepts and deduces claims about concrete societies from there, ending up with what Margret Archer has rightly criticised as "downwards conflation" (Archer 1995, 81). While the mode of presentation of *Capital I*, starting with the commodity as the most abstract-simple concept, seems to affirm a deductive approach, Marx's mode of inquiry is neither deductive nor inductive but retroductive. The point of departure for his materialist method is the "real concrete" (immediate appearance of society), which by way of abstraction is understood and criticised as "thought concrete" (reconstructed appearance) (see Hall 2003, 127; Ollman 2003, 60). Thereby the objective of critique is twofold. On the one hand, it exposes the fallacies and contradictions of existing scientific and common sense explanations. On the other hand, it challenges the social injustices that characterise the object of investigation.

Arguably, the most comprehensive discussion of methodology in Marx's work is to be found in the introduction to *Grundrisse*. In this chapter, he explicitly rejects essentialist and naturalist conceptions of political economy to argue that all abstract categories, like production, distribution, exchange, and consumption, "form the members of a totality, distinctions within a unity" and "[m]utual interaction takes place between the different moments. This the case with every organic whole" (Marx 1973, 99f.). The whole is thus internally differentiated (we could also say shattered or fractured) and constituted by the dynamic interaction between all these moments. In other words, it is a "complexly structured differentiated totality" (Hall 2003, 127; see also McNally 2015; Ollman 2015). Marx consciously does not treat capital, labour, and value (to name but three important categories) as separate, independent factors. Rather, capital *is* value in motion, labour *becomes* (variable) capital under certain relations of production, labour *takes on* a specific value form, etc. In other words, these are no essentialised categories but relational concepts that are in constant flux and, precisely because of their conditioned relationality, embody different categories in one way or the other. It does so, however, based on a stratified ontology and various levels of abstraction, signalling a different relevance of specific concepts. The purpose of his method, then, is precisely to uncover why this relationality exists in exactly this way, how it is organised and what effects, including contradictions, it produces.

If there was one central claim that runs like a red thread through Marx's critique of political economy, it is the analytical shortcoming of classical political economy in essentialising and naturalising economic categories, failing to grasp their historical and thus inherently social, contingent and contested character. Marx claims that "all science would be superfluous if the form of appearance of things directly coincided with their essence" (Marx 1981, 956). For instance, the financial inclusion discourse assumes that not having a bank account (a form of appearance) is a crucial problem for the global working poor (essence). However, Marx's method rejects self-sufficient entities to argue that every appearance, like lack of money amongst specific segments of society, is always "the sum of many, prior determinations" (Hall 2003, 115). And scrutinising these relations changes what the essential problem is. In this sense, dialectic is primarily understood as an epistemological strategy. It does not refer to any obscure motor force of history that predicts the ways of the world. Dialectics is a mode of thinking that allows replacing "the common sense notion of 'thing' (as something that has a history and has external connections with other things) with notions of 'process' (which contains its history and possible futures) and 'relation' (which contains as part of what it is its ties with other relations)" (Ollman 2003, 13). While a common-sense perspective suggests that certain economic phenomena, say economic growth, must imply wealth and therefore undermines its opposite (poverty), a materialist dialectic claims that economic growth produces both wealth (capital accumulation) and poverty (immiseration of labour through exploitation/expropriation) *at the same time*, and one cannot conceive of one side without its relation to the other (McNally 2015; Ollman 2015; Selwyn 2017).

Such a view has profound implications for some of the most common concepts in science, including our understanding of causal claims. Rather than assuming "logical independence and absolute priority" of discrete entities, this form of dialectical thinking suggests that "there can be no cause that is logically prior to or independent of that which it is said to give rise and no determining factor that is itself not affected by that which it is said to determine" (Ollman 2003, 71). The conventional understanding of causation as self-sufficient entities that collide to produce an effect is thus replaced with an analysis of specific mechanisms that emerge from the social structure and express themselves in distinct effects or events dependent on spatiotemporal conditions (Sayer 2000). In this context, different levels of abstraction are key to specific knowledge claims. For instance, the appropriation of surplus labour may be a general characteristic of class rule, but it "can occur in multiple configurations, under a variety of conditions, buoyed by a diverse set of institutions, narratives of justification, and social practices" (Bohrer 2019, 185f.). In other words, the claim that capital exploits labour remains an "empty abstraction" (Marx 1973, 96), an "external determination of lifeless entities" (McNally 2015, 136) if the concrete conditions, that is, the processes and relations that constitute specific labour processes in distinct spatiotemporal settings, are left unexplored.

These processes and relations cannot be deducted from the general level, and they are necessarily diverse in the concrete. They must be reconstructed historically and empirically to turn from the "real concrete" (immediate appearance) to the "thought concrete" (reconstructed appearance) (see Hall 2003, 127; Ollman 2003, 60). In other words, the directly observable must be thought through internally, differentiated through related layers of abstractions, and traced historically backwards to become meaningful beyond its superficial appearance in common sense.

The Irreducibility of Structure and Agency: Tracing History Backwards

Tracing history backwards requires differentiating structure and agency. Following Margret Archer's critical realist approach, I maintain that (a) structure and agency are irreducible to one another; (b) that structure are emergent entities and necessarily pre-date those actions which transform it; (c) and that structural elaboration necessarily post-dates those actions (Archer 1995, 76). To argue that structure and agency possess different properties and powers allows us to investigate their relationship methodologically, explaining why things are the way they are (and not otherwise) (Archer 1995, 64f.). The question of temporality is crucial in this regard because structure and agency operate at different time intervals. Only through time (and space) can we specify *whose* activities acted upon *what* social structure and *which* structural elaboration resulted from this specific conjuncture. What may sound obvious is indeed eschewed by conflationary social sciences. Whether we assume that structure determines agency (downward conflation), that agency determines structure (upward conflation), or that both are co-existent (central conflation), all approaches preclude a sequential analysis in which structure and agency are profoundly interrelated and yet irreducible to one another (Archer 1995, 163ff.).

These statements are perfectly compatible with the ontological assumptions discussed above. In contrast to general claims of critiques that historical materialism cannot sufficiently account for the diversity of human agency, a social, stratified and relational ontology highlights the processual, and thus conditional and open-ended, nature of structure and agency, requiring researchers to focus on the reproduction and transformation of specific structures (of thought) and practices in a given historical period (Bakker and Gill 2003, 20). As Marx famously declared in the *Eighteenth Brumaire*, "[m]en [sic!] make their own history, but they do not make it as they please; they do not make it under self-selected circumstances, but under circumstances existing already, given and transmitted from the past" (Marx 1937, 8). In this sense, the properties and powers of (social) structures constrain human agency, but they do not determine it. Reciprocally, the agency is always located within social structures, reproducing or transforming the latter. Still, it never creates structures entirely anew (as for example imagined by the liberal invocation of a natural state).[3]

As a consequence, a critical realist epistemology must not only be reflexive (of the conditioned and relational nature of social reality), but it must also be historicist to account for the irreducible and yet interconnected relationship between structure and agency (Bieler and Morton 2018, 48). In this sense, we can think of structure and agency as "abstractions form a single set of historical processes" (Bakker and Gill 2003, 22). It is impossible to precisely predict structural elaboration ex-ante, even if one consciously reflects on a given structure and agent's interests, because there are infinite combinations in which the agency of a multiple subjects come together, producing various potential outcomes. Yet, it is possible to trace the conditions, constraints and interactions of structure and agency backwards ex-post, making sense of the present (structural elaboration) through history (structural conditions and social interactions). Of course, such analysis can never claim absolute truth. Knowledge production remains inherently fallible, amongst other things, because it is always embedded in what it tries to make sense of (Bhaskar 2008; Sayer 1992, 5f.). Moreover, structure and agency are irreducible and fundamentally complex and diverse as embedded forms of consciousness (Bannerji 2020, 8). Therefore, knowledge must always stand the test of critical reflection and debate to prove its ex-

3 Margeret Archer thus argues that society is not simply what we choose to make (of) it, "for generically 'society' is that which nobody wants in exactly the form they find it and yet it resists both individual and collective efforts at transformation – not necessarily by remaining unchanged but altering to become something else which still confirms to no one's ideal" (Archer 1995, 95).

planatory value and context-specific relevance both in the concrete contexts in which it emerges and afterwards.

Against this backdrop, a historical materialist critique of financial inclusion cannot be limited to criticising the predatory aspects of lending money to the poor. Financial *exclusion*, understood as preventing people from accessing credit, is not a desirable cure for the exploitative dynamics that drive increased indebtedness. Rather, one must identify the processes and relations that explain why and how subaltern working classes in many parts of the world have become so desperately reliant on chronic borrowing to make ends meet, criticising and challenging exactly these dynamics instead of their superficial appearance. The critical aspect of this approach lies in its emphasis on reflexivity, in rejecting to accept the observable appearance (i.e. poor households lack money) as given, without rejecting the real existence of the social fact that an increasing share of the global working class is structurally indebted to sustain their livelihood.[4] The task of critical political economy lies in scrutinising the myriad *presuppositions* that constitute this real condition. In other words, it must trace the present's determinations theoretically, historically, and empirically. That is precisely the main goal of this book.

In sum, determinations are vital to critical research. At the same time, determinism is firmly rejected as a mode of inquiry, both in the form of deducing the concrete from the abstract or suggesting a teleological development. Determinations allow us to mediate between different levels of abstraction, study different parts while at the same time relating them to a broader whole, break up the entrenched binaries of the individual/social, micro/macro, or voluntarism/structuralism through focussing on differentiated, conditioned and relational phenomena in specific spatiotemporal configurations. In this regard, the historical materialist method is "not eurocentric, however, but anti-eurocentric" because it "demands that the specificity of all societies and contexts be apprehended *on their own* terms" (Gruffydd Jones 2012, 225, own emphasis). As such, this rich and diverse research tradition provides a promising starting point for studying the global political economy as a differentiated whole. This is not to deny that there are many internal relations and hidden connections that Marx insufficiently addressed or misread. But the methodological foundations of the paradigm require it to internalise reflexivity and criticism as central modes of self-development. In other words, Marx's critique of political economy remains an "open-ended critique" (Foster 2018), and feminist, anti-racist, postcolonial and ecological internal critiques have greatly enhanced the explanatory power and strategic horizon of historical materialism in recent decades. If anything, this chapter attempts to contribute modestly to precisely this mode of internal criticism and advancement. To this end, the following parts will engage with the theoretical

4 This categorisation builds on the useful distinction from Cox (1981) between problem-solving and critical theory.

substance of the research design, that is, a combination of Marx's conceptualisation of money, finance and class rule, social reproduction feminism and racial finance capitalism, which together allow us to trace the history of financial inclusion in India backwards.

Chapter 5
Marx on Money, Finance, and Power in Capitalism

Money is a concept as central as it is contested in economics research.[1] Mainstream economics usually defines money as all assets which fulfil the monetary functions of medium of exchange, unit of account, and store of value (Mankiw 2012, 324). Although foundational to markets, orthodox approaches assume "monetary neutrality" (Mankiw 2012, 370): money affects nominal but not real variables of the economy. Despite being dominant, this perspective has become increasingly under scrutiny in recent years, especially after the great financial crisis of 2008. For instance, political economy scholars have challenged the functional definition, criticising that it does not reveal anything about the "nature of money" (Ingham 2004). Popular critics have argued that money is not a thing but a social relation, specifically, a credit-debt relationship (Ingham 2004; Pettifor 2017). Commercial banks create money "out of thin" air in modern capitalism by issuing credit (Lavoie 2020; Werner 2014). Notably, modern governments have delegated the power to produce money to commercial banks, which is an important dimension to understanding contemporary inequalities (Desan 2014; Pistor 2019; Wullweber 2019). As such, these criticisms eschew the dominant understanding of money as a neutral economic institution, politicising the power of (producing) money and highlighting the inequality between creditors and debtors. Arguably, these basic assumptions are the foundations of a 'new critical orthodoxy'.[2]

It would seem that such a critical approach is useful for understanding the rise of commercial microfinance and the proliferation of household debt in the global South. However, understanding money primarily as a social relation of debt limits

1 The history of the philosophy of money is rich and diverse and cannot be discussed here at length. For an overview, see e.g. Eich (2022). Rather than summarising different theories of money, this section makes the case for engaging with Marx's understanding of money, finance, and power to understand the structural violence of financial inclusion in the present.

2 I borrow the term "new critical orthodoxy" from Brand (2016), who uses it to criticise the emergence of critical sustainability studies engaging with escalating climate change and the necessity of changing the fossil fuel-based growth model without challenging the power relations underpinning the present political ecology of inequality.

the explanatory capacities of credit theories substantially. First, it focuses on financial relations as isolated from the broader political economy. Second, in foregrounding the credit-debt relation, (micro-)finance is primarily studied as a relationship between borrowers and creditors, ignoring the relevance of the labour-debt nexus. Third, focussing exclusively on the power of commercial banks to produce money, these approaches usually imply a mono-dimensional understanding of power, confined to the creation of credit money. Moreover, equating money and credit implies a flat ontology in which all kinds of debt (whether from moneylenders or microfinance organisations) are the same.

Engaging with this criticism, this chapter argues that reading Marx's philosophy of money, finance and power in capitalism presents a promising foundation for studying the proliferation of commercial microfinance. Interestingly, the new critical orthodoxy draws on diverse canonical thinkers like Georg F. Knapp, Alfred Mitchel-Innes, Max Weber, Georg Simmel, and John M. Keynes but refrains from a deeper engagement with Karl Marx. It is often claimed that Marx's (commodity) theory of money is naturalist, claiming that gold *is* money and that his theory of value is essentialist, simply maintaining that labour *is* value (Ingham 2004, 61f.). These interpretations are partly grounded in existing ambiguities, blind spots, and contradictions in Marx's voluminous writings and partly in failing to understand the different levels of abstraction employed in *Capital I*.[3] The following seeks to demonstrate that Marx's understanding of money and finance remains relevant to date because it explains *why* and *how* money can perform diverse functions in capitalist social formations, providing the basis for a deeper critique of the old orthodoxy.[4] Therefore, I will first engage with Marx's understanding of the nature of money and how it is not a social relation of debt but rather a societal relation of oppression. Then, I will continue discussing the monetary foundations of finance capitalism and how this perspective explains the structural violence of financial inclusion.

---

3 On the one hand, Marx analyses the basic forms of the capitalist mode of production in its ideal historical average, arguing on a highly abstract level of social theory. On the other hand, he frequently uses empirical examples of specific institutional configurations that marked the political economy of capitalism as it appeared in his time. And at times, he conflates these two levels of abstraction or insufficiently distinguishes between them, laying the ground for numerous misinterpretations. This is the case for several parts where he equates money with gold.

4 Marx explicitly discusses various functions of money, most importantly money as means of circulation (exchange), as measure of value, as store of value, as means of deferred payment, and as world money. However, these functions cannot explain the nature of money. Rather, the nature of money explains why money can perform these functions in the economy. Therefore, the various functions of money in Marx's work will not be discussed in detail here. For an overview see Marx (1976, 188ff.), and for a detailed discussion of its relevance to understanding contemporary capitalism see, for example, Harvey (2006a, 11ff.) de Brunhoff and Foley (2006), Jessop (2013), and Ivanova (2020).

Money as Everything and Nothing

For Marx, the nature of money cannot be understood by defining it on its own terms. He was very aware of the fluid and opaque character of money, paying specific attention to its peculiar *social* form. Hence, he suggested studying the nature of money in relation to the reproduction of society at large. In *Grundrisse*, Marx speaks of money as "an essential relation of production" to highlight the way in which forms of money change over space and time:

> "Various forms of money may correspond better to social production in various stages; one form may remedy evils against which another is powerless; but none of them, as long as they remain forms of money, and as long as money remains an essential relation of production, is capable of overcoming the contradictions inherent in the money relation, and can instead only hope to reproduce these contradictions in one or another form." (Marx 1973, 123)

But what are these fundamental contradictions that, according to Marx, are inherent to any money form? This is where the nature of commodities, and in particular their contradictory character, must be taken into consideration. Not because money *is* a commodity (e.g. gold) but because, as Marx famously declares in the opening passage of *Capital I*, commodities are the "elementary form" in which wealth appears in "societies in which a capitalist mode of production prevails" (Marx 1976, 123).

Thus, money is a peculiar *social form of value* in which value is expressed independently of a product's specific qualities. This expression of value is tied to the dual and contradictory nature of commodities. Only because products can be expressed in a value abstracted from their inherent qualities (as use values) do they become commodities. The social form of commodities (exchange value) exists in the form of money, while the physical form (use value) exists naturally. This process is far from straightforward since it entails that entirely different things, which seem to have nothing in common, are made commensurable by abstracting from their specific and concrete existence. In other words, the particular qualities of commodities as use-values are "extinguished" in the *money form*, just as the difference of the production process creating these specific use-values is rendered invisible so that they can be expressed independently as quantitative relations, and they can exist as values autonomously (Marx 1981, 516).[5] From this perspective, money is not only abstract money of account or measure of value, as stressed by credit theorists. Money, though

5 Marx uses the expression of money as *selbständiger (Tausch-)Wert* at various points in *Grundrisse* and *Capital*. The English version usually translates *selbstständig* as *independent* to highlight the existence of (exchange) value alongside the use-value qualities of commodities. However, the German word *selbstständig* also means *autonomous*, emphasising that commodity's (exchange) values develop a life of their own.

tied to all commodities, is different from the latter, for it is the immediate *expression* of value, it's specificity being value (Heinrich 2001).[6]

To emphasise the coordinating role money plays in any complex society, characterised by a certain degree of division of labour, is not the same as to say money emerged from barter. Quite to the contrary, exchange in the money form and barter are qualitatively different processes. The latter, which Marx referred to as "real exchange", is characterised by *specific* products with *distinct* properties that may only be exchanged if they fulfil particular conditions. Barter thus creates a unique, qualitative relationship between exchanged products. No complex real economy could be sustained on this premise, where exchange-relations are based on goods' physical and natural properties (McNally, 2011, 122). The peculiarity of exchange in the money form is that a commodity becomes related to *all* other commodities as an independent expression. It becomes countable, "equally divisible", and "always exchangeable" as value as if thrown into a melting pot that creates as common texture for entirely different things:

> "As a value, a commodity is an equivalent for all other commodities in a given relation. As a value, the commodity is an equivalent; as an equivalent, all its natural properties are extinguished; it no longer takes up a special, qualitative relationship towards the other commodities; but is rather the general measure as well as the general representative, the general medium of exchange of all other commodities. As value, it is money" (Marx 1973, 141)

Understanding money as every*thing* and no*thing* highlights its transient character, embodying both the *immateriality* of value and the *material* form in which commodities as bearers of value appear in the process of valorisation. In this sense, "[a]ll commodities are perishable money; [and] money is the imperishable commodity" (Marx 1973, 149). Thus, money is "the form in which all commodities equate, compare, measure themselves; into which all commodities dissolve themselves; that which dissolves itself into all commodities; the universal equivalent" (Marx 1973, 142). It follows that value is nothing inherent *in* commodities but rather a relation *between all* commodities – a contradictory relation between qualitatively distinct things that are incomparable in every sensuous aspect but made comparable by abstracting from their individual qualities.

Since the process of equalising different commodities is also the equalisation of different labour processes necessary to produce these commodities in the first place, Marx claimed the substance of value is *abstract labour*.[7] The equality of differ-

6 Heinrich (2001) thus speaks of a "monetary theory of value".

7 This does not imply that labour *is* money. Rather, the concept of 'abstract labour' seeks to highlight how the atomised labour of commodity producers must become social labour in order to facilitate commodity exchange, and for this to happen the concrete labour must take

ent labour can only exist as an abstraction of their actually existing inequality by reducing commodity's qualities to the only common character they possess, that is, being products of human labour, hence abstract (social) labour. In this sense, the alienation of individual producers from their social relationships is a prerequisite for money to emerge (Nelson 1999, 4ff.). To say a commodity's use value, its uniqueness, its concreteness is extinguished in the money form also means that the specific, unique and concrete labour process creating this commodity is extinguished, only appearing as a portion of total value:

> "When we equate coats, linen and gold, therefore, we are equating weaving, spinning and mining – each of which is a qualitatively distinct work-process. We are saying that each of these unique labour-processes, however much they differ concretely as productive activities creating distinct use-values, have produced the same intangible thing: a certain quantity of value, measurable by money" (McNally 2011b, 123)

In other words, money is the direct form of existence of abstract labour, for only in this form can private labour be socially recognised as value-producing labour in exchange (after production). As such, money is far more than a unit of account or means of circulation. It is a necessary *medium of socialisation* under capitalist social relations (Heinrich 2001).

If critiques argue that Marx's theory of money or the labour theory of value is based on the nature of commodities or the assumption that social labour produces value and that it is, therefore, naturalist, essentialist or reductionist, they fail to understand the centrality of the *societal* character of labour producing commodities, which distinguishes Marxist approaches from classical political economy. As Michael Heinrich emphasises, the distinctiveness of commodities as exchange value has nothing to do with their physiological character and has everything to do with the specific social form of labour that underpins their production. The existence of value in commodities only is a "phantasmal concreteness" (Heinrich 1994, 10). It appears as an independent expression of things, although it does not have any objective basis in these things. Its value objectivity is the result of social recognition, not as an individual or intentional act, but as the effect of a particular form of socialisation.

These thoughts are no mere philosophical exercise. They have profound implications for understanding the power of money. For the new critical orthodoxy, the power of money is expressed in the inequality of creditor-debtor relationships and in the privilege of certain financial institutions, like commercial banks or a central bank, to create money by way of credit. As outlined above, such a perspective stresses

---

an independent value form, i.e. money, for it to be commensurable with other commodities and labour processes (Heinrich 1994; Saad-Filho 1993).

the role of the sphere of circulation while remaining blissfully ignorant towards the sphere of production and the role of labour therein – let alone the sphere of social reproduction. The following section will outline the basic characteristics of money's social power.

Money, Power, and Class Rule

In his earlier writings, like the *Paris Manuscripts (1844)*, *Economic and Philosophical Manuscripts (1844)*, and *Grundrisse (1857)*, Marx speaks of money as an 'object of eminent possession', as an 'almighty being', a 'real God', as 'bond of all bonds', as 'confusion and exchange of all things', as the 'estranged essence of men's existence' and as the 'alienated ability of mankind'. How can one make sense of the rich metaphorical language? Do all these definitions and images highlight the inconsistency and derangement of Marx's monetary theory? Or are they rather an expression of how Marx consciously developed a creative, multi-layered, and fantastic conceptualisation of money, because only in doing so could he understand what the classical political economists did not see and what the new critical orthodoxy also fails to comprehend.

Money is everything and nothing because commodities in economic space can only relate to each other by expressing themselves in a general referent, by taking a "social existence *separated from the natural existence* of the commodity." (Marx 1973, 145). The wider the economic space of commodities is, the more powerful money becomes. Although money, commodities, and capital have existed for centuries and long before the advent of an emerging capitalist world market in the long sixteenth century, the power of money was circumscribed by the social production underpinning the reproduction of societies. The capitalist mode of production, in contrast, is defined by its inherent drive to accumulate, and accumulation only works through (self-)valorisation (Marx 1976, 254).

Marx speaks of capital as "money which begets money" (Marx 1976, 256) to highlight that money is not capital *per se*. It only becomes capital in specific social relations in which money is valorised, whether in production, trade, or finance. In other words, money only is *potential* capital (Marx 1981, 477). In this context, the power of money is contingent upon the social relations of production. Only in capitalist social formations does money become an 'almighty being', not because money, commodities, or capital didn't exist before, but because the relations of production under capitalism are such that they build on and intensify the relentless movement of value (thus capital as value-in-motion). Its nature as a medium of socialisation successively turns money into an 'almighty being' and, eventually, into a condition of existence, revealing a dimension of power that credit theorists fail to acknowledge:

> "By possessing the property of buying everything, by possessing the property of appropriating all objects, money is thus the object of eminent possession. The universality of its property is the omnipotence of its being. It therefore functions as the almighty being. Money is the pimp between man's need and the object, between his life and his means of life. But that which mediates my life for me, also mediates the existence of other people for me. For me it is the other person." (Marx 1988, 136)

Money's omnipotence is inscribed into its value form as a universal equivalent, but the effectiveness of its power is contingent upon the universalisation of the commodity form, that is, the expansion of capitalist social relations, in particular, the commodification of economic space. Therein, money becomes a condition of existence, mediating human life and obscuring the fact that our existence is mediated by other human beings and, in fact, their labour. This is what Marx famously describes as the "money fetish" in *Capital I,* a concept that only becomes fully apparent through understanding the "fetishism of the commodity" underlying it (Marx 1976, 163).[8]

Moreover, money expresses a structural break between life and the means of life. As such, it also embodies a central aspect of what I call fractured lives. Under capitalist social relations, money literally turns into something natural, a means of existence and necessity for life – just as humans require oxygen or water to live. As such, money creates and sustains capitalism's second nature, "money replaces nature as the essential condition of human life", dictating "that access to the necessities of life shall depend upon money – and sufficient quantities of it at that" (McNally 2011b, 148–49, see also 2020, 46). In this regard, the coercive and violent nature of money becomes apparent. Money is not only a means of socialisation. It is a coercive and divisive form of socialisation, expressing and reifying unequal power relations in society, i.e. class relations and hierarchies between nation-states.[9] In *Economic and Philosophical Manuscripts,* Marx summarises this coercive and divisive aspect brilliantly by defining money as 'bond of all bonds', consisting of the contradictory character of it being simultaneously a 'binding agent' and an 'agent of divorce':

8 Here again, the English translation is incomplete, it simply speaks of the 'money riddle' and the 'commodity riddle'. In the German version, Marx highlights that the 'money riddle' is the visible expression of the 'riddle of the commodity fetish'.

9 Class is here understood not as a fixed category that derives automatically from income or wealth. Rather, it describes the positioning of social groups within the given relations of production. It thereby also establishes a relation between different classes in a distinct mode of production. And finally, class is essentially produced through the struggle over the relations of production, including the means of revenue through labour, ownership of capital and/or land (Harvey 1998; Skeggs 2022).

> "If money is the bond binding me to human life, binding society to me, binding me and nature and man, is not money the bond of all bonds? Can it not dissolve and bind all ties? Is it not, therefore, the universal agent of separation? It is the true agent of divorce as well as the true binding agent – the [universal] galvano-chemical power of Society." (Marx 1988, 138)

Fractured lives, hence, not only refer to the fracture between life and means of life at the individual level. It also highlights the fractures that run through the social body and allow money to wield such enormous power in society. The social power of money is grounded in its property as 'bond of all bonds', and it can be appropriated privately. In the words of Marx, the "social power [of money] becomes the private power of private persons" (Marx 1976, 230). Since money is an independent expression of value with a separate social existence (alongside its natural existence as a commodity) as much as a relation of production, that is, its power is an expression of any given relations of production in society, it necessarily also reflects the class relations characterising such social formations. Therefore, money is a class-based form of power in which the social power of money is unevenly appropriated (Clarke 1988, 17; Harvey 2006, 24; 256; Lapavitsas 2003, 66). When Marx argues that with money, "[t]he individual carries his social power, as well as his bond with society, in his pocket" (Marx 1973, 157), he emphasises how class rule becomes obscured, ordinary and naturalised through the peculiar nature of money.[10] As such, money is not simply a social relation. Instead, it is best understood as a *societal relation of oppression*.

Why are these foundational relations of political economy so difficult to grasp? Marx grappled with this question in many of his writings and delivered some convincing explanations. These are once again linked to the peculiar *social* form of money. Money, as 'bond of all bonds', does not *appear* as a social bond, less so as a social bond of class rule. Instead, "money presupposes the objectification [*Versachlichung*] of the social bond; in so far, that is, as money appears in the form of collateral which one individual must leave with another in order to obtain a commodity from him" (Marx 1973, 160). The trustworthiness of this collateral is, however, based on *objectified* exchange value, which in turn is based on the alienation of labour turning into "a mutual relation between people's productive activities" (Marx 1973, 160). Put differently, what underpins the money form as *social* value (in circulation), is the appropriation through alienation (in production). The nature of money can only be understood as a cyclical process: Money emerges as an independent expression of a

10 Simon Clarke (1988, 17) emphasises that the "social power of capital is not embodied in the person of the capitalist, but in the social power of money". In this regard, money is not simply a tool of power of ruling classes. It is an "autonomous social power" and as such expression "of the subordination of all human needs to the needs of capital, to the capitalist thirst for profit." (Clarke 2003, 35).

commodity's value in circulation but must be based on the 'abstract labour' in producing this commodity, which in turn can only be socially validated in circulation. Thereby, money already anticipates the movement of capital as value-in-motion, which is why Marx speaks of money as *potential* capital.[11]

What characterises capitalist social formations is that money does not primarily rule based on personal dependency but as objective domination (*sachliche Herrschaft*), in which individuals are governed by abstractions. Make no mistake in taking this for an idealist position. Quite to the contrary, "[t]he abstraction, or idea, however, is nothing more than the theoretical expression of those material relations which are their lord and master" (Marx 1973, 164). By governing through concrete abstractions, money conceals its class-based form of power, which is much less apparent than class relations in the labour process (Harvey 2006, 17; Soederberg 2015, 21). Even more importantly, the objectification of social relations suggests that there is no privileged position of the exploited and expropriated classes to understand the complexity of their oppression because it does not *appear* as such (Heinrich 2001, 5).

To make it short, the abstraction, alienation, and objectification that constitute money as a peculiar value form make its common understanding so difficult. Speaking of money as everything and nothing acknowledges what money *is* and *does*. As an "active concept of value", money "confounds and exchanges everything. It is the general *confounding* and *compounding* of all things – the world upside-down – the confounding and compounding of all natural and human qualities" (Marx 1988, 140). Money beholds a creative and fantastic power to "turn an image into reality and reality into mere image" (Marx 1988, 139) because it allows those who possess it to acquire all things to fulfil their desires – especially those they could otherwise not have.[12] Though imaginary, immaterial, and opaque, money embodies specific social relations of production, i.e. material relations of exploitation, and hence is described by Marx as the "alienated ability of mankind" (Marx 1988, 138).

Reading his earlier writings makes it abundantly clear that Marx developed a *relational* ontology of money, in which money's property and essence can only be understood in relation to social activities, which in turn are conditioned by specific material circumstances. In his perceptive critique of one of the leading classical political economists, James Mill, Marx writes:

---

11 In this sense, "[c]irculation is the movement in which the general alienation appears as general appropriation and general appropriation as general alienation." (Marx 1973, 196).

12 In *Economic and Philosophical Manuscripts*, Marx illustrates this truly creative power vividly: "If I long for a particular dish or want to take the mail-coach because I am not strong enough to go by foot, money fetches me the dish and the mail-coach – i.e., it converts my wishes from the realm of imagination, it translates them from their meditated, imagined or willing existence into their *sensuous, actual* existence, from imagination to life, and from imagined being into real being. In effecting this mediation, money is the truly creative power." (Marx 1988, 139).

> "The essence of money is not, in the first place, that property is alienated in it, but that the *mediating activity* or movement, the *human*, social act by which man's products mutually complement one another, is *estranged* from man and becomes the attribute of money, a *material thing* outside man. [...] It is clear that this *mediator* now becomes a *real God*, for the mediator is the *real power* over what it mediates to me. [...] This *mediator is* therefore the lost, estranged *essence* of private property, private property which has become *alienated*, external to itself, just as it is the *alienated* species-activity of man, the *externalised mediation* between man's production and man's production." (Marx 1844a)

This proposition consciously refutes money's essence to a property, even if this property was alienated. Instead, the essence of money can only be grasped by studying the social act of commodity exchange as an alienated social form of relating entirely different labour processes to one another, as if they were of the same kind. Furthermore, Marx stresses how this process of economic socialisation enabled by the money form of value is ultimately also the alienation of humankind's species-activity, i.e. labour. Thus, the progressive spatial and temporal extension of the commodity economy builds on money as its "lifeblood" while simultaneously intensifying its contradictions, including the alienation "from our species-being, our cooperative and imaginative potential" (Haiven 2020, 108).[13]

Hence, the materialism of Marx's monetary theory has nothing to do with money being a tangible, material thing and has everything to do with uncovering, explaining, and criticising the ordinary, seemingly natural dehumanisation and violence inherent in the commodity and money form. As David McNally reminds us, ultimately, the social power of money in capitalist social formations in the form of "capital directs and labour obeys" expresses the social power of money rooted "in the domination of their bodies (as repositories of labour)" (McNally 2020, 46). As a divisive and coercive form of socialisation, money implies structural violence, governing human lives *and* deaths in a god-like fashion:

> "Money degrades all the gods of man – and turns them into commodities. Money is the universal self-established *value* of all things. It has, therefore, robbed the whole world – both the world of men and nature – of its specific value. Money is the estranged essence of man's work and man's existence, and this alien essence dominates him, and he worships it." (Marx 1844b)

The disenchantment of the money veil is foundational for Marx's critique of political economy, which always is a critique of both scientific inquiries, i.e. bourgeois political economy, and a critique of the violence of capitalist social relations.

---

13 For a detailed discussion of Marx's 'alienation theory of money', see Nelson (1999, chapter 2).

In sum, we can speak of money as everything and nothing in several senses. Historically, different 'things' have taken the value form of money (e.g. shells, hides, cattle, precious metals, paper, etc.), at least in fulfilling partial functions. Yet, none of these things *is* the nature of money, for they only represent value relations in each period, reflecting the social relations of production. Although Marx equates gold with money in several instances in his writings (especially in *Capital I*), his theoretical framework offers ways to think through money in a non-reductionist and non-essentialist way, and particularly his early writings on the philosophy of money stand in stark contrast to a 'crude materialist' interpretation of gold as money.[14] Marx recognised that gold and silver could be replaced by other forms of money, such as bank notes or mere symbols, as with electronic money, "because material money as mere medium of exchange is itself symbolic" (Marx 1973, 212).[15] In this sense, we can talk of money as every*thing* and no*thing*.

Theoretically, understanding money as everything and nothing allows us to approach the creative, multilayered, and fantastic nature of money from various angles. The commodity is foundational for Marx's theory of money, not because money *is* a commodity but because money *is* the only possible, separate, independent, *social* existence of the commodity's value in exchange. The money form allows the impossible, "allowing all substantial variety to be wrapped up in its formal quality as the common referent; money is so to speak, a *socially constructed substanceless nothing*. Yet without nothing no-one is worth anything." (Altvater 1997, 49). The latter point speaks to the way power and money are inseparably related in capitalist social formations since, as the universal equivalent, money also is "the very incarnation of social power" (Harvey 2006, 245). As such, it allows for objective domination (*sachliche Herrschaft*), which characterises capitalist class rule.

Practically, to speak of money as everything and nothing recognises how, under capitalist social relations, money as the reincarnation of social power, allows for the unequal possession and appropriation of wealth, which is always linked to the dehumanisation and violence inflicted on labourers producing such wealth. Moreover, since every *thing* can take on the commodity form and can become purchasable and saleable by putting a price tag on it, money conceals what has been transformed into it – the so-called "money fetish" (Marx 1976, 187). The limits to what can be expressed in monetary value seem to be indefinite, especially in today's world, where

14 Of course, there are different interpretations as to whether money must be a commodity in Marx's theory of money. While many prominent Marxist theorists claim money must be a commodity, Marx indicates at various points how money as independent expression of value develops an autonomous dynamic.

15 There are many other instances where Marx explicitly rejects a 'crude materialist' understanding of money or value, and where he emphasises the symbolic nature of both: As such, value is a "mere symbol, a cipher for a relation of production, a mere symbol for its own value" (Marx 1973, 141; see also 1981, 516).

everything from ecosystem services to the death of human beings is measured by the same standard – monetary value – as if these processes were comparable. As an independent expression of value, money is characterised by a relative autonomy that takes on a dynamic of its own, one which takes on even more creative and fantastic forms through the development of credit and finance. To this end, the following section will discuss the role of credit money and the topsy-turvy world of finance capital.

The Topsy-Turvy World of Credit and Finance Capital

In contrast to a credit theory of money, Marx offers a monetary view of credit. Credit money emerges from two distinct but interrelated processes. It is primarily linked to money's function as a means of payment, which implies the possibility of sale and purchase at different points in time (Marx 1976, 232ff.). Such commercial credit (money) comes into being every time a seller allows a buyer to acquire a commodity in the present (sale) while the payment is due at a defined future date (purchase). In such a case, the commodity is not sold for money but for a recorded "promise of paying" (Marx 2012, 469), specifying a date for final payment. This seemingly simple process entails a complex social form. Money as means of payment acts as a measure of value and unit of account in contractually determining the price of a purchased commodity, and fixing it as a debtor's obligation, anticipating the social validation of a commodity's value (Ivanova 2020, 140). In this sense, we can speak of a pre-validation of social labour through credit money. A commodity's actual social validation, however, depends on its realisation in the market and can only occur once money as means of payment performs its second function as the final means of settlement (Ivanova 2020, 140). Throughout history, credit money has not only emerged as commercial credit. It has also appeared as relatively autonomous financial institution when professionalised moneylending mediates and manages capital in the money form for active capitalists (Heinrich 2020, 292f.). Ultimately, both channels merge in the modern banking system and coalesce into what credit theories stress as the "production of [credit] money" (Pettifor 2017). While Marx did not share the positions of the nominalists (his description of credit theories at the time), he was influenced by some of their thoughts[16] and recognised the power of credit creation obtained by commercial banks as well as the contradictory public-private character that credit money takes in the modern era:

16 For a more detailed account of Marx's critique of the Banking School and Utopian Socialists proposing a labour-money, see e.g. Anitra Nelson (2005) and Stefan Eich (2022).

> "A banknote is nothing more than a bill on the banker, payable at any time to its possessor and given by the banker in place of private drafts. This last form of credit seems especially striking and important to the layman, firstly because this kind of credit money emerges from commercial circulation into general circulation and functions here as money; also because in most countries the major banks that issue notes are a peculiar mishmash between national banks and private banks and actually have the government's credit behind them, their notes being more or less legal tender; and because it is evident here that what the banker is dealing in is credit itself, since the banknote merely represents a circulating token of credit." (Marx 1981, 529)

In other words, Marx was acutely aware of the existence of credit produced by private banks out of thin air. He also acknowledged that such credit money is simply an IOU in a hierarchy involving private and central banks. And finally, he stresses how such a private IOU potentially becomes legal tender because of the public-private "mishmash" that underpins the modern monetary, financial *and* state system (Marx 2012, 474).[17] This private act is a dynamic process in which debts are continuously produced and cleared, in which "[c]redit money is perpetually created and destroyed through the activities of private individuals" (Harvey 2006, 236). Yet, Marx was cautious to understand credit money as money because credit (money) depends on money (income) which in turn only emerges once it "enters the domain of social production as an embodiment of the value of social labour or social purchasing power" (Ivanova 2020, 142).

Following Marx, scholars have argued that, with the development of the capitalist mode of production in general, and the credit system in particular, the relative importance and eventually dominance of money as *means of payment* vis-à-vis money as a *means of purchase* increases, implying that credit monies such as bills of exchange, bank notes, or loans become increasingly important vis-à-vis state-issued coin or paper money (Eich 2022, 110f.; Ivanova 2020, 140). Some scholars even hold that only fiat money is adequate for the developed capitalist mode of production, and credit money had not fully unfolded during Marx's lifetime (Heinrich 2020, 304). Credit money allows the expanded reproduction of capital to occur more dynamically, increasing the scale of production and the extraction of surplus value and turnover time, accelerating the development of technology and the creation of the world market (Vasudevan 2019, 242). Yet, it simultaneously increases the contradictions inherent in the social forms of money, particularly the falling apart of sale and purchase, anticipating the accumulation of contradictions which ultimately erupt as monetary crises rooted in an "ongoing chain of payments [which] has been fully

17 A detailed historical analysis of this public-private mishmash and how the monetary, financial, and nation state system emerged, including its intimate relationship to colonialism and slavery can be found in McNally (2020, 121ff.).

developed, along with an artificial system for settling them" (Marx 1976, 236). Critics have argued that the post-Bretton Woods monetary order indicates the de-commodification of money, rendering Marx's monetary theory irrelevant. While the former part is right in a formal sense because dollars cannot be exchanged against gold at a fixed rate anymore, this conclusion is hardly convincing. As David McNally argues, "the dollar can be readily exchanged for gold or any other commodity at prevailing market rates" (McNally 2020, 218). In contrast to understanding money *as* credit, the monetary foundations of credit explain how debt encounters individuals and institutions as seemingly external and objective power while obscuring and deepening processes of alienation, including the alienation of labourers from the means of existence and human beings in general from their species-being (Haiven 2020; Nelson 1999).

Credit money's successive development and growing significance already point towards the fundamental role of capitalist banking and finance. While a detailed analysis of finance capital is beyond the scope of this section, the remainder of this chapter discusses two fundamental concepts, interest-bearing and fictitious capital. The distinction between these two is critical for understanding contemporary microfinance for several reasons: First, it explains why and how income-generating and consumption loans imply different financial flows. Second, the notion of fictitious capital illustrates how the financialisation of poverty connects microfinance borrowers within the operations of transnational financial markets. Finally, discussing these concepts makes the separation between pre-capitalist usury and capitalist finance evident.

The notion of interest-bearing capital complicates our understanding of the dynamics of money and finance. As Marx writes in *Capital III*, money can be turned into capital only because it is an independent expression of value, whether it exists in money or commodities (Marx 1981, 459). As capital, however, the independent expression of value is transformed into self-valorisation, hence value-in-motion. The use value of money is thus not only that it functions as a general equivalent but also that money *can* work as capital. And it is this capacity that allows "capital as capital [to] become a commodity" (Marx 1981, 463). In this context, it is of vital importance to distinguish between form and content. Credit relations appear as primarily contractual and juridical relations between a creditor and a debtor. Yet, this social form does not tell us much about the social content of these relations. Marx introduces the notion of interest-bearing capital to explain why and how credit money becomes a pivotal process for capital accumulation, seemingly disparate but interwoven with commodity production. If, in *Capital I*, Marx highlighted that capital primarily exists in commodity production, not in circulation, his notion of interest-bearing capital in *Capital III* complicates this suggestion. The movement of interest-bearing capital is a multi-layered process (M-M-C-M'-M') wrapped around the simple form of capital (M-C-M'). Contrary to the simple form, money in this process is spent *as capital* with the use value to produce surplus value (M-M), and it returns as *realised capital* (M'-M') (Harvey 2006, 256). Put differently, interest-bearing capital functions as capital already in circulation, turning capital into a commodity *for others:*

> "Capital appears as a mysterious and self-creating source of interest, of its own increase. [...] The social relation is consummated in the relationship of a thing, money, to itself. Instead of the actual transformation of money into capital, we have here only the form of this devoid of content. [...] Thus it becomes as completely the property of money to create value, to yield interest, as it is the property of a pear tree to bear pears. And it is as this interest-bearing thing that the money-lender sells his money" (Marx 1981, 516)

Marx emphasises at various points in his work that the character and nature of interest-bearing capital is no social form confined to the modern era.[18] Like merchant capital, usury as "archaic form of interest-bearing capital" (Marx 1981, 728) belongs to the oldest forms of capital that have existed long before the dominance of the capitalist mode of production over the global economy, and thus appear "[...] to the popular mind as the form of capital *par excellence*." (Marx 1981, 744). These "antediluvian forms of capital" represent "capital's mode of exploitation without its mode of production" (Marx 1981, 728, 731), anticipating the self-valorisation of money (M-M').

In contrast to premodern forms, however, merchant and interest-bearing capital become increasingly embedded in the overall dynamics of capitalist development, simultaneously enhancing the capacities for capital accumulation and feeding surplus value produced in commodity production through, for example, fees and interest. This contradictory nexus is specific to the capitalist mode of production, with important implications for economic development: Interest-bearing capital in the form of usury generally tends to ruin individual producers through indebtedness, generally associating more debt with more dependence and poverty on the side of the debtor and increased power and wealth on behalf of the creditor (Marx 1981, 730). In contrast, the modern capitalist banking and credit system may provide an incentive for productive debts: A commercial bank granting a loan for a corporation investing in new production capacities would be a classical case, in which a sum of money is lent (not sold!) as capital, i.e. money with the property to create more money (M-M), allowing the borrowing company to expand its production (and thus exploitation of labour, M-C-M'), and to pay back the loan with an interest (M-M'), while potentially also retaining an own profit.[19] In such cases, indebtedness can

18 Most notably, chapter 36 in *Capital III* discusses the relevance of pre-capitalist relations and how they become subordinated.

19 It is important to remember that the money capitalist remains the owner of money capital and simply lends the properties of capital (as commodity) to a functioning capitalist who invests it into commodity production. The profit that emerges from the appropriation of sur-

be productive, liberating and wealth-generating on behalf of the debtor (functioning capitalist), while simultaneously increasing the scope and wealth of the creditor (owner of money capital).

Interest-bearing capital then refers to all types of financial assets (like loans or property titles) which use money capital to create a source of regular revenue by enabling the expanded reproduction of capital. Overall, the development of the credit system, with interest-bearing capital at its centre, fulfils several essential functions for capitalist development, including the mobilisation of money as capital, reducing the cost and time of turnover, allowing for fixed capital formation, equalising the profit rate across economic space, and centralising capital (Harvey 2006, 260ff.). Analytically, interest-bearing capital sheds light on how capital as a whole is organised, with specialised functions of the entire processes divided amongst different factions of capital, including contradictions and tensions. Marx refers to interest-bearing capital as the "mother of every insane form" (Marx 1981, 596), reaching its "most superficial and fetishized form" (Marx 1981, 519) because the production of surplus value "appears as a purely occult quality [of self-valorising money]" (Marx 1981, 744). In its fetishised appearance, interest-bearing capital conceals the power of money, foregrounding the power of banks and financial institutions. However, "although it is the latter who wield the power of money, it is the *power of capital* in its most abstract form" (Clarke, 1988, 5). Credit theorists are often blinded by the powerful appearance of finance capital, without acknowledging how this power is part of and based in the broader relations of production beyond the glass towers of mighty financial institutions. Therefore, many contemporary credit theories of money arbitrarily highlight the power of finance without conceptually or empirically linking it to power relations characterising the overall political economy.[20] While at times it may seem that interest-bearing capital creates a smooth symbiosis between different factions of capital (basically win-win-situations in the sense of complementary division of labour within the capitalist class), it is rife with tensions and contradictions (Harvey 2006; Lapavitsas 2014).

There is a particular form of interest-bearing capital that, although long neglected and generally poorly understood, is particularly relevant for the investigation at hand: fictitious capital.[21] The concept of fictitious capital can become

---

plus value is consequently split into interest (for the owner of money capital), and a company profit (for the functioning capitalist).

20 Moreover, our understanding of class relations becomes refined, for instance, when considering that interest-bearing capital is not primarily opposed to labour but primarily acts in a contractually antagonistic relationship with functioning capitalists (Heinrich 2020, 287). The latter, in turn, also seems to stand in no direct antagonistic relationship to labour, because he does not *own* the employed capital.

21 There are multiple reasons for the neglect of Marx's notion of fictitious capital in critical social theory until rather recently, including the unfinished character of his notes on fictitious cap-

meaningful only when exploring *why* capital may be considered fictitious and *what* the implications of this process are. Marx uses the term in two interrelated ways. First, it describes a sum of money treated as capital although it is not invested productively, turning it into "illusionary capital" (Marx 2012, 523). For instance, public debt is generally not spent as capital but for investments in public services, like education, health care or public infrastructure. Yet, for sovereign bond owners, the tax-based interest payments seem to stem from their invested capital. This peculiarity points to a general confusion that interest-bearing capital creates: Every regular revenue of money in capitalist social formations appears as the interest of invested capital, regardless of whether interest payments spring from capital (Marx 2012, 520).

Marx's second contention on fictitious capital refers to the illusionary expression of value. The sovereign bond mentioned above seems to express value (in German: *Wert*papier, literal 'value paper') and can be sold and bought in secondary markets, i.e. it becomes a tradable asset. Through fictitious capital, it seems as if capital exists twice – once as the capital value of the respective property title and once as the value of the employed capital on which the property title is based (Simon 2021). Accordingly, the value of such securities describes an independent movement, and the price of these tradable claims becomes autonomous. The value of fictitious capital is entirely based on expected revenue. Since the current valuation of expected future payments can change all the time, depending on numerous socio-cultural, political or economic processes and information about them, they are the most speculative form of capital. To be sure, capital is always speculative in the sense that capitalists can never be sure that the invested monetary value is also realised with a higher profit – be in commodity production or beyond. However, by defining an independent movement of capital value, the buying and selling of such property titles become a market with profit opportunities of its own and, in general, considerably higher price volatility than in other markets, turning financial accumulation into a potentially lucrative alternative investment of moneyed capital.[22] As such, fictitious capital potentially augments the speed and scope of capital accumulation by producing debts and securities as a means of profit-making. The *differentia specifica* of fictitious capital – in contrast to the broader notion of interest-bearing capital – lies in the dynamic of capitalising "discounted income streams that can be traded in specialized markets" (Jessop 2015, 28) and that these tradable titles "constitute claims on

ital as well as methodological problems (for a detailed account see e.g. Breda 2021; Heinrich 2020, 289).

22 In this regard, David Harvey emphasises the contradictory and crisis-prone nature of fictitious capital since "future surplus value production is uncertain and varies according to the state of competition, the pace of technological change, the rate of exploitation and the overall dynamics of accumulation and overaccumulation" (Harvey 2006, 267).

future flows of income and surplus" (Vasudevan 2019, 77). This second dimension is crucial for understanding the structural re-organisation of global capital accumulation since the 1970s, commonly discussed under the buzzword financialisation.

Following Céderic Durand, we can understand fictitious capital as the 'nodal point' of various processes that are associated with the neoliberal transformation of the world economy since the 1970s. These include the global expansion and deepening of financial markets with new actors, institutions and guiding principles, escalating corporate, household and government debt, the tendency toward privatisation of social security systems and of nature, the fragmentation of the worker's movement (including the casualisation of wage work), and the proliferation of financial crises (Durand 2017; see also Lapavitsas 2014; McNally 2011a). Speaking of financialised accumulation, finance-led or finance-dominated capitalism then refers to a specific phase and geography of capital accumulation that is significantly driven, if not dominated, by the imperatives of "accumulated claims upon production [and revenue]" (Marx 2012, 524), including a leading role of moneyed capitalists and their respective institutions in shaping capitalist development and re-organising the social fabric. Durand usefully distinguishes between "elementary forms of fictitious capital" such as government bonds or shares, and a "new generation of sophisticated forms of fictitious capital" (Durand 2017, 65) which has become particularly relevant with the rise of global finance in recent decades. These include a variety of derivatives like futures, options, and swaps and financial innovation based on the securitisation of assets. The latter allows for the repackaging of income streams from all types of loans (from mortgage loans to microfinance) into tradable securities (Bryan, Martin, and Rafferty 2009; McNally 2011a, 99), usually associated with the transformation of banking and, most importantly, the rise of shadow banking (Guttmann 2016). David McNally summarises the implications of securitisation for the transformation of banking as follows:

> "Securitization radically changes this model of banking. Instead of making loans, like a twenty-five-year mortgage, and holding them on its books, a bank now makes the loan and, for a fee, sells it off to an institution that specializes in creating "financial products," such as mortgage-backed securities. In this system, banks move loans off their books almost as fast as they make them, collecting a fee every time they sell them to an investment bank or similar institution. In the process, they take themselves off the hook in the event of default. No longer is the mortgage (or credit card, or student loan) originator stuck if the borrower defaults. That risk is now passed on to the new owners of these debts, wealthy individuals and institutions who have purchased these debt-based securities. Securitization also means that a growing share of bank profits derive not from years of interest payments on mortgages and the like, but from the fees they make by selling such loans to investors." (McNally 2011a, 99)

A monetary perspective of financial capital accumulation is necessary and analytically fruitful because it highlights how in contemporary capitalism, financial products like derivatives allow for the management of all kinds of risks – from currency fluctuations to default of microfinance borrowers – as if these risks were comparable, and in fact, commensurable. Just like incomparable commodities become commensurable by taking on the money form of value, entirely unrivalled types of risks (for profitability) are turned into tradable financial assets as if they were all of the same types. Only by abstracting concrete risks from their unique and complex context can these securities suggest to objectively measure and compare them, as if they were of the same kind. In other words, the value form of money allows fictitious capital to create complex chains of debts and securities of entirely incomparable social processes and relations, wrapping them together into a common texture that is "equally divisible" and "always exchangeable" (Marx 1973, 141), as in the case of derivatives. In this sense, abstract risk mimics the underlying dynamics of abstract labour as the social substance of value, including its fundamental contradictions (see also Bryan, Rafferty, and Jefferis 2015; McNally 2011a, 115).

Since financial securities are nothing but claims on future income streams, financialisation allows for extending the commodity principle along the axis of space and time. Phytos Lysandrou (2016) has referred to the latter process as the "systematic occupation of the future" or the "colonization of the future", removing pressures of institutions (like governments and corporations) in the present (see also Blackburn 2006). His argument criticises most heterodox economics approaches, including many Marxists, for treating financialisation as a primarily dysfunctional and temporary phase of capital accumulation. Whilst failing to acknowledge how financialisation – despite inherent contradictions – allows to reconcile real and financial sector interests, "in that governments and corporations, on the one hand, need to issue increasing amounts of securities to maintain their *capacities* for production or service provision, and in that large institutional investors, on the other hand, need to absorb increasing amounts of these securities to maintain their *capacities* for asset management" (Lysandrou 2016, 464; own emphasis).

Despite its independent and fantastic nature, fictitious capital has profound real effects. After all, such securities represent "claims upon production" (Marx 2012, 524). As such, they are also claims on future labour power. To a significant extent, banking capital engages in accumulating money capital by facilitating such "claims upon production" and accumulating the market prices (the illusionary capital value) of these claims. Consequently, financial accumulation contributes to the disciplining and casualisation of labour, for example, by the shareholder-value orientation of joint-stock companies (Boyer 2005; Lazonick and O'Sullivan 2000). It seems, however, that Marx underestimated – or, at least, insufficiently discussed – the role of violence involved in financial accumulation *beyond* production. Concerning escalating household and sovereign debt in the neoliberal era (Lazzarato 2015; Martin 2002), fictitious capital represents claims on revenue beyond production rather than upon production. It thereby exerts pressure on state apparatuses and households to generate revenue *by any means necessary*. Naturally, these dynamics have implications for the domination and exploitation of labour beyond the production process.

The Exploitative Dynamics of (Micro)Finance

This section discusses the relevance of subordination and exploitation of labour through financial accumulation, shedding light on the labour-finance nexus. In doing so, I draw on recent debates on a concept from Marx that has long been sidelined in critical political economy: the notion of secondary exploitation (Dörre 2012; Lapavitsas 2009; Dos Santos 2009).

Marx refers to "secondary exploitation, [as process] which proceeds *alongside* the original exploitation that takes place directly within the production process itself" (Marx 1981, 745; own emphasis). In discussing the relevance of money lending, advance payments, or rents, he highlights how these processes resemble "capital's mode of exploitation without its mode of production" (Marx 1981, 732). The qualitative difference between these two types of exploitation has much to do with the social form of value appropriation. Exploitation of wage labour in commodity production, generally considered a key characteristic of the capitalist mode of production, entails a mystified relation: From the exchange perspective, labour power is exchanged as equivalent for a wage. Only by entering the "hidden abode of production" (Marx 1976, 279) does the secret of profit-making become apparent, in which owners of capital systematically appropriate newly generated surplus value from wage labourers in commodity production.

Profits from secondary exploitation are qualitatively different from this, in that there is no exchange of equivalents in the sphere of circulation, and possibly there is no appropriation of newly created surplus value. Rather than profits that emerge from the flow of newly created value, financial expropriation implies a "re-division of money revenue streams, typically taking the form of interest" (Lapavitsas 2014, 143). Landowners, moneylenders or retail merchants who engage in such secondary forms of exploitation "are indifferent as to whether the rent [or interest] they receive is a deduction out of wages of labour, out of excess or even average profit of capital, or out of any other form of revenue" (Harvey 2006, 342). The contractual nature of these economic processes may suggest a relationship of equivalence between, for example, a creditor and a debtor. Yet, these contractual parties do not meet as equals in the marketplace. Quite to the contrary, as will be discussed in Part III and Part IV, access to credit is mediated by unequal relationships of power that run through the social body.

To be sure, financial accumulation is not always synonymous with financial expropriation through interest-bearing loans. The latter becomes primarily relevant regarding household and government debt. In contrast, interest as claims upon surplus value in productive sectors, dividends on shares, fees and commissions for services, and speculative capital gains that result from fluctuations in equity's purchase price and its sale price are further significant channels of financial profit (Durand 2017, 92). However, in recent decades, the transformation of banking and the financialisation of capital accumulation has increased the scope for financial expropriation as a powerful new type of secondary exploitation (McNally 2011a, 122; Dos Santos 2009). In the context of declining real wages and the privatisation of social infrastructure, working-class households have turned into a profitable market segment which is exploited in production and beyond:

> "Financial expropriation, then, is a source of profit that has emerged systematically during the recent decades. It should be clearly distinguished from exploitation that occurs in production and remains the cornerstone of contemporary capitalist economies. Financial expropriation is an additional source of profit that originates in the sphere of circulation. In so far as it relates to personal income, it involves existing flows of money and value, rather than new flows of surplus-value. Yet, despite occurring in circulation, it takes place systematically and through economic processes, thus having an exploitative aspect" (Lapavitsas 2009, 133)

Such profits from financial expropriation are reminiscent of redistributive aspects of poverty/wealth creation through "archaic forms" of interest-bearing capital that Marx discusses in *Capital III* (Marx 1981, 728ff.). As such, secondary forms of exploitation may be more vicious, intrusive, and violent than exploitation in commodity production because, generally, they may appropriate *all* surplus value from petty producers and landed proprietors (for example, through exorbitant interest rates), also *beyond* the needs of labouring populations (Marx 1981, 730).

Despite many convergences, there is an essential distinction between archaic and capitalist forms of interest-bearing capital: While financial accumulation through usurer's capital is usually entangled with personal relations of power and dependency, as observable in the case of local moneylenders in India, the domination of interest-bearing capital suggests a fetishised form in which the abstraction, alienation and objectification of social relations turn into an impersonal power relation seemingly beyond human relationships – as if the power of debt resides in the property of money. This differentiation is crucial in understanding how the power of so-called informal moneylenders and the power of financialised microfinance corporations at present is a continuum which contains similar forms of class exploitation and domination (see also Part IV). Moreover, it is critical to highlight that pre-capitalist and capitalist forms of interest-bearing capital may co-exist and that the relevance of usurer's capital can by no means be relegated to the past. In *Capital III*, Marx summarises various situations that underline the continuous relevance of usurer's capital *within* the capitalist mode of production, including non-capitalist producers (small peasants and artisans) and "where borrowing results from individual need, as at the pawnshop" (Marx 1981, 735).

The thin line between usury and financial expropriation points to the multiple ways in which financial accumulation is linked to processes of continued forms of so-called primitive accumulation. That is, the enclosures of commons, the privatisation of public goods and the commodification of ever more spheres of life through the spatial extension of (financial) accumulation (Dörre 2009; Durand 2017, 102f.; Harvey 2003). Contrary to the mainstream financial inclusion discourse, such a perspective may explain how individuals and communities become integrated into the money nexus as debtor or creditor, not based on isolated household decision-making (as most liberal theories assume), but because of broader dynamics related to land ownership or access to social provisioning force specific populations into debt-based survival strategies (Arboleda 2015b; Bernards 2021; Breman 2019).

Financial expropriation has important implications for labour. In *Grundrisse*, Marx outlines how financial accumulation, premised on the money form of value, reorganises the exploitation of labour: "Money, then, in so far as it now already in itself exists as capital, is therefore simply a *claim on future (new) labour* [...] As a claim, its material existence as money is irrelevant, and can be replaced by any other title" (Marx 1973, 367; own emphasis). This passage is significant for contemporary analysis in at least two ways. On the one hand, it draws attention to the creative powers of finance to produce a multi-layered system of titles and claims that allow the "colonization of the future" through financial innovation and accumulation. On the other hand, Marx anticipates the implications of the "spatialization of the future" (Lysandrou 2016, 464) through financial accumulation, expanding capital accumulation spatially in the present by creating and colonising future terrains through the accumulation of claims upon future labour capacities, production and revenue.

To realise such claims, the ruling classes must develop ways of exploiting, controlling, and disciplining labouring classes that run parallel to those in commodity production. Financial expropriation explains contemporary processes of secondary exploitation. However, the concept does not account sufficiently for the impact this has on class formation and class struggle, especially in postcolonial contexts. Moreover, it remains confined to the neoliberal era, ignoring the formative role of fictitious capital and financial expropriation for the subordination of colonised populations and their adverse incorporation into the capitalist world market (Banaji 1977, 2013). Expanding the explanatory horizon of these two concepts, Part III will reconstruct the continuities and changes in governing access to credit on the Indian subcontinent.

Understanding class formation in India, and arguably for most of the world's population, requires engaging with different and changing degrees of proletarianisation, combining agrarian subsistence, petty commodity production and precarious wage labour (Bernstein 2010, 54f.; Breman 2010; Lerche and Shah 2018; van der Linden 2014). In other words, a hybrid diversity of forms of labour constitutes the livelihoods of a significant share of the global working class. Henry Bernstein has aptly described the complexity this reality poses for critical social theory:

> "The working poor of the South have to pursue their reproduction through insecure, oppressive and typically increasingly scarce wage employment and/or a range of likewise precarious small-scale and 'informal economy' survival activity, including marginal farming. In effect, livelihoods are pursued through complex combinations of wage employment and self-employment. The social locations make for ever more fluid boundaries and defy inherited assumptions of fixed and uniform notions of 'worker', 'farmer', 'petty trader', 'urban', 'rural', 'employed', and 'self-employed'." (Bernstein 2010, 111)

This is particularly relevant for analysing precarious migrant labourers in South Asian metropolises. Moreover, the concept counters the idealised image of the unbanked (see Part I), highlighting how multiple fractures run through the social body, the working class, and individual lives. Following Marcel van der Linden (2014), we can understand this diverse population as a "subaltern working class".[23] The term seeks to highlight three critical aspects for studying migrant labourers in India: First, it highlights the multiple modes of labour which converge in a household economy. Second, it emphasises the historical continuum between free and forced labour within the capitalist world economy, which continues to shape many labour processes in India (see also Banaji 2020; Breman, Guérin, and Prakash 2009; Linebaugh and Rediker 2000). And third, it acknowledges that individual workers often combine different modes of labour in everyday life, producing ambiguous class positions and multiple fractures that mark their lives. Significantly, the prefix subaltern complicates the notion of class structure through, for example, gendered and racialised oppression while simultaneously maintaining that, despite these real

23 There are many alternative conceptions which partly overlap with this understanding, including "informal proletariat" (Davis 2006, 178), "classes of labour" (Bernstein 2010, 110), and "surplus labour" (Bernards and Soederberg 2021; Sanyal 2007). However, for the study of migrant labourers in India, the notion of subaltern working class seems most precise to me. In contrast to Breman's rather descriptive understanding of "footloose labour" or "labour circulation" (Breman 2010, 2019) is extremely valuable, but conceptually detached from broader class analysis in political economy.

and important fragmentations, they are all part of a class that is free of sufficient means of subsistence and must thus sell its labour power directly or indirectly.[24]

The concepts of fictitious capital and financial expropriation are critical to understanding subaltern working-class indebtedness in India. Fictitious capital is vital in the dual sense played above, i.e. money used as money, not capital, hence "illusionary capital" (Marx 2012, 523), and the financialisation of the microfinance sector, including the securitisation of loan portfolios (Kar 2018; Mader 2015; Soederberg 2012). The lending of such fictitious capital involves the appropriation of disposable incomes of respective households through financial expropriation. As such, the financialisation of the global economy since the 1970s has been a powerful mechanism in the "unmaking of the established working class" (Silver 2014, 49), eroding living standards and the positioning of respective households within the given relations of production. To foreground these dynamics means moving beyond the study of the actual labour process, arguing that parallel processes of exploitation and domination through financial means may be critical for understanding the complexity of class formation.

Stressing the relevance of class rule by financial means expands rather than supplants the complexity of class analysis. It highlights new contradictions and instabilities that are helpful to understand class struggle in a broader sense. On the one hand, class struggles around land ownership, public infrastructure, and decent work directly impact the need for money (as credit). On the other hand, there is a thin line between chronic indebtedness that still allows for the generation of continuous revenues and that which entails complete destitution. This balancing act can be politicised and turned into a powerful lever for collective action. For instance, in the context of increasing household debt in the US, Andrew Ross has argued that debts have turned into the "wages of the future" (Ross 2013, 28) and that in challenging precarity in the neoliberal era, struggles over debt become the frontline conflict of our time. These observations can also apply to other contexts beyond the US and neoliberal contexts. In other words, analysing class rule through financial means can uncover how debt struggles are important sites of class struggles in modern capitalist formations. Contributing to this hitherto unheeded debate in critical political economy, Part III and Part IV will engage with these questions empirically.

---

24 The term 'subaltern' has been used by Antonio Gramsci in the prison notebooks to make sense of the specific class domination and subordination in the Italian context. It was popularised by the South Asian Subaltern Studies Group and Postcolonial Studies more broadly since the 1980s, which expanded its meaning to refer to all types of marginalised and oppressed social groups. A detailed discussion around the controversies of the term can be found in Green (2011). For this research, I use "subaltern class" and "subaltern working-class" mostly interchangeably, referring to the categorisation provided by van der Linden (2014) for the present, while acknowledging that the constitution of the subaltern (working) class has changed over the course of history.

Finally, the coalescence of usury and fictitious capital in the present era is a powerful analytical entry point to understanding the multiplicity of debts and their entanglement with class rule within a fragmented whole. Most critical studies on financial inclusion have studied the rise of (commercial) microfinance on its own, rarely examining the systemic relationships with existing forms of money lending. The perspective outlined above suggests that local moneylenders' operations are based on personal dependency and the accumulation of power and wealth of individual capitalists, including landlords and employers. In contrast, corporate MFIs are characterised by the rule through alienated debts which are governed by the (global) dynamics of financial markets, including the volatility associated with it. In these cases, labour is subordinated more subtly and indirectly through the objectified, mystified, and alienated power of monetary debts. Both are capitalists and yet moneylenders and corporate MFIs have different positions and interests within the circuits of financial capital. Against this backdrop, formal and informal debt, productive and reproductive use of money, and monetary and non-monetary debts overlap, reinforce and blend into one and the same household economy, producing distinct and yet converging modes of domination and exploitation (Bernards 2021, 90f.). To engage more thoroughly with these divisions in the household economy, the following part discusses the relevance of social reproduction feminism in expanding the study of subaltern indebtedness.

Chapter 6
A Shift in Perspective: Social Reproduction Feminism

Whereas many Marxist studies tend to reduce material reality to capitalist commodity production, Marxist feminist scholars insist on broadening the analysis by understanding "material reality as referring to the ensemble for social relations upon which human survival depends" (Hennessy 2017, 101). It may sound unpretentious, but it is an essential fact that "humans need to exist in a material-corporeal form before they can make and produce history" (Mies 2014, 214). More than a biological necessity, Marx claimed labour was a species-defining characteristic, for only through the exercise of labour power have human beings historically appropriated non-human natures to survive. The labour process is a process in which humans confront nature as a "force of nature", changing and shaping non-human natures while at the same time changing his/her *own* nature (Marx 1976, 283). From this perspective, human labour, in *all* its social forms, is crucial for creating and sustaining life. From a materialist perspective, the necessity of subsistence, and the essential role of labour in safeguarding the former, including a definite social division of labour and the appropriation of surplus labour by dominant classes, is a general characteristic of all societies. However, capitalist social formations imply a peculiar and historically novel structural separation between a productive economy and a vast realm of essential work sustaining human life (Fraser 2017; Katz 2001; Laslett and Brenner 1989). Engaging with Marxist feminism, this section shifts the perspective of our investigation, looking at money, credit, and finance primarily from the perspective of social reproduction. It first discusses some foundational premises of the labour-life-nexus, discusses the peculiar role of value and social reproduction, and finally engages with the notion of the financialisation of social reproduction as promising vantage point to understand subaltern indebtedness in India. In doing so, this section expands and refines the theoretical substance of Marx's approach to studying money and finance outlined in the previous chapter.

The Life of Labour and the Labour of Life

Since the 1970s, feminist critiques of political economy have highlighted a basic, though often still neglected, insight: Capital accumulation is premised on living labour. But labour-power does not just exist; it must be produced and maintained. And this production and maintenance requires work like cooking, cleaning, or other forms of physical and emotional care. Moreover, labour power as a peculiar commodity is not separately packageable like a bag of rice or a bottle of milk. It is necessarily embodied as a living capacity of human beings and a fundamental part of their existence. In contrast to looking at the care economy, and care work as a separate sector, as often proclaimed by liberal feminists, unitary theories developed by Marxist feminists in the 1970s have insisted on theorising patriarchal and capitalist social orders in an integrated fashion, paying close attention to the conflictual and contradictory nature of their co-evolution, while rejecting functionalist explanations (Arruzza 2016; Bannerji 2020; Bhattacharya 2017b). Social reproduction is no onerous appendage to capitalist development. It is and remains any economy's undeniable point of origin and capital's necessary precondition – its socio-economic base. Feminist political economy is thus equally interested in the life of labour beyond the factory gate and the work of producing and sustaining life beyond the market.

In this context, social reproduction refers to the "production of life itself" (Luxton 2018, 37), and the labour involved in producing and maintaining both labouring bodies in specific and human life in more general. Despite slight differences in emphasis, most Marxist feminists agree with a variegated conceptualisation of social reproduction, consisting of different internally related daily and inter-generational dimensions of labour (Bakker 2007; Bezanson and Luxton 2006; Hoskyns and Rai 2007; Katz 2001). These include the biological dimension of literally producing life and guaranteeing the reproduction of the species; the social provisioning of goods and services that recreate labour power and maintain life, including subsistence, education, and healthcare; and all other forms of care work, like sexual, emotional, and affective services crucial to maintain social relationships. Barbara Leslett and Johanna Brenner have summarised these aspects in their seminal paper on gender and social reproduction, arguing that social reproduction allows to understand the gendered division of labour by analysing the

> "[...] activities and attitudes, behaviors and emotions, responsibilities and relationships directly involved in the maintenance of life on a daily basis, and intergenerationally. Among other things, social reproduction includes how food, clothing, and shelter are made available for immediate consumption, the ways in which the care and socialization of children are provided, the care of the infirm and elderly, and the social organization of sexuality." (Laslett and Brenner 1989, 382f.).

The peculiar social form of surplus labour appropriation under the dominance of the capitalist mode of production is premised on a structural and hierarchical relationship between different types of work, including a gendered division of labour (Ferguson 2020, 16). From this, we can conclude that social reproduction is necessary for capitalist development. However, despite being a precondition, it is structurally and ideologically rendered invisible (Davis 1982, 234; Vogel 2013, 144). We can speak of an 'inverse hierarchy' in which social reproduction seems secondary to capitalist production, while it is precisely the reverse. Social reproduction has an inherent logic and cannot be reduced to capital's machine-like and expansive automatism. Marxist feminism fundamentally diverges from liberal and post-modern approaches by emphasising how capital's relentless imperative to accumulate essentially shapes the *social* form of subsistence and production of life, constantly provoking "boundary struggles" (Fraser 2014a, 68) in search to manage its contradictions. Social reproduction feminism thus proposes a "complex, necessary, and contradictory interaction, arguing that patriarchal relations both shape and are shaped by economic dynamics of dispossession and accumulation" (Ferguson 2020, 86).

Far from a natural or idyllic phenomenon as is portrayed in patriarchal narratives, the gendered division of labour, the devaluation of reproductive work, and the domination of women is a history written "in the letters of blood and fire" (Marx 1976, 875). Feminist scholars have demonstrated how what Marx discussed as so-called primitive accumulation – the enclosures of the commons, the expropriation of the peasantry and land privatisation, the violent colonial expansion of European empires, and the terror of racial slavery – were crucial for creating and maintaining a structural separation between production and social reproduction, and for subordinating, disciplining, and exploiting women, including their bodies and therefore labour capacities (Federici 2004; Mies 1986). From this angle, violence in all its facets, like torturing and burning "witches" or rape and other forms of sexual violence, is a crucial mechanism that underpins the inverse hierarchy mentioned above (Dalla Costa 1996). Such forms of violence also extend to modern discourses that naturalise women (and enslaved people or non-white populations) as part of nature, as property possessed by free men, who must control their irrational character and discipline their unruly nature (Mies 2014; Patel and Moore 2017). In her landmark study *Caliban and the Witch*, Silvia Federici (2004) demonstrates how the physical enclosures of land and territory were deepened by a process of social enclosures in which reproductive work would be confined to the family in the household (Federici 2004, 84), producing what Maria Mies has called "housewifization" (Mies 1986, 2014) for a significant share of women. As a result, the apparently natural social order entrenched and justified a gendered division of labour, including its oppressive and exploitative aspects. By restructuring the entire process of social reproduction, capitalist relations not only changed the social form and division of labour but also transformed "our sense of identity, to space and time, and to our social and sexual life" (Federici 2020, 70). If reproductive labour was this essential, how can its relative irrelevance in quantified economic terms be understood? To engage with this puzzle, we must remember the analytical power of the previously employed social value form analysis.

Valuing Reproductive Labour

The inverse hierarchy mentioned above is reflected in the wage form and the money form of value. As Wally Seccombe remarked half a century ago, "domestic labour figures substantially in the relative value of labour power, but is no part at all of its equivalent, expressed in the wage" (Seccombe 1974, 10). Put differently, the wage form and, ultimately, the value form of money explain the structural devaluation and unrecognised nature of a substantial part of necessary labour in capitalist social formations. From a relational perspective, the question of valuation has nothing to do with the inherent qualities of specific types of work. Instead, the value of work is contingent upon the *social form* of labour. Reproductive labour comprises a vast spectrum of distinct and necessary types of work that reproduce workers and safeguard human life more generally. It can be commodified, as is increasingly the case with care work, but it can also remain non-commodified, which still accounts for most of this labour. In either case, reproductive labour is necessary and concrete, producing a use value. But only in the former does it also take an *independent* social appearance as monetary value (abstract labour), relating to *all* other commodities in the market. As outlined above, only in its abstracted form, in which the concrete and unique character of labour is extinguished, is labour socially recognised as value-producing labour in exchange. Nonetheless, assuming that non-commodified reproductive labour is irrelevant to value creation would be grossly inappropriate. It "contributes directly to the creation of the commodity labour power while having no direct relation with capital" (Seccombe 1974, 9). As such, reproductive labour is not only a subsidy of wage labour and capital in a symbolic sense. Rather, it reduces the actual and average costs for profitable commodity production by reducing necessary labour time and enhancing individual and societal productivity (Elson 2015; Patel and Moore 2017). At the same time, the relationship between capital and reproductive labour is complex and contradictory because the latter also constrains respective labourers from using their time and energy to be offered as labour power in the market (Vogel 2013, 161).

At the heart of Marx's conception of exploitation is the subordination of a concrete labour process under the abstract valorisation process – the labour process relations and the money relations are part of a unity (Elson 2015, 172). In the case of unpaid care work, for example, the concrete labour process is indirectly subordinated to capital's value regime. Necessary labour is thus not confined to commodity production. Reproductive work represents another vital component of necessary labour, albeit mainly outside capitalist production (Vogel, 2013, 159). Importantly, the dynamics of wage labour and unpaid reproductive work are intimately connected. For instance, the extension of the working day, a classical method of increasing absolute surplus value, is not limited to the workday in factories or other locations. It also includes extending the working day for all labour necessary to reproduce the labour power (Hensman 2011). Put differently, externalising reproductive costs and burdens, pushing subsistence levels below critical thresholds, allows for cheapening labour power, as is visible for many highly precarious (migrant) labourers in the world economy (Breman and van der Linden 2014; Shah and Lerche 2020). Moreover, controlling reproductive sites beyond the home-workplace dichotomy (for example, in hostels), taking intergenerational reproduction in rural settings for granted, or subordinating homeworkers to global value chains are other relevant mechanisms which obscure the relevance of informalised and gendered labour for capital accumulation – particularly in the global South (Hensman 2011; Menon 2019; Mezzadri 2019).

As discussed above, labour power necessarily comes with a body attached since it is a living capacity of human beings. And the expanded reproduction of capital has always relied upon existing forms of social oppression that divide and subjugate bodies according to race, gender, sexuality, and more, allowing for a differential appropriation of surplus labour (Ferguson 2020, 115; Hall 1986, 24). In this context, the "accumulation of differences and divisions within the working class" (Federici 2004, 63) becomes a crucial analysis that adds complexity to the dynamics of capitalist development. Consequently, the shift in perspective that social reproduction feminism has for a materialist monetary theory lies in highlighting how the social power of money is rooted in the domination of living labour beyond commodity production:

> "The process of capital accumulation – the transformation of life (living work and nature) into commodities, money, and steadily increasing capital – is polarising and irreversible. In other words, money and capital can grow out of life, but no new life can grow out of capital and money. Life always has to be added to capital in order to make it palatable and bring it to life. Money that 'breeds' more money out of itself (as through interest) is a myth" (Bennholdt-Thomsen and Mies 1999, 21)

This statement adds another critical layer to the above-outlined argumentation. Not only is the exploitation of wage labour in commodity production concealed and mystified by capitalist relations. Likewise, social reproduction is a continuous precondition for money to circulate as value-in-motion, albeit this fact is fetishised and turned upside down by real constraints in capitalist social formations, prescribing money as capital's "second nature" (McNally 2011b, 147f.), as a precondition to access the means of subsistence. Furthermore, this perspective adds another set of foundational contradictions to the crisis-prone dynamics of capital accumulation. While social reproduction remains an undeniable condition for sustained accumulation, capital's expansive accumulation tendencies tend to destabilise the processes of life-making on which it relies (Federici 2012; Ferguson 2020, 112; Fraser 2016). To speak of re/production thus acknowledges the entrenched separation between a valorised productive economy and a devalued reproductive economy, which, despite their separation, are a unity at the level of social formation.

Historically the household has been a privileged site where much of this work occurs. The household is a promising entry point to investigating the indebtedness of subaltern classes in capitalist social formations because it reveals how most people exist by combining various forms of labour, including wage labour and unpaid domestic labour, to maintain themselves and their families/communities.[1] This approach fundamentally diverges from microeconomic studies focusing on household decision-making without relating these processes to broader political, economic and cultural dynamics. Looking at the global political economy through the households, it becomes evident how different forms of labour "are part of the same socio-economic process" (Luxton 2006, 32). The household can be considered an "income-pooling unit" (Mohandesi and Teitelman 2017, 40), where various sources of income are bundled to create, maintain and restore labour power as a peculiar commodity and human life more generally. This is particularly important for researching contexts like India, where most households sustain themselves through a mixture of agricultural subsistence and petty commodity production, self-employment, and precarious wage labour in the so-called informal economy (Basole and Basu 2011a, 2011b; Breman 2019; Naidu and Ossome 2016). Marcel van der Linden suggests understanding these as a "strategic repertoire" (van der Linden 2023, 118) of working-class households to manage their subsistence. Unravelling such household strategies requires investigating the labour relations, social networks of family members and the "institutional environment which facilitates or impedes the various components of a strategic repertoire" (van der Linden 2023, 118).

From this perspective, the household is capitalist and non-capitalist, a site of consumption and production involving monetised and non-monetised labour. It is

1 Albeit a broad consensus on the privileged position of the household for social reproduction exists, Marxist feminists have always insisted that the family-household itself a historic production of capitalist social formations, and that within capitalism, there have always also existed other crucial sites where labour-power is produced and the workforce is replenished (Vogel 2013, 144ff.). Reproduction always also takes place at workplaces and other sites beyond the household/workplace. For instance, in the case of (seasonal) migrant labourers in India, there are multiple "invisible economies of care" (Shah and Lerche 2020).

a site where the contradictions of capital accumulation and the fractures of capital's coercive and divisive mode of socialisation become particularly apparent. On the one hand, the generalisation of the commodity form, often associated with violent enclosures and processes of expropriation, forces people to organise their reproduction through the market, i.e. to buy the means of subsistence, like food, shelter, and other essentials. On the other hand, feminist scholars have time and again called attention to the fact that most of the work associated with social reproduction is still uncommodified, unpaid, unrecognized, and overwhelmingly performed by women in households and communities. Despite the trend to commodify, mechanise, automatise, and digitise reproductive work, feminist scholars have pointed to the relative irreplaceability of unpaid care work (Hensman 2011). Most of this work is highly labour-intensive. It cannot be mechanised or paid for because it involves creating and maintaining human relationships, and the complete commodification of this vast sphere of work would diminish the prospects of profitable commodity production (Vogel 2013, 162). Moreover, continuous resistance against the commodification of (the conditions of) life as well as social struggles for the reappropriation or collectivisation of reproduction, are a crucial social limit and a threat to capitalist expansion (Federici 2012; Fraser 2014b).

Against this backdrop, our understanding of finance in capitalist societies becomes refined. As second nature, money becomes a necessary means of subsistence, mediating between production and social reproduction. As such, it also obscures the inverse hierarchy between these two seemingly distinct spheres. For precarious working-class households' reproductive debt, that is, credit not for valorised investment but for ensuring immediate subsistence needs like housing, food and water, health, education, etc., may turn into a critical household strategy to safeguard survival. The previous chapter discussed how, in this regard, the productivity of fictitious capital is ultimately rooted in an exploitative dimension of ensuring repayments by any means necessary. A social reproduction perspective can expand this understanding by highlighting how processes of financial expropriation imply the subordination of unpaid care work, including the caring for debts. In investigating this contradictory relationship, I suggest speaking of re/productive finance. This rather general argument has been debated intensely in recent years as a significant feature of the neoliberal era of capitalist development under the banner of the financialisation of social reproduction.

The Financialisation of Social Reproduction

From a historical materialist perspective, it seems logical that the contradictory and crisis-prone relationship between capital and social reproduction must be studied not only on an abstract-simple level but equally through more concrete spatiotemporal configurations. In this regard, Nancy Fraser has suggested the notion of "regimes of social reproduction-cum-economic production" (Fraser 2016, 104), pointing to different institutional forms and normative orders that organise and shape this relationship. It is widely acknowledged that the global political economy underwent significant changes since the 1970s, which are associated with the transnationalisation of production and the hierarchical organisation of global value chains, the re-organisation of global governance in line with the liberalisation of trade and finance, a shift in policymaking on privatisation of state-owned enterprises, and commodification of social provisioning (Harvey 2005; McMichael 2017). Dubbed under the ideological banner of neoliberalism, this class struggle from above was centred around breaking the power of organised labour in many parts of the world and curbing the political and economic ambitions of former colonial states, with the prospect of restoring profitability in the context of multiple crises (McNally 2011a, 25ff.; Prashad 2012).

Feminist scholarship highlighted that the aggressive and state-backed antiunion strategies also extended to relations beyond the workplace. The assault on crucial areas of social reproduction, through the downscaling and privatisation of social services in the name of structural adjustment, the externalisation of costs and responsibilities onto households and communities, has led to declining living standards amongst the global working class (Bhattacharya 2017a, 90; Federici 2014a). Moreover, the "reprivatisation of social provisioning" turned households into crucial sites increasingly imbricated, dominated by capital's present-day enclosures and the alienation of common social property (Bakker and Gill 2003, 19; LeBaron 2010). The Fordist class compromise in core capitalist countries, which a male breadwinner model complemented, successively eroded, and gave way to a neoliberal regime of financialised capitalism, where two-earner households increasingly struggled to make ends meet – provoking a new crisis of social reproduction (Fraser 2016, 2017). Thus, working-class households became an important new frontier for the ascent of global finance (Cooper and Mitropoulos 2009; Lazzarato 2012; Martin 2002a).

In this context, feminist scholars have suggested understanding the financialisation of capital accumulation as a significant part of a neoliberal regime of social reproduction (Federici 2014b; Fraser 2016; Roberts 2016). Under finance-led capitalist development, debt has emerged as a "new normal" to temporarily manage the costs of social reproduction (Bayliss, Robertson, and Fine 2018; Roberts and Soederberg 2015; Young 2010a). Notably, the expansion of transnational finance rests on targeting customer segments that remained untapped before by way of gendered and racialised forms of "predatory inclusion" (Dymski, Hernandez, and Mohanty 2013; McNally 2011a; Wang 2018). Those populations excluded from accessing commons or public infrastructures through privatisation and commodification are being included through commodified and financialised services, including, most importantly, loan products. In these cases, inclusion into market processes, including those offering financial services, turns into "exclusion through incorporation" or "adverse incorporation" (Ghosh 2015; McNally 2011a; Phillips 2017b). Those dynamics reveal how debt is a class-based *and* gendered means of exploitation in contemporary capitalism, and how present forms of financial expropriation turn capital's indirect relation to household and domestic work into a direct one: "Financialisation, in fact, is a political strategy, a shift in the modality of the exploitation of female work, from indirect, under the supervision of the male wage earner, to direct, under the control of capital through the banks" (Federici 2018, 180).

The "new normal" (Roberts and Soederberg 2014) of indebtedness hides the structural gendered violence and social inequalities it produces and presents the broadened access to credit as benevolent inclusion of poor women. At the same time, it creates novel dependencies and dilemmas for respective social groups. Four interlocking dimensions are crucial to understanding how the financialisation of social reproduction modifies patterns of capitalist domination and exploitation: (a) the changing role of the state and governance; (b) the shifting means of dominating and exploiting labour; (c) the way debts are lived through, including the production of new subjectivities; and (d) the contradictions and conflicts this new constellation provokes. Let us look at these points in order.

The state's role is key to the ongoing financialisation of social reproduction. Susanne Soederberg has developed the concept of a "debtfare state" to highlight the connections between rising household debt amongst the working poor, austerity policies, the privatisation/commodification of social provisioning, and the expansion of financial capital that underpin the "normalisation of a poverty industry" (Soederberg 2015, 46). As such, it helps to conceal how conflictual, contradictory, and oppressive social relations and modes of exploitation have expanded from the realm of production to the realm of exchange (and, thereby, also to the realm of reproduction), where the processes of class power and exploitation are less visible (Bhattacharyya 2018, 151f.; Soederberg 2015, 46). The notion of a debtfare state resonates with the financialisation of social reproduction because it explains how public policies and state-funded welfare programmes "help[s] construct the reliance of the working poor on privately created money (credit) to meet social subsistence needs, and thereby top up their living wages" (Hembruff and Soederberg 2015, 8). This trend also resonates with the new geopolitics of Development, which has increasingly turned into "De(bt)velopment" (Casolo and Doshi 2013) in recent decades (see also Part I). The dynamics of debtfare and de(bt)velopment policy may also intersect. For instance, the "collateralization of social policy" (Lavinas 2018) has become a critical feature of new social security schemes in the global South as discussed in the introduction. Populations considered unbankable before may access credit from financial institutions because their status as welfare recipients guarantee the creditor a regular cash flow necessary to repay (micro-)loans.

Financial expropriation thus not only takes place through appropriating worker's incomes and savings but also through mobilising their entire livelihoods and reorganising them in the service of debt repayment, including reproductive labour and access to welfare services (Cavallero and Gago 2021, 48f.; Soederberg 2015, 37). This brings us back to how financial capital accumulation allows for the colonisation of the future, thereby dominating and exploiting populations beyond the direct exploitation of wage labour. However, this trend includes the disciplining of various types of labourers, exerting pressure "to accept any type of work to pay the obligation to the future. In this sense, it drives precarisation from 'within'" (Cavallero and Gago 2021, 9). To understand the societal implications of these shifts and how they affect the re-organisation of social reproduction, one must abstract from individual cases and assessments of specific loan contracts and debt relations. Gargi Bhattacharyya has summed up the consequences to the point:

> "What matters here is not so much the extent of the loan, although there are loans that crush life, but the sale of future. Entering into the loan relationship presents a route for capital to extract value from the spaces of social reproduction directly, without the mediation of the waged worker. In order to become self-managing and entrepreneurial, that is, in order to gain access to the consumer economy and move beyond subsistence, the debtor of the poor world must mine practices of social reproduction to provide payments to service the loan. One part of what previously was undertaken to keep families alive must be diverted to loan payment" (Bhattacharyya 2018, 173f.)

Amongst other things, the quote shows how chronic indebtedness is not just a condition. It is a continuous process thatworks through the household economy's contradictions. At this point, the notion of fractured lives gains traction once more. Living through reproductive debts may be a vital household strategy, but it is no magic bullet. Individualising risk, responsibility, and guilt require constant work, negotiations, and trade-offs on behalf of debtors. In this context, "caring for debts" has emerged as an important reproductive work, without which debts may become non-performing loans, producing risks for increasingly sophisticated debt chains (Karaagac 2020; Montgomerie and Tepe-Belfrage 2017). The systemic importance of caring for debts is particularly conspicuous in microfinance, where women's social capital, time and labour are expended in group meetings and further engagements to ensure a profitable business model (Rankin 2002; Weber 2014; Wichterich 2012, 410).

Moreover, a feminist perspective highlights that household debt is a lived and embodied experience involving complex psychological and emotional dimensions, something "one lives through as sustaining life" (Karaagac 2020, 9). Indebtedness produces specific subjectivities, for example, of financially responsible women through discursive imaginaries in advertisements, rituals of debt monitoring, or participation in financial literacy programmes (Haiven 2017; Wichterich 2017). These imaginaries render women's labour particularly susceptible to commodification and exploitation (Kar 2018, 132f.; Roberts 2015). Furthermore, such imaginaries serve to legitimise the moral economy of debt. The operations of financial expropriation navigate a thin line between discursively produced good debts to bad debts based on gendered and racialised stereotypes and notions of responsibility, rationality and worthiness (Guérin 2014; Seamster 2019). As long as repayments are regular, the image of the extraordinary entrepreneurial skills of poor women is showcased. At the same time, the latter's irrationality and infantile nature is invoked when loans cannot be serviced anymore.

The notion of caring for debts thus also highlights how women must deal with these contradictory ascriptions and how loans, although necessary to make ends meet, potentially become "for women a source of fear, anxiety and shame, ending with seclusion in the home" (Federici 2018, 183). Caring for debts, including the emotional burdens associated with it, is even passed onto women even if they are no direct borrowers. For instance, the infamous wave of farmer suicides in post-liberalised India bears witness to how the debtor's widows continue to struggle with the afterlives of their husbands' debts (Neelima 2018; Vasavi 2014). The imaginative dimensions of everyday financialisation are not limited to depressive and repressive logic. As Max Haiven argues, "financialization works not because it feels like an inescapable dystopian nightmare but because it offers us a set of metaphors, narratives, tools, and measurements that feel empowering and enlivening. We might suggest that, from one angle, financialization represents a form of storytelling about ourselves and the world we inhabit that makes certain forms of highly delimited freedom possible" (Haiven 2017, 355). In this sense, microfinance frames women borrowers as innovative entrepreneurial subjects, concealing how much of their entrepreneurial success in terms of regular repayments is, in fact, unrecognised, unpaid, and devalued reproductive labour, interwoven with economic spaces that are rendered invisible.

Caring for debts and related processes of alienation are not limited to borrowers. Sohini Kar (2018) has argued that loan officers, usually employed as precarious wage labourers, serve as "proxy-creditors" in Indian microfinance and must engage in direct, frequent, and often emotional relationships with borrowing women in regular meetings and beyond to recover loans (Kar 2018, 82ff.). Various forms of labour are thus crucial for the operations of financialisation, although the fetish character of money usually disguises them:

> "Like other commodities, debt instruments do not magically enter the lives of poor borrowers in India or homeowners in the United States, and capital does not appear in the books without the work of intermediaries. However, once fetishized,

> the loan is no longer seen as a product of labor tied to relations of productions but as a mysterious, powerful, and almost natural thing that circulates freely. In its commodity form, the debt can be alienated from its producer and finally moved to the balance sheets of the company" (Kar 2018, 88)

Against this backdrop, it appears that one cannot infer any one type of financialised subjectivity. Instead, feminist political economy is most persuasive when examining the specificity and uniqueness of lived indebtedness on a concrete level of abstraction without denying a structural and universal tendency of alienated debts on a more abstract level. In this regard, Lucí Cavallero and Verónica Gago point to the analytical necessity of investigating multiple subjectivities of indebtedness in concrete contexts:

> "[W]e see a critical need to affirm that there is not a singular subjectivity of indebtedness that can be universalized nor a sole debtor-creditor relation that can be separated from concrete situations and especially from sexual, gender, racial, and locational difference, precisely because debt does not homogenize those differences, but rather exploits them" (Cavallero and Gago 2021, 4)

How capital accumulation, in general, and alienated debts, in particular, work through the exploitation of differences is a topic we will explore in more detail in the following chapters. To do so, I suggest engaging with contemporary debates on racial (finance) capitalism. This third and last step in developing the theoretical substance of this research is necessary to account for another aspect of fractured lives that characterises the chasm between benevolent rhetoric and structural violence in financial inclusion: the role of racialised capital accumulation.

Chapter 7
A Strategic Intervention: Racial Finance Capitalism

Racial capitalism has recently experienced a stellar ascent in social sciences and public debates.[1] This section discusses the notion of racial (finance) capitalism, eschewing the binary between a culturalist and an economistic reading of capitalist development. The former may be associated with Cedric Robinson's *Black Marxism*, a foundational reference in contemporary debates.[2] According to Robinson, "Marxism is a Western construction" (Robinson 2010, 2), unable to analytically grasp the racial character of the emergence of the modern world market. He maintains that racialism, understood as "the legitimation and corroboration of social organization as natural by reference to the 'racial' components of its elements" (Robinson 2010, 2), already permeated feudal Europe and thus formed capitalist development. In reviewing the emergence of capitalism, Robinson argues that the "bourgeoisie that led the development of capitalism were drawn from particular ethnic and cultural groups; the European proletariat and the mercenaries leadings states from others; its peasants from still other cultures; and its slaves from an entirely different world" (Robinson 2010, 26). In this process, existing regional and subcultural differences were apparently turned into racial ones. While Robinson raises an important question concerning the continuities and breaks between feudalist and capitalist social orders and the relevance racial oppression played in this transition, his account of racialism and capitalism, as well as their interrelationship, remains conceptually and empirically ambiguous (Levenson and Paret 2022; Ralph and Singhal 2019; Virdee 2023).

1 For a concise overview over the conjunctural uses of racial capitalism and the contradictions of current debates, see Levenson and Paret (2022) and Kundnani (2023).

2 I would like to acknowledge that the primary aim of Robinson's *Black Marxism* was not to develop a theory of racial capitalism, although some currents engage in this fantasy. In fact, racial capitalism is only discussed in the first chapter and is largely developed through a historic review without much conceptual underlabouring. Instead, the main aim of the work is to challenge the silencing of Black Marxists within academic and public discourse, using W.E.B Du Bois, C.L.R James and Richard Wright as intriguing cases.

In contrast, David Harvey, arguably one of the most read contemporary Marxist intellectuals in the world, acknowledges that the history of capitalism is an "intensely racialised and gendered history" but still claims that these relations "are not specific to the form of circulation and accumulation that constitutes the economic engine of capitalism" (Harvey 2014, 7). He justifies this statement in a contradictory way: "The intersections and interactions between racialisation and capital accumulation are both highly visible and powerfully present. But an examination of these tells me nothing particular about how the economic engine of capital works, even as it identifies one source from where it plainly draws its energy" (Harvey 2014, 8). If, as Harvey argues, racialisation is a source from which capital accumulation draws its energy, scrutinising this process should also tell us something specific about the actual operations of capital in general and in the neoliberal era particularly (Issar 2021; Kundnani 2021).

Ironically, Harvey and others, who usually emphasise the enigmatic appearance of capital, fail to fully de-fetishise its economistic appearance in relation to racial oppression and thereby only sustain the fantasy of the "objective character of capitalist development" (Robinson 2010, 9). However, while a sophisticated engagement with Eurocentricism and racial silence within Western Marxism is undoubtedly needed, a culturalist reading of capitalist development, as employed by Robinson, primarily contributes to ignoring or obscuring the fundamental workings of this specific mode of production. Both positions represent the broader tensions in conceptual controversies around racial capitalism. In a critical review, Julian Go (2020) has usefully discussed three contradictions within current debates: (a) the sketchy and often superficial use of race and racism, (b) an imprecise or vague understanding of capitalism, and (c) a controversy on whether the relationship between race and capitalism is contingent or logically necessary. In addressing these and other criticisms, this section seeks to clarify how racial capitalism may be analytically helpful to understanding the indebtedness of subaltern working classes in India. Therefore, I will first discuss the relations between race, racism, and racialisation in the capitalist mode of production. Second, I will expand this perspective by engaging with a relational understanding of caste and race. Finally, I will outline why and how racialisation analytically contributes to understanding financial expropriation.

Race, Racism and Capitalist Development

Racial capitalism does not refer to a specific historical or geographic constellation that is distinguishable from otherwise non-racial capitalism. Rather than a residual feature, racialisation/racism is constitutive of the capitalist mode of production. In this regard, I follow Robinson's general assertion that race is a powerful rationalisation for the domination, exploitation, and extermination of those defined as Others

(Robinson 2010, 27). Contemporary scholarship on racial capitalism has claimed that all capitalism *is* racial capitalism because "the key dynamics of capitalism—accumulation/dispossession, credit/debt, production/surplus, capitalist/worker, developed/underdeveloped, contract/coercion, and others—become articulated through race" (Jenkins and Leroy 2021, 3). To substantiate these claims, we must first understand what race is and how it is systemically imbricated with capitalist development.

Race, broadly understood, is a power-ridden category of naturalised human difference, typically rooted in perceived physical appearance and presumed ancestry, constructing populations as groups within a hierarchy of worthiness (Pailey 2021, 31; Reed 2013, 49; Wilson 2012). A fundamental puzzle marks it. On the one hand, race is a modern social construction and ideology which does not have any natural existence, although it appears as such. In this regard, postcolonial scholars have rightly pointed to the phantasmal nature of racism, which "consists, most of all, in substituting what is with something else, *with another reality*" (Mbembe 2017, 32; own emphasis). On the other hand, despite this constructed nature, it has profound effects on racialised populations which in many cases marks the difference between life and death. Because it ascribes particular lives with less value, race makes the suffering or death of distinct populations more tolerable – or even justified (Wilson 2012, 157). Violence in all its forms remains a constant characteristic of racial orders because it is only through the permanent excess of violence that the legitimacy, necessity, and rationality of race as a modern relation of domination can be upheld, despite its inherently phantasmal, unstable and contested nature (Gilmore 2007, 247; Mbembe 2017, 46f.).

Race is analytically important because it draws our attention to the "politics of difference" (Pandey 2016), that is, the question of how amongst a myriad of potential differences between human beings, only some differences acquire meaning and thereby become socially significant (Hall 2017, 50). As such, racism is not only about exclusion. It is equally a matter of including social groups, and also about how both oppressors and the oppressed understand themselves and their position within the *same* world. Wulf Hund thus speaks of "negative societalization" to highlight how racism denies certain human beings social acceptance as equally human and thereby groups them into a homogeneous entity, allowing the perpetrators to understand themselves as a collective (Hund 2010). Likewise, Etienne Balibar has suggested understanding the heritage of colonialism and the relationship between racism and nationalism in the postcolonial era as "a fluctuating combination of continued exteriorization and 'internal exclusion'" (Balibar 1991b, 42f.). These thoughts point to the variability of racism, changing forms in different contexts.[3]

3 Historically, the phantasmal mobilisation of biological difference and its pseudo-scientific legitimation was essential for the rationality of race. While this continues to play an important role in actual practices of racialisation, many scholars have emphasised that cultural aspects

Figure 6: Racialisation, Racism and Race

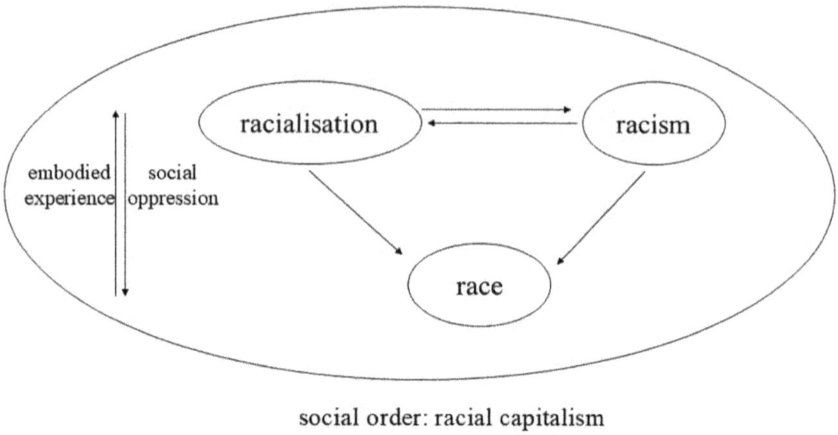

Source: own elaboration.

I suggest understanding race as a product of the twin dynamics of racialisation and racism to engage with the abovementioned puzzle. Race does not exist prior to or independent of racialisation, that is, "a continuous process of ascription whereby humans are grouped (and self-grouped) according to assigned qualities that are assumed to be biologically innate" (Ranganathan 2021, 4). In other words, racialisation, in its most abstract-simple form, is the hierarchical differentiation of humanness that cuts through the social body. As such, it is a social practice involving discursive and material dimensions. Moreover, racialisation is shaped by and shapes racism, understood as the institutional ensemble of habits, hegemonic common sense and knowledge production, laws, and policies that maintain, justify, and safeguard a seemingly rational double-standard to oppress distinct social groups founded on the fiction of race.

The interrelation between racialisation and racism allows us to understand the historical and geographical malleable category of race. Figure 6 suggests the causality does not flow from pre-existing racial differences to racism as an oppressive social structure. Instead, the mobilisation of existing power relations prevailing in a social order produces changing dynamics of racialisation, racism and race. From a historical materialist point of view, production relations are foundational to understanding social stratification. Therefore, it only seems consequent that such a perspective of racism understands the production of race not simply or primarily

have increasingly dominated racialisation/racism in the post-colonial era (Balibar 1991a; Hall 2017).

as an ideology but as a distinct social relation of oppression, which despite its specificity, is rooted in questions of land ownership, division and exploitation and labour, and modes of appropriating of wealth (Camfield 2016; Virdee 2023). Moreover, although racism is lived through and embodied individually, it always targets the entire racialised group.

If, as was argued above, the twin dynamics of racialisation/racism work through the prevailing power relations in specific social orders, we can understand the systemic linkages between race and capital accumulation as a relative necessity. Jodi Melamed has summarised this point accurately:

> "Capital can only be capital when it is accumulating, and it can only accumulate by producing and moving through relations of severe inequality among human groups – capitalists with the means of production/workers without the means of production, creditors/debtors, conquerors of land made property/the dispossessed removed. These antinomies of accumulation require loss, disposability, and the unequal differentiation of human value, and racism enshrines the inequalities that capitalism requires. Most obviously, it does this by displacing the uneven life chances that are inescapable part of capitalist social relations onto fictions of differing human capacities, historically race" (Melamed 2015, 77)

Against this backdrop, I maintain that there are three significant channels through which racialisation/racism/race and capital accumulation are systemically linked.

First, racialisation and racism organise the division and subordination of labour, facilitating differential surplus extraction through dehumanisation and devaluation of human beings (as bearers of labour power). For instance, the racial fracturing of the global workforce by the nineteenth century – the high-time of European industrialisation and the purported end of slavery – into slaves, coolies, bonded labourers and sharecroppers, or precarious wage workers was an expression of how racial capitalism has been the "animating spirit" (Manjapra 2020, 7) of modern colonialism and imperialism, based upon differential exploitation and appropriation of a fragmented class of labourers (see also Linebaugh and Rediker 2000; Lowe 2015; Virdee 2019). This racialised subordination of labour under capital has not withered away with the end of formal colonialism. It has reinvented the justification and maintenance of inferior working conditions, devaluation of labour processes, and denial of fundamental citizenship rights (Bonacich, Alimahomed, and Wilson 2008; Camfield 2016). At present, the super-exploitation of workers, broadly understood as the appropriation of surplus labour beyond the subsistence needs of labourers and, therefore, the cheapening of commodified labour power is arguably amongst the most significant manifestations of racialised accumulation within an imperial world order (Gilbert 2022; Latimer 2021). In these cases, the fiction of race creates a rational double standard whereby differential treatment, rights, and privileges of racialised groups become naturalized and de-historised (Hall 2017, 58ff.; Kundnani 2021, 65f.). In this context, race must be understood as a general logic of depreciation which is highly adaptable and often works through the state but always is integral to the valorisation of capital. Nikhil Pal Singh has succinctly summarised this point:

> "Embodied in the figures of the slave, the migrant worker, the household worker, the chronically unemployed, and the like, appropriation encompasses zones of both privatized and publicly sanctioned coercion and ethicopolitical devaluation that are inseparable from capitalist processes of valorization" (Singh 2016, 40f.)

The racialised (and gendered) operations of capital produce a fracturing and fractioning of the working class, informing distinct processes of class formation and dividing the class struggle internally, despite being part of the general form of the class struggle (Hall 1996, 339). In this sense, the dynamic of capital accumulation is also premised on the "accumulation of differences, inequalities, hierarchies, divisions, which have alienated workers from each other and even from themselves" (Federici 2004, 115; see also Hall 1986, 24, 2017, 118f.). This poses strategic challenges for organising labour and defining goals for radical politics. Thus, acknowledging the relevance of fractured lives through racialisation/racism becomes a promising starting point for analytically understanding the complexity of class oppression and strategically engaging with it.

Second, racism mediates the articulation of various relations of production, justifying and rationalising the extinction or adverse incorporation of pre-existing modes or relations of production in the context of an imperial world order. Thus, the structural violence of racial capitalism is closely interrelated with the expansionary nature of capital accumulation, invoking continuous and variegated processes of expropriation or what Marx describes as so-called primitive accumulation (Fraser 2018; Singh 2016).[4] For instance, thousands of contemporary socio-ecological conflicts around land, water, and other natural resources, in which local communities struggle against corporate capital and state-backed development policies, can be understood as imperialist relations between capitalist and non-capitalist modes of re/production (Shah 2019). In these struggles for commons, racialisation/racism is frequently mobilized to draw boundaries between productive and inefficient use of resources, work and non-work, and transformation social and society-nature relationships (Federici 2004, 61ff.), ultimately legitimising the displacement of communities in the name of progress, wealth, and civilisation (Gilmore 2007, 243). In all these cases, "capitalism must justify and mystify the contradictions built into its social relations – the promise of freedom vs. the reality of widespread coercion,

---

4 Expropriation is not simply theft or dispossession. It refers to the (strategic) integration of the dispossessed into the valorising logic and practice of capital accumulation (Fraser 2018).

and the promise of prosperity vs. the reality of widespread penury – by denigrating the "nature" of those it exploits: women, colonial subjects, the descendants of African slaves, the immigrants displaced by globalization" (Federici 2004, 17).

Third, racism manifests not only within the "engine of capital accumulation" (Harvey 2014, 7) but permeates capitalist social orders more broadly. Consequently, practices of racialisation and racist structures are not confined to the exploitation and expropriation of labour. Rather, they develop a relatively autonomous dynamic integral to imagining and maintaining nation-states, hegemonic modes of governing civil society and world order (Acharya 2022; Hall 1986). While it is hardly possible to understand modern racism without scrutinising its internal relation to capitalist relations of production, racism cannot be reduced to a derivate function of capital accumulation (Camfield 2016; Hall 1996). There are many instances where racism is systematic and yet not primarily functional to capitalist development. Two such key processes are exclusion and extinction. For example, racialised border regimes organise the uneven mobility of a fragmented global workforce, but the fortification of these border regimes is highly contingent upon the political dynamics of nationalism, cultural supremacy, and variegated forms of racism (Balibar 1991a; Fekete 2001; Walia 2021).[5] The racial management of migration is, of course, linked to the dispossession associated with uneven capitalist development, where imperial wars, development-induced displacement and the effects of neoliberal policies underly migration patterns. Yet, the exclusion of migrants from basic citizenship rights and labour markets can also run contrary to corporate interests. Likewise, extinction, as visible in genocidal violence, can significantly harm profitability and markets, revealing another dimension in which racism cannot be reduced to a derivative function of capital accumulation. This third dimension acknowledges that not only capital superimposes its logic on processes of racialisation and racist structures. Rather, racial oppression characterising specific social orders also informs the trajectory of capitalist development in respective contexts (Bhattacharya 2017a, 87; Bhattacharyya 2018, 103).

While Marx highlighted the commodity fetish, in which the actual labour necessary for the existence of the commodity becomes disguised by its value form appearance, a similar process can be observed regarding the mystification of racialised and gendered violence and oppression underpinning labour exploitation. Capital can never exist only in the abstract, and no labour process takes place in a social

5 Xeno-racism describes the increase of anti-migrant racism since the 2000s, in which projections of asylum seekers and other migrants are associated with culturally coded forms of devaluing entire social groups, as in the case of Muslim migrants in Europe, the US or India (Fekete 2001; Natrajan 2021).

vacuum (Bannerji 2020, 12).[6] However, the structural gendered and racialised violence concerns the concrete labour process, and these concrete characteristics are "extinguished" as abstract social labour. They do not appear as part of the commodity production but are fetishised as cultural specificity or exception from an otherwise neutral economic process. Both racial infantilisation in the form of unruliness, irrationality, the requiring of guidance, supervision and protection or feminised racialisation (the beast within, absence of reason, primordial innocence and heathen influences) constitute both the lived experience of (different) labourers as well as their vulnerability and availability to exploitation and expropriation (Bhattacharya 2017a, 89; Santiago-Valles 2005, 60).

Thus, racial capitalism allows us to understand fundamental capitalist dynamics, like "expropriation, impoverishment, alienation and formation class consciousness and expression [...] not [only] as abstractions or the residual effects of a system of production but as *living categories*." (Robinson 2010, 80). In sum, the perspective of fractured lives and a focus on the gendered and racialised process of class domination and exploitation allows us to acknowledge the politics, production, and accumulation of difference as inherent parts of a fragmented whole. The strength of a historical materialist approach to racism is in understanding the social existence and social consciousness as an internally related ensemble (Camfield 2016, 43). Himani Bannerji has aptly summarised this point:

> "As it stands, 'race' cannot be disarticulated from 'class' any more than milk can be separated from coffee once they are mixed, or the body divorced from consciousness in a living person. This inseparability, this formative or figurative relation is as true for the process of extraction of surplus value in capitalism as it is a common sense practice at the level of social life. Economic participation, the value of labour, social and political participation and entitlement, and cultural marginalisation or inclusion are all part of this overall social formation." (Bannerji 2020, 12)

Moreover, the methodological implications of historical materialism outlined in chapter 4 provide a coherent framework to acknowledge the malleable nature of racism as part of the unfolding history of capitalism, accounting for a plurality of geographically and temporally specific forms of racism. As such, it also challenges the hegemonic currents of Anglo-American academia reducing racial capitalism to anti-Black racism that emerged in the context of the transatlantic slave trade (Ince 2022; Virdee 2019). To understand why and how racial capitalism also offers

---

6 This is methodologically important because otherwise Marx's theory of capital (exploitation) would be treated like a neoclassical model, rather than an abstract concept that tries to explain a concrete reality.

analytical insights into the Indian context, the following section will engage with the relationship between caste, race, and capitalist development.

Caste, Racialisation and Racial Capitalism

There is a particularity about caste, a mystic fog that makes it look like something ancient and incomprehensible. In contrast to race, gender, or religion, caste receives scant scholarly attention in development studies (Mosse 2018). The mystic fog around caste is so thick that even the UN Sustainable Development Goals (SDGs) speak of reducing inequalities and promoting "the social, economic and political inclusion of all, irrespective of age, sex, disability, race, ethnicity, origin, religion or economic or other status" (United Nations 2015b, 21) – not mentioning caste at all. Likewise, the Government of India (GoI) has fiercely defended the position of the non-existence of systematic caste oppression for decades, including at the UN World Conference Against Racism in Durban (2001), arguing that the constitution outlaws caste discrimination, and hence cannot be a systemic issue in post-colonial India (Natrajan and Greenough 2009).[7] Nonetheless, caste inequality has been remarkably persistent and continues to adversely shape the livelihoods of a fifth of the world's population (Deshpande 2018; Mosse 2018; Rao 2005).

In countering this widespread ignorance, this section explores how the persistence of caste can be understood through the lens of racial capitalism. To do so, we first need to understand what caste is, how it relates to, and yet differs from race. Based on these foundations, we can explore how the notion of racial capitalism focuses our attention on the processes of the fundamental role of caste in the exploitation, expropriation, and exclusion of the working class in India. Finally, this engagement will help us to understand how poverty (finance) is "not just a question of having no money or no possessions. Poverty is about having no power" (Roy 2014, 51).

The mystification of caste is intimately related to its long history and the complexity of its character. Caste is arguably the oldest, most elaborate and fetishised system of social stratification and related oppression (Bag and Watkins 2021, 56; Yengde 2019, 7). Generally speaking, it refers to "a mode of hierarchically arranged, closed endogamous strata, membership to which is ascribed by descent and between which contact is restricted and mobility impossible" (Teltumbe 2010). In practice, it simultaneously exists as thousands of regionally specific castes and sub-castes that have historically been linked primarily to generational occupation

7 In public and academic debates, caste is often made invisible by relegating it to the past or describing it as a uniquely cultural issue of India. This line of reasoning has a long (colonial) tradition and has been very effective in depoliticizing caste oppression (Krishna 2015, 153; Wilson 2012, 43).

(jati) and the hierarchical ordering of these actually existing categories into four basic classes *([chatur]varna)* that emerge from Hindu scriptures: the Brahmins (the priestly classes), Kshatriyas (the warrior/fighting castes), Vaishyas (the business/trading castes), and the lower-rung Shudras (the working classes: artisans, agriculturalists, food gatherer, hunters, fisherfolk, etc.).[8]

Importantly, there are two significant social groups that are not part of the four basic classes (*chaturvarna*) and yet are affected by its hierarchical order. The first one is the Dalits (*avarna*), who are beyond the pale of the varna system but still live in physical proximity to it.[9] The Dalits are not only "the Untouchables, the Unseeable, the Unapproachable – whose presence, whose touch, whose very shadow is considered to be polluting by privileged-caste Hindus" (Roy 2014, 24). At the same time, they are the undeniable basis of a social order from which they are excluded because they perform the most menial jobs necessary to reproduce society, like carrying away excrement, disposing of animal corpses or working as landless agricultural labourers. The second social group is India's indigenous population (*Adivasis*), who are organised in tribes and worship a variety of gods or cultivate a form of spirituality beyond Hinduism. Historically, they have lived in the subcontinent's dense forest and mountain regions rather than in villages and towns, but with the enclosures of commons since the late eighteenth century under British colonial rule, many tribes lost their means of subsistence and became eventually integrated as outcasts (Breman 1974; Verghese 2016).

Crucially, the caste system is not a "federation of mutually exclusive units" but rather the "parcelling of an already homogenous unit" (Ambedkar 1917), in which (Hindu) culture creates the notion of homogeneity, while at the same time hierarchically fragmenting this homogeneity. In this sense, it resembles the "negative societalization" that Wulf Hund uses to characterise racism (Hund 2010). This seemingly paradox constellation is tied together by what Ambedkar describes as "graded inequality" of endogamous groups. The caste system creates a social structure where even the low is privileged in comparison to the lower, providing a contradictory stability to this stratification (Roy 2014, 51). Brahmanism is thus not limited to the tiny fracture of Brahmins at the top of the social hierarchy, but it is an institution that enables the near impossibility of maintaining order through coercive practices like "imitation and excommunication" amongst all *varnas* (Ambedkar 1917; Yengde 2019,

8 The classification of varnas is something to be found under different nomenclature in many other regions of the world and is not uniquely Indian (Mukherjee 1999). Moreover, even though the *varnas* provide a hierarchical framework in which the *jatis* align themselves, it is important to note that the fixation of social groups is far from being static or straightforward. Historically, the social rank has been much more fluid and ambiguous than often acknowledged, with contradictory claims regarding the *jati-varna* affiliation (Deshpande 2018).

9 The Dalits are not a homogenous group but are, again, ordered hierarchically into subgroups/*jatis*.

21). The notion of purity/pollution dictating permissible food, occupation, marriage, and social interaction is particularly relevant for preserving endogamy.

Importantly, caste-based violence is systematically gendered. Because endogamy is central to maintaining caste hierarchy/purity, the "degree of control men exercise over women and the degree of passivity of the women of the caste" (Kannabiran and Kannabiran 2005, 254) structure the social order. Rather than being epiphenomenal, structural violence, including atrocities from upper castes as well as violence within the patriarchal family they inhabit, is necessary to socialise, normalise and depoliticise the gendered nature of caste oppression:

> "Subjugation of women both within and outside one's caste groups then becomes a necessary condition not only for the subsistence of patriarchy but also for the maintenance of caste purity and therefore the need to control women's sexuality through the practices of endogamy, discourses of honour etc. to maintain and reproduce norms of upper caste respectability. On the other hand, humiliation of women of lower caste becomes a means through which hierarchies are maintained." (Banerjee and Ghosh 2018, 5)

Linking these insights to the previous discussion on the gendered nature of social reproduction, caste allows us to understand the concrete operations of patriarchy and capitalism in India (Menon 2019; Rao 2005). If the gendered caste hierarchy has been fundamental for the reproduction of society for centuries, a historical materialist perspective must explain the specificity of how "Brahmanical patriarchy" (Chakravarti 2005) works within the current relations of production.

It should have become clear from the description provided above that simply understanding caste as race or substituting one with the other would be historically inappropriate, analytically flawed, and politically problematic. Caste is not defined by ethnicity, nationality, religion, immigrant status, or descent from a colonised or indigenous people; it is a unique relation of social oppression (Bag and Watkins 2021; Teltumbe 2010; Yengde 2019). Yet, over the last century, the distinctions and similarities between race and caste have been intensely debated among scholars and activists.[10] Despite profound differences, I claim that understanding caste and race

10 Scholarly debates on the difference and similarity between caste and race are vast, diverse and date back more than 100 years. In the late nineteenth century, for example, Indian scholars conceptualized caste along racial lines, linking it to Aryan/Dravidian distinctions (for an overview see Nigam 2019). Reputed scholars like Bhimrao R. Ambedhkar or Oliver C. Cox have strongly criticised the view of subordinating caste as a form of race as "gross perversion of the facts" (Ambedkar 2014). In recent years, academics from the United States have increasingly suggested that racism against Afro-American population can and should be understood through the lens of caste (for a critical review see Gidla and Horn 2021). These debates will not be reviewed here in detail. For my argument, it suffices to focus on the general similarities and differences between 'race' and 'caste' and how they can and should be understand as

in a relational way, that is, in relation to one another and in relation to the capitalist mode of production, is promising and necessary for several reasons.

Firstly, both include cultural aspects but cannot be reduced to them. They are malleable and yet persistent because they are inscribed into the relations of production and broader social order. If the analysis of caste is reduced to the religiously sanctioned practices of inter-marriage, inter-dining, purity-pollution and other such customary behaviour and perceptions, it seems sensible to understand it primarily as cultural characteristic, as "caste in itself".[11] However, historically caste has always been as much about land ownership, labour exploitation and possession of wealth. The distinguished caste scholar Anand Teltumbe has summarised this point aptly:

> "Castes [...] were neither born out of religion nor sustained by religion alone. Religion was merely one of the contributors to their sustenance. The major factor was that it provided material power to the dominant castes, in a cascading manner, which gave the descending levels of the hierarchy a diminishing stake in its continuance. Castes are thus homomorphous with the social structure itself and have enough resilience to adapt to changes in it" (Teltumbe 2018, 115f.)

Likewise, in *Annihilation of Caste*, Ambedkar seems to foreshadow debates on how race fragments the working class, arguing that "[t]he caste system is not merely a division of labour. It is also a division of *labourers*" and "it is a hierarchy in which division of labourers are graded one above the other" (Ambedkar 2014, 234). In other words, caste is inseparably linked to the foundations of political economy, to the processes of class formation, accumulation strategies and modes of exploitation that constitute and shape the relations of re/production over time. The ordinary, naturalised character of caste (just like race in other contexts) serves to rationalise "the intensification of the extraction of surplus value of the Dalits [and lower castes in general]" (Karat 2017) and to facilitate the "segregation, containment, and disciplining of Dalit labourers in space" (Ranganathan 2021, 4). As such, like gender/sexuality, both race and caste are embodied forms of oppression, shaping the (de-)valuation of a fragmented workforce in capitalism (Chakravarti 2019; Menon 2019). Thus, racial capitalism may call our attention to how capitalist development in India works *through* caste oppression and the associated racialisation of Adivasi and Muslim communities.[12] In the words of Jens Lerche and Alpa Shah, these relations of op-

---

oppressive social relations intimately bound up with the dynamics of the modern capitalist world economy.

11 For a detailed critique of approaching "caste in itself", "caste and class" or "caste in class", see Mukherjee (1999).

12 The racialization of Muslims has become particularly pertinent in recent years under the hegemony of Hindutva. This trope deserves attention, but it will not be systematically in-

pression have become "integral and systemic to capitalism" (Lerche and Shah 2018, 933). They inform the concrete operations of capital accumulation through inherited inequalities of power associated with land ownership, access to capital and education, political representation and state capture, and they are pertinent in the super-exploitation of casual migrant labourers who overwhelmingly come from low-caste, Dalit and tribal segments of society (Breman 2010; Lerche and Shah 2018, 937; Shah and Harriss-White 2011). As such, a racial capitalism perspective highlights how caste oppression explains the key characteristics of the "subaltern working class" (van der Linden 2014), including the continuum between free and forced labour within the capitalist world economy.

Secondly, both race and caste are social relations of oppression that fragment the social body hierarchically, essentialising this difference through naturalising certain characteristics, thereby grading the humanness of social groups. Yet, despite their natural appearance, neither caste nor race "do things in the world" (Bhattacharyya 2018, 103); that is to say, they do not exist naturally. Of course, this does not mean that they are mere illusions. Quite to the contrary, they have profound effects on human beings and communities, which in many cases mark a difference between life and death. But these effects must be explained as a result of the twin processes of racialisation and racism/Brahmanism rather than as inherent in a pre-existing race/caste. (see Figure 7).

Like race, caste is informed by racialisation as a continuous process of ascriptive difference informed by unequal relations of power, resources, and knowledge (Ranganathan 2021, 4). Simultaneously caste is sanctioned and normalised by Brahmanism as a socio-cultural structure, including state-sanctioned and, in many cases, state-led mystification and objectification of caste (Natrajan 2021; Teltumbe 2010, 2018). Brahmanism is also sometimes described as casteism and refers to the graded *savarna* supremacy based on the logic of infection/imitation. Speaking of racism/Brahmanism as social structures and racialisations as a social practice is primarily an analytical distinction that helps understand the malleability and persistence of race/caste over time.[13] Ultimately the (re-)production of caste through racialisation and Brahmanism adds to our understanding by rendering visible and politicising the "continuous and not fixed process of recalibrating and reinstating caste hierarchy through legal, spatial, economic, and cultural logics to serve capitalist accumulation" (Ranganathan 2021, 4).

tegrated into the present analysis for pragmatic reasons. For a relational account of racialization of Muslims, Adivasis and Dalits see Natrajan (2021).

13 Methodologically, the distinction between of structure and agency is necessary to investigate the "structural elaboration" (Archer 1995) of race/caste over time.

Figure 7: Relational Understanding of Race and Caste

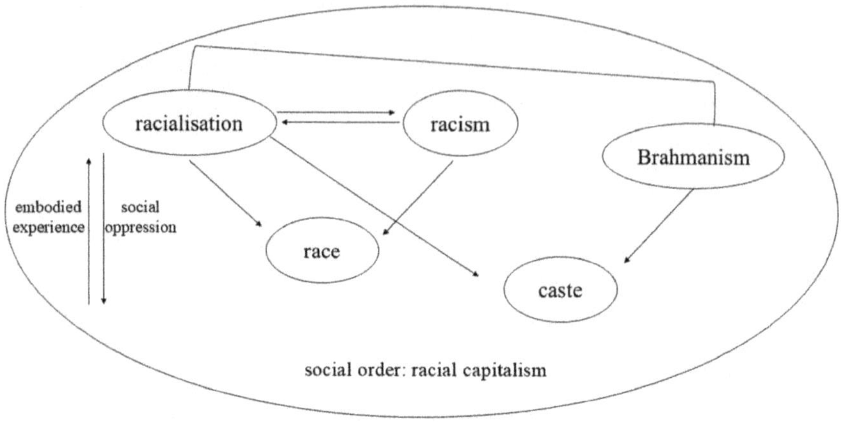

Source: author's elaboration.

The materiality of caste is the everyday dehumanisation, the reduction of human beings into "nonpersons, monsters, or things" (Natrajan 2021, 5) that allow for, legitimise and underpin the structural violence unleashed against these social groups. However, it is worth noting that this violence is not reducible to the economic function of racialised class exploitation, expropriation, and exclusion though it is also never entirely disconnected from the latter (Hall 1996; Natrajan and Greenough 2009, 30). In both cases, various forms of violence (lynching, rape, dispossession, etc.) serve to stabilise the phantasma of a naturally graded humanity, denying racialised groups the same entitlement and treatment (Roy 2014, 98). In this sense, racism and casteism/Brahmanism, though distinct, have similar effects (Deshpande 2018; Natrajan and Greenough 2009, 18).

Thirdly, race and caste have different historical roots, and yet the modernisation of caste must be understood in relation to European colonialism and India's integration into the capitalist world economy. The term caste is a distinctly modern appearance. It neither derives from any Indian language nor does it have a direct translation to one. Its etymological roots can be traced back to the Portuguese 'casta', which was used first by Portuguese colonisers and later by other Europeans to make sense of the subcontinent's diverse and unique social order.[14] Moreover, British colonial rule crucially codified and institutionalised the caste system within the state apparatuses, systematising and organising Indian civil society through "racial difference"

14 Virdee (2023) argues that the popularisation of terms like raza (race), casta (caste) and linaje (lineage) emerged since the fifteenth century on the Iberian peninsula in the context of the Reconsquista.

(Wilson 2012, 43). Therefore, some post-colonial scholars have suggested that European colonisers have performatively created a caste society (Chakravorty 2019; Dirks 2001). However, most caste scholars have criticised this narrow perspective, arguing that the fundamental practices of the caste system have existed for centuries, dating back to the Indus Valley civilisation (Ambedkar 2014; Bag and Watkins 2021; Teltumbe 2010).

Although the claim that British colonialism invented caste is problematic for several reasons, there are robust arguments that it played a major role in modernising, racialising and entrenching caste to churn capitalist profit (Mukherjee 1999, 1759; Ranganathan 2021, 5; Wilson 2012, 43f.).[15] It did so, however, in collaboration with the domestic upper-class/caste, as will be discussed in more detail in Chapter 9. This point has important implications for contemporary debates on racial capitalism. Most contributions have focussed rather narrowly on transatlantic slavery and the plantation economy to highlight the racial nature of modern capitalism. Yet, Europe's colonial expansion in Asia and the forceful subordination of respective regions into the capitalist world economy in the eighteenth and nineteenth century, has been paralleled by a regional-specific set of racial logics which were entwined with the caste system (Ince 2022; Khan 2021).[16] In this sense, a relational perspective of race and caste not only politicises the contemporary public and academic silence around caste. It can also broaden the US-centric debates on racial capitalism through understanding historically and geographically specific modes of racialised accumulation.

Finally, these analytical questions have important strategic implications. They point to the complexity of class analysis and struggle. Labourers are not an undifferentiated homogenous social group but a fragmented class (Menon 2019, 140). Especially feminist researchers have emphasised that these processes are not only manifestations of social oppression. They are also "embodied experiences" which crucially shape the formation of subjects, their positioning in the world, and their motivation and perception to act in particular ways (Bhattacharyya 2018; Menon 2019). Freely adapted from Stuart Hall, we can maintain that in India, caste "is [...] the modality in which class is 'lived', the medium through which class relations are experienced, the form in which it is appropriated and fought through" (Hall 1996, 341). If this is the case, then the multiple forms of oppression that run through the social body necessarily produce fractured lives.[17] And this poses a serious challenge for organ-

15 Likewise, Arundathi Roy has powerfully argued that "[d]emocracy hasn't eradicated caste. It has entrenched and modernised it!" (Roy 2014, 37).

16 Arguably, the subordination of Asia has been the major breakthrough when the capitalist mode of production became truly globally dominant (Anievas and Nişancıoğlu 2015; Parthasarthi 2011).

17 Significantly, racial and caste oppression can also overlap to produce ambiguous subject positions which are simultaneously privileged in some settings and oppressed in others.

ising labourers. As Arundhati Roy notes: "Brahmanism precludes the possibility of social and political solidarity across caste lines" (Roy, 2014, 51). In the Indian context, one must therefore acknowledge the relevance of "graded/Brahmanical patriarchy" (Chakravarti 2005, 2019) "in class" (Mukherjee 1999) to be able to challenge the prevailing social order. As Brinda Karat, the former general secretariat of the All-India Democratic Women's Association (AIDWA), remarked:

> "No class struggle in India can succeed without at the same time challenging the birth based hierarchical caste system against Dalits or the specific issues that Adivasi workers face. [...] Thus, class consciousness must necessarily include the consciousness of the specific exploitation that workers may face because of their caste or racial origins or because of their gender" (Karat 2017)

The complexity and contradictions of class struggle will be further discussed in the following chapters. The remainder of this chapter will synthesise the previous thoughts of racial capitalism in India, discussing how this analytical perspective is useful in scrutinising finance capitalism.

Racial Finance Capitalism in India

There is a broad consensus that the financialisation of the world economy is a significant characteristic of the contemporary era of capitalist development. While there are certainly specificities about the current type of finance-led accumulation, including the increased complexity of financial market operations through revolutions in information technology, the notion of racial finance capitalism challenges certain presentism in contemporary analysis. The term emphasises the "inseparability between racial hierarchy and the financial architectures and mechanisms of capitalism" (Ranganathan 2019, 2) as foundations of modern colonial and imperial infrastructures. The colonial expansion of European powers since the long sixteenth century, the imperialist rivalry, violent dehumanisation turning millions of Africans into commodities shipped over the Atlantic and the racialised exploitation on modern plantations has been essentially facilitated through financial innovations, like the creation of modern (central) banks, joint-stock companies, modern insurance and securitised debt (Gruffydd Jones 2013; Haiven 2020; McNally 2020).

Far from over or merely a background condition, the coloniality of finance for (capitalist) development has been reinvented under the banner of sustainable finance (Haiven 2017; Perry 2021). In these contexts, race not only serves as a logic of depreciation. It also constructs different forms of investability and bankability for financial capital seeking investments (Kish and Leroy 2015; Rankin 2013; Tilley 2020). In the global South, poverty finance is the key mechanism which enfolds subaltern working-class households into the circuits of (financial) capital accumulation (Bernards 2022; Kar 2018).[18] The notion of financial inclusion redefines the key problem of Development (poverty) into a financial opportunity (access to credit) by constructing ideal types of financial subjects (the unbanked). The construction of underdevelopment (lack of capital), however, relies on the essentialisation of this development problem along racial lines, depoliticising and obscuring the root causes and racialised inequalities that structure the global financial system (Alami and Guermond 2022; Torkelson 2021).

Moreover, as was outlined above, financialised accumulation is increasingly premised on innovative financial tools (like derivatives) that render all kinds of qualitatively different risks into a single metric, which allows for the commodification of risk (McNally 2011a, 110). In this process, the money fetish also conceals how different social groups are (involuntarily) turned into risk-bearers, and how the uneven distribution of risks, responsibility, integrity and bankability associated with indebtedness are glossed over by racialised and gendered discourses, including the financially underserved poor (Alami and Guermond 2022; Bhattacharyya 2018, 71ff.; Wang 2018, 125). Against this background, the political talk of financial inclusion as benevolent, modernising, and rational acts of development appears in a different light. Despite much talk of cooperation, participation, empowerment, and sustainability, a critical political economy can unveil the structural politico-economic conditions which allow for the present-day development discourse of democratising credit to appear as sensible, rational, and beneficial – but really ignoring, consolidating and, in many ways, reinforcing gendered and racialised expropriation-cum-exploitation of working-class households in global finance capitalism (Chakravartty and Silva 2012; Fraser 2018).

Racial finance capitalism thus draws our attention to the simultaneous dynamics of racialised exclusions and inclusions that underpin the contradictory expansion of predatory lending. As such, the concept enables us to understand how matters of financial inclusion/exclusion are contingent, contradictory, and conflictual. There is no a priori rule that racialised subjects must always be excluded or included. Rather, capital accumulation works through the politics of difference in myriad ways. The shift in housing policy and debt in the US can illustrate this point. In the mid-twentieth century, during the so-called golden age of Fordist capital accumulation, the practice of "redlining" allowed for the financial exclusion of Blacks from mortgage borrowing in the context of rapid suburbanisation (Taylor

18 The proliferation of household debt through microfinance must be understood in relation to sovereign debt (crises), in which neoliberal austerity policies shift costs and risks to vulnerable populations (see Chapter 2). Importantly, the nexus between sovereign and household debt did not start during the neoliberal counterrevolution but already extends to colonialism (Haiven 2020; Zajontz 2022).

2019). Several decades later, at the high peak of neoliberal hegemony in the early twenty-first century, the aggressive "expropriation through financial inclusion" (Wang 2018, 134) of Black and Latinx subprime borrowers paved the way for the biggest financial crisis in a century. In both cases, capitalism worked through its respective spatiotemporal conditions and contradictions, leading to entirely different ways of how financial exclusion/inclusion can be racialised. Likewise, Part III traces the shifting dynamics of subaltern indebtedness in India, highlighting how poverty lending has worked through different spatiotemporal conditions and contradictions.

Although Marx did not stress the racialised or gendered nature of capitalism, his understanding of "money as universal agent of separation" (Marx 1988, 138) helps us to clarify the power of money not only as a class-based form of power but equally as one that is inherently articulated with other forms of social oppression, like colonialism/imperialism, racism/Brahmanism, and heteropatriarchy. Put differently, the coercive and divisive mode of socialisation that the money form of value implies renders not only the classed-based form of power on which it is premised invisible but also the gendered and racialised conditions upon which its dynamic expansion rests. Understanding money as "the bonds of all bonds" (Marx 1988, 138) remains a powerful perspective to scrutinise contemporary financialised capitalism and its contradictions because it allows us to explain how alienated debts constantly "dissolve and bind" social ties as part of the subordination of concrete labour processes under the abstract valorisation process. Money binds us to human life, but it does so in different ways. Importantly, this is not a *quantitative* difference but primarily a *qualitative* one that often makes a difference between life and death. This veiled difference is a difference between labourers and social forms of labour (much broader than just wage labour). Notably, racial finance capitalism may unearth how the uneven distribution of financial risks is mediated by debts and systemically linked to the depreciation of labour(ers). Consequently, profits emerge from exploitation in the sense of contractually siphoning off surplus labour in the relatively visible sphere of commodity production and from the violent nature of expropriating fractured lives.[19] In *Comments on James Mill*, Marx offers an intriguing perspective for understanding this violence as a source of value underpinning alienated debts:

> "Within the credit relationship, it is not the case that money is transcended in man, but that man himself is turned into *money*, or money is *incorporated* in him.

---

19 In analysing the globalisation of the plantation system after the abolition of slavery in the nineteenth century, Kris Manjapra summarises this point well: "The abstract, exchangeable, sovereign, and accounted financial form of money veiled 'off the books' profits and erased extractions of life-power from colonized and terrorized flesh, blood, and soil" (Manjapra 2018, 382).

> *Human individuality*, human *morality* itself, has become both an object of commerce and the material in which money exists. Instead of money, or paper, it is my own personal existence, my flesh and blood, my social virtue and importance, which constitutes the material, corporeal form of the *spirit of money*. Credit no longer resolves the value of money into money but into human flesh and the human heart. Such is the extent to which all progress and all inconsistencies within a false system are extreme retrogression and the extreme consequence of vileness." (Marx 1844a)

By understanding how monetary debts and repayments are intimately bound up with "personal existence, [my] flesh and blood, [my] social virtue and importance", Marx highlights the ordinary, structural violence of debt relationships as a systemic feature rather than solely as a power relation between creditor and debtor. If we reckon that money is "the alienated and exploited energies and potentials of the working class now returned to them in punitive, extortionate, and, indeed, *vengeful* form" (Haiven 2020, 95), we can unmask the social violence underpinning such seemingly normal, legitimate and legal household debt. It is entirely consistent and, as I have argued above, necessary to explicitly acknowledge the gendered and racialised violence as a systemic feature of proletarian indebtedness.

How do these considerations relate to the focus on understanding reproductive debts in India? First, it is important to acknowledge that reproductive labour is far less mechanised, commodified, and state-subsidised in India compared to OECD countries (Hensman 2011; Rao 2021). Social reproduction is largely privatised, and a racial lens is important because it highlights that the labour of (reproducing) lives "remains largely the work from India's marginalised castes and classes" (Rao 2021, 49). As a result, there is a much higher dependency on commons and turning non-human natures and the physical environment for food and shelter, and increased labour time expended on fetching water, preparing food or cleaning dishes. Hence, struggles around land acquisition of land, forests, or water bodies for commercial and development interests (mining, transport infrastructure, special economic zones, etc.) are intimately bound up with understanding the crisis of social reproduction, adversely affecting communities' ability to safeguard their reproduction.

In such a context, the violence of finance capitalism in relation to working-class household debt is most visibly expressed in the vicious cycle between accumulation, dispossession, subsistence-related distress and debt (Agarwal 2021).[20] To speak of

20 Moreover, these dynamics extend across space. Households are traditionally not only nuclear families, and stretch across the rural-urban-divide, including processes of circular/seasonal migration or the relevance of urban remittances to sustain rural livelihoods (Breman 2010; Harriss-White et al. 2013; Shah and Harriss-White 2011).

racial finance capitalism in this context is to highlight that the systemic cycle of accumulation, dispossession, distress, and debt is at all stages informed by racialised and gendered patterns. For instance, the dispossession of India's subaltern population is fundamentally linked to the dynamics of exclusionary growth facilitated by development projects and has further increased the caste divides in many cases (Agarwal and Levien 2020). Moreover, chronic indebtedness emerges as an important survival strategy to manage subsistence-related distress (Agarwal and Levien 2020; Guérin et al. 2022). As a result, financial expropriation must be understood as a gendered and racialised process entangled with the broader dynamics of class exploitation, expropriation, and exclusion.

Rather than revoking money's occult power rooted in class domination, the notion of racial finance capitalism helps to refine the operations of monetary credit by acknowledging the fragmentation of the working class and the accumulation of a systematic process. This also includes scrutinising the variety of creditor institutions and concrete dynamics of exploitation that cuts across the formal-informal divide and a variety of incomes and forms of labour necessary to service these debts (see Part IV). Analysing the case of Argentina, Verónica Gago has called this the "capture of subaltern networks", emphasising that "it doesn't matter what type of work you do, what matters is that you pay your debt" (Gago 2018).

These arguments should be understood as strategic interventions into contemporary debates on the financialisation of development, tackling some of the existing blind spots and thereby opening new avenues for "Marx's open-ended critique" (Foster 2018). Money's divisive and coercive form of socialisation in the form of 'illusionary capital'[21] is a promising starting point for investigating contemporary microfinance, where credit is used primarily as reproductive debt. Moreover, the notion of crises of social reproduction helps to understand the affirmative proposition of microfinance as an existential safety net, and as a dominant development strategy to tackle the contradictions of financialised capital accumulation. Finally, the notion of racial finance capitalism helps to situate these dynamics in a broader history of racialised accumulation, highlighting how caste domination in India underpins the debt-distress cycle, which creates the demand for credit.

21 That is, the first dimension of fictitious capital, where money is used as money not capital, hence illusionary capital.

Chapter 8
Investigating Regimes of Re/Productive Finance

At the beginning of chapter 4, I argued that any research necessarily involves abstractions to reduce complexity and make inquiries practicable. However, I also highlighted that the process of abstraction is no one-way road. It must relate back to concrete realities to become meaningful. In this sense, this part discusses how the rich theoretical substance discussed in previous chapters relates to the concrete research process. I will first introduce the method of incorporated comparison and regime analysis to operationalise the notion of re/productive finance. Then I will reconstruct the empirical research process, including sampling, data collection and analysis.

Incorporated Comparison as Relational Research Strategy

Many studies on financial inclusion would be categorised as comparative research.[1] Drawing on indicators like bank account ownership of adults, incidence of borrowing in the past year, or use of digital financial services, such studies compare the progress of financial inclusion in different countries throughout the world (see Chapter 2). These comparisons usually impress with vast databases consisting of many observations, allowing for statistically rigorous explanations. This research is particularly appealing for academics, policymakers, and public debates because it allows us to identify precise stages of development regarding financial inclusion in respective contexts.

Despite its attractiveness, this type of research faces some fundamental problems. First, the unit of analysis (e.g. bank account ownership) is used as a data category and theoretical category, conflating observational and explanatory units (Ragin 2014, 8f.). If we observe a lower share of bank account ownership amongst adults in

1 While all empirical research is comparative to a certain extent, comparisons in social research usually refer to identifying similarities and differences between large macrosocial units (Ragin 2014, 6).

India compared to Germany, the World Bank and other proponents adopting such methodology jump to the conclusion that bank account ownership *explains* the level of financial inclusion/exclusion. This leads to a second fundamental problem of positivist comparisons: Assuming that their unit of analysis are somewhat discrete entities that a common metric can measure, this type of research abstracts one-sidedly from the historically and socially conditioned reality. In the end, the reasoning employed seems overly simplistic and unable to understand why, under which conditions and with what purpose people in India/Germany choose to (not) open a bank account. Finally, these criticisms are linked to a third problem this research strategy faces. By parcelling out neat indicators, the latter do not relate to other indicators in a constitutive way. Consequently, the policy prescriptions suggest that increasing bank account ownership or widening access to credit is necessarily beneficial and promotes financial inclusion, irrespective of how these measures impact people's real lives through interacting in complex ways with other indicators.

This section suggests a different type of comparison sensitive to historical and social embeddedness of investigated phenomena. Philip McMichael developed the "incorporating comparison" (1990) to avoid both the upward conflation immanent in most mainstream comparative social research and downward conflation – in the form of structural determinism – predominant amongst some critical political economy approaches, like world-system theory. Rather than juxtaposing discrete cases or indicators to identify common and contrasting patterns of variation, an incorporated comparison proceeds through an internal "historical inquiry, where process-instances are comparable because they are historically connected and mutually conditioning" (McMichael 2000, 671). In contrast to focusing on an external analysis that contrasts similarities and differences of given instances, it prioritises a focus on "internal dynamics" of those social and historical relations that form an evolving whole. Such a research strategy implies that the composition and context of the units of analysis (e.g. access to credit amongst different social groups) do not exist prior to or are independent from the investigation of the relations through which it comes into being. Finally, this framework allows to explore both spatial and historical relations that underpin observable phenomena (McMichael 1990, 2000, 2019).

In line with the distinction between determinations and determinism outlined above, the mode of explanation and exploration does not eschew generalisations but highlights that every generalisation is historically contingent "because the units of comparison are historically specified" (McMichael 1990, 386). Hence, tracing presuppositions of the present whole must necessarily engage with historical reconstruction. The central claim of re/productive finance that subaltern working classes in India must organise their livelihoods through indebtedness because of a structural subsistence crisis is a generalisation. However, rather than taking this claim for granted, it must be historically, theoretically, and empirically reconstructed to have any validity. This includes showing how this general characteristic differs significantly over time and in concrete contexts when looking closer at, for example, the interplay between the creditor institutions, the borrower needs, the accumulation dynamics, the mediation through state institutions, and the agency of social forces.

By investigating the historical and social relationality of the present configuration, the incorporated comparison allows us to trace determinations of social change in a non-teleological and non-totalising way, opening promising pathways to integrate the postcolonial critique of modern science (Hart 2016). It thereby acknowledges how different regions and scales in the global political economy are interconnected, rejecting any form of "methodological nationalism" or "methodological Fordism" prevalent in some political economy analyses (Gallas 2023; McMichael 2019). This interconnection pertains to the fundamental role of the capitalist world market (including class struggles, formation of nation-states, etc.) and their systematic imbrications with colonialism and imperialism (Hart 2016). In practice, regime analysis has often used the incorporated comparison explicitly or implicitly in critical political economy.

Regimes of Re/Productive Finance

Regime analysis can be considered a rather young tradition within critical political economy. In recent years, several innovative studies have emerged around *labour control regimes regimes* (Anner 2015), *regimes of social reproduction* (Fraser 2016), *Sweatshop Regime* (Mezzadri 2017), *regimes of dispossession* (Levien 2018) or *hydrosocial regimes* (Goldman and Narayan 2019), to name but a few. However, the precursors of this type of regime analysis date back to the 1980s, including most prominently Harriet Friedman's and Philip McMichael's *food regime analysis* (McMichael 2009) or Michael Burroway's notion of *factory regimes* (Buroway 1985). Rather than engaging with the particularities of each of these approaches, the following seeks to outline some general features that characterise regime analysis as methodological perspective.

Despite differences in focus and application, these approaches all seek to investigate present-day empirical phenomena while keeping in mind the broader political economy and historical contexts. They usually start from ordinary questions related to concrete reality, like What food is produced by whom and under what conditions? Who oversees and who is subjected to the exploitation of labour in global value chains that produce the clothes, electronics, and food we consume daily? How is the provisioning of (clean) water organised in rapidly growing metropolitan areas? Which conditions impel labourers to resist exploitation? Based on these ordinary entry points, they employ historical, theoretical, and empirical modes of investigation to construct a complex argument which explains the current configuration as a result of specific social and historical relations.

In this sense, the first characteristic of a regime analysis in critical political economy is its focus on the relative coherence and stability of a governance configuration related to a specific issue, for example, subaltern indebtedness in India. Methodologically, these regime analyses operate at a level of analysis which is more concrete than general features and abstract concepts that characterise the global political economy but more abstract than empirical investigations into people's daily lives (see Figure 8). As such, it allows to explore a specific spatiotemporal configuration by linking it with both general (abstract) and distinct (concrete) features. In this context, the notion of regime is useful to point to multiple actors and institutions, as well as dynamics of power, oppression, and resistance, which converge in a defined spatial and temporal context to produce a distinct political economy that governs everyday life. It is intimately linked with projects and processes of state building, but it also comprises the political power of capital, labour, and civil society. As such, it allows us to transcend the liberal binary between state and market or politics and economy to produce more complex understandings of different manifestations of governance.

The second defining characteristic of a regime analysis is its relational nature. Respective approaches seek to uncover depoliticised processes and institutions by revealing the hidden connections between seemingly disparate processes. In his seminal contribution, *The Politics of Production*, Michael Burawoy argues that specific factory regimes are not only about organising the division of labour. They also include political and ideological apparatuses of production which secure and obscure the appropriation of surplus value (Buroway 1985, 8). As such, a critical regime analysis shifts our attention to those relations, processes and institutions which usually appear as normalised or naturalised background conditions. As Mezzadri (2017) demonstrates in the case of India's garment industry, regime analysis is not confined to a particular workplace, set of workers, commodities, or business strategies. Rather, it focuses on the *interrelations* of all these seemingly disparate processes and agents, demonstrating the significance of their coalescence. In this regard, a regime analysis provides a practicable toolbox to explore why and how certain relations have become depoliticised and normalised in distinct social configurations. Moreover, it can assess the continuities and changes within the political economy that governs everyday life in the long run.

Finally, a regime analysis not only provokes questions about social change but explores opportunities and obstacles that different social agents face in specific contexts. As such, it takes the irreducibility of structure and agency seriously, engaging with the temporality of what Margret Archer calls "social elaboration" (Archer 1995, 71). The notion of labour control regimes, for example, has been usefully employed in labour studies on global value chains to make sense of the variegated structural hindrances to organising labour and struggling for decent work (Anner 2015; Pattenden 2018). Importantly, a regime analysis allows for an incorporated comparison, outlining the specificities of state-, market-, or employer-dominated labour control regimes, while maintaining that they are part of a fragmented whole. As such, a regime analysis not only mediates between different levels of abstraction, it also potentially shows sensitivity to the temporal coalescence and yet difference between structural constraints and agent's strategies. Likewise, studying (resistance to) regimes of dispossession in post-colonial India, Levien (2018) has argued that the political apparatus for coercively redistributing land, and the forms of resistance against it, have changed between the state-led regime of dispossession up until the 1980s, and the neoliberal market-led regime of dispossession since the 1990s.

In sum, a regime analysis provides a useful tool for critical political economy by linking more abstract methodological and theoretical concerns with historical and empirical research without super-imposing one on the other. What makes this type of regime analysis critical is its potential to challenge prevailing explanations in social sciences while simultaneously questioning those oppressive and power-laden social structures it investigates. As such, it follows Marx's call to not take the forms of appearance for granted but to investigate and explain them as a result of specific social relations. It is an obvious reality that throughout the world, hundreds of millions of households lack sufficient money to live a decent life. If one takes this as unproblematised starting point of analysis and policymaking, it might make sense to expand access to credit for respective households and to incorporate them into the formal financial system. If, however, this apparent, concrete reality is investigated as a social and historical product, and the demand for money is rooted in a chronic subsistence crisis which is associated with the interlocking dynamics of (super-)exploitation, expropriation, and exclusion, the entire financial inclusion discourse becomes at least contradictory, if not nonsensical. Therefore, such analysis helps to politicise what is taken for granted in academia, public policy, and common sense, provoking necessary questions for radical change.[2]

In consciously using abstractions, I draw on Ollman's (2015) distinctions between three necessary abstractions for any research project: (a) the abstraction of extension, (b) the abstraction of generality, and (c) the abstraction of vantage point. The question of extension defines the boundaries of which of the innumerable internal relations one conceives of actively. As such, it delineates both the spatial and temporal limits of investigation, making the research process feasible. This research focuses on India as one of the most dynamic microfinance markets in the world and an important territory for the development project of financial inclusion (see Part I). It focuses its investigation roughly on the past 200 years to embed

2 Radical change is meant in a literal and etymological sense here, that is questions and discussion around the *root* causes and obstacles to a decent life for all.

contemporary critiques of financial inclusion into a *long durée* perspective, considering the profound changes and legacies that British colonialism triggered on the subcontinent in the nineteenth century.

The abstraction of generality substantiates the layers of abstraction that come into focus. This research operates on three levels of abstraction (see Figure 8). At the most abstract level, it draws on and develops concepts that characterise general features of the capitalist mode of production and its imbrication with colonialism, i.e. money as societal relation of oppression, social re/production, or racialised capital accumulation. At a more concrete level, it uses both modular forms of the incorporated comparison. Part III engages with the "multiple form" to compare how distinct regimes of re/productive finance in modern India are "products of a continuously evolving process in and across time" (McMichael 1990, 389). This analysis enables a systemic view of access to credit for subaltern working classes since the late eighteenth century, contextualising the rather recent rise of commercial microfinance within a broader history of racial finance capitalism. Based on this overview, Part IV zooms in on the contemporary regime of re/productive finance at a more concrete level of abstraction. Investigating the livelihoods of diverse migrant labourers in the south Indian metropolis Bengaluru, it employs a "singular form" of incorporated comparison, understanding their "shattered story" as variations in space within a specific conjuncture (McMichael 1990, 389).

Figure 8: Investigating Regimes of Re/Productive Finance through Levels of Abstraction

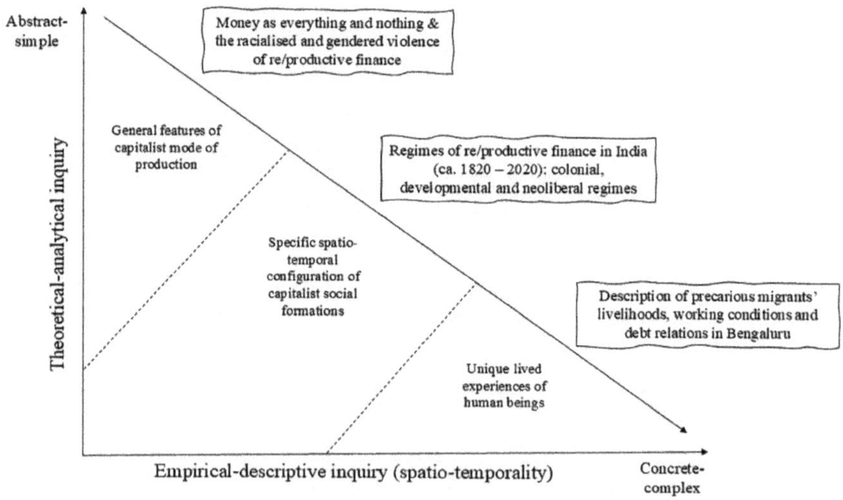

Source: own illustration.

The notion of re/productive finance allows us to understand the continuities and changes related to the gendered and racialised proletarian indebtedness through the interlocking dynamics of expropriation, exploitation, and exclusion. It highlights the multiple fractures that run through the social body, the working class, and individual lives and how financial expropriation is based on the "accumulation of differences, inequalities, hierarchies, divisions" (Federici 2004, 115). As such, it can conceptually grasp the chasm between the benevolent rhetoric and structural violence of financial inclusion outlined in the introduction. Proponents of financial inclusion advertise the widened access to credit as a win-win situation. Low-income households receive money to smooth consumption expenditure, and financial markets and institutions can expand their reach. In contrast, understanding this development strategy in the context of a historically specific regime of re/productive finance brings into view the multiple relations of domination and oppression which constitute the demand for money. Re/productive finance describes the tendency of (subaltern) working-class households to use debt as a strategy to manage the costs of social reproduction while repayment is ensured, amongst other things, by pushing the cost of living below a certain subsistence level. As such, it builds on the notion of the financialisation of social reproduction, expanding it to account for the longer history of racial finance capitalism.

In Part III, I will argue that it is possible to identify three distinct regimes of re/productive finance in modern India: a colonial regime (ca. 1820 – 1940), a developmental regime (ca. 1940 – 1990), and a neoliberal regime (ca. 1990 – present). To investigate the difference of subaltern working class indebtedness over a long time span and to delineate them from one another, I suggest employing an incorporating comparison based on three interlocking dimensions: (a) the changing (global) political economy and specifically, the distinct accumulation regime; (b) the social stratification and effects this type of accumulation produces for subaltern classes, including the link between a chronic subsistence crisis and debt relations (c) the shifting modes and means of governing access to credit, including the specific forms of dependency and exploitation and contradictions it entails.

The final necessary abstraction of the vantage point refers to the perspective the inquiry takes, specifically from where it starts. In accordance with the theses outlined above, I start from the vantage point of chronic indebtedness, particularly but not exclusively visible amongst India's large and growing rural-urban migrant labour force, to trace the historical presuppositions of distress-driven indebtedness backwards. In this process, I change vantage points to sometimes look at processes and relations from the borrowers' perspective, creditor institutions' point of view, or other major actors shaping and dealing with the dynamics of changing access to credit, like civil society organisations and policymakers. The shift in vantage points is not arbitrary. It acknowledges a commonplace in radical feminist research, namely that knowledge is always an "embodied practice" by particular groups of people in specific settings (Connell 2007, 217). Of course, it is impossible to fully explore all these vantage points in their entirety. There are considerable limits put forth by the collection and interpretation of my primary data. Hence, the following section will reconstruct the qualitative research process, reflecting on data collection and processing.

Windy Roads to Sampling

This research emerged within an interdisciplinary research project that investigated the socio-ecological changes in peri-urban Bengaluru as one of the fastest-growing metropolises in Asia. Initially, one of the sub-projects aimed to find out how access to credit amongst the peri-urban population had changed over time. Therefore, in the nascent stages of the research, a survey format was conducted to find out about the socio-economic characteristics, current access to financial services (esp. credit), changes in the past decades as well as how households coped with shocks affecting their livelihood (like crop loss, land loss, deaths, etc.) along a spatial gradient stretching from rural Bengaluru to urban Bengaluru, and comprising different villages/settlements. From this first round of field research, two findings stood out. Firstly, talking about money and debt was extremely sensitive and interviewing people in a survey format seemed to be of limited use, despite the voluntary participation of interviewees. Although I explained the purpose of the research and how the data will be used, people seemed reluctant to share details and the information given on credit (amount, sources and purpose of loan) was often contradictory and changed decisively during the interview.[3] I realised that in addition to being hesitant in talking about money with strangers, chronic indebtedness, especially comparatively low sums for household reproduction, was normalised to such an extent that many people did not mention them as anything significant worth talking about.

The second finding that changed the course of the research was the significance of social stratification. In the broader research project, investigating the peri-urban was largely defined in spatial terms, comparing different locations in their size and proximity to the urban centre. The idea behind it was to understand the stages of urban development in terms of vegetation, land use, access to credit, etc. – as if these played out in a linear way. Put differently, a Modernist understanding informed it,

3 For example, interviewees would say that they don't borrow credit at all, or that they borrow credit only for agricultural purposes, like digging a borewell or buying fertilisers. However, when asked specifically about whether they had faced any shocks that adversely affected their livelihood in the past decade and how they had coped with such events, most mentioned that they had borrowed money. Yet only few were willing to talk more about the sources, conditions and implications that borrowing had on their household economy.

assuming that a higher degree of urbanisation (measured in population density, infrastructure, valuation of land, etc.) would automatically lead to widened access to credit. Such an account, however, is ill-fit to grasp the differences that both dynamic processes of urbanisation and changes in access to credit have on various segments of society. In other words, the Modernist paradigm tends to ignore the relevance of how social positioning matters and how it informs the way debts become significant in people's lives. From a critical social sciences perspective, relations of power and exploitation that shape differential experiences, opportunities, and impacts are turned into a crucial starting point to investigate social phenomena.

At the empirical level, this problem became apparent when comparing upper-caste farmers with more than four acres of land in rural Bengaluru with low-caste migrant workers without land ownership in urban Bengaluru. While the former had taken a loan for Rs. 150.000 from a cooperative society to invest in irrigation facilities and facilitate a change in crop towards silk production, the latter struggled as a domestic worker to secure small loans from a local SHG, an MFI and moneylenders. While the former – though residing in the distant urban hinterland – had no difficulties in accessing and repaying a large loan due to his land ownership and caste affiliation that matched the governance structure of the local agricultural cooperative, the latter – though living within the busy boundaries of the megacity – accessed small sums through various sources and constantly struggled to serve them. Where they lived on the rural-urban gradient was almost irrelevant to understanding how access to and use of credit shapes their livelihood. What was significant instead is the social positioning and how, in the latter case, this related to spatial patterns of rural-urban migration that may stretch several hundreds of kilometres from a village in Raichur (Northern Karnataka) to a makeshift settlement in urban Bengaluru.

I thus changed the methodological approach rather quickly during the first round of field research. By engaging with critical urban ethnography and critical agrarian studies, I began to focus on precarious migrant labourers in Bengaluru as an entry point to investigate rural-urban interlinkages. As a significant and increasing population, circular and seasonal migrant labourers provide a unique, relational, and complex understanding of rural-urban linkages in contemporary India. Following qualitative methods developed in critical geography, I incorporated space not just as a given background condition but as something that is being socially produced in relation to time, embodiment and daily practices, which thus helps to investigate the changing nature of access to credit (Kuntz 2012; see also Venegas and Huerta 2012). In this sense, observations and explorations of where and how migrant labourers living in makeshift settlements access water may turn into important vantage points through which debt relations can be traced and connected with, for example, the privatisation of land (including lakes and other water bodies) and other broader political and economic dynamics. Parallel to this adjustment, the research design and strategy also became increasingly refined as one centred around regimes of re/productive finance, using the multiple and single modular forms of incorporating comparison.

Picture 1: Kodigehalli Lake, October 2002

Source: GoogleEarth.

Picture 2: Kodigehalli Lake, October 2018

Source: GoogleEarth

Importantly, the household interviews were not pre-arranged, but the sampling happened spontaneously and yet planned through geolocation. Prior to the field trips, I assessed two regions (polygons) in the North and East, focussing on three main criteria: Firstly, these locations were on the outskirts of the city twenty years ago but are now well incorporated into the boundaries of the city, testifying to the production of urban space. Secondly, both locations have a high number of scattered slums, where predominantly migrant labourers reside. Thirdly, these areas are marked by several branch offices of major microfinance institutions (MFIs), making it likely that borrowers also live in the surrounding. Inspired by Krishna et al. (2014), I used satellite images from Google Earth to construct polygons in different areas of the city which matched these three criteria. Pictures 1 and 2 demonstrate how the land-use change can be visually traced over time, showing how lakes dry out, agrarian land becomes increasingly occupied by concrete housing, and makeshift settlements emerge.

Based on this preliminary desktop sampling, the field research was influenced by ethnographic strategies, like spending a long time at the research sites, talking to those who are present, observing and documenting the living conditions, and, of course, conducting narrative interviews (Venegas and Huerta 2012).

The Purpose of Interviews: A Relational Account

The overall research question grounding this project was why and how microfinance could expand at such a rapid scale in recent years. To understand how microfinance works, I suggest embedding the workings of microfinance in the broader investigation of regimes of re/productive finance, which trace access to credit for India's subaltern working class. To account for the basic premises of regime analysis, I consciously shifted between different vantage points, including migrant labourer households, microfinance institutions (MFIs), civil society actors (CSA), and the Reserve Bank of India (RBI). Accordingly, the field research navigated narrative and expert interviews to explore the unique perspective each actor group offered. In total, the research built on 68 household and 21 expert interviews (see Appendix).

The primary objective of household interviews was to gain knowledge of how debt shapes and is shaped by their livelihood. It tried to understand why and how microfinance works from the perspective of migrant labourers. Thus, narrative interviews seemed more promising than the initial survey format. The former foreground the life stories of these migrant workers and "aims at using the more detailed, contextualized and personal style of talking in storytelling to enrich the interview data" (Flick 2022, 238). However, the concrete application is best understood as focused narrative interviews or episodic narrative interviews (Mueller 2019). Instead of letting interviewees narrate their entire lives, it focused on the relevance of indebtedness, focusing on specific significant episodes, like the reasons for labour migration.

This hybrid method allowed me to overcome the obstacles of the survey format, allowing for a more trustful and accessible interaction (less structured and distanced) and providing an in-depth account of the relevance of debt in migrant labourer's lives while staying open to understanding people's living circumstances in their own terms. Despite acknowledging the uniqueness of every single story and how individuals experienced distinct episodes, this method allows for the layering of narratives, discerning patterns that occur across participants' experiences (Mueller 2019). A relative saturation of interviews was indicated by the fact that similar tropes, patterns, accounts and concerns emerged from the narratives, indicating that general mechanisms seemed to be at work.

Importantly, the interviewees were not addressed as microfinance customers. Rather, the role of debt was focused by embedding it in their life stories, while their significant commonality was being precarious migrant labourers residing in an urban slum. Moreover, I consciously chose to investigate them through their household economy rather than as individuals, acknowledging the theoretical framework of social reproduction feminism. The latter assumes a privileged position of households to explore the power-laden, contradictory, and conflictual relationship between the different and yet inseparable spheres of the economy and types of work. The field visits were conducted during the day when many daily labourers were out for work. But given the inconstant nature of daily work, there would always be workers staying home, usually ready to tell their stories. Significantly, those staying back were often women and children. Primarily interviewing women matched the research objectives for two reasons. On the one hand, almost all borrowers involved in debt relations through self-help groups (SHGs) or microfinance institutions (MFIs) are women. On the other hand, they share multiple burdens of care and waged work, having a different knowledge and experience of how household debts are lived and worked through, both productive and reproductive. But there were also patriarchal constraints to this sampling approach. Being a foreign man, despite being accompanied by a local female research assistant, a certain socio-cultural distance constrained the depth of narrative interviews. In some cases, women were eager to talk about the reasons for migration, how they struggled at work (usually construction or domestic work), and what burdens of unpaid labour they shouldered on a daily basis. However, when talking about sources and types of debt, they replied that their husbands oversaw those monetary issues and that they didn't know anything about it.

While this hybrid approach certainly had advantages compared to the initial research design, I don't intend to portray it as one without flaws.[4] Perhaps most importantly, as a non-native with no relevant knowledge of Kannada, Tamil and Hindu – the three most common languages spoken by interviewed migrants – I had to rely on local research assistants for translation. And instead of recording interviews, which made people anxious, I limited documentation to taking detailed notes during and after each interview, and to reflecting on the field research experience in a diary. Following the standard ethnographic approach and spending several months in one or two specific locations would have certainly enriched the collected data, based on more trustful and deep social relationships, as well as a more complex understanding of people's livelihoods. And recordings of people's accounts in their own words would have certainly been more accurate. However, the approach taken had pragmatic reasons, which were informed by several real-world constraints I faced as PhD researcher, including limited time in the field (two rounds of field research for each two months), personal sickness during this time, financial constraints, and my involvement in teaching and care work in Germany.

Despite these shortcomings, the household interviews are one significant pillar of the overall research design. Employing a single form of incorporated comparison, I focused on three types of migrant labourers, namely construction, domestic and garment sector workers. On the one hand, these are the largest occupations for migrant labourers in Bengaluru and thus represent a large share of the city's slum population and subaltern working class. On the other hand, they are also different in many respects, especially with regard to how their labour and the broader sector are positioned within the overall political economy. Rather than comparing these three as self-sufficient entities, I use them as vantage points that shed light on a specific aspect which – despite its specificity – speaks to the broader conditions of indebtedness amongst rural-urban migrant workers. In this sense, the unique experience of migrant workers and the patterns that emerged from layering their narratives were complemented by semi-structured interviews with academics, civil society actors, microfinance institutions and the Reserve Bank of India (RBI). These interviews were pre-arranged, conducted in English, and recorded consensually.

The use of expert interviews formed a second major pillar of the research design. Semi-structured interviews are commonly used to explore complex dynamics through rather simple entry points that relate to the interviewees lived reality while prescribing a certain dramaturgy of events and allowing to compare the contents among different institutions (Flick 2022, 65). Importantly, the reasoning for interviewing such diverse actor groups was to get a more comprehensive account of the

4 On the general difficulties of doing research in the "shadows of the global political economy" see also Phillips (2017a).

political economy of subaltern working-class indebtedness by engaging with different perspectives. For example, interviewing top-management staff in MFIs could provide an in-depth account of changing business strategies, including customer targeting or diversification of loan products, or how repayment crises are dealt with from their end. I specifically focussed on Bengaluru-based organisations, and particularly on two institutions, Ujjivan and Janalakshmi, which both emerged in the mid-2000s as slum-based MFIs and had evolved into large corporations with millions of customers throughout India and strong ties to domestic and international capital within few years. By the time I conducted my field research in 2018 and 2019, both were underway to becoming Small Finance Banks (SFB), a category the Reserve Bank of India (RBI) had newly created to acknowledge the fact that India's largest MFIs had turned into quasi-banks. Since the rapid rise of microfinance had attracted much attention and research in the past two decades, many of which were critical of the former's operations, access to staff was difficult and required a detailed explanation of the purpose and context of the study.

In addition, interviews with various departments of the Reserve Bank of India (RBI), most importantly the Financial Inclusion and Development Department (FIDD) and the Department for Non-Banking Supervision (DNBS) in Bengaluru and Mumbai, were conducted. The RBI is arguably the most important public policy body when it comes to financial inclusion and access to credit and a crucial interface to global discourses and institutions promoting financial inclusion. Since it focuses on the entire country, their perspective helped to contextualise specific developments and contradictions in Bengaluru in a broader context and shed light on how access to credit is governed.

Finally, I interviewed various local civil society actors from trade unions and NGOs who work with construction, domestic and garment workers in Bengaluru, as well as academics who researched microfinance and migrant labourers, to learn more about specific patterns of exploitation and resistance in various sectors of the urban economy, the gendered and caste-based differentiation within the working-class, and the obstacles of migrant labourers to access public services. Importantly, all these general concerns were related to the problem of chronic indebtedness amongst migrant labourers in Bengaluru. Since most of the interviewed institutions have existed for decades, they could provide a historical account, highlighting significant changes over time. Particularly some of the senior interviewees had been working in this field since the 1980s and thus provided invaluable insights into some neglected aspects of microfinance research, namely the post-independence era.

Despite their inherently worthy perspectives, the expert interviews should not be understood as merely additive accounts of one and the same story. Rather, these groups relate to the investigated phenomena in vastly different ways, and they are invested in the object of research through unequal power relations (Flick 2022, 23).

All provide a different account of why and how microfinance works, but no perspective is innocent because each actor group is imbricated with the dynamic expansion of credit-debt relations in different ways. If one takes the epistemological and ontological positions outlined above seriously, it follows that despite the fact, that each of the diverse interview partners is an expert for a specific aspect of the complex whole, and as such has a certain privileged understanding, none of these can claim absolute or neutral knowledge of the object under investigation. Therefore, "active listening" both in the form of being attentive and reflexive of the social positioning of the interviewer and interviewees, was crucial for doing interview research (Fuji 2018). Hence, no coherent narrative appears automatically from such a diverse body of interviews. Constructing one, remains a task of (critical) analysis, which is why a robust theoretical substance is crucial for this research.

The interviews were transcribed and coded with MAXQDA. Initially, many thematic domains were identified through in vivo coding[5], acknowledging interviewees' diverse experiences, positioning, and interests. This first round already revealed some patterns across the answers. In the second step, using the creative coding tool, the initial codes were thematically clustered, merged, and hierarchically ordered to find superordinate categories (Flick 2022, 328). In this process, the number of codes was substantially reduced, and the in vivo codes were read through the theoretical concepts that underpinned this research. The analysis is now required to identify specific explanations and causal mechanisms of the identified patterns. Following a critical realist understanding, retroductive reasoning suggests moving back and forth between theory and evidence without superimposing one on the other (Belfrage and Hauf 2017). The overall research process aims at first identifying and describing regularities concerning the investigated phenomena (e.g. rural indebtedness due to adverse conditions in agriculture as a reason to migrate to the city), then constructing causal mechanisms which explain this pattern with the help of theoretical concepts (indebtedness through fictitious capital facilitates the making and subordination of India's subaltern working class), and then qualify the existence of this causal mechanism by using primary and secondary data, as well as reflecting on the practical strengths, contributions, weaknesses and limitations of the study's design and conduct (Blaikie and Priest 2017, 188f.).

In practice, this translates into a "reflexive iterative research strategy" (Montgomerie 2017, 102), emphasising the movement of research, including its non-linear, messy, and pragmatic nature as well as its constant wrestling with the underlying research ethics and objectives. In this sense, the critical aspect of this research refers to reflecting and challenging common-sense explanations and dominating arguments amongst scholars and policymakers in line with the overall paradigm and

5 In vivo coding derives codes directly from the data/transcripts, reflecting the language and terminology of interviewees.

theoretical framework. But it also refers to criticising the very existence of an unjust social reality, uncovering those relations of power and other real mechanisms that shape these inequalities to overcome them.

Part III: Regimes of Re/Productive Finance in Modern India

"[W]hat the new economic system did permit small farmers to do was to live on, and by, credit – which was itself a valuable source of subsistence"
– *David Washbrook (1994)*

"The poor women must have rupees in their own pocket, so they are no longer bound without her will to the local moneylenders, contractors, landlords and social structure"
– *Ela Bhatt (1998)*

"We have mainstreamed
the underbanked"
– *Kshama Fernandes (Sinha 2018)*

Chapter 9
The Making of the Indebted Peasant

In the previous chapters, I laid out the methodological foundations for studying the fractured lives that emerge from the chasm between benevolent rhetoric and the violent practices of financial inclusion. I argued that tracing history backwards provides a fruitful pathway to gain a broader understanding of how and why commercial microfinance became successful in recent years. But how far and deep must we explore the history of subaltern indebtedness to gain a meaningful understanding of the present? And how can we engage in such an endeavour without getting lost in the complexity and unevenness of history?

I suggest limiting the investigation to modern regimes of re/productive finance, starting with British colonisation of the subcontinent in the eighteenth century, for two reasons. First, India's subordination under the British-dominated world economy signalled a significant shift in the (global) political economy, which fundamentally altered the social structure on the subcontinent and crucially affected both the chronic subsistence crisis and related indebtedness of subaltern classes. Second, British colonial rule also gave rise to a centralised modern state that would govern access to credit on the subcontinent for the first time. This is not to deny that there were also usurious moneylending practices in pre-colonial India or that the developments described below played out unevenly throughout the vast landmass and diverse population. Instead, it emphasises that despite different pre-conditions and variations, a common thread underpins the shattered story of India's unbanked people, one which is intimately bound up with uneven capitalist development. And this is the experience of managing a chronic subsistence crisis through re/productive finance.

This part is divided into three major chapters and an interim conclusion. We will begin in this chapter with exploring the formation of the first modern regime of re/productive finance under British rule during the nineteenth and early twentieth centuries. Chapter 10 investigates the post-colonial era and describes how, under the leadership of the Indian National Congress (INC), a second regime replaced the imperial political economy while simultaneously reproducing some of its contradictions. In a third step, Chapter 11 covers the contemporary neoliberal regime and discusses why and how the rise of commercial and financialised microfinance must be understood in relation to the legacy of the previous two regimes. Finally, the fourth chapter part summarises key insights of this regime analysis for studying microfinance and financial inclusion.

For the longest time in the past 2,000 years, Asia has been the epicentre of the world economy, with China and India constituting the most extensive manufacturing base in the world and accounting for a significant share of the world's total income (Nayyar 2016; Parthasarthi 2011; Pomeranz 2000). This trend only radically changed relatively recently, with Europe's imperial expansion and subordination of the world under an emerging capitalist world market, which began in the long sixteenth century but had manifested itself only in the late nineteenth century. India's subordination under the British-dominated world economy was a critical strategic success in Europe's rise to global supremacy (Anievas and Nişancıoğlu 2015, 245ff.). If there is a single overarching feature of this imperial political economy, it is the plunder of the East India Company (EIC), which appropriated returns that "no other investment of comparable size, industrial or otherwise, could ever have generated" (Arrighi 2010, 215; see also Patnaik 2017; Reinhard 2017). Engaging with this political economy of plunder is crucial for understanding the history of India's unbanked populations, the roots of the modern subsistence crisis of subaltern classes, and how they managed it through chronic indebtedness. This chapter starts by outlining the colonial political economy of plunder, continues with an exploration of what I describe as a contested moneylender-state nexus, and concludes by describing the roots of the unbanked, including the ambiguous introduction of credit cooperatives on the subcontinent.

A Political Economy of Plunder

When the British Atlantic system was in decline towards the end of the eighteenth century (amongst other things because of the abolition of slavery and the independence of the United States), the imperial expansion to Asia became ever more important to back the political economy of Britain's empire. This shift was both geopolitically and geoeconomically motivated, as can be illustrated by the case of the cotton trade. During the seventeenth and eighteenth centuries, cotton textiles were the most important manufactured goods in world trade, and India clothed the whole world "from Mexico to the Philippines and from England to Java" (Washbrook 2007, 90). As a result, massive amounts of precious metals (esp. gold and silver, but also copper) and cowrie flowed to the subcontinent as a means of payment:

> "A very conservative calculation reveals that between 1600 and 1800 about 28,000 tons of bullion in silver equivalents (and much of it actually silver), which repre-

> sented roughly a fifth of the world's production of 142,000 tons, flowed into the Indian subcontinent. In this period, the major silver producers in the world were the Americas, which added 132,000 tons of bullion, in silver equivalents, to world supplies, and Japan, which accounted for about 10,000 tons" (Parthasarthi 2011, 46)

Private merchant companies, the so-called East India Companies of England, Holland, France, and Denmark, facilitated the import of textiles from South Asia, both for consumption in Europe and to pay for enslaved Africans who would toil on the plantations in the Caribbean. However, these transnational corporations remained largely dependent on local traders (*banias*) who would run a decentralised network, sourcing the much sought-after fabric from villages in the hinterland. Consequently, the weavers "had control over the rhythm and organization of their work, owned their tools, just as they had for centuries, and even retained the right to sell their products to whomever they pleased" (Beckert 2014, 34). Moreover, their living standards were generally higher than those of their counterparts in England – measured in calorific terms and financial security (Parthasarathi 1998, 82; Washbrook 2007, 90).

In an attempt to dominate the vibrant trading activities and source manufacturing goods and other resources more directly, the British East India Company (EIC) expanded its military presence on the subcontinent and waged decades of wars against different local rulers since the mid-eighteenth century (Manjapra 2020; Robins 2012). This expansion was accompanied by a broader paradigm shift amongst the ruling classes in Britain from mercantilism to liberal political economy, "which prioritized the command of the worldwide movements of goods, capital, and people, and which increasingly treated territorial occupation as a means to this end rather than as an end in itself" (Lowe 2015, 109). Increasingly, the Company approached weavers directly through its own agents and imposed draconian measures, like flogging and other corporeal punishment, on weavers who produced for private merchants.

As a result, the producer's share in revenue from cloth had declined to a minuscule share of about six per cent toward the end of the eighteenth century, while it had been roughly one-third a hundred years earlier (Beckert 2014, 45). In the words of Irfan Habib, after controlling ever more territories on the subcontinent, the Company lived every merchant's dream: "to be able to buy without having to pay, and yet to be able to sell at the full price" (Habib 1975, 25). This was only possible since the Company declared all revenue it generated in India as gross profits, deducted expenses necessary for the colonial administration, paid out dividends to European creditors, and 'invested' in Indian commodities with the remaining net profits (see also Bagchi 2010, 150; Habib 1975). In a piece written for the *New York Daily Tribune* in June 1853, Marx highlights that the East India Company's stock rose significantly with its transition from a "commercial into a military and territorial power [...] and dividends were paid at the rate of 12 ½ per cent" (Marx 1853b). This was not just a speculative fancy. The miraculous power of fictitious capital, which the stocks of the EIC and other joint-stock companies undoubtedly were, was rooted in the productivity of plunder on which the colonial political economy rested (Banaji 2013; McNally 2020).

In contrast to other imperial expansions of European capitalist powers, England hardly used its biggest colony as a market to sell their own goods in the early decades of colonial rule. Imports from East India surged from 1.5 million to 5.8 million pound sterling in the second half of the eighteenth century and accounted for up to one-fourth of all imports. At the same time, exports to India had risen comparatively slowly during this period (Habib 1975, 26). This would radically change a hundred years later when the Company had established a firm grip over the continent, and the British Crown banned Indian textiles on the island to protect its emerging cotton manufacturing, crushing India's cotton mills through discriminatory tariffs, effectively facilitating a process of "deindustrialisation" (Bagchi 2010, 179). While the British cotton industry thrived, India's cotton imports reached unbelievable levels. By the late nineteenth century, British cotton yarn and piece-goods accounted for between 40 and 50 per cent of the total Indian imports (Bagchi 2010, 179). The new trading imbalance created a problem of tribute realisation (Habib 1975). Indian made goods (esp., cotton textiles) had served as a tribute to the colonial motherland before, now this was hardly possible. Indigo exports from India increased rapidly with rising demand from the growing British textile industry but could hardly reverse the new trade imbalance.

In this context, opium emerged as India's most significant export good, accounting for roughly one-third of total exports in the late 1850s (Habib 1975, 40). The Company's monopoly over opium production and trading from the subcontinent quickly turned it into the world's largest drug dealer. It was crucial for financing the colonial administration and (indirectly) balancing trade relations with England. In the second half of the nineteenth century, the opium monopoly was the second largest revenue of the colonial state, accounting for between 16 and 17 per cent of total revenue (Bose 2019, 140; Reinhard 2017, 794). Perhaps even more critical, opium exports from India to China – heavily backed by another set of year-long and brutal wars – were crucial to securing imperial tribute and balancing trade relations between England and China: "In 1855, England consumed tea and silk to the value of £ 8.5 million, while exporting a mere £ 1 million of goods to the country. The balance was sheer gain obtained through Indian exports of opium, which in 1855 amounted to £ 6.23 million" (Habib 1975, 40).

The transformation of the agrarian economy in northern India backed these macroeconomic relations. The Opium Department of the Company was one of the largest enterprises on the subcontinent and had a monopoly over the opium trade.

Despite the meagre prospects to make a living from growing the cash crop, an estimated 1.5 million small peasant households cultivated the labour-intensive poppy. This was because they would receive interest-free advances when committing to produce at a set price for the Company and because the colonial administration exercised extensive pressure through local elites, like landowners, forcing indebted peasants into cultivation (Banaji 2013; Bauer 2019). Based on a detailed regional study on poppy cultivation in Northern India, Bauer (2019, 5) concludes: "[E]ven if we take the highest possible gross income and the lowest possible costs of poppy cultivation, we must conclude that the peasants produced opium at a loss". Subordinating these peasants allowed the Company to extract enormous profits while simultaneously balancing the trade between England and China through opium exports from India (Banaji 2013; Bose 2019).

By the end of the nineteenth century, India's status as a major manufacturing hub in the world economy (accounting for a quarter of the world's manufacturing in 1750) had dwarfed to less than two per cent, while the country had become a supplier of labour-intensive primary products with little added value, including raw cotton, raw jute, tea, coffee, and wheat amongst others (Bose 2019; Habib 1975; Simmons 1985). The Deccan Districts experienced a massive commodity-expansion in the second half of the nineteenth century, exporting a substantial share of its agricultural produce to Europe (e.g. cotton, sugarcane, groundnut) and to Bombay (e.g. cabbage, potatoes and other fresh vegetables). In total, the share of commercial produce to overall agricultural production in the region increased sharply from roughly one-quarter to two-thirds (Banaji 1977). But contrary to what one might expect, the increasing commercialisation of India's agrarian economy and its integration into the capitalist world economy led to the deterioration of the livelihoods of the masses, especially for artisans, weavers, agricultural labourers and small peasants (Bagchi 2010, 145; Washbrook 2007). Between 1757 and 1947, there was no increase in India's per capita income, while it is likely that incomes and living standards declined significantly in the last half of the nineteenth century (Davis 2011, 329; Prasannan Parthasarathi and Riello 2014). Moreover, the colonial plunder that sustained the drain of wealth from the subcontinent extended well beyond unequal trade relations and the production of cheap goods for export.

Around one-fifth of India's land area was covered by forests, which provided livelihoods for "nomadic, pastoral and gathering economies [which] were as significant as peasant farming" (Bayly 1985). By the end of the nineteenth century, India's forests were entirely enclosed by the imperial state, mainly for commercial logging activities, extracting resources, expanding agricultural plantations, and building infrastructure, such as railway sleepers (Bayly 1985, 593; Damodaran 2002, 143; Davis 2011, 345). These enclosures were legally warranted by the Indian Forest Act of 1865, which gave the colonial administration total control over the Indian forest land, turning the Company's Indian Forest Department effectively into one of the largest forestry enterprises in the world (Rangarajan 1994; Roy 2023). Since gathering wild food resources, firewood, and fodder was primarily a responsibility of women according to the prevailing gendered division of labour, it was them who were hit hardest by this trend, many resorting to agricultural labour as a livelihood alternative (Damodaran 2002; Patnaik 1983). Moreover, these enclosures adversely affected Adivasi (tribal communities) and other forest dwellers and threatened their subsistence: "Corporations, like those involved in the timber trade or iron mining, entered areas where *adivasis* had lived and were granted a monopoly right over forest produce. Once a forest area was officially reserved, *adivasis* no longer had any claim to these lands and were charged fees for collecting produce or grazing in these areas" (Verghese 2016, 1633).[1]

In addition to commercial interest, enclosing forest and hill lands was also important for subordinating the subcontinent's diverse population under a centralised state bureaucracy, suppressing vagrancy and banditry (Damodaran 2002; Mayaram 2003; Verghese 2016). In the early 1870s, entire communities, especially from lower castes and nomadic tribes, were designated as habitual criminals by the Criminal Tribes Act (CTA). Regardless of whether individuals had committed any criminal offence, they were registered and under surveillance simply because they belonged to a certain community that was deemed as a class of hereditary criminals, turning them effectively into outlaws (Nigam 1990; Verghese 2016). Likewise, transgender people, commonly known as *hijras*, who performed songs, dance and other performances in public as a means of subsistence (esp. on markets and festive occasions like weddings or religious ceremonies), were often policed under the CTA, with the mission to erase them from the public (Hinchy 2014). It is estimated that between three and four million people had been notified under CTA upon independence in 1947 (Schwarz 2010). Policies like the CTA were crucial in dissecting the social body, creating manageable units that hierarchised the subordinated population and entrenching racialised notions of caste.

As much as the rise of the capitalist world economy under British hegemony was linked to the spread and sophistication of commerce and finance, the empire crucially relied upon the racialised exploitation of agro-industrial labour in an increasingly globalised "plantation complex" (Arrighi 2010, 180f.; Lowe 2015, 77; Manjapra 2020, 71–99). Labour control regimes became increasingly sophisticated after slavery had been abolished officially in the first half of the nineteenth century. The

1 Expropriating land for commercial purposes was not restricted to forest areas. With the Bengal Regulation Act (1824) which would later culminate in the Land Acquisition Act (1894) pertaining to the entire subcontinent, the British introduced the principle of eminent domain in India. Henceforth, private land could be forcibly acquired for a 'public purpose', that is, extracting mineral resources, growing plantation crops, constructing roads, canals or other public amenities with a minuscule compensation (Levien 2018; Roy 2023).

role of indentured labourers from Asia – who, in contrast to their white counterparts, were referred to as *coolies* – was of particular relevance in this regard (Behal and van der Linden 2007). Export-oriented production, such as tea plantations in Northern India, coffee plantations in Ceylon, rubber and petroleum production in Burma and Malaya, or newly emerging mines for coal, tin and other raw materials in South (East) Asia, were all based on contracted *coolie labour*. Liberals celebrated the new contract system as advancement of free wage labour. Though indentured labourers were no commodities like slaves, brute force played a vital part in subordinating and disciplining them, which is why scholars have referred to these labour relations as "second slavery" (Zeuske 2017): "Being recruited, collected, concentrated, transported, physically exploited until exhaustion, and corporally punished were all characteristics of the indentured labor system" (Mann 2011, 128). In addition, humiliation in forced medical examination, omnipresent gender-based violence, hardship of long-distance transport with insufficient foodstuffs and widespread diseases all characterised the new form of 'free wage labour' (Anderson 2009; Behal and van der Linden 2007).

Far from marginal, this emergent migrant working class sustained the imperial political economy for more than a century. Komlosy (2018) suggests that at least 30 million Indian *coolies* and another five or six million labourers from other Asian regions worked to supply European industrialisation between 1830 and 1930 through the supply of primary goods. Vagrant communities and those in increasing despair to provide for their livelihoods were a crucial and abundant source for contractors and recruiting agencies, while policies like the CTA further increased their vulnerability by fragmenting and segmenting the subaltern population (Damodaran 2002; Kaur 2011; Mann 2011; Sharma 2009; Varma 2017). However, the vicious indentured labour system also fed on the chronic indebtedness of the small peasantry and the widespread deprivation of landless labourers. Within this broader context, the first modern regime of re/productive finance took shape on the subcontinent.

The Contested Moneylender-State Nexus

In *The Accumulation of Capital*, Rosa Luxemburg discusses capital's imperial nature, annihilating and disintegrating all other forms of reproduction whilst spreading on the globe. Rather than a technical or purely economic process, she describes the expansion of capital as deeply political, based on force, unequal trade relations and oppressive taxation (Luxemburg 2003, 349). While the previous section has discussed the role of political force and unequal trade relations in detail, this section will explore how oppressive taxation was essential to plundering the subcontinent and maintaining colonial rule while simultaneously exacerbating the indebtedness of the peasantry. Throughout the nineteenth century, land tax contributed, on average, half of all state revenue, securing the costly military expansion on the subcontinent and the imperial tribute to the British Crown and the shareholders of the EIC (Reinhard 2017, 794). Perhaps even more important, the tax reforms under colonial rule fundamentally and permanently altered the social structure by creating regionally distinct property titles to land, intensifying caste-based class inequalities and vulnerability to indebtedness.

The land tax had already been a central source of revenue for the Mughal Empire, which relied on regionally dominant, hereditary upper-caste landowners (*zamindars*) who had the right to collect taxes. With the Permanent Settlement of Bengal in 1793, the EIC both subjugated *and* incorporated these landed classes under colonial rule by turning the *zamindars* into an intermediary institution between the rural masses and the colonial administration. This incorporation of domestic elites in Bengal, Bihar and Orissa was a crucial mechanism in dividing colonial subjects, with obedient elites being rewarded with land titles, while those who resisted the Company's rule and fought against the colonisers were sentenced to death or imprisoned (Nigam 1990; Yang 2007).[2] The liberals, who increasingly gained the upper hand in the Company, criticised this feudal arrangement and pushed for direct taxation of peasants, presumably creating incentives to invest in land and enhance productivity (Dutt 2001). Eventually, the so-called *ryotwari system* was introduced in Madras and Bombay Presidency in the early nineteenth century. Under this system, the peasant households (*ryot*) were required to pay their dues directly to the colonial state.

Despite differences, both the *zamindari* and *ryotwari* system had a significant commonality. Rather than creating a steady title on immovable property for landlords, occupiers of land or cultivators, the security of land ownership was contingent upon paying land tax, which, in turn, sustained the colonial state (Bagchi 1992; Washbrook 1994). In other words, the inability to pay would effectively lead to land expropriation and transfer in expanding land markets. Moreover, in the pre-colonial era, land taxation was fixed as a share of the crop and varied according to the crop cultivated, with the state occasionally supporting cultivation through loans, tax remissions, or fostering irrigation (Habib 1975). In contrast, under the colonial system, land tax was calculated on the average potential yield of the land, which would inevitably lead to the impossibility of all cultivators to produce sufficient output, especially for less irrigated plots and regions particularly affected by recurring droughts or crop failure (Bagchi 1992; Bose 1994; Reinhard 2017). Since most peasants could not accumulate surpluses under the new system, they lacked the means to invest in

2 Yang (2007) shows how collaborating and obedient local elites in Southern India were rewarded with property and status as landlords, while those who openly resisted imperial rule were sentenced to death or imprisoned and exiled to outposts of the British empire – though retaining a higher social status, since they were generally not forced to work like subaltern classes had to.

traditional irrigation and water storage systems, while the colonial administration reduced public financing for such means (Davis 2011, 327; Hardiman 1996).

The absence of banks or government programmes that would support agrarian production through (subsidised) access to credit or investments in irrigation meant that both cultivators and landlords were usually dependent on moneylender's advances, whose business practices increasingly monetised (Bose 1994; Habib 1975). In the pre-colonial era, merchant-moneylenders usually provided advances in seed-grain, foodstuff and other necessities and demanded a share of their produce upon harvest (Hardiman 1996). Most peasants were also trapped in continuous and exploitative debt relations (Habib 1964; Hardiman 1996). However, these were generally personal and only partly monetised, rarely leading to eviction, while monetised debts' abstract and non-negotiable value reigned supreme in the new system. In an article for the *New York Daily Tribune* from June 1853, Marx succinctly summarises the ambiguous dynamic the land taxes had brought about:

> "The Ryot is subject, like the French peasant, to the extortion of the private usurer; but he has no hereditary, no permanent title in his land, like the French peasant. Like the serf' he is forced to cultivation, but he is not secured against want like the serf. Like the *métayer [sharecropper]* he has to divide his produce with the State, but the State is not obliged, with regard to him, to advance the funds and the stock, as it is obliged to do with regard to the *métayer*. In Bengal, as in Madras and Bombay, under the *Zemindari* as under the *Ryotwar*, the Ryots-and they form 11–12ths of the whole Indian population — have been wretchedly pauperized" (Marx 1853a)

Against this backdrop, rising rural indebtedness during the nineteenth century must be understood as a response to the insufficient subsistence produce, pressures from land taxation, export-oriented commercialisation of agriculture, and a lack of other income opportunities (Bagchi 1992; Banaji 1977; Bose 1994). As David Washbrook summarised it: "Small peasants, in effect, reproduced themselves and their cultivation, from day-to-day and season-to-season, through the credit system" (Washbrook 1994, 150).

Notably, the power of moneylenders was rooted in the reform of the judicial system, modelled after the British one. In pre-colonial times, disputes between creditors and debtors were often resolved through locally based, communal institutions such as village councils (*panchayat*). While these can hardly be imagined as democratic institutions, even upper-caste peasants who dominated such assemblies tended to be sceptical of moneylenders if they were not part of the village community (Habib 1964; Hardiman 1996). In contrast, the colonial *ryotwari system* was based solely on written contracts, which in turn were considered the basis of jurisprudence. Most peasants could not read the agreements and terms, nor did they have access to lawyers who could represent them in court. Even the British politician Thomas Macaulay, a central figure in the colonial education policy on the subcontinent, described the introduction of the British judicial system in South Asia in an essay as a "reign of terror" in which arbitrariness triumphed over reason and arrogance over understanding: "[The reign of terror] consisted of judges not one of whom was familiar with the usages of the millions over whom they claimed boundless authority. Its records were kept in unknown characters; its sentences were pronounced in unknown sounds" (Macauly 1965, 449).

In effect, the new legal system gave unprecedented power to the creditors as long as they could provide written proof of the debt, while no policy was in place that regulated moneylending anyhow. Even borrowing small amounts (Rs. 10) could add up to massive debts within ten years (Rs. 330), turning credit both into a vital mode of surplus appropriation and facilitating cheap agricultural labour at the expense of peasant household's subsistence (Bagchi 1992, 38; Bose 1994; Washbrook 1994, 155). The chronic subsistence crisis and vulnerability to crop failure were intensified by the increased indebtedness and the erosion of protective systems. Though far from idyllic or egalitarian, the old patron-client relationships in rural areas usually entailed safeguarding the subsistence of oppressed classes/castes. This "right to subsistence" (Hardiman 1996) increasingly eroded under British colonial rule and gave way to new forms of dependency mediated by monetised debts, while the colonial administration restrained from any measures to protect the social reproduction of the rural masses (see also Breman 1974).

This wilful ignorance is perhaps best illustrated by the devastating consequences of recurrent famines in the nineteenth and twentieth centuries. Between 1876 and 1908, famines killed around 20 million people in British India, despite millions of tons of grain in commercial circulation and modern railroads that could have reduced rather than exacerbated regional grain shortages (Bagchi 2008; Bose 2019; Washbrook 2007). The fatal consequences were distributed rather unevenly. For instance, in Madras Presidency the great famine of 1876–78 took the lives of 10 per cent of the population, with a larger percentage of landless labourers and small peasants (Roy 2005, 28). Since the imperial political economy and colonial administration had significantly exacerbated these population's vulnerability to droughts and crop failures, and failed to prevent mass deaths, Mike Davis has referred to the series of famines as late Victorian Holocausts: "Millions died, not outside the 'modern world system', but in the very process of being forcibly incorporated into its economic and political structures" (Davis 2011, 9). These famines not only provided a testament for the profound subsistence crisis of subaltern classes in British India. They also exacerbated the indebtedness and provided a vital trigger for widespread and sustained unrest.

Increasingly, credit formed the advances "for the reproduction of [his] labour-power" and social reproduction of agrarian households more generally, with many households from the lower segments being indebted to multiple "monied capitalists", especially during recurring droughts and famine (Banaji 1977, 1373). While a share of borrowing would always also be for cultivation, purchasing bullock, and paying the land tax, the relevance of borrowing for other reproductive needs (including social functions) and the repayment of old debts increased over time (Bose 1994, 282). This also implied new forms of dependency and exploitation:

> "Once indebted to a bania, it was difficult [for them] to avoid being caught up in a vicious circle, whereby debts generated more debts—and the debtor who objected to the arrangement always had the threat of a civil suit hanging over him. In this way the bania, without whose finance cultivation could hardly have continued at all, prospered at the expense of the agrarian population, simultaneously keeping agriculturists alive and impoverishing them" (Cheesman 1982, 462)

The rise of professional moneylenders fed primarily on caste-based class inequality. On the one hand, large families from merchant castes (known as *baniya*, *marwari* or *mahajan* depending on the region), who guaranteed the flow of goods and finances between towns and villages, were often also moneylenders (*sahukar* or *sowkar*). Frequently, they travelled long distances to establish networks along caste lines. The power of these merchant-moneylenders grew greatly under British colonial rule and was not regulated in any way until the early twentieth century (Bagchi 1992; Hardiman 1996; Saikia 2010; Warner 2020). Moreover, the commercialisation of agriculture and changes in land property allowed for the increasing land concentration in the hands of a relatively small rural class of landowners and large farmers, who lent money to the small and middle peasantry and hired the impoverished as agricultural labourers (Banaji 1977; Washbrook 1994, 152).

The concentration of land ownership exacerbated the subsistence crisis of subaltern classes and provided one of the most pertinent legacies of colonial rule. The region of Punjab, long considered the land of small farmers, vividly illustrates the profound effects. At the end of British colonial rule, about half of the land belonged to a relatively small landowning class, about four per cent of the rural population, while 80 per cent of the population sought to secure their livelihood as impoverished small farmers, landless tenants, or wage labourers (Hamid 1982). Notably, powerful landlords were not necessarily cultivators. The roughly 2,000 principal village officers in Bellary district, one of the driest districts in South India, were bestowed 22 per cent of land through a feudal title equivalent to that of the *zamindars* in 1804. Six decades later, their landholding amounted to 60 per cent, covering nearly 400,000 acres (Washbrook 1994, 136). The rising agrarian inequality also meant that an increasing share of the rural population became landless and had to sell their labour power as agricultural labourers in order to survive. While this trend was already visible towards the end of the nineteenth century, it gained rapid momentum in the early twentieth century (Saikia 2010). In the Madras Presidency, which then covered much of southern India, the proportion of landless agricultural labourers rose from about 12 to 52 per cent between 1871 and 1931 (Patnaik 1983, 7). Finally, the chronic indebtedness of the small peasantry and the destitution of landless labourers also fed into the vicious indentured labour system that sustained the global plantation complex discussed above (Manjapra 2018, 376).

In contrast to today's prevailing development discourse, in which informal moneylenders usually appear as exploitative evils from pre-modern times, the rise of these moneylenders was closely linked to the power of the colonial state as well as caste-based class formation under British rule. On the one hand, access to credit was an important tool for large segments of peasant households to guarantee their subsistence and pay taxes to the state. If they were unable to pay the taxes, they faced eviction or imprisonment (including forced labour). On the other hand, informal credit relations were *de facto* formalised by the new judicial system because moneylenders could be sure that the courts would guarantee payment of debt service with state force as long as creditors could produce a written document. Informal moneylenders were thus central, sustaining the colonial state and its drain of wealth. In Surat, for example, an administrative district north of Bombay (now Mumbai), approximately 85 per cent of the land taxes payable by the peasantry were advanced by moneylenders in 1900 (Reinhard 2017, 796).

Thus, a moneylender-state nexus developed under British colonial rule that expressed the violence of racial finance capitalism on the subcontinent as a fusion of colonialism, capitalism and casteism, re-ordering the social structure. This nexus describes the simultaneous deepening of political power on the part of the colonial state and economic power in the fusion of capital and casteism – a process that particularly favoured merchant castes and (emerging) landlords, who now became professional moneylenders. In other words, the moneylender-state nexus describes a colonial class compromise that was built on the prevailing caste hierarchy. Amiya Kumar Bagchi has aptly summarised this process: "As British domination of the rural economy grew, so did the power of the moneylenders" (Bagchi 1992, 29). The growing power of merchant-moneylenders and landlord-moneylenders was also possible because the colonial bureaucracy did nothing to regulate usurious lending, land transfers and debt bondage until the end of the nineteenth century, while creditors could be sure that the liberal rule of law guaranteed them payment of the debt, including interest, as long as the loan contract was in writing (Kumar 2018, 209).

Though a powerful expression of class domination within the imperial political economy, the moneylender-state nexus was contested by appeals, protests, and peasant rebellions across the subcontinent. Many peasants were acutely aware of the significance that colonial policies (esp. land revenue) had on their lives, calling upon the British administration to revoke the law or at least transfer judicial responsibility from Court Laws back to the *village panchayat*. In a petition from 1840, the *ryots* could not have analysed the situation more clearly: "Under the present government, by the sale of our immovable property, we are reduced to a starving condition in the same manner, as a tree when its roots are pulled out, dies. [...]" (Kumar 1965, 616). Moreover, speculative grain trading during famines further fuelled rural unrest, which was, in many cases, led by the middle peasantry (Arnold 1979; Bagchi 1992). Between 1770 and 1970, there were at least 77 peasant rebellions. The smallest of these comprised several thousand peasants in active support or in combat, while about 30 revolts must have affected tens of thousands and about twelve several hundreds of thousands (Gough 1976). Ranajit Guha suggests that these uprisings were an "antithesis of colonialism" because they were directed against the "triumvirate" that dominated the rural masses, that is, the colonial administration, the moneylenders, and landlords: "By directing his violence against all three members of this trinity irrespective of which one of them provoked him to revolt in the first place, the peasant displayed a certain understanding of the mutuality of their interests and the power on which this was predicated" (Guha 1999, 27).

Although certainly diverse in triggers, form and dynamics, these peasant insurgencies were not random or individualised outbreaks of violence. In many cases, social and economic boycotts of moneylenders, particularly from upper-caste cultivators, preceded more direct actions, including the destruction of debt records in moneylender's homes, courts, and registries, as well as the looting of police stations and other symbols of British rule (Bagchi 1992; Gough 1976; Kumar 1965). As such, these rebellions must be understood as strategic acts of enforced debt cancellation in the context of chronic indebtedness. Destroying account books or mortgage records was crucial in this endeavour because these documents symbolised, legalised and entrenched the domination and exploitation of the rural masses (Hardiman 1996, 144). As such, rioting must be understood as "established form[s] of protest, coercion and revenge to which the poor and underprivileged not infrequently resorted in defence of their material interests and their continued subsistence" (Arnold 1979, 114). The moneylender-state nexus became increasingly contested throughout the nineteenth century and pressured the colonial administration to provide alternatives for accessing credit.

Colonial Roots of the Unbanked

The contemporary financial inclusion discourse takes the existence of the unbanked as a given characteristic of so-called developing economies (see Chapter 2). Yet, the emergence of a modern banking system is intimately rooted in the violent history of European colonialism and imperial expansions – both in core capitalist countries and the peripheries (Gruffydd Jones 2013; Manjapra 2020; McNally 2020). The exclusion of the masses of peasants and labourers from these institutions was no coincidence. It was rooted in the extractive imperial political economy described above.

Towards the end of colonial rule, it increasingly expressed the growing power of a small but powerful class of domestic capitalists. In this context, the colonial state's growing preoccupation with governing access to credit for the rural masses through establishing credit cooperatives turned out to be an ambiguous strategy navigating between the growing unrest of the masses and the co-optation of domestic political and economic elites. These developments cast their shadows well into the post-colonial era.

India's modern banking system emerged during the nineteenth century under the dominance of metropolitan capital. European agency houses and joint-stock companies dominated public finance, the financing of export-oriented businesses, and trading with foreign exchange (Bagchi 1985; Chandavarkar 1983). Their business was confined mainly to the Presidency towns (Calcutta, Bombay, and Madras) and hardly interacted directly with ordinary Indians. These institutions were critical to realising imperial tributes and facilitating the drain of wealth on which the imperial political economy relied. This is particularly visible in the case of the few powerful Exchange Banks, which were either well-known British banks based in London, such as Oriental Bank Corporation (OBC), the National Bank of India, or other 'imperial banks' that specialised in trade of their respective countries with India, like the Deutsch-Asiatische Bank (German), Yokohama Specie Bank (Japanese), or International Banking Corporation (American) (Chandavarkar 1983, 782).

The Exchange Banks had access to money markets in London and elsewhere and retained a monopoly over the profitable business of facilitating foreign exchange and trade. Moreover, they were tightly connected with powerful institutions of the British Empire, such as the Bank of England, the Treasury, and the India Office (Bagchi 1985; Chandavarkar 1983; McGuire 2005). Their business activities comprised, for example, opium trade with China, investing in coffee plantations in Ceylon or sugar plantations in Mauritius, where indentured labour was exploited, or using privileged access to cheap money in London to profit from lending in South Asia (Banaji 2013). Though not directly interacting with the rural masses, the Exchange Banks assumed the role of a "final link in the chain whereby the surplus of the cultivating peasantry was extracted in a range of different forms and fed into the larger circuits of capital that linked the domestic to the global economy" (McGuire 2007, 87). Undoubtedly, facilitating the drain of wealth was extremely profitable, with European shareholders earning the highest dividends and bonuses amongst all London-based banks at the end of the 1850s by investing in the OBC (McGuire 2005, 147, 2007, 91).[3]

---

3 A second type of joint-stock banks were government-backed commercial banks that effectively operated as central banks on the subcontinent in term of public debt management and acting as banker's bank, while they were precluded from any authority over monetary policy or dealings in foreign exchange. These three Presidency Banks were founded in the

While domestic bankers were largely excluded from the commanding heights of the imperial political economy, there were numerous Indian banking houses from upper-class mercantile castes who usually ran them as family businesses (Bagchi 1985; Chandavarkar 1983). Traditionally, these larger Indian banks were fusions of commercial and financial capital, engaging in facilitating trade, manufacturing, and financing the extravagances of domestic elites. Towards the early twentieth century, there was a notable nexus between emerging domestic industrial capitalists and proliferating Indian joint-stock banks, many of which would support the nascent nationalist movement to protect "indigenous capital" and further their political and economic interests (Birla 2009, 206; Goswami 1998, 628). But none of these engaged directly and to a significant extent with the Indian peasantry. There were connections between professional moneylenders who provided working capital and subsistence finance to cultivators, and artisans in rural areas and larger Indian banking houses, but these were regionally confined and remained overall limited (Bagchi 1985).

In the 1870s, there had been lively debates amongst the colonial elites on creating a state-sponsored or joint-stock bank, specifically focussing on agricultural credit for the Indian peasantry. A proposal by William Wedderburn, who would later become a founding member of the Indian National Congress (INC), clamoured for establishing agricultural banks in Bombay. It was later declined by the Government of India as it seemed too worrisome to build-up a large credit network that would penetrate rural areas, and too risky to support a banking industry with an indebted peasantry as primary customer base (Robert 1970). However, the prolonged resistance in the forms of riots, robbing, vagrancy, and political mobilisation increasingly forced the British to act upon mass indebtedness, the carnage of colonial famines and the cumulating agrarian crisis. Toward the end of the nineteenth century, the colonial administration introduced several new legislations and schemes that sought to tackle these issues through improved access to agricultural credit, a ceiling of land transfers and ordering that interest payments should not exceed the principal (Dantwala 1952; Kumar 2018; Unger 2018).[4] Yet, these interventions failed to contain the destructive dynamics that had been unleashed decades ago and remained marginal, if not insignificant, for the rural masses. The extended state-backed loans amounted to not more than one per cent of the total credit supply in rural areas, primarily reaching the agrarian middle and upper classes

---

first half of the nineteenth century, first in Calcutta (Bank of Bengal), then in Bombay (Bank of Bombay) and Madras (Bank of Madras), and later merged into the Imperial Bank of India in 1920, which after nationalisation in 1955 would eventually become India's largest public bank in the post-colonial era: the State Bank of India (Bagchi 1987).

4 These measures included, for example, the Deccan Agriculturalist Relief Act (1879), Land Improvement Loans Act (1883), Land Alienation Act (1900), and Usurious Loan Act (1918).

(Dantwala 1952; Kamenov 2019). Moreover, there were neither sufficiently effective institutions on the ground, nor the political will to implement ceilings of land deals or regulate moneylending, then leading to continuous land transfers in which moneylenders cooperated with dominant landlords who, in turn, disguised land ownership through intermediaries (Hamid 1982; Islam 1995).

At the end of the nineteenth century, the increasing organisation of fractured resistance into a nationalist movement increasingly threatened British dominance on the subcontinent. The formation of the Indian National Congress (INC) in 1885 and the popularity of the Swadeshi movement, which sought to protect local industries from imperial domination and increasingly called for self-rule, were considered particularly dangerous for the British ambitions on the continent. Headed by middle-class intellectuals, with support from domestic business elites, this nationalist movement could potentially channel the widespread anger of the rural masses and orchestrate nationwide resistance (Goswami 1998). Within these broader developments, the establishment of credit cooperatives rooted in the agrarian economy turned out as a panacea for the colonial administration to effectively and efficiently deal with mass indebtedness and the power of moneylenders on the one hand, and discontent, riots and political mobilisation on the other hand, while at the same time neither investing nor risking much economically (Kamenov 2019; Unger 2018).

A distinguished civil servant called Frederick A. Nicholson was commissioned by the Madras Government in the 1890s to draft a report on the possibility of introducing land and agricultural banks in the Madras Presidency and to compare rural banking structures in Europe and India. Since his studies on credit relations in rural Madras demonstrated that the preponderance of loans was based on mutual trust and made in kind between *ryots* for small sums negotiated on a short-term basis, he enthusiastically suggested the introduction of cooperatives according to the *Raffeisen* model, which had been successfully applied in rural Germany to revive the agrarian economy during famine and sluggish growth prospects a few decades earlier (Robert 1970, 165). Nicholson's report was deemed "radically unsound", "dangerous", and "naïve" and hence rejected by the Madras Board of Revenue (Robert 1970, 176). However, his ideas were revived only a few years later at the all-India level after another series of devastating famines killed millions of Indians, with landless labourers and poor *ryots* being disproportionately affected (Bose 2019; Roy 2005).[5] Against this backdrop, Nicholson and other reformers would draft legislation on cooperatives, which came into effect as the *Cooperative Credit Societies Act* in 1904.

The cooperative framework seemed to offer a perfect mixture of a decentralised system that worked through intimate knowledge amongst borrowers and lenders and thus reduced risk and excessive expenses for the colonial state. At the same time,

5 The official death toll for the famines of the 1890s were as high as 4.5 million, while unofficial estimates claimed up to 16 million deaths (Bose 2019).

it blended perfectly with the civilisational mission of colonial rule to educate their subjects in terms of economically rational and accountable behaviour, introducing "a good dose of Victorian morality" (Bose 1994; Robert 1970, 167; Unger 2018). A community in a village had to raise Rs. 2,000 to register a credit society and could usually borrow another Rs. 2,000 from the state (Kamenov 2019, 226). The credit would be dispersed through a pyramid of credit institutions, with primary societies at the village-level receiving low-interest long-term loans (up to 10 years) from district central banks, which in turn were financed by the central urban bank for the whole Presidency (Robert 1970). The growth of credit cooperatives was certainly impressive. There had already been roughly 2,000 registered primary credit cooperatives in 1906, and the number spiked to 100,000 in 1930. In Bengal, the average debt per family increased at least threefold in this period, while the percentage of debtless families decreased from 55 to 17 (Iqbal 2017, 225). Yet, despite the stunning outreach, the cooperative movement neither tackled the entrenched class inequalities nor did it prevent the rural masses from being trapped in indebtedness. Three reasons may explain this.

First, since its inception, credit cooperatives were designed by the British as effective tools to contain anti-colonial resistance (Iqbal 2017; Kamenov 2019; Unger 2018). Notwithstanding the political rhetoric of crowding out usurious moneylenders and the displayed concern with mass indebtedness, cooperatives were never implemented to raise living standards for the bulk of the rural population. Ifthekar Iqbal has summarised colonial attitude in Bengal as follows: "While the initial years of the cooperative movement saw the government trying to use it to contain the swadeshi political tide, later on the threat of terrorist movement, communism and economic depressions informed the government attitude towards the movement" (Iqbal 2017, 234). The swadeshi movement that gained momentum rapidly around the turn of the century, became increasingly incorporated into the cooperative movement, for example, by integrating "competent leaders" (Iqbal 2017, 228).

Second, the governance structure of cooperatives reflected local or regional class and caste hierarchies and further entrenched these through selective access to credit. In effect, wealthy peasants, landlords or local merchant-moneylenders, who were all usually from upper castes, would head the society's village council (Iqbal 2017; Shah, Rao, and Shankar 2007). The colonial government encouraged wealthy and influential peasants in the village to become leading members both to set an example for 'idle' ones and to contain uprisings locally. Cooperative leaders proved mostly loyal to British rule, but their 'service' came at a price. Like the share that *zamindars* would keep for collecting land tax, many cooperative leaders appropriated wealth through the control of the local credit business. When the nationalist movement gained momentum, the participation of Indian politicians in government affairs increased. The 'elite capture' of credit cooperatives was now increasingly tainted by political ambitions. In the Madras Presidency, ministerial reforms in 1919 meant that the Cooperative Department fell into the hands of Indian politicians. In this process, cooperative societies became a political steppingstone as much as they were a vote bank for emerging Indian politicians, with presidents of credit cooperatives becoming politicians or endorsing candidates (Robert 1970). Moreover, the lower ranks of the rural population, including tenants, landless labourers, and small farmers, were largely excluded from equal participation (Iqbal 2017, 231).

Third, cooperative societies were never able to compete with moneylenders. On the one hand, demand for credit was simply so high that even the rapid growth of the cooperative movement seemed little compared to the vast debt business that had emerged in recent decades. Despite considerable outreach, credit supply through cooperatives amounted to less than ten per cent of total credit amongst rural households (Bose 1994, 277; Kumar 2018; Robert 1970). On the other hand, cooperatives adhered to accountancy standards, which moneylenders did not follow in the same way. Cooperatives could not be as flexible with regard to long-lasting overdue credit by their members since much of their working capital was borrowed (Kamenov 2019, 227). Issues with mass default built up during the 'credit cooperative boom' and became particularly apparent after the economic chain reactions of the Great Depression in the United States led the British to implement strict austerity measures, including reduced investments in the cooperative credit system (Robert 1970). As a result, default rates reached 80 per cent in 1934–35 in most districts of Bengal, and Rs. 30 million of the Rs. 40 million of cooperative loans were defaulted in 1940 (Iqbal 2017). Moreover, cooperatives seemed to have grossly misunderstood the increased relevance of reproductive debts for the rural masses: "One of the major causes of the failure of rural credit cooperatives in India to compete with the moneylenders is their doctrinaire aversion to provide consumption credit to cultivators" (Chandavarkar 1983, 803).

In sum, the credit cooperatives provided the first large-scale attempt to govern access to credit for the rural masses across the subcontinent. Their impressive growth within a few decades testified to the massive demand for financing both cultivation and subsistence, which almost exclusively relied on various moneylenders. However, contrary to the colonial presumption that these were primarily welfare institutions freeing the peasantry from the stranglehold of moneylenders, the previous sections demonstrated that the rise of moneylenders and rural indebtedness was a result of colonial policies and India's subordination under the British-centred world economy. As such, the credit cooperatives did not signal the start of a new regime of re/productive finance. Rather, it must be understood as a significant shift within the formation of the first modern regime. Put differently, the introduction of credit cooperatives can be understood as a early form of development policy ("big D") working through the contradictions of uneven capitalist development ("small d"), seeking to pacify widespread unrest and searching for a new compromise with the nascent nationalist movement.

The exclusion of subaltern classes from modern banking was no accident and certainly no result of a lack of financial means. The vibrant financial flows on the subcontinent, including the commercialising of agrarian production, investments in export-oriented plantations, or building of infrastructure like railways, were dominated by European joint-stock companies and exclusively geared towards securing British dominance and the imperial drain of wealth. Meanwhile, the larger share of the peasantry was exposed to increasing indebtedness with merchant-moneylenders and landlord-moneylenders, fostered by reforming the land tax and judicial system. The legacies of this political economy of plunder, to name a few, include the impoverishment and chronic indebtedness of the rural masses, the excessive power of moneylenders, a massive concentration in landownership amongst few upper-caste elites, and a corrupted infrastructure of credit cooperatives. These were the foundations upon which the second regime of re/productive finance would emerge.

Chapter 10
The State of Financial Inclusion

India's independence in 1947 marked a watershed moment in the country's history and had a significant impact on the broader shifts in the global political economy. However, just like other colonies, independence did not end the struggle for self-rule (Getachew 2019; Hansen and Osterhammel 2013). Of course, there were significant changes, like drafting a new constitution and establishing a parliamentary democracy. Yet, the new rulers of the INC also came to terms with continuities in the centralised administration and bureaucratic apparatus, the military and, in part, the legal system. India's economy had been dominated by metropolitan capital and commodities for over a century. British colonial rule also rested on support from landed property and domestic big business. Transforming the colonial state thus meant engaging with a strategy for a new political economy, including the question of securing support from domestic elites without compromising on popular support.

In this context, the second modern regime of re/productive finance took shape. It sought to address the mass indebtedness and impoverishment of the rural masses through state-led investments in agriculture, improved access to credit and redistributive measures. These efforts were significant and changed the monopolistic power that moneylenders had enjoyed during British colonial rule. In the three decades after independence, the share of non-institutional lenders in rural credit, primarily moneylenders and landlords, has rapidly declined, while the share of institutional sources, mainly credit cooperatives, regional rural banks, and commercial banks, has soared from below 10 per cent in 1951 to more than 60 per cent in 1981 (see Figure 9). Moreover, the share of agricultural credit to agricultural GDP increased from 0.5 to 8.3 per cent in the first three decades after independence (Joshi 2006, 26). This significant success of the state-directed political economy under the leadership of the INC was centred on the promotion of credit cooperatives, particularly in the early years, and the re-structuring of the banking system through nationalisation, restrictions of licensing and quotas for lending to agriculture and other priority sectors. Thus, the state turned into a primary agent for financial inclusion in a broad sense.

Figure 9: Share of Credit Sources in Rural India, 1951 -2012 in %

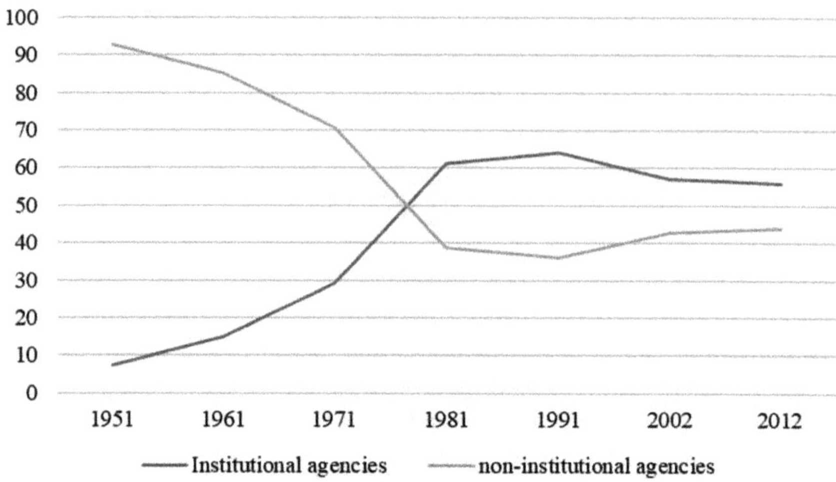

Source: adapted from Sriram (2018).

Notwithstanding these changes, the new state-directed regime reproduced some of the contradictions of the colonial regime. From the perspective of subaltern classes, this success story is less gloomy. This chapter traces the continuities and changes in India's political economy, the social structure and subsistence crisis of subaltern classes, and how access to credit related to these shifts. It starts out by describing the profound transformation of the political economy, how the promotion of credit cooperatives fit into these developments, and what effects this had for small and marginal peasants as well as landless agricultural labourers. We will then continue to look at the significance of the nationalisation of major banks in the late 1960s, how this was related to a new agricultural policy and the extension of subsidised credit as an anti-poverty measure. Finally, the third section outlines the slow erosion of the developmental regime of re/productive finance, including the formation of alternative credit institutions that would challenge the state-directed approach and pave the way for the rise of specialised microfinance institutions.

The Contradictions of Post-Colonial Development

Debates on the trajectory of post-colonial development had already started prior to independence. In the mid-1930s, the INC set up a National Planning Committee with leading business leaders and other experts, and Jawaharlal Nehru served as the chairperson. The overarching aim of their plan for economic development in independent India was to raise the living standards of the masses by enhancing economic growth through state-directed investments and ensuring redistribution through governance of capital and credit (Bose 2019; Chakravarty 1987; Joshi 2006). Meanwhile, the domestic business elite began to articulate their own ideas for the future of India's political economy. The so-called Bombay Plan of 1944 was a comprehensive intervention of corporate capital in the enfolding debate on how to govern the independent country. It consisted of two documents which influential industrialists, like G. D. Birla, J.R.D Tata, Lala Shri Ram, Purshotamdas Thakurdas and others had drafted. Interestingly, it endorsed the necessity for planning large-scale public investments to accelerate capital accumulation while respecting private property. The initiative was disdainfully regarded as a "capitalist's plan" amongst left-wing critics within and beyond the Congress, and there are continued debates today on the strategic nature of this initiative (Chibber 2006; Kudaisya 2014; Lockwood 2012). On the one hand, the plan confirmed the necessity of a strong state in fostering capital accumulation and the emancipation of domestic from metropolitan capital (Bose 2019; Kudaisya 2014; Sanyal 2007). On the other hand, the degree and scope of state intervention remained a controversial issue throughout the post-colonial era amongst different factions of Indian business, within Congress and its social base, and between capitalist classes, state bureaucracy and leading politicians. In contrast to the 'developmental state' experiences in Southeast Asia, the Indian capitalist class constantly evaded state regulations and lacked the discipline to abide by the state's plans (Chandrasekhar and Ghosh 2002; Chibber 2006).

Nonetheless, the interests of Congress leadership and the industrialists converged on the call for an independent, centralised state which would build public infrastructure, promote (heavy) industries through a mixture of protective measures and cheap credit, and introduce a land reform of the *zamindari* and *ryotwari* system with the aim of promoting a class of peasant proprietors. Gandhi's popular critique of modern technology, commercialisation, and centralised state power as evils of modern civilisation and British colonialism secured widespread nationalist mobilisation in the early twentieth century. Yet, his vision of an independent India centred on self-sufficient village economies and decentralised governance played no significant role in these discussions (Bose 2019; Kudaisya 2014). There was a broad consensus amongst the Congress leadership that bolstering economic growth and import-substituting industrialisation were crucial means to build a sovereign nation and tackle the poverty of the masses.

What came to be known as Nehruvian socialist planning thus aimed at balancing a thin line: On the one hand, it aimed at keeping the market principle in check because the political elites were afraid it would lead to excessive consumption amongst high-income groups and underinvestment in essential sectors, further exacerbating mass poverty and inequality. On the other hand, it built on socialist rhetoric but refrained from redistribution of productive assets and developing institutions to discipline private capital to abide by its plans, fearing this would endanger growth prospects and undermine support from domestic economic elites (Chakravarty 1987; Chibber 2006, 127ff.). As a result, economic planning became the central means for disentangling industrialisation from anti-colonial rhetoric and depoliticising development into a techno-bureaucratic project of India's young democracy. Essentially, planning allowed experts and bureaucrats to determine the "priorities on behalf of the 'nation' [...] a modality of political power outside the immediate political process itself" (Chatterjee 2002; Sanyal 2007).[1] Ultimately, this depoliticisation was linked to containing class conflicts in a "fragmented multiclass state" (Kohli 2004, 260) through a mixture of incorporation and demobilisation of various social groups.[2]

One of the few points where Gandhi's emphasis on decentralised self-governance and Nehru's vision of economic development converged was the continuous relevance of credit cooperatives for providing access to the rural masses. As discussed above, India's banking system was dominated by metropolitan capital and entirely geared towards facilitating the drain of wealth with hardly any relevance for the agrarian economy. Upon independence, the share of banks in rural credit was less than one per cent (Shah, Rao, and Shankar 2007, 1353). In the early years, the Congress government nationalised the Reserve Bank of India (RBI) and the Imperial Bank of India, now rechristened as the State Bank of India (SBI), but refrained from larger nationalisation of the banking sector. Instead, the colonial infrastructure of credit cooperatives was revamped as "people's institutions" (Sriram 2018). At the village level, Primary Agriculture Cooperative Societies (PACS) would govern access to credit, while district and state cooperative banks functioned as superordinate entities and clearing houses, providing guidance and state-backed refinancing. Importantly, the cooperative structure was relatively autonomous and did not come under the direct supervision of the RBI.

The promotion of cooperatives led to extended outreach of public credit in rural areas, although occurring geographically unevenly. By the early 1970s, cooperative societies dominated rural areas as a major creditor institutions (Bhende 1986; Shah, Rao, and Shankar 2007). Their share in rural household credit increased from 3 per cent in 1951 to more than 20 per cent in 1971 (Table 2). However, despite significant outreach, the cooperatives had not led to the previously hoped effects on agricultural productivity, rural poverty and unemployment, and socio-economic inequal-

1 The power of the Planning Commission was limited by the relevance of the Planning and Development Department set up under late colonial rule (Bose 2019, 147).

2 For decades, Congress had led a heterogenous mass social movement against British rule. After independence, a significant share of the left-wing section within the party became increasingly absorbed into the politics of planning and navigating the administrative apparatus inherited from the British, becoming ever more estranged from the labouring masses, and thereby manifesting the dominance of conservative party elements more closely aligned with business (Chibber 2006, 111).

ity. To clarify, agricultural production did grow in the 1950s and 1960s, but this was largely a reflection of increased labour input (growing population) and use of additional land facilitated in part by new public investments in irrigation systems (Kohli 2004). Moreover, cooperative banking was not the self-sufficient grassroots movement Nehru and others had aspired to. It was driven mainly by government action, and borrowing was primarily financed through public means, not from member's savings (Vaidyanathan 2013). Perhaps most importantly, the effects of cooperative banking on poverty, unemployment and inequality remained limited because one of the key contradictions of the colonial cooperative banking structure was never seriously tackled. Rather than sites of decentralised democratic decision-making, wealthy peasants, landlords, and political party leaders primarily benefitted from these institutions and used them as an opportunity "for acquiring power and patronage for personal and party gain by managing these funds" (Vaidyanathan 2013, 32).

Table 2: Share of Rural Creditor Institutions, 1951 – 1991

	1951	**1961**	**1971**	**1981**	**1991**
Relatives and friends	14.2	6.8	13.8	9.0	6.7
Moneylenders*	69.7	60.8	36.9	16.9	15.8
Landlords and Traders	7	8.6	17.3	7.4	11.1
Commercial Bank (incl. RRB)	0.8	0.4	2.2	28	29
Cooperative Societies	3.1	9.1	20.1	28.6	18.6
Government	3.3	5.3	6.7	4.0	5.7
Others	1.9	9	3	6.1	12.9

Source: adapted from Sriram (2018). *Moneylenders, incl. professional and agricultural moneylenders.

First and foremost, the power of credit cooperatives centred on dominating small and marginal peasants though a mixture of exclusion and dependency. They resemble the characteristics of usurious capital discussed in Chapter 5 with one important addition. The accumulation of political power and personal enrichment through PACS is a state-sanctioned and publicly subsidised means of exploitation. An NGO representative working on rural development in the late 1970s elaborates on this point:

> "What did I find at the cooperatives? I used to go to the meetings. I talked to people and I found, people you have a president, secretary, but there was not much discussion. Because the three top people were also the biggest farmers, there were also in politics, they were the power. They held political power, they had status, they were upper-caste, and they also had resources. So people used to borrow from them and they depended on them. That's why there was hardly discussion. [...] So then I discovered that this top three chaps were taking loans from 6–7% from the cooperative and lending to everyone else at 40%. And nobody was asking a question. After doing that, they also said: If you want to get a loan, you have to come and work on my farm first" (CSA_7, Pos. 22)

The idea of local democratic institutions providing subsidised credit seemed to provide a perfect match between the Gandhian emphasis on decentralised political and economic governance and the Nehruvian emphasis on modern institutions as drivers for economic growth. However, it ignored the practice that the Indian village and related institutions, like the panchayat or credit cooperatives, were essentially also sites of oppression.[3] Thus, access to public credit did significantly increase, but this access was mediated by the dominant rural classes who used these institutions primarily as vehicles for consolidating their power and wealth (see also Unger 2018).

Moreover, the credit cooperatives did not account for the increasing share of agricultural labourers. The Congress government launched socialist rhetoric of land reform and abolished feudal tenures by paying handsome compensations, but it did not challenge the power of rural landlords significantly (Bagchi 1982, 157; Kohli 2004, 262).[4] In most states, the concentration of land ownership continued despite reforms implementing land ceilings because landlords were able to evade transfer of ownership, for example, by claiming to cultivate the land directly through hired labour or transferring it nominally to friends, relatives and servants (Ahuja and Ganguly 2007; Patnaik 1983, 9). Twenty years after independence, in 1967, unequal land ownership had remained essentially the same, with 5 per cent of rural households owning 40 per cent of the land, while nearly 58 per cent cultivated either no land or less than 2.5 acres (Ahuja and Ganguly 2007, 253).

The relevance of industries and the public sector in general increased considerably, but it did not absorb the labour surpluses in agriculture (Kohli 2004). With no other employment opportunities, the number of agricultural labourers rose. While

3 This argument draws on Jodhka's (2002) distinction of how independence leaders viewed the Indian village differently as site for authenticity and self-rule (Gandhi), backwardness (Nehru) and oppression (Ambedkar).

4 Sukhamoy Chakravarty, a long-standing member of the Planning Commission, notes: "Unlike the Russian revolution, the Indian independence movement and the subsequent transfer of power did nothing significant to curb the pre-existing power of these groups [e.g. rich landlords and big business]" (Chakravarty 1987, 14).

roughly a quarter of total cultivators and labourers in India worked as agricultural labourers in 1961, their share had increased to 38 per cent ten years later (Patnaik 1983, 14).[5] The agrarian inequalities were also reflected in terms of access to credit, entrenching the power of landlords and traders. According to some estimates, their share in the borrowing of cultivator households increased more than fourfold in the first decade of planning, reaching a high of 14.5 per cent in 1961 (Joshi 2006, 27).[6] The overall relevance of moneylenders may well have declined in this period, but taking the role of landlords and traders into account dilutes the impression that exploitative debt relations have faded (see Table 2). Against this backdrop, the success of institutional vs. non-institutional creditors portrayed in Figure 9 needs further qualification. In spite of significantly extending the outreach of public credit, the relative share of rural credit has a bias towards wealthier households. On average, their loan sizes are much higher, thus adding disproportionately to the statistic. In contrast, small and marginal farmers and landless agricultural labourers usually borrow small amounts with moneylenders, landlords, and traders, adding comparatively less to the overall lending.

Studying the transforming landlord-labour relationships in Gujarat, Jan Breman maintains that "de-patronisation" was underway, where agricultural labourers were paid in monetary wages rather than in kind and labourers were not necessarily bound to one landlord. However, this process, which already began under the colonial regime, left agricultural labourers isolated from protective measures which neither the landlords nor the Indian state filled, and hence became increasingly mediated by (monetary) debts:

> "The living standard of the agricultural laborers, low to begin with, deteriorated further when allowances in kind were replaced by money wages. Most of them are continually indebted, and this is the main reason why, in budget calculations of households of agricultural laborers, expenditure always turns out to exceed income. The debt binds the Dublas [Adivasi tribe] and provides the landlords with a means of pressure. In the long term it is cheaper and safer for the landlords to give a limited loan to a farm servant than to hire day-laborers. Moreover, they select the most industrious and obedient laborers for farm service" (Breman 1974, 225)

5 Although occurring unevenly, this increase occurred across India. It was particularly pronounced in central and south India, including the states of Kerala, Madras, Andhra Pradesh, Mysore, and Maharashtra.

6 This number deviates from Table 2 which draws on the calculations of Sriram (2018), although both are based on various rounds of the All India Debt and Investment Survey. Despite differences in magnitude, both testify to the entrenched power of landlords and traders in the post-Independence era.

Understanding the debt-bondage as a feudal relic thus misses a crucial point. Forms of debt-bondage have certainly shifted. But this does not preclude the modernisation of bonded labour, in which new forms of exploitation and dependency are mediated increasingly, though not exclusively, in monetary terms. The depiction of wages as loans may be a strategic means for controlling and disciplining labour in capitalist relations, whether dominated by individual capitalists (wealth farmers/landlords) or corporate capital (Banaji 2010, 150).[7]

The persisting problem of debt bondage was acknowledged by the Indian government. Under the leadership of Indira Gandhi, it outlawed this practice by passing the *Bonded Labour System (Abolition) Act* of 1976. However, legally abolishing caste discrimination or labour does not necessarily translate into eradication, if there is no appropriate enforcement. A survey of 1000 villages in 10 states from the late 1970s shows that there still were at least 2.6 million bonded labourers in India (primarily in agriculture), of whom 86.6 per cent were Dalit or Adivasi (Srivastava 2005, 4).[8] When understanding the emergence of new forms of bonded labour not as a feudal relic, it may well be that the developmental growth strategy contributed to Dalit and Adivasi labourers' vulnerability and isolation. The complete neglect of basic social provisioning (education, healthcare, etc.), alternative employment opportunities, and continued forms of enclosures preventing them from using common land and resources, ultimately rendering them susceptible to exploitative labour and debt relations (Breman, Guérin, and Prakash 2009; Guérin 2013).

For instance, the four major public-sector-led integrated steel towns which were built in the 1950s and 1960s acquired more than 90,000 acres of rural lands that primarily included agricultural land and forests, displacing a population of roughly 185,000 (Roy 2023, 36). Building on the colonial *Land Acquisition Act* of 1894, involuntary acquisitions and forced displacements were justified for public purposes, frequently without resettlement or adequate compensation (Ahuja and Ganguly 2007; Levien 2012). Although there are no exact figures, it is estimated that the developmental regime dispossessed at least 25 million people in the four decades after independence, primarily for the construction of dams, steel towns, infrastructure and mining (Levien 2018; Roy 2023). Tribal communities (*Adivasis*) and other marginalised social groups living in resource-rich mountain and forest areas were the most affected by these dispossessions (Ahuja and Ganguly 2007, 264). Therefore, rather than resolving the problem of surplus labour through rapid industrialisation and rural employment opportunities, Indian planning has "produced as wasteland of dispossessed" (Sanyal 2007, 166), vulnerable to multiple forms of exploitation.

---

7 We will return to this aspect in Part IV, when discussing the sourcing of migrant construction workers in the contemporary era.

8 Although most bonded labourers worked in agriculture, the phenomenon was also observable in other sectors, including brick kilns, seaports and prostitution (Srivastava 2005)

Social Banking: Ambitious and Ambiguous

The government's disillusion with cooperative credit societies in the mid-1960s had less to do with their oppressive mode of governance and more with the lack of fostering agricultural productivity. India's apex food security scheme, the Public Distribution System (PDS), was dependent on food imports. Though recurring droughts and crop failure did not lead to the devastating effects of the famines under colonial rule, hunger and malnutrition continued to be major problems. In this context, two significant policies decisively influenced the governance of access to credit. Firstly, the nationalisation of commercial banks and, secondly, the new agricultural policy commonly known as the Green Revolution. Both were connected but had their separate political and economic dynamics.

The 1960s marked a crisis of legitimacy for the Congress party, which had been in power since independence. The party-left pushed for socialist demands like bank nationalisation, effective land ceilings, and collective farming but at first could not universalise their position against the dominant leadership (Sen 2016). After a historic loss of support in the 1967 general elections, prime minister Indira Gandhi picked up the idea of bank nationalisation as a crucial policy to gain popular support and manifest her position within the divided Congress leadership (Sen 2016; Torri 1975). The essential critique centred around commercial banks focusing on large-scale investment in industries while neglecting agriculture and small and medium enterprises. The share of commercial banks in rural credit was marginal in the 1950s and 1960s (see Table 2), and the top three per cent of shareholders owned nearly half the shares of the leading banks (Torri 1975, 1079).

In 1969, the Congress government nationalised 14 major commercial banks, which together accounted for 45 per cent of banking business. Moreover, it controlled both the physical outreach of banking in rural areas and the diversification of their portfolio.[9] The transfer in ownership was followed by introducing Priority Sector Lending (PSL), prescribing banks to lend at least 40 per cent of their portfolio to agriculture and small and medium enterprises. Moreover, the licensing policy was adjusted, requesting banks to open three (later four) new branches in rural areas for every new branch created in cities. In addition, the government introduced Regional Rural Banks (RRB) as new institutions that were more locally rooted than commercial banks, had higher PSL quotas and soon developed an impressive branch network (Chavan 2017; Joshi 2006; Sriram 2018).

There can be no doubt that these policies significantly impacted the structure of rural credit and fostered financial flows between commercial banks and the agrar-

9 The State Bank of India (SBI) which had been nationalised in 1955, controlled roughly 30 per cent and the remaining 25 per cent of small and foreign banks were exempted from nationalisation (Sen 2016, 137).

ian economy. In the two decades after nationalisation, the number of bank offices increased from 1,443 to over 30,585 (Shah, Rao, and Shankar 2007, 1345). Moreover, the share of commercial banks and RRBs in rural credit skyrocketed from 2 per cent in 1971 to 28 per cent in 1981 (see Table 2). Therefore, the post-nationalisation period is commonly referred to as the "social banking era" (Chavan 2017; Joshi 2006; Sriram 2018). However, the massive extension of public banking services in the agrarian economy does not necessarily imply the even distribution of financial resources. To assess how social public-sector banking really was, one needs to understand its ground workings, particularly where most of the credit flowed. This analysis brings us to the intersections between bank nationalisation and the second major policy-shift in the late 1960s, the new agricultural policy.

The shift towards a new agricultural policy can be partly attributed to domestic factors, including the efforts amongst governmental officials and scientists to develop new ways of increasing agricultural productivity. But it also had a geopolitical context: India's dependency on food imports made the country vulnerable to foreign interests. In the early 1960s, the PDS, offering subsidised food grains to the rural masses, was almost entirely dependent on wheat imports, including from the US. The latter used this leverage to advance its interests on the subcontinent by making food aid contingent on recipients for broader US foreign policy goals, including fostering the Green Revolution (Gupta 1998; Patel 2013).

Essentially, the US-driven Green Revolution was an imperialist strategy in the context of the Cold War, keeping the Red Revolution, that is, communism, peasant insurgencies and radical politics in Third World countries in check through technological modernisation and increased agrarian productivity, while opening markets for US agribusiness (Cleaver 1972; McMichael 2017; Patel 2013). It started with experiments of the Rockefeller and Ford Foundation on new grain varieties in Mexico and later the Philippines, which, under heavy use of fertilisers and irrigation, could produce substantially higher yields than traditional varieties. The programme quickly attracted support from the US government, US corporations, UN bodies and the World Bank, and was introduced in numerous Third World countries in the 1960s (Gupta 1998, 52ff.; McMichael 2017, 73ff.). This new agricultural policy required shifting public financing from large irrigation projects to small tube wells and energised pump sets, and offering credit to farmers for increasing the rate of fertilisers, high-yielding seeds, pesticides, fossil energy sources, and machinery (Chakravarty 1987, 24; Joshi 2006). This is where bank nationalisation and the Green Revolution converged.

Overall, development planning, including the new agricultural policy, succeeded in increasing agricultural productivity and output in the post-independence era significantly, especially in wheat, making India food self-sufficient by the mid-1980s (Patnaik 1991). During the two decades following the Green Revolution and bank nationalisation, capital accumulation in agriculture kept pace with capital formation in the rest of the economy (Basole and Basu 2011b, 53). Yet, similar to the case of cooperatives, growth itself is not necessarily social and does not automatically translate into higher living standards for the subaltern classes.

To begin with, the Green Revolution deepened regional inequalities. The high-yielding varieties of wheat and rice required reliable irrigation. However, during this time, only about 20 per cent of cultivated land was under irrigation, and only half of that had assured water supplies (Cleaver 1972, 181). Consequently, the adoption was focused on only 20 out of 300 districts and remained largely confined to the North Indian states of Punjab and Haryana. With massive public support, these regions experienced a rapid rise in food production per head of the total population up to the mid-1980s, whereas per-head food production in the rest of India stagnated or declined. The food surpluses were, however, not distributed evenly. Instead, most of it was accumulated as government stocks and channelled through the PDS, while a minor share went into exports (Patnaik 1991). Yet, the PDS was notoriously famous for a corrupt bureaucracy, hoarding of food grains amongst dominant rural classes, and the sale of food grains on the black market (Ahuja and Ganguly 2007, 254). Moreover, the unequal rates of growth favoured some crops, particularly wheat, over rain-fed crops like "*bajra*, *jowar* or *ragi*, which are the staple diets of the poor in many regions, or pulses, which are the main source of protein for the poor" (Bagchi 1982, 1975).

In addition, the new agricultural policy was not sensitive to the extensive class inequalities that marked the agrarian economy, further entrenching the concentration of land (Bagchi 1982, 176; Ladejinsky 1970; Patnaik 1983). Focusing on high-yielding variety seeds required costly complementary inputs, like fertilisers, diesel/electricity, and machinery. Wealthy farmers could easily access cheap credit, allowing for varied investments (Cleaver 1972, 182). In 1970, the bulk of agrarian producers (including the lower strata of the middle peasantry), that is, roughly 185 million peasants, would earn between Rs. 190 and Rs. 250 annually, and had landholdings of less than 5 acres, making working capital investments of Rs. 10,000 – 12,000 for Green Revolution agriculture practically impossible (Ahuja and Ganguly 2007, 256; Ladejinsky 1970, 763). This problem was further exacerbated by the fact that purchase orders had to be approved by bank officials and was only valid with some dealers, who used their privileged position to sell old seeds and fertilisers to peasants, trapping them in a cycle of debt (Gupta 1998, 196). Unequal land ownership was both a cause and consequence of the uneven agrarian accumulation. For instance, a longitudinal study of two villages in the Mandya district of Karnataka, situated between Mysuru and Bengaluru, revealed that caste-based class inequalities had increased between 1950 and 1977, with upper-caste Lingayats and traditional peasant castes steadily increasing their share of land ownership at the expense of declining land holdings amongst the Dalits (Adikarnataka) (Dhanagare 1988, 139).

Similar trends are also observable for prestigious large-scale infrastructure projects. For instance, India's longest canal, the Indira Gandhi Canal, stretches over 600 kilometres, channelling water from Punjab and Himachal Pradesh into Rajasthan, "greening" the Thar desert and enhancing agricultural productivity in one of India's poverty-ridden states. It was conceived shortly after independence and was approved by the Planning Commission in 1957. However, the mega-project was being built until the early 1970s and attracted foreign funding, including from the World Bank, to create "thousands of private plots irrigated by the canal and supplied with Green Revolution inputs" (Levien 2018). The effects on local people's livelihoods were bleak. While wealthy landowners who settled at the main canal arteries benefitted from producing high-yield crops, the majority of small farmers down the waterway "suffered from an absence of water, sand-choked canals, failed crops, high indebtedness, and government negligence" (Goldman 2005, viii; see also Ramanathan 1991), while semi-nomadic pastoralists who had used the common grazing land were robbed of their livelihoods.[10]

In sum, bank nationalisation and the Green Revolution increased public banks' outreach into the agrarian economy, enhancing productivity and output. However, the accumulation of agrarian capital was highly uneven and did not generally lead to reasonable employment opportunities for the rural masses. On the contrary, it is likely that it entrenched the dynamics of labour attachment for the lowest ranks of the rural population. In 1969, roughly one-fourth of the total rural population of 434 million were landless (Ladejinsky 1970). For these populations, overwhelmingly low-caste, Dalit and Adivasi, the uneven agrarian accumulation intensified the means of wealthy farmers and landlords to uphold labour bondage. Even at the heart of the Green Revolution, in Punjab and Haryana, where the share of agricultural labourers was below average, Utsa Patnaik finds that "indebtedness is built into the wage contract itself and that labourers fail to reach the 'poverty-line' levels of consumption" (Patnaik 1983, 16). The persistence of the severe subsistence crisis of the rural masses and widespread criticism and unrest pushed the Congress government under the leadership of Indira Gandhi to address this issue more seriously.

The rhetoric of land reform was discarded, but after her successful re-election in 1971, Indira Gandhi stressed employment generation, livelihood diversification, and anti-poverty measures as central national policy concerns in the Fifth and Sixth Plan (1974 – 1985). The flagship scheme of this period was the Integrated Rural Development Programme (IRDP). In contrast to the Green Revolution, it explicitly focused on small and marginal farmers, agricultural labourers, rural artisans and all other households with an annual income below the nationally defined poverty line.

10 Moreover, the Green Revolution increased the political ecology of inequality in various other ways (Patel 2013; Shiva 1993; Shrivastava and Kothari 2012).

The government would provide subsidised working capital of Rs. 3,000 per household for three years, primarily through public sector banks, to acquire assets, like milk animals or sewing machines, that would help these populations enhance their household incomes and cross the poverty line (Kurian 1987; Rath 1985). As such, it had striking similarities with other global experiments with income-generating loans in the 1970s and 1980s (see Chapter 2). The magnitude of the programme was significant. It targeted around 15 million poor households in rural areas and earmarked Rs. 15 billion in government grants, while public banks contributed the larger share with Rs. 30 billion (Kurian 1987).

The programme quickly came under scrutiny from critiques, which, similar to most government schemes, pointed out massive leakages, elite capture, mis-targeting, and inefficient bureaucratic processes hampering the effective delivery of these substantial resources (Dreze 1990; Mathur 1995; Rath 1985). Although a minor share of the targeted families seemed to have benefited from the programme through improved livelihood opportunities and increased household incomes, more than half of the credit was not paid on time, and almost one-fourth of all beneficiaries had overdue amounting to more than Rs. 1,000, while inadequate incomes were the primary reason for the inability to pay (Kurian 1987; Rath 1985). More importantly, however, the philosophy of asset-based credit as effective anti-poverty measures entailed at least two major flaws, which foreshadowed the contradictions of current microfinance initiatives.

The first is the naïve assumption that access to working capital will be a sufficient condition for creating enhanced incomes through self-employment, and that this could work on a large scale. There were also parallel schemes that provided public employment for the rural poor during seasons of unemployment. Still, often, these did not provide a minimum livelihood security. Since priority was given to asset-based anti-poverty measures, the employment opportunities only reached a minuscule share of the working-age population amongst poor rural households (Rath 1985, 245; Sanyal 2007, 136).[11] As a result, instead of understanding poverty as a chronic crisis of social reproduction of specific social classes rooted in unequal production relations and a lack of employment opportunities, the IRDP reduced poverty to a lack of access to capital. Yet, most poor households were in desperate need of income to secure their social reproduction, and not for working capital that would expose them to multiple additional risks given the power asymmetries in the agrarian economy. In a scathing critique, Jean Dreze summarised this key contradiction

11 For instance, the National Rural Employment Programme (NREP) and the Rural Landless Employment Guarantee Programme (RLEGP) were launched in the 1980s, and were early predecessors to the Mahatma Gandhi National Rural Employment Guarantee Scheme (MGNREGS) introduced in 2006.

as follows: "Why a poor entrepreneur vulnerable to the uncertainties of the market, lumbered with a crushing debt to the local bank and exposed to bureaucratic caprices should be considered more 'self-reliant' than a person entitled to employment in times of need is a mystery to me" (Dreze 1990, 96).

The second flaw of the IRDP was the failure to recognise the immediate needs of the rural masses, including the logic of reproductive debts. Although the programme's name suggested otherwise, major dynamics that impacted poor people's livelihoods, like land ownership, access to common property resources, safe drinking water, sanitation, and access to education and health care, were side-lined (Dreze 1990; Rath 1985). But even for entrepreneurial active populations, increased access to credit is not exclusively or primarily used for business activities, especially when households face acute income shortages to safeguard the social reproduction of household members. Everett and Savara (1984) investigated credit form public sector banks for poor women in Mumbai in the early 1980s. One of the women they interviewed expressed how the paradigm of income-generation loans fails to acknowledge the pervasiveness of reproductive debts:

> "The banks do not realize that we need money most often in time of crisis and [...] for purposes of survival. Yes, I understand that banks give money for work [business investment] only, but what happens is something like this. At times of crisis when we need money immediately, we borrow from a moneylender. We have to go there because who knows when the bank loan will come. Then when the bank loan does get sanctioned, we repay the moneylender." (Everett and Savara 1984, 290)

This point can be further substantiated by drawing on Maria Mies' case study of lace makers in Andhra Pradesh. In the 1970s, home-based production of lace for export rapidly expanded in Narsapur, providing a vital source of income for tens of thousands of women in the region. Wages for women workers were chronically low (below Rs. 1/day), with agents, traders and exporters accumulating the bulk of revenue. Even though, on average, lace makers worked 13–15 hours a day, with roughly half of the time spent on lace making and the rest on other work, including housework, the combined household income of women and their husbands – who would usually work as agricultural labourers – was chronically below the expenditure for food and other essentials (Mies 2012, 149ff.).[12] Since patriarchal norms prescribed women as

12 Moreover, the "housewifisation" of women workers associated with home-based work entrenched their oppression through atomisation and disorganisation, limiting prospects to negotiate for better pay. This trend spread across generations because daughters were often integrated early one in home-based production rather than send to school (Mies 2012, 199).

responsible for safeguarding the reproduction of household members, three-quarters of the surveyed lace makers were forced to pawn their jewellery or other assets they had received as dowry and turn to moneylenders, primarily to ensure day-to-day expenses for food, social functions, and health (Mies 2012, 158ff.).

Both cases vividly demonstrate how multiple debt relations converge in the household economy and how power hierarchies in the agrarian economy entrench the demand for credit due to a chronic subsistence crisis and the dependency on moneylenders. A subsidised loan scheme cannot compensate for the lack of decent working conditions, insufficient livelihood opportunities, and unsatisfactory social provisioning. Even with substantial public investments, the strategy of income-generating credit as an anti-poverty measure for the masses "merely provide[s] channels through which new ties of dependence and exploitation are established" (Everett and Savara 1984, 284) if the root causes of the subsistence crisis are not systematically tackled. Arguably, the 1980s marked the period in the post-independence era with the most ambitious attempts on behalf of the state to engage with the crisis of social reproduction amongst subaltern classes, including large-scale subsidised loan schemes and public work schemes for the rural poor. At the same time, this decade also saw the slow erosion of the developmental regime of re/productive finance.

Signs of Erosion and the Expansion of Civil Society

By the 1980s, India's political economy was haunted by its colonial past. The developmental regime had succeeded in fostering economic growth, building a diversified industrial base, expanding the public sector significantly, and overcoming the devastating famines of the colonial era. However, the concentration of land ownership and other assets in the hands of few persisted, and decent employment or livelihood opportunities for the majority of the rural population were virtually non-existent. Poverty and hunger remained the grim reality of a significant share of the population. In macroeconomic terms, this created a problem: domestic demand was overall weak, and the state had to spend to maintain a growth stimulus. Yet, the developmental state had never managed to discipline big business and create sufficient revenue by way of taxation (Chandrasekhar and Ghosh 2002; Chibber 2006). In addition to this fiscal deficit, the current account deficit increased mainly as a result of the demand amongst domestic businesses and the urban middle class for goods from abroad, depleting the country's foreign exchange reserves (Chandrasekhar and Ghosh 2002). Hence, the government started to liberalise imports and significantly increased its external indebtedness to finance the increasing public expenditure (Patnaik and Chandrasekhar 1995, 3007). Eventually, these contradictions would culminate in high inflation and a balance of payment crisis, which would pave the way for the neoliberal restructuring that had already began to spread across the globe.

Moreover, there were also signs of institutional changes in the governance of access to credit. During this time, the RBI increasingly withdrew from its function to plan and refinance agriculture and rural development and instead created specialised institutions, like the National Bank for Agriculture and Rural Development (NABARD), responsible for promoting and facilitating access to credit in the agrarian economy (Sriram 2018). With advice from international development agencies, NABARD started to support the local women's group-lending model (see below).

Meanwhile, the Indian left became ever more divided along strategic questions and organisational forms of how to respond to the persistent subsistence crisis of subaltern classes adequately. In 1967, a section of the Communist Party of India (Marxist) engaged in a peasant rebellion in Naxalbari, a small village in West Bengal. The police quickly crushed the uprising, but in the following decades, the so-called Naxalites, an alliance between revolutionary Marxist intellectuals and impoverished peasants, particularly from tribal communities, gained a foothold in many states (Ahuja and Ganguly 2007; Das 2010; Verghese 2016). They called for a "New Democratic Revolution" and challenged the power of landlords, moneylenders and the post-colonial state through armed attacks and guerrilla warfare. As such, they built on the legacy of anti-colonial peasant insurgencies, giving them more or less a coherent ideological underpinning, disciplinary organisation, and strategic outlook (Parashar 2019; Sundar 2011). Their agitation would be most successful in precisely those regions that were affected worst by skewed landownership, chronic impoverishment, indebtedness, and hunger. Despite extensive state repression, the Naxalites continued to grow. However, another entirely different type of activism would prove to challenge the foundations of the developmental regime of re/productive finance more permanently: the rise of civil society organisations.

Two broader trends favoured this development. First, a new generation of educated middle-class Indians had emerged in cities and was eager to challenge persistent poverty, hunger, and inequalities through new types of organisations and forms of interventions. Disillusioned with the factional conflicts of party politics and traditional trade unions, some of these started to create alternative structures of mobilising women in local groups and experimented with group lending.[13] Second,

---

13 I'm drawing on the experiences of SEWA and MYRADA in this section as the two most prominent examples. The general arguments put forth also apply to other civil society organisations that experimented with SHGs and group lending, like the Association for Sarva Seva Farms (ASSEFA), the Professional Assistance for Development Action (PRADAN), and later, the South Asia Poverty Alleviation Project (SAPAP) or the Development of Humane Action (DHAN) Foundation (Mahajan 2005; Nair and Gandhe 2015; Singh 2008)

these initiatives were enthusiastically endorsed and supported by Western development institutions, which increasingly discredited state-subsidised targeted lending programmes in the global South as top-down, ineffective and too expensive and endorsed group lending experiments as financial innovation (see Chapter 2). Moreover, they were also backed by new state institutions, like NARBAD. Eventually, these initiatives, which began in the mid-1970s and picked up in the 1980s, signalled the decline of the state-led regime of re/productive finance and provided the basis for the rise of a neoliberal regime.

Interestingly, these civil society initiatives returned to the vision of credit cooperatives as decentralised and democratic institutions owned by the impoverished masses while recognising that the existing cooperative structure oppressed instead of empowered them. For instance, Aloysius Prakash Fernandez, who was a key figure in pioneering the self-help group (SHG) model through an organisation called MYRADA, argues that the village-based cooperative societies "tend to further the oppressive relations in traditional society that prevent the poor from increasing their incomes and diversifying their livelihoods" (Fernandez 2018, 138). Likewise, Ella Bhatt maintains that founding the Self-Employed Women's Association (SEWA), a union for unorganised workers and peasants, was an essential part of the struggle for 'second freedom' (*doosri azadi*), that is, the economic freedom of the masses which had not materialised in independent India despite three decades of freedom from colonial rule:

> "The poor women must have rupees in their own pockets, so they are no longer bound without her will to the local moneylenders, contractors, landlords or social structure. The poor women must also be equipped to shed the sense of inferiority because of gender, caste, illiteracy and poverty by building their organised strength through self-managed, self-owned and viable economic organisations" (Bhatt 1998, 26)

Essentially, these civil society initiatives provided the organisational means through which women's individual savings could be pooled and held in a safe space. Encouraging regular savings would provide the means through which groups could borrow lump sums to members or, as in the case of SEWA, a specialised bank.

Initially, these groups were not limited to facilitating savings and credit management. Rather, they worked on a broad range of issues, including skill-sharing, enabling market linkages for produce, challenging domestic violence, and securing access to public health care or other social infrastructure. SEWA was even founded as a trade union for unorganised workers who were not represented by the traditional unions (Bhatt 1998; Webster 2011). However, the pervasiveness of reproductive debts cutting across these issues soon became apparent, which is why developing an alternative financing mechanism gained momentum quickly. Importantly, the

NGOs recognised the relevance of reproductive debts from the beginning. These women needed loans without collateral and a flexible repayment schedule that they could draw on for day-to-day needs and in times of crisis. As such, they mimicked the moneylenders but removed the exploitative part of high-interest rates and sustained dependency through debt by mobilising savings in solidarity groups and borrowing from each other. Recalling a field experience from the 1980s, Fernandez highlights that women in the villages frequently opted for moneylenders not only because alternatives were lacking but because they offered the type of credit they needed most: "[The moneylender] is on call for any emergency not just financial; he lends for any purpose and the amount of loan is not standardised [...]; he allows us to reschedule repayments if we have a genuine problem and to pay in lump sum when we have the cash; this suits us as our income is not steady" (Fernandez 2018, 109). Thus, the purpose of loans would not be restricted. Even when SEWA created its own bank in 1983, the latter would offer loans not only for business activities but also for home improvement, social functions, health and other emergencies.

This strategy recognised that even for self-employed women, just as in the case of lace makers discussed above, business was generally a supplementary household income, while they were also working as precarious labourers and engaging in cultivation, none of which could sustain the household economy on its own (Duvendack 2015, 188; Webster 2011, 110). So, while the aspect of savings and investment played a crucial role, what precarious women workers, responsible for safeguarding the social reproduction of all household members, needed most, was a source of income – which indebtedness provided temporarily – that would help manage household expenses related to illness, deaths and marriages, housing, and basic needs (Kabeer and Noponen 2005).

The new civil society organisation's intervention in the state-directed regime of re/productive finance was ambiguous. It recognised the oppressive nature of the agrarian political economy, the limits of the social banking approach, and the importance of reproductive debts for subaltern classes, opting for organising grassroots groups as a basis for alternative institutions. Yet, similar to the NGOisation of social movements, this middle-class activism remained primarily "problem-solving" (Harriss 2005). It focussed on providing an alternative savings and borrowing institution, supporting groups in terms of skill development and livelihood diversification, and helping marginalised sections of society to claim their rights within the prevailing norms. However, these initiatives did not have a strategic vision for broader political mobilisation of these local groups that could join with other social forces to challenge the root causes of the entrenched subsistence crisis: unequal distribution of land ownership, lack of employment opportunities, barred access to common resources and insufficient social provisioning related to basic needs.

This dilemma became further exacerbated by the dependency of these initiatives from external donors. It is hardly surprising that the need for reproductive debts exceeded the means these groups could create from their savings (Fernandez 2018; Nair 2015). Thus, scaling up the group-based loans model without collateral was contingent on development agencies supporting and financing these experiments or acquiring support from the state. For instance, SEWA has received vital funds from key institutions that fostered the Green Revolution, like the Rockefeller and Ford Foundation, USAID, the World Bank, and many others (Kerswell and Pratap 2017). MYRADA has scaled up its success with support from NABARD, which encouraged the SHG model in the late 1980s and would adopt it into a vital strategy during the neoliberal transformation. As such, these experiments not only signalled the decline of the developmental regime of re/productive finance, but they also prepared the ground for the emergence of microfinance between state and market capture, a topic we will further engage with in the following chapter.

Chapter 11
The Ascent of Market-Based Reproductive Debt

The 1980s and 1990s marked the neoliberal counter-revolution in the global political economy, burying the hopes of post-colonial states for a new international economic order and ushering in the much-quoted 'end of history' (see Chapter 3). These profound transformations were also witnessed in India. This chapter outlines the key characteristics and dynamics of the neoliberal regime of re/productive finance while maintaining alertness to the legacies of the earlier regimes. In this sense, I follow Aseem Shrivastava's characterisation of the present as an "era of nested eras" (Shrivastava 2016, 78). All key creditor institutions of the past, the moneylenders, credit cooperatives, commercial banks, and emerging SHGs converge into a new regime and articulate with commercial microfinance, which has strategically banked on reproductive debts.

I will start this chapter by exploring how the neoliberal reforms impacted the growth-model and labour relations, exacerbating the chronic subsistence crisis of India's subaltern working-class households. The second section investigates the expansion of (commercial) microfinance as a hybrid structure pushed by both state and market interests, manifesting a unique form of a debtfare state. This forms the background to understand the rapid rise of corporate MFIs since the mid-2000s who, contrary to the previous discourses on income-generating loans, endorsed themselves as services to manage the chronic subsistence crisis. Finally, I will discuss the contradictions of India's contemporary re/productive finance regime by investigating the expansion of reproductive debts through privatised and financialised health care.

Neoliberal Reforms and the Contemporary Crisis of Social Reproduction

India's political economy underwent significant neoliberal restructuring during the 1990s, including greater freedom for (international) capital in both productive and financial sectors, extensive liberalisation through reduced state control over economic resources and prices, privatisation, incentives for investors, including subsidies and tax cuts, and curbing public expenditure to service debts (Chandrasekhar and Ghosh 2002; Patnaik and Chandrasekhar 1995). Financial liberalisation was vital to the project of neoliberal restructuring. After all, India's banking sector was almost entirely dominated by public banks since nationalisation in the late 1960s. The policy changes comprised a wide range, including reduced controls on interest rates, allowing private banks (both foreign and domestic) to enter the sector, expanding the sources and instruments through which financial institutions can access funds, and easing conditions for the participation of both firms and investors in the stock market (Chandrasekhar 2007, 195ff.; Chandrasekhar and Ghosh 2002, 97ff.). Some radical proposals, like the privatisation of RRBs or the removal of priority sector lending (PSL), were not implemented, but the definition of PSL became increasingly diluted. For instance, with an eye on India's increasing entanglement with the global corporate food regime, corporate food and soft drinks production was accepted as PSL (Chavan 2017).

In essence, the liberalisation policies marked the beginning of a highly uneven growth model. While most of the population depended on agriculture, the sector's share of GDP substantially declined (Ghosh 2015; Kannan and Raveendra 2009). Moreover, quotes on bank branches were removed, adversely impacting access to credit in rural areas. Directed credit and investment for particular sectors and populations were replaced by praising the efficiency of competitive markets, and banking increasingly turned "away from facilitating commodity production and investment to lubricating trade and promoting personal consumption" (Chandrasekhar 2007, 198). The bank branch network in rural areas declined during the 1990s, while metropolitan and urban areas, where most of the profitable customers lived, experienced a massive increase (Sriram 2018, 11). As a result, liberalisation drove financial exclusion in terms of supply and demand of credit amongst the rural masses. In the two decades after liberalisation, the relevance of public banks in rural areas declined, rural credit dried up, particularly for the lower rural classes, while moneylenders experienced a spectacular return (Chavan 2005; Shah, Rao, and Shankar 2007). Importantly, these new moneylenders were not confined to landlords, traders, and wealthy farmers, but with escalating income and wealth equality across the country, members of the petty bourgeoisie, like government servants or lawyers, also entered the lucrative business of informal moneylending (Basole and Basu 2011a, 53). Small, marginal, and effectively landless farmers were more prone to become trapped in usurious debt relations, intensifying their vulnerability to exploitation as cheap labourers in agriculture and beyond, fostering new forms of debt-bondage and labour attachment (Guérin 2013; Harris-White and Gooptu 2001; Pattenden 2010).

While manufacturing stagnated as a share of value-added GDP, economic growth primarily benefitted the corporate-dominated services sector, with finance, insurance, real estate (FIRE), information and communication technologies as key winners of this uneven growth model (Ghosh 2015). India's growth pattern and sectorial transformation is thus based on the persistence of "jobless growth" (Kannan and Raveendra 2009; Shrivastava and Kothari 2012). In the 25 years following liberalisation, the number of formal employment has been resiliently stagnant, rising imperceptibly from 26.7 million in 1991 to just below 30 million in 2016 (Shrivastava 2016). The uneven growth in the neoliberal era has been accompanied by the expansion of the informal sector and the casualisation of formal sector work, which provides a livelihood for the overwhelming share of the country's population. Nearly 80 per cent of Indian households do not own a regular wage or salary, and the vast majority of rural and urban workers have no formal written contract, no paid leave, and no access to any social security benefits (George and Sinha 2017; Mishra and Bhattacharya 2017). Of course, these general characteristics should not imply there is no "division of labourers" (Ambedkar 2014).

India's working class is fragmented and segmented by caste, ethnicity, gender and region. They experience multiple forms of exclusion, exploitation and expropriation, cumulating to what Lerche and Shah (2018) call "conjugated oppression". For instance, in 2011–2012, a staggering 81 per cent of Adivasis and 64 per cent of Dalits – who together account for roughly 300 million of India's population – are working in agriculture, hunting and forestry or construction, that is, the sectors associated most with below subsistence wages, hardly any security, and little bargaining power of labour (George and Sinha 2017). Moreover, the trends of casualisation are also witnessed in public employment with a particular gender bias. For instance, more than 1.5 million women are working as Anganwadis and nearly one million as Accredited Social Health Activists (ASHA) who together form the backbone of primary childcare and health services in rural areas. The former are paid wages but do not have permanent employment with social security benefits comparable to other government staff. And despite being essential for the immunisation of children, treating basic illness, or improving village sanitation, ASHAs are considered voluntary activists who do not receive a regular wage or honorarium at all but a meagre compensation below the legal minimum wage (Ghosh 2015; Sathi 2023; Sreerekha 2017).

Despite the multiple fragmentations and segmentations, the essential livelihood characteristic of the majority of Indians represents quite precisely what Marcel van der Linden describes as the "subaltern working-class" (van der Linden 2014): Various household members must engage with multiple types of work in different sectors, at different times, with shifting degrees of freedom and dependency to secure their livelihood. From a different perspective, we can maintain that the highly uneven capital accumulation in the neoliberal era requires the majority of Indians to diversify their livelihoods. However, this diversification is clearly distress-driven, and it is hardly associated with substantially improved living standards. Over a decade after the liberalisation of the Indian economy started, three-quarters of all rural households had marginal landholdings of less than 2.5 acres. For these, incomes from cultivation had to be complemented by animal husbandry, non-farm business activities and, most importantly, wage labour, which contributed nearly half of the total income for marginal farmers and almost two-thirds for effectively landless households (Basole and Basu 2011a; see also Naidu and Ossome 2016). But even this pooling of various income sources into the household economy was grossly insufficient to meet necessary expenditures.

Table 3: Monthly Income and Consumption Among Rural Classes, 2003 in Rs.

	Wages	Income from Cultivation	Income from Animals	Non-Farm Business Income	Total Income	Subsistence Surplus (Income – Expenditure)
Effective Landless (>1 acre)	999	223	86	260	1,568	-798
Marginal (1.01 – 2.5 acres)	720	784	112	193	1,809	-863
Small (2.51 – 5 acres)	635	1,578	102	178	2,493	-655
Middle (5.01 – 10 acres)	637	2,685	57	210	3,589	-96
Large (> 10 acres)	496	5,195	26	531	6,248	1367

Source: Basu and Basole (2011a).

Table 3 shows the pervasive crisis of social reproduction amongst rural classes. Except for large landowners and the upper parts of the middle peasantry, who can accumulate surpluses, all rural households experienced higher consumption expenditures than their total incomes. Nearly 90 per cent of the rural population belongs to the lower three categories, which all experienced a subsistence gap between monthly consumption expenditures and total incomes, amounting to between Rs. 655 and Rs. 863 in nominal terms. This subsistence gap was as high as half of their monthly income for the marginal and effectively landless households, constituting roughly two-thirds of the rural population. Another decade later, in 2012–2013, the picture had not substantially changed, despite record levels of economic growth in the 2000s and numerous national welfare schemes introduced during this period (see below). Two-thirds of rural households were still caught between de-peasantisation and semi-proletarianisation, depending on mainly precarious wage labour and cultivation/animal husbandry, augmenting the household economy with incomes from non-farm business, while on average experiencing a subsistence gap of 20 per cent of their total incomes (Naidu and Ossome 2016, 55).

It is hardly surprising, in this context, that the prevalence of hunger and malnutrition remains a grim reality for a significant part of the Indian population. While food grain availability per capita slowly increased in the three decades after independence, liberalisation policies revoked this achievement. While food exports were soaring at the turn of the millennium, food availability per capita had declined to the levels of the early 1950s. An estimated three-quarters of the rural population had insufficient incomes to meet the minimum food intake of 2,400 calories per day (Patnaik 2007, 115ff.). Even according to more conservative estimates, the share of undernourished in the population has only marginally declined between 2000 and 2021. Indicators like the prevalence of wasting (low weight-for-hight) among children under five years have not improved at all during this time – even though the Indian government has launched numerous welfare schemes in the 2000s (von Grebmer et al. 2021). Meanwhile, following liberalisation, wealth inequality has increased dramatically between rural and urban areas and between the top 10 per cent and the majority population, especially driven by unequal ownership of land and buildings, and particularly benefiting urban elites (owners, managers, professionals) and rural rentier classes (moneylenders and absentee landlords) at the expense of unskilled urban workers, marginal farmers and agricultural labourers (Anand and Thampi 2016; Vakulabharanam 2010).

These trends have led to speculation of a vast "surplus population" that capital has no need to employ (Sanyal 2007). The problem of labour surplus is indeed a pressing issue, one, as we have seen, that has already marked the early post-colonial era. Sanyal's separation between most of the Indian population living in the "need economy" rather than the "accumulation economy" (Sanyal 2007, 70ff.) reflects the entrenched crisis of social reproduction amongst the subaltern classes. Yet, the latter is also a systemic dynamic on which the uneven growth model works. A significant share of India's working class, estimated at between 100 and 140 million, became "footloose" in recent decades, shifting between regions and states and resorting to seasonal, circular or steady migration in search of a livelihood (Basole and Basu 2011b; Breman 2010; Corbridge and Shah 2013; Lerche and Shah 2018). While labour migration is certainly distress-driven, it also provides an important condition for cheap labour in urban areas. As will be shown in more detail in the following chapter, many of these migrant workers build the city's infrastructure, maintain middle- and upper-class households through domestic work, or produce garments for export, which, in turn, realise much sought-after foreign exchange. Rather than surplus, they are an undeniable foundation upon which India's booming economy rests.

In sum, the neoliberal regime is marked by a highly uneven growth model which has no means to tackle the chronic crisis of social reproduction amongst India's masses. For most Indians, the chronic crisis of social reproduction is rooted in the convergence of the intersecting trends described above (Rao 2021; Rao and Vakulabharanam 2019). First, the agrarian crisis manifests in low agricultural growth rates, unviable cultivation for the masses of small and marginal farmers, and increased vulnerability to external shocks. Second, the agrarian crisis is paralleled by jobless growth and the informalisation of work in the manufacturing and services sectors, forestalling the opportunity for sustained employment and access to social security. Third, corporate-driven and state-backed grabbing of land and resources intensified the (indirect) displacement of vulnerable populations. Still, insufficient public social provisioning and welfare schemes were stalled in the name of austerity during the first decade and a half after liberalisation. Against this backdrop, the rise of microfinance as a form of debtfare became increasingly institutionalised.

Between State and Market Capture: The Foundations of India's Debtfare State

The uneven neoliberal growth model increased the demand for money (credit) amongst the rural masses due to an entrenched crisis of social reproduction, in which most households had chronically higher expenditures than their combined incomes (see Table 3). In this context, the group-based savings and credit model that was pioneered in different regions in the 1980s was incorporated by both state and market actors, creating a unique form of what Susanne Soederberg (2015) has described as neoliberal "debtfare state" (see Chapter 6). This emerging debtfare state also paved the way for the rise of commercialised and financialised microfinance in the 2000s, a topic we will discuss in the following section.

The first pillar of India's emerging debtfare state was the recognition and scaling of SHGs, linking them with the existing banking system. Based on earlier experiments with local credit management groups, NABARD set up the Self-Help Group Bank Linkage Programme (SHG-BLP) in 1992. The basic idea was to integrate the SHGs with commercial banks, reducing the latter's transaction costs for borrowing microloans in rural areas, by outsourcing a substantial part of the work in building trustworthy debt relations to the women's groups and the NGOs that promoted them (Rankin 2013; Wichterich 2017).[1] The group's regular interactions, savings, and disciplining were offered as creative forms of collateral to access a bulk loan from NABARD, which could be used freely according to their needs. This shift was part of a broader trend in the 1980s and 1990s, where development agencies and DFIs enthusiastically financed and promoted diverse forms of group lending, linking these

1 Theoretically, there were three possibilities of linkage: Banks could directly promote SHGs, NGOs acted as facilitator linking SHGs and banks, or NGOs acted as intermediaries lending money to the groups. In practice, only the latter two were used.

to the broader banking system (see Chapter 2).[2] Although the SHGs were no legal entity and did not have conventional collateral, the RBI supported this expansion by granting loans to respective groups as priority sector lending (Fernandez 2018; Nair 2015; Sriram 2018). Therefore, SHG members could either resort to intra-group lending based on their savings or avail of bank loans through the group once they had been successfully linked.

Initially, the expansion of SHGs was primarily driven by NGOs. However, by the end of the 1990s, the government had turned the SHG architecture into the backbone of its revamped rural development programme. The Swarnajayanti Gram Swarozgar Yojana (SGSY) merged and replaced numerous previous rural development schemes, including the IRDP, to provide subsidised loans to women's groups subject to ceiling per group or per capita.[3] Moreover, the programme integrated the creation and organisation of SHGs with district and local government bodies, cooperating with NGOs (many of whom were funded by foreign aid). This was strategically significant because it allowed central and federal states as well as local and international development agencies to use this decentral infrastructure to launch further development interventions (Nair 2015). It took more than a decade to link one million SHGs to commercial banks and credit cooperatives. However, in the new millennium, the outreach of the programme was exceptional, turning the SHG-BLP into the world's largest microfinance scheme. Two decades after its start, it reached almost 5 million SHGs, representing an estimated 70 million households across India (Tankha 2012).

However, the growth of groups was regionally very uneven and mostly concentrated in Southern states. Subsidised credit was not linked to capacity building on the ground, and about half of the groups never accessed a bank loan once (Sinha and Navin 2021). Therefore, the SGSY was reformed in 2011 under the National Rural Livelihood Mission (NRLM), which provided all SHGs who had documented regular group meetings, savings, intra-group borrowing and timely repayment with an incremental corpus of Rs. 10,000 – 15,000 to meet member's credit needs and catalyse further lending.[4] In 2022, there were about 7.67 million operative SHG accounts, arguably reaching around 142 million families across India. Together, these groups hold Rs. 470 billion (US$ 6 billion) in savings with commercial banks, RRBs and credit cooperatives, and access loans annually with a cumulative value of Rs. 1.511 billion

---

2 For instance, the German GTZ had pioneered a similar bank linkage programme in Indonesia at the end of the 1980s and the World Bank promoted such ideas in the World Development Report 1989 (Nair 2015).

3 The subsidy amounted to half of the project costs and was ceiled at Rs. 125,000 for entire SHGs or Rs. 10,000 per capita (Nair 2015, 9).

4 When it was launched in 2011, the NRLM had a budget for US$ 5 billion, of which US$ 1 billion came from a World Bank credit (World Bank 2011).

(US$ 19 billion) (Sriram et al. 2022).[5] The substantial gap between loans disbursed and savings indicates that the financial needs of SHG members are much higher than their accumulated savings (Sinha and Navin 2021, 38).

One of the main reasons why SHGs took off rapidly was that these loans were not attached to any purpose, there were no standardised repayment schedules, and groups could decide on the interest rates that members had to pay (Nair 2005; Sriram 2018). Although the SGSY translates into Golden Jubilee Village Self-Employment Scheme and the NRLM continues to emphasise self-employment as primary poverty alleviation strategy, it is well documented that most SHG loans, particularly amongst the lower classes are predominantly used for reproductive purposes, that is, to pay for food, home improvement (incl. sanitation, electricity, water supply), medicine, education, social functions, and for the repayment of other debts, while the share for business activities is comparatively small (Garikipati 2013; Guérin et al. 2015; Kabeer and Noponen 2005; Pattenden 2010; Rajasekhar, Manjula, and Suchitra 2017). In the context of the pervasive subsistence gap that most rural households face, both intra-group and publicly subsidised loans provide critical means to manage precarious livelihoods. Recognising the need for reproductive debts, the NRLM even has a Vulnerability Reduction Fund (VRF), which provides resources to SHG Federations at the village level to address food insecurity, unexpected health expenses or other emergencies. Since the central bank regulations did not consciously specify the purpose for lending, and most loans were taken to safeguard the household's social reproduction, reproductive debt essentially became qualified for the 40 per cent PSL quota that commercial banks had to fulfil.

Yet, even if used for income-generating activities, these loans by themselves hardly provided a successful strategy for substantially increasing household incomes for the masses. Average loan sizes for SHGs were usually between Rs. 2,000 and Rs. 4,000, hardly sufficient to invest in an enterprise (Mahajan 2005; Singh 2008). Moreover, intra-group lending was limited by meagre savings. In an interview with an NGO that used to organise Dalits into SHGs, a civil society activist reflects on one of the core contradictions of this intervention:

> "Many of the SHGs never took off because you can't be earning Rs. 2 and saving ten paisa, and you're going to create capital out of that – it never works. Every time they did some income-generating activities, they failed because of lack of capital, or someone would fall ill and then they would take more loans and go deeper into debt. After about ten to fifteen years, we realised that it was not working. Self-help groups, as a concept itself, was disempowering people. Because in their own mind,

5 A detailed assessment of the SGSY/NRLM, including its specificities and regional variation in implementation lies beyond the scope of this analysis. Instead, this section focuses on the general aspect that the promotion of SHGs has created a state-backed decentralised infrastructure for the rural masses to access reproductive debts.

> we were telling them if you save, you can come up. Which was not happening. While we were constantly reinforcing this idea that it is because of your lack of savings, and lack of being thrifty that you are going down." (CSA_4, Pos. 8)

Eventually, the NGO discontinued promoting SHGs and instead advocated for rights-based government welfare schemes and supporting the working poor in accessing respective programmes. The statement is indicative because it points to the fundamental dilemma of microfinance rhetoric and practice. Despite being advertised as having the potential for income generation lifting poor households out of poverty, the actual practice is one in which SHGs primarily add another creditor source to manage reproductive debts without addressing any of the root causes that trap subaltern working-class households in a subordinate position. This finding is also true for the second key pillar of India's emerging debtfare state, which rose in the shadows of the first.

While some NGOs stopped the promotion of SHGs and instead focussed on rights-based campaigns centred around economic and social participation, others used the SHG-BLP to become professional financial intermediaries, often with support from international DFI and donor agencies. These so-called NGO-MFIs were specialised institutions that still built on women's groups but used them exclusively as joint-liability groups (JLGs), which, following the Grameen model, would ensure regular and timely repayment. Thus, the emerging MFIs in the late 1990s, though mostly registered as non-profit organisations or new forms of cooperatives, were external debt agencies which decided the loan size and repayment schedules, following a credit-driven rather than savings-led approach (Fernandez 2018; Nair 2015; Sriram 2018). Importantly, they rode on the legitimacy and outreach of the SHG model (Roy 2018; Shah, Rao, and Shankar 2007). Although growing fast, their operations were regionally confined and mostly concentrated in Southern states, particularly Andhra Pradesh.[6]

In Chapter 2, we discussed how publicly subsidised group lending became increasingly under attack from proponents of a financial system's approach, maintaining that group-based lending must be profitable, with market interest rates and strict repayment schedule, and how the Grameen model provided an avenue to do so. Only then could microcredits become successfully integrated into the rhythms of the banking system and financial markets. This was no different in India. At the turn of the millennium, many MFIs had turned into noticeable financial institutions with significant loan books, despite having no equity and still being registered as non-profit organisations. Therefore, many started to create separate entities that would

6 Examples include Basix, Swayam Krushi Sangham (later SKS Microfinance), Spandana (later Spandana Spoorthy Financial Services Limited), Share (later Share Microfin Limited), and Asmitha Microfin Limited.

focus exclusively on poverty finance (Sririam and Upadhyayula 2004). Meanwhile, a broad coalition of government institutions, international DFIs and private commercial banks in India urged the NGO-MFIs to transform into profit-driven financial institutions, continuing their lending at market rates.[7] Hence, most are registered as Non-Bank Financial Corporation (NBFC), which would not allow them to deal with deposits but continue lending.

In essence, the twin pillars of the emerging debtfare state depoliticised the SHGs, instrumentalising women's groups primarily as an extended arm of rural development and welfare and as a source of profitable lending in the name of empowerment and poverty eradication (Pattenden 2010). An NGO worker describes the narrowing of most SHGs through the rise of increasingly commercial MFIs as follows:

> "I'm familiar with the labour rights and human rights sector since the 1980s, and the one trend that I have seen between the 80s and 90s, was a shift from self-help groups to microfinance groups. The SHGs as a model itself changed. Before, NGOs established these groups in an area because they were fighting a particular issue, it may be a land issue, caste issue, or an ethnic issue. Then you start getting organised and you have people, Sanghas, in each village and you dealt with many issues. And because the cash flow with women was very minimal, and along with gender-based violence, they also started saving, and add one more layer of security. SHGs dealt with a lot of different local issues, and they were a safe space for women to come together, discuss issues, and deal with everything. Saving money was added as a layer much later in the process. Whereas, the microfinance model depends on a very quick expansion. You need to add a lot of people quickly, to add value. Then the process is not a priority. It's the credit and debt. If you look at any of the microfinance units, they will have 20 books, tracking the money, but they have not a single book looking at gender violence, health of women, or other things." (CSA_2, Pos. 22)

The increasing shift of women's groups from ambiguous political entities to debt management circles should, however, not be conflated with the exclusive dominance of the JLG model. I suggested understanding the state-promoted rise of SHGs and the capital-induced growth of the JLG model as twin pillars of India's emerging debtfare state. Doing so acknowledges three critical points. Firstly, in the wake of the neoliberal transformation, the scaling of a state-subsidised group model provided the crucial conditions upon which the market-led model could flourish (CSA_11, Pos. 49). In many cases, SHGs are also JLGs or women move

7 The Small Industries Development Bank of India (SIDBI) was a prominent advocate for this and received support from international DFIs like UK's DIFD and the German KfW, and ICICI Bank (Nair 2015; Roy 2018).

from one to the other. Secondly, though different in terms of group governance, loan size, and repayment schedules, both types of loans are pooled into the same household economy, and it is common to use SHG loans to repay MFIs (Guérin et al. 2015; Sinha and Navin 2021). The subsidised and less coercive borrowing through SHGs, with overall higher delinquency rates and losses on parts of the public banks involved, also subsidises the for-profit model indirectly. Finally, both pillars are a crucial means to safeguard the reproduction of India's subaltern working class. To explore this latter point in more detail, the following section will outline how the rise of microfinance is rooted in the financialisation of the pervasive subsistence gap amongst the Indian masses.

Financialising the Subsistence Gap

Based on the neoliberal reforms and state-backed expansion of a nationwide SHG infrastructure, MFIs have experienced exponential growth since the mid-2000s. Between 2006 and 2016, the average active borrower grew more than eightfold from below 5 million to nearly 40 million (see Figure 10). The commercialisation and financialisation of the group-lending model were crucial for this success (Kar 2018; Mader 2015; Sriram 2010; Taylor 2012; Wichterich 2017). The NGO-MFIs turned to for-profit companies to expand their business, which could more easily attract funding from the banking system and financial markets. However, high growth rates and profitability are a prerequisite to attract equity capital and favourable conditions for loans from banks and other financial institutions. Hence, this transformation meant adopting business management techniques to focus exclusively on financial performance, introducing digital technology to bring transaction costs down, and scaling and diversifying lending portfolios to become an attractive asset class (Mader 2015; Nair 2015; Roy 2018). As discussed in Part I, microfinance portfolios in India and other parts of the world increasingly became an autonomously valued asset through securitisation because repayment rates had proven to be high and stable, portfolios of small-size loans were diversified, and there was a low correlation with other asset classes (see also MFI_5, Pos. 55–57). Of roughly US$ 15.4 billion loaned to microfinance customers in India in 2017, less than one per cent came from non-profit NGOs (Sririam 2017). These trends speak to the productivity of fictitious capital (M-M') under finance-dominated accumulation (see Chapter 5).

Figure 10: Average Active MFI Borrowers in India, 1999 – 2019, in Million

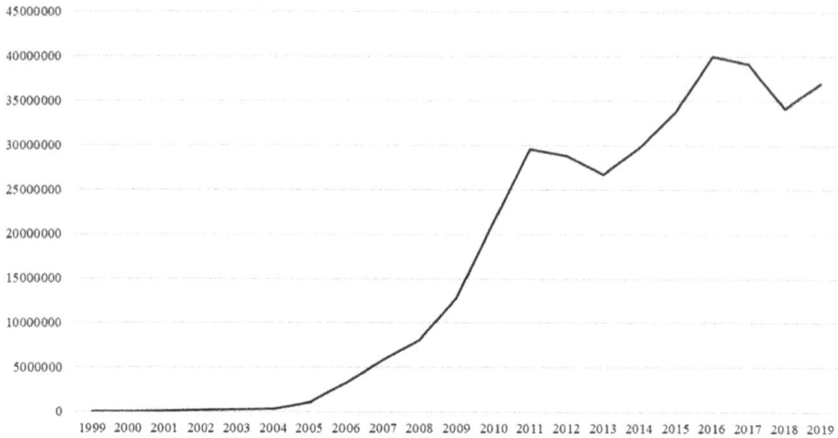

Source: MIX Market.

The first time the exponential growth was hampered was after a home-made crisis in Andhra Pradesh.[8] The aggressive growth of for-profit MFIs was regionally concentrated, completely unregulated by the RBI and feverishly supported by DFIs and institutional investors, ultimately leading to a Ponzi scheme with multiple institutions borrowing from the same household, often at ridiculously high interest rates (Mader 2015; Taylor 2012; Wichterich 2012). While the dynamics of the crisis and its causes, including the reckless expansion, usurious interest rates, coercive recovery methods, and lack of regulation, are well described in these studies, there is one aspect which has received far less attention. That is the systemic role of reproductive debts in the growth dynamic of commercialised and financialised microfinance, both before and after the Andhra crisis.

As will be argued below, a new generation of NBFC-MFIs strategically banked on the pervasive crisis of social reproduction, and, contrary to widespread interpretations, the sector's regulation after the Andhra crisis has contributed to normalising and institutionalising this trend. To substantiate this argument, a closer look at

8 The second crisis followed, Demonetisation the ad-hoc decision of Prime Minister Narendra Modi to demonetise all Rs. 500 and Rs. 1000 banknotes in early November 2016, allegedly to counter corruption, reduce illicit financial flows and promote cashless transactions. It affected the informal economy adversely, and can rather be seen as another strategy to push for financialisation (Chandrasekhar and Ghosh 2017). The third is not visible in the chart. More recently the COVID-19 pandemic (2020 – 2022) and related lockdown measures affected the informal economy and, particularly, migrant workers adversely, also impacting the MFI sector. These two episodes cannot be discussed here at length, but both will be touched upon briefly in the following chapter.

the debt relations around the crisis is necessary. A 2010 study commissioned and published by IFMR Capital provides intriguing insights on this issue. IFMR Capital (now Northern Arc Capital) was set up in 2008 as a specialised institution mediating between NBFC-MFIs and global institutional investors as well as DFIs through, for example, facilitating securitisation deals. The company will likely be the country's largest structured finance company specialised in microfinance and a critical backbone of market-based poverty finance.

The study is not only indicative because of the company's privileged position. It was also taken up by the RBI and the so-called Malegam Committee responsible for drafting regulations for MFIs after the crisis. Until the Andhra crisis, the RBI trusted in the self-regulation of the sector and did not provide any specific regulations.[9] The committee recommended creating a separate category for MFIs (the NBFC-MFIs), which would come under the supervision of the RBI. These for-profit companies would be defined by offering small short-term loans (1–2 years) without collateral to poor households. To address usurious practices, the committee further suggested to cap interest rates and fees, though leaving a margin of between 10 and 12 per cent depending on the size of the MFI. Hence, MFIs could borrow credit at 12 per cent from commercial banks and on-lend this at 24 per cent to their customers. Moreover, three-quarters of the company's portfolio was to be given as income-generating loans. This latter point was justified on drawing on the aforementioned study, which provided ample evidence that income-generating loans hardly played a significant role in MFI/SHG lending in Andhra Pradesh.

Table 4 is based on the data from the IFMR Capital study. It provides an overview of loan utilisation across various creditor institutions. Three observations are particularly relevant to the present investigation. First, the data illustrates the pervasiveness of reproductive debts, that is, loans used for consumption (food, water, cloths, consumer durables), health, education, home improvement (incl. sanitation, electricity), and social functions, which form the backbone of demand for credit, especially amongst MFIs, SHGs, and the broad category of informal sources. This also links up with findings from the SHG-BLP discussed above and other studies (Guérin et al. 2015; Young 2010a). Of course, there are notable differences within this general observation, pointing towards a certain division of labour amongst creditor institutions from the perspective of borrowers. For instance, in case of health emergencies, it might be easier to acquire loans from informal sources or intra-group lending of SHGs than from MFIs or banks. Moreover, acquiring loans to repay other debts is an important dimension of microfinance, especially for SHGs and MFIs. An estimated 84 per cent of rural households had two or more loans outstanding (Johnson and

9 Anticipating the necessity for a more structured and transparent framework to secure the viability of poverty finance, some MFIs started to organise before the crisis, for example, the Association for Karnataka Microfinance Institutions (AKMi).

Meka 2010). This finding may point to over-indebtedness, as was clearly the case in Andhra Pradesh (Mader 2015; Taylor 2012; Wichterich 2012). However, it may also indicate the necessity for juggling different types and sources of reproductive debts (Guérin 2014), a phenomenon we will engage with in more detail in the following chapter.

Table 4: Prevalence of Reproductive Debts Across Creditor Institutions, 2010 in %

	Banks	MFI	SHG	Informal*
(Potentially) Income Generating	66	32	31	26
Consumption	27	32	50	25
Repayment of old debt	15	25	20	7
Health	11	11	19	25
Home improvement	10	22	13	14
Social functions (marriages, deaths, festivals)	5	9	7	19
Education	4	4	6	5
Other	2	2	3	2

Source: Johnson and Mekha (2010). Based on 1920 households in 64 villages across 8 districts of Andhra Pradesh. Note: Shares might add up to more than 100% as loans may be used for multiple purposes. *Includes moneylenders, landlords, employers, and friends.[10]

Second, Table 4 debunks the myth of income-generating loans as the primary purpose of SHG/MFI lending. It may be argued that this is different for credit from banks (incl. RRBs and cooperatives), since income generation is the primary use of such loans. Yet, this category requires further qualification. Almost all of these loans are used to buy agricultural inputs, with only a minor share borrowed to purchase stock, livestock, or to start a new business. In fact, the share of loans used for new businesses is between one and three per cent, with purchases for agricultural inputs dominating the category across all creditor institutions. Considering the previous explorations of highly uneven landownership and the increased commercialisation of agriculture, we can understand borrowing for agricultural input as an ambiguous strategy, which may backfire, especially for small and marginal farmers.

10 The table is not representative for the entire country, because it focuses only on Andhra Pradesh. But given the fact that this was the most vibrant state, heading the way for rapid growth of MFIs, it can speak to a broader trend. This is especially the case, because many of the key findings emphasised below are also found in other regional studies.

Buying agricultural inputs, like HYV seeds, fertilisers, and pesticides, may increase productivity at the expense of adverse ecological consequences, but only under certain conditions. The bulk of small and marginal farmers stand to lose out from such investments, especially if they cannot safeguard stable irrigation, lack capacities to market their produce, and remain dependent on middlemen. It is no coincidence that the epidemic of farmer suicides in neoliberal India is rooted in over-indebtedness with various creditors due to agricultural inputs.[11] According to official numbers, between 1995 and 2012, nearly 300,000 farmers, overwhelmingly low-caste small and marginal landholders, committed suicide, with most of these cases occurring in the semi-arid zone in the southern and central parts of India (Basu, Das, and Misra 2016; Dandekar 2016; Nagaraj et al. 2014; Vasavi 2009). Against this backdrop, it seems reasonable to categorise loans for agricultural inputs amongst small and marginal farmers as potentially income-generating at best. For clarity, credit for agri-inputs is not reproductive debt in a strict sense. Yet, as the table clearly shows, they cannot be separated from the remaining household economy and the pervasive subsistence crisis.

Third, of course, access to creditors is not distributed evenly. The share of reproductive debts and the share of borrowing from generally more exploitative creditors is clearly segmented by class. Basole and Basu (2011a) argue that effectively landless households across India used nearly 60 per cent of outstanding loans exclusively for consumption purposes, whereas this figure was as low as 20 per cent for middle and large farmers (see also Guérin et al. 2015; Pattenden 2010). Therefore, it may not be a surprise that the incidence of indebtedness in rural households was highest for the broad category of informal sources (82%), followed by SHGs (54%), commercial, regional rural and cooperative banks (38%) and MFIs (11%) (Johnson and Meka 2010). This finding also indicates that despite massive growth, there was still substantial potential in 2010 to further expand the frontiers of commercialised and financialised microfinance. This is even more the case at the country-level, since the data refers to the state with the highest density of MFIs.

The pervasiveness of reproductive debts is no particularity of the Andhra crisis. Rather, banking on reproductive debt has been the main driver of the microfinance growth miracle. This can be illustrated by looking at the practices of the third generation of MFIs that started out in the mid-2000s as profit-driven NBFC-MFIs and underlined the sector's exponential growth. In Chapter 5, we explored how finance capital tends to speed up the process of capital accumulation, increasing the tendency for market concentration and monopolisation. This is evident in the case of Indian microfinance. Though only founded in the mid-2000s, Janalakshmi and

11 Of course, these suicides cannot be reduced to a single factor, but chronic indebtedness is mentioned in most studies as vital explanation for this systemic phenomenon (Basu, Das, and Misra 2016; Dandekar 2016; Nagaraj et al. 2014; Vasavi 2009).

Ujjivan served 5.5 million customers out of 40 million in 2016 (Sa-Dhan 2016). Both founders, Ramesh Ramanathan and Samit Ghosh, had previously worked for years in leading positions of investment banking at Citigroup, amongst others. Their contacts, reputation, and experiences from this career as investment bankers helped to scale for-profit microfinance, inter alia in acquiring initial equity from international investors (Roy 2018).

Both adopted the credit-driven model of joint-liability groups with two notable changes. First, they primarily focused on the urban working poor as a rapidly growing target segment, starting from the slums of Bengaluru. This strategy seemed to recognise that with the devastating consequences of the uneven neoliberal growth model on the rural masses, the number of migrant workers in search of a livelihood in the Indian metropolis rose drastically. One of the strategies to successfully engage with the working poor in urban areas was the creation of a separate non-profit NGO (Parinaam and Jana Urban Foundation) that would work in the slums of the city, surveying the living conditions, preparing customers through financial literacy workshops, and building trust amongst respective communities through other interventions (Roy 2018, 103ff.). Second, both recognised that scaling financialised microfinance would only be possible by surpassing the focus on income-generating activities. Instead they enthusiastically embraced reproductive debts as profitable business case. In an interview, Samit Ghosh confirmed that it "[...] is somewhat of a myth, that microfinance is only for income-generating loans", explaining the success of his company as follows: "Typically, microlenders want their funds to be used for income-generating activities and will only lend to self-employed women. Ujjivan, though, lent to salaried urban workers too, even extending credit for children's school fees or medical expenses, provided the borrower had the capacity to make repayments" (Kazim 2018). Within less than a decade, Ujjivan had three million customers across India and went public with an IPO that was oversubscribed 41 times (Sririam 2017, 126).

While the second-generation MFIs (Basix, SKS, Spandana) had moved from non-profit to for-profit MFIs, the third generation (Ujjivan, Janalakshmi, Equitas) started out as for-profit NBFC-MFIs with close ties to transnational finance capital, creating non-profit NGOs to facilitate profitable lending in urban slums. From the beginning, reproductive debts were crucial to their business model, and this continues to be the case. As an industry insider remarks: The "next big thing is healthcare and housing, both are very necessary, huge demand and Parinaam has already worked as a tester in this field" (CSA_10, Pos. 46). Ujjivan's focus on reproductive debts is not unique. Most corporate MFIs offer loans for home improvement, sanitation, health, and education. From the systemic perspective of regimes of re/productive finance, this is not a "mission drift" (Kulkarni 2017), as some have suggested. Instead, it emphasises corporate MFI's strategic engagement with the pervasive subsistence crisis that India's subaltern working class faces.

The previous sections have shown how India's neoliberal transformation was associated with a highly uneven growth model, providing no sustainable livelihoods for the subaltern working class, which, despite pooling different livelihood strategies into the household economy, could not accrue sufficient income to make ends meet. It is these insecure working-poor households that have turned into the key market segment for commercial microfinance. Of the 1.2 billion people living in India in 2010, roughly 820 million can be considered as part of the poor and vulnerable population, while 380 million have middle and high incomes (George and Sinha 2017; Kannan 2017, 271). A KPMG study on the potential growth market of microfinance argues that commercial financial institutions could reach around 169 million households in India (Figure 11). Assuming an average household size of four, this figure almost exactly matches the 820 million who, due to lack of landownership, precarious employment opportunities, and insufficient access to social security, can be considered in a poor or economically vulnerable position with one exception. The most impoverished (rural) households, that is, the bottom quarter of India's poor and vulnerable population, are considered to be no reasonable business case.

Figure 11: The Potential for Commercial Microfinance in India, 2018

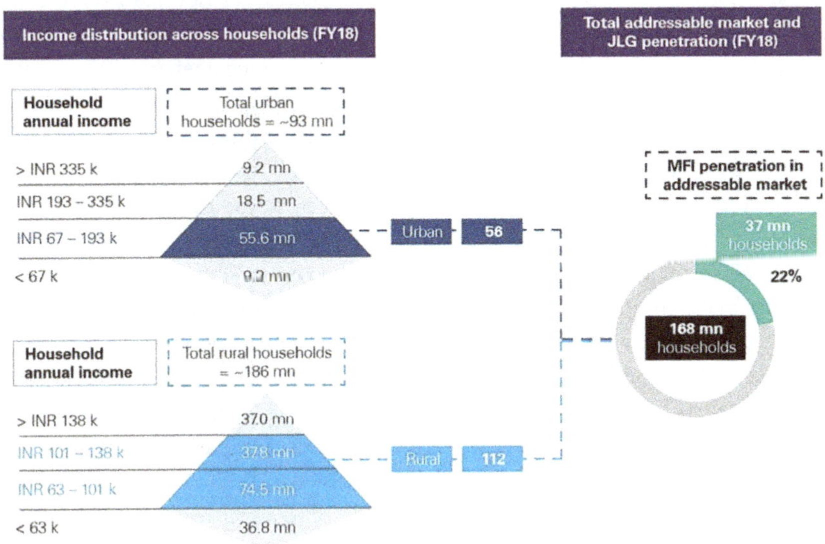

Source: KPMG (2018).

About two-thirds of this potential is in rural areas, whereas one-third is estimated to come from urban areas. This is remarkable since the distribution of poor and vulnerable households is more unevenly concentrated in rural areas. However, the assessment may reflect the increasing trends of distress-driven rural-urban migration, whether circular, seasonal or steady. The business models of third-generation MFIs, like Ujjivan and Janalakshmi, who consciously started from the slums of a metropolis, may underline this reasoning. The mass of rural-urban migrants who work as precarious (daily) wage labourers would live in a household with a total monthly income between Rs. 5.500 – Rs. 16.000, which exactly matches the envisaged market segment for commercial microfinance (see Part IV). Focussing on this group is a sensible business case for financial capital for at least two reasons: First, wages in urban areas are generally higher, potentially allowing for more secure returns. At the same time, the demand for money is also considerably higher in urban areas. The contemporary uneven and jobless growth model exacerbates this demand at the lower ranks through increased privatisation and financialisation of social infrastructure, like housing, health care and education. Taking into account these actual (rising) household expenditures, Bhattacharya (2015) argues that the poverty ratio in India would be as high as 76 per cent for urban and 90 per cent for rural areas. Second, with the cumulating agrarian crisis, rural-urban migration is likely to grow in the future: "All of these metropolises are also migration magnates. It's not like I serve a million people, and I have reached my agenda. Because by the time I have that number, 100,000 new people will have arrived. So that's an ongoing agenda." (CSA_11, Pos. 60). Of course, borrowing is not limited to precarious migrant workers and demographic pressures also feed into this dynamic, but establishing this link is important for the investigation following in Part IV.

In concluding this section, let us briefly return to the thesis that regulating the MFI sector has contributed to normalising and institutionalising reproductive debts. While the cap on interest rates and borrowing might initially seem like a setback, many companies endorsed the regulations because they helped set transparent standards, avoiding instability and high volatility while allowing substantial manoeuvre for profits.[12] The declaration of lending 75 per cent for income-generating loans has been shown to be nothing but lip service to maintain the discourse of entrepreneurial microfinance. The RBI has no means, capacities, and ambitions to check up on the loan utilisation of this vast sector. As the case of Ujjivan and Janalakshmi has shown, the rapid growth of commercialised and financialised microfinance since the 2000s has been achieved by strategically moving beyond

12 Under the new regulations, NBFC-MFIs could, for example, borrow money at 12 per cent p.a. from commercial banks, and lend this money to working-class households at 24 per cent p.a. For commercial banks this is also a good deal, since borrowing to MFIs falls under the 40 per cent PSL quota they must fulfil.

the focus of income-generating loans in rural areas to embracing the relevance of reproductive debts for India's vast subaltern working-class. The practice of for-profit reproductive debt has not only become normalised by the regulations. Since the mid-2010s, the largest NBFC-MFIs have become incorporated into the banking system through merger and acquisition by granting them a proper banking license or turning into a new type of Small Finance Banks (SFBs), as is the case with Ujjivan and Janalakshmi.

Finally, the coercive repayment methods, rooted in disciplining women's groups through peer pressure and shame, have never been seriously challenged by the regulations and continue to form the basis for the for-profit business model. As an industry insider put it: "From a crude form of coercion [moneylenders], we have come to a more sophisticated form of coercion [MFIs]. That is the basic paradigm shift. Otherwise, there's nothing." (CSA_11, Pos. 66). Although there is much talk of "keeping the human touch" (KPMG 2018), the coercive nature of practices is rooted in the rhythms of fictitious capital accumulation which care little for people's subsistence crisis:

> "If it [microfinance] was supposed to make women less insecure, it only looked at the banking part of it. And delineating everything else as something that added inefficiency to the system. Because if you start relating to people's crises, you can't enforce repayment. You can't write off loans. You can't even support them for a long enough time so that it becomes sustainable. So, the type of transactions changed quite a bit. In many places, it's just a post-work kind of support system, where people come and drop off the money at a point, you don't even meet as a group." (CSA_2, Pos. 24)

Significantly, the more sophisticated forms of coercion do not necessarily replace the crude forms. As was shown above, multiple borrowing is frequent and meeting the strict repayment schedules of MFIs – which have zero tolerance for default – often requires borrowing from moneylenders or other sources. In other words, multiple debts and degrees of exploitation and dependency build on the fragmentation and segmentation of India's subaltern working class and converge in the household economy. This is particularly visible in the case of health care.

Healthy Profits: The Contradictions of India's Debtfare State

In the early 2000s, the enthusiasm for neoliberal reforms amongst India's political and economic elites and the urban middle classes was embittered by deteriorating living standards and widespread discontent amongst the rural masses. At the end of the 2000s, the Naxalite insurgencies stretched over 180 out of 640 districts across ten states of India, accounting for about 40 per cent of India's landmass (Das 2010). With increasing support of the impoverished masses, the Maoists' strategy of worker-peasant alliances to overthrow the power of landed classes, post-colonial state bureaucracy, and corporate capital through armed revolutionary struggle was increasingly framed as the 'single biggest national security threat' (Sundar 2011). Accordingly, the Government of India responded with harsh repression and militarisation of respective regions (Chandra 2014; Parashar 2019). Meanwhile, diverse social movements and civil society organisations have launched campaigns against the widespread exclusion of rural and urban poor from India's growth model (Roy 2023). The INC, which had been at the helm of neoliberal policies in the early 1990s and had to give in to the Hindu-Nationalist BJP in the 1999 elections, launched an effective electoral campaign in 2004, picking up widespread unrest promising to merge economic growth and social justice.

Together with smaller left parties, The United Progressive Alliance (UPA) introduced several significant welfare schemes between 2004 and 2014. Thus, in contrast to the experiences in core capitalist countries, neoliberalisation in India has been accompanied by the expansion rather than retrenchment of welfare services since the mid-2000s. The government scaled up existing schemes and turned them into a right for the impoverished masses, including the extension of primary education and mid-day meals in schools, the strengthening of PDS as apex food security infrastructure, the expansion of primary health care in rural areas and health insurance for informal workers, and employment guarantee securing 100 days paid public work for unemployed rural workers.[13] This resurgence in popular social welfare policies has led some observers to attest India's democracy is a "quiet revolution" based on the successful "politics of the poor" (Roy 2023).

Undoubtedly, the increase in welfare policies has made a difference in the lives of millions of Indians. However, what is far less clear is how these schemes have ameliorated the entrenched subsistence crisis amongst India's subaltern working class. Critiques have pointed out that the resurgence in welfare policies was almost exclusively focused on prioritising social protection while ignoring the dismal condition of social provisioning of basic services (Kannan and Breman 2013; Kapur and Nangia 2015). Moreover, despite the substantial allocation of budgetary sources, the implementation of these schemes is still prone to elite capture because none of them has addressed the underlying problems of massive wealth inequalities, including skewed land ownership (Corbridge and Srivastava 2013). Finally, these schemes

13 These schemes were grounded in the National Rural Health Mission (2005), Mahatma Gandhi National Rural Employment Guarantee Act (2005), Unorganized Workers Social Security Act (2008), Right to Education Act (2009), and National Food Security Act (2013). This list is not comprehensive but comprises only the flagship schemes which are amongst the largest in the world in terms of outreach.

seemed to follow a strategy of "welfare without work or wages" (RoyChowdhury 2018).[14] This section does not aspire to give a comprehensive overview, let alone an assessment of India's emerging welfare state and its effects on the working poor.[15] Instead, it traces some of the core contradictions of the contemporary regime of re/productive finance by demonstrating how welfare schemes intersect with reproductive loans, without providing any means to escape chronic indebtedness. This is particularly visible in the health care sector which serves as illustrative case for India's contemporary debtfare state.

In Chapter 2, we discussed the intimate connection between sovereign debts, neoliberal SAPs, and the push for market-based finance both at the state and household level. Since the late 1980s, the World Bank has pushed for the privatisation of health care in the global South as part of the SAPs. The World Development Report 1993 *Investing in Health* urged governments to bet on households' responsibility, foster the role of private sector service providers, and reduce public health expenditure as part of fiscal adjustment (Nuruzzaman 2007). Following the neoliberal reforms, India's already low government expenditure in health care almost halved between the mid-1980s and mid-1990s, from 1.5 to 0.7 per cent of GDP (Duggal and Jadhav 2018). In the years following liberalisation, between 1992 and 1993, the budget allocation to health care was slashed by 20 per cent (Nambiar et al. 2014, 32). The consequences of outsourcing risks and responsibilities to households in the form of user charges are catastrophic, especially for low-income households. As the World Health Organization (WHO) recognises, lower government spending in health care is associated with higher out-of-pocket spending (OOPS), that is, expenditure for diagnosis or medicine patients have to pay directly upon treatment (World Health Organization 2022, 6).[16]

By the mid-2000s, more than three-quarters of total health expenditure in India came from OOPS (Berman, Ahuja, and Bhandari 2010). This leads to a contradictory dynamic of inclusion and exclusion. On the one hand, user charges for diagnostics and medicine lead to the exclusion of those households that are unable to pay. In urban areas, about 20 per cent of untreated illness episodes remain unattended because of financial constraints (Shahrawat and Rao 2012, 218). On the other hand, borrowing money turns into a vital coping mechanism to access healthcare for households without sufficient incomes and savings. In rural areas, almost 14 per cent of all

14 This claim can even be uphold in the case of MGNREGA, because daily wage rates paid for public work in Karnataka and many other states are below those of daily wage labourers in agriculture, resulting in employment below minimum subsistence (RoyChowdhury 2018, 57).

15 For such assessments, see e.g. Kannan and Breman (2013), Dreze and Khera (2017).

16 In almost all countries where government expenditure on healthcare accounts for more than 6 per cent of GDP, the OOPS are below 20 per cent of total health spending. In contrast, in countries with public investment of less than 2 per cent of GDP, the OOPs are considerably higher, in some cases up to 80 per cent.

households met OOPS *exclusively* through borrowing, and in urban areas, the number was estimated at just below 10 per cent (Flores et al. 2008, 1401). It can hardly be a surprise that this dynamic is experienced unevenly across classes. For the lowest income quartile, borrowing was the most prevalent financial coping mechanism in both rural and urban areas, while savings were only second, and sale of assets third. Consequently, studies estimated that up to 40 million people in India are pushed into poverty due to health payments annually (Shahrawat and Rao 2012, 214). The affirmative literature on financial inclusion acknowledges financial vulnerability as a chronic feature of significant shares of the population in the global South. However, it primarily takes this vulnerability as given without scrutinising how the privatisation and financialisation of D/development have significantly deepened this vulnerability (see Chapter 1).

The World Bank has been much more than just an initial trigger for the privatisation of health care. The Bank's IFC has been crucial for investing and facilitating public-private partnerships across the global South. More than a quarter of the IFC's global health budget is invested in India. Between 1997 and 2022, the IFC pumped US$ 523 million into private hospitals and clinics, supporting some of India's biggest corporate hospital chains (Taneja and Sarkar 2023). Ironically, these are primarily high-end urban hospitals out of reach for most Indians.[17] Since the 2010s, there is a significant increase in (private) equity investment in India's booming privatised healthcare system, testifying to the potency of market-based finance. Major DFIs, like the IFC, UK's Commonwealth Development Corporation (CDC) or the German KfW/DEG, and large institutional investors increasingly bought shares or acquired private healthcare providers (Chakravarthi et al. 2017, 52). In 2023, the hospital industry, which accounts for the largest share of the total healthcare market, was valued at US$ 132 billion and is expected to grow significantly in the coming years (Taneja and Sarkar 2023). The financialisation of public provisioning, such as health care, creates the conditions for a market in which financial services like credit and insurance seem reasonable interventions to support low-income households.

The privatisation of India's healthcare system was paralleled by the realisation amongst commercial MFIs that loans beyond income-generating schemes were necessary to deepen market penetration and to bank on the reproductive needs of working-class households. Consequently, many MFIs started offering health and emergency loans or water and sanitation loans (see above). Borrowing for OOPS was already frequent. However, most of this lending happened in the informal sphere, particularly borrowing from friends and family, but also from moneylenders or employ-

17 Often these projects are also state backed, with governments granting land for the development of health facilities for free or minimal costs, demanding the private service providers to attend to the local poor. However, reports show that such agreements are regularly violated (Taneja and Sarkar 2023).

ers (Berman, Ahuja, and Bhandari 2010; Flores et al. 2008). The World Bank's Global Findex database shows the vast potential of reproductive debt in India, grounded in financial vulnerability that has been exacerbated through neoliberal policies. Currently, more than half of all adults in India are very worried about not having enough money for monthly expenses, education, medical costs, and old age (see Figure 12). Health care stands out since almost two-thirds of all adults stated they were very worried about not being able to cover costs, that is, OOPS, in case of illness or accidents.

Figure 12: Financial Vulnerability in India, 2021

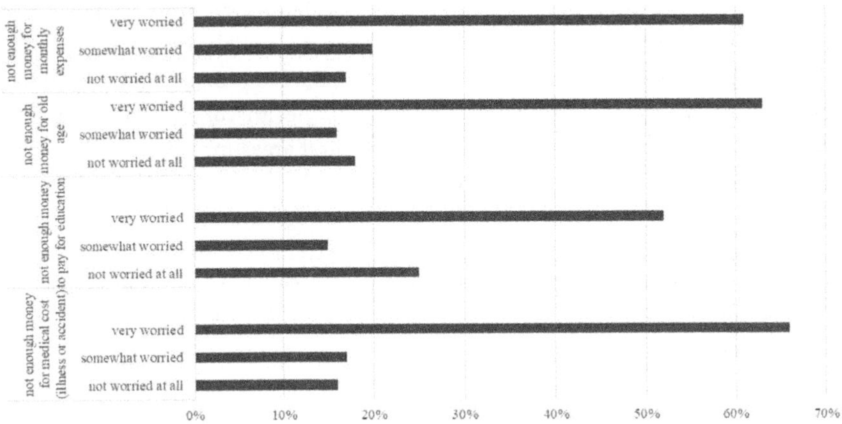

Source: Global Findex Database.

Of course, the cumulating health crisis has not remained unnoticed by policymakers. Amongst other initiatives, various state governments have initiated publicly financed health insurance schemes for the poor since the mid-2000s.[18] Following the Unorganised Workers Social Security Act, the UPA government introduced a national health insurance programme in 2008. The Rashtriya Swasthya Bima Yojana (RSBY) covers hospitalisation costs for BPL families in the unorganised

18 In this context, it is important to highlight the uneven public provisioning of health care amongst states. The average public per capita expenditure in India is only about Rs 1,500 per year (2017–2018). However, some smaller states spend between Rs 4,000 – Rs. 7,000 per capita, including Arunachal, Sikkim, Goa, and Mizoram, contributing to robust health indicators and strong primary health-care services. In Mizoram, for example, there is practically universal public health care, without user charges and private sector firms. (Duggal and Jadhav 2018). However, three quarters India's population lives in only ten out of 26 states, and all these have public per capita expenditure below the national average, many even below 1,000 per capita (Duggal 2017).

sector up to Rs. 30,000 annually.[19] The central government would pay three-quarters of an annual premium of Rs. 750 per household, while state governments matched this sum with the remaining 25 per cent. Although the programme is envisioned to reach all families below the poverty line (BPL) by 2012, the official number more than a decade after the programme started is that about half were reached. However, other estimates that the actual outreach is significantly lower because private service providers have created bogus beneficiaries to earn the premium subsidy from governments, and about half of the enrolled households do not belong to the BPL category (Ghosh 2018). Moreover, the general government health expenditure has only nominally increased but remained between 1 and 1.5 per cent of GDP between 2000 and 2020. Increased resources, however, are not necessarily used as social means. Especially the centre's funds are often geared towards the promotion of public-private partnerships and special programmes for public employees and formal sector workers (Gupta and Chowdhury 2014; Sundararaman, Mukhopadhyay, and Muraleedharan 2016). Meanwhile, India's public health workers, predominantly women, are sustaining primary health care in rural areas for payment below the legal minimum wage (Sathi 2023; Sreerekha 2017).

Perhaps most importantly, many studies have argued that a publicly financed health insurance scheme in a healthcare delivery system which is dominated by private profit-oriented providers is inherently contradictory and has "failed to address the issue of access and financial risk protection" (Ghosh 2018; Gupta and Chowdhury 2014; Shahrawat and Rao 2012). This is because the national health insurance scheme has not substantially reversed the high OOPS. RSBY/PMJAY covers costs for inpatient care, which can be very high and catastrophic for working-class households. However, the bulk of OOPS, about 82 per cent, stems from outpatient treatment and medicines which are not covered by public insurance (Shahrawat and Rao 2012, 216). For the increasing mass of urban poor, outpatient care for respiratory infections, skin problems, diarrhoea infections and nutrition-related health problems are a constant financial burden. Since public facilities often have limited hours open and workers need to take a day off to wait for treatment, many precarious wage workers prefer treatments in private hospitals (Nambiar et al. 2014; Sharma et al. 2020).

---

19 The NDA government has introduced the Pradhan Mantri Jan Aarogya Yojana (PMJAY) in 2018. Under the scheme, around 500 million Indians are eligible for cashless inpatient care in secondary and tertiary hospitalisation up to Rs. 500,000 per family annually. While the scheme certainly addresses the pressing issue of catastrophic health expenditure in cases of inpatient care, a few years after the introduction there are no signs of substantial financial risk protection for beneficiaries and a systemic review of studies points to similar issues to previous publicly financed health insurance schemes (Reshmi et al. 2021).

This case illustrates how the neoliberal drive for privatised and financialised health care creates the conditions in which demand for reproductive debts increases.[20] Hardly surprising, most working-class households, experiencing fluctuating incomes, absence of social security and overall, much higher exposure to various health risks related to adverse working and living conditions, face the fatal choice between non-treatment and indebtedness. Both demands for and access to such reproductive debt is gendered and racialised, with women, particularly from Dalit, Adivasi and other marginalised communities, being the worst affected. Together, these observations point to the systemic nature of structural violence associated with reproductive debts and India's contemporary debtfare state. The following part will engage with the livelihoods of migrant workers in Bengaluru to shed more light on the concrete dynamics involved. Before doing so, however, the following chapter will summarise the main insights of the review of the three regimes of re/productive finance in modern India.

20 Similar dynamics can be observed for other areas of social provisioning, including housing and education.

Chapter 12
Synopsis: A Systemic View on Re/Productive Finance

The previous chapters have outlined three distinct though interconnected regimes of re/productive finance. This synopsis discusses how this broader history helps us to comprehend the rapid rise of microfinance in recent decades and what this implies for the contemporary discourse on financial inclusion.

The analysis of the imperial regime of re/productive finance challenges the predominant understanding of financial exclusion as a given feature of countries in the global South. Instead, it reveals how exclusion from modern banking is a colonial legacy rooted in an imperial political economy of plunder, in which financial flows were consciously orchestrated to facilitate a drain of wealth. The rise of moneylenders and their unconstrained power during British rule was no coincidence. It was rooted in a class compromise in which the colonial administration extracted disproportionate land revenue from the peasantry without supporting their livelihoods, driving them into the hands of moneylenders (traders, landlords, wealthy farmers), who increasingly safeguarded their subsistence through chronic indebtedness, while simultaneously oppressing them. The colonial administration exacerbated the power of moneylenders not only by driving the agrarian inequality. It also refrained from regulating usurious moneylending and escalating land transfers (based on indebtedness), while the reformation of the judicial system along British lines, based on written contracts and debt records, generally guaranteed creditors the backing of state power. This constellation, which I have called the moneylender-state nexus, fundamentally questions the modern categories of formal/informal finance and inclusion/exclusion on which today's dominant development discourse rests.

Second, the history of India's unbanked is not only a matter of financial exclusion. Theirs is a shattered story of uneven capitalist development based on the fragmentation and segmentation of the subaltern classes and the dispossession, super-exploitation, and adverse incorporation into market-mediated social reproduction. Put differently, the demand for credit is rooted in a chronic subsistence crisis, fundamentally shaped by the broader political economy, including class-based, gendered and racialised stratification. As discussed in Part II, money's power as "second nature" (McNally 2011b, 147) is contingent upon the commodification of economic space. The subordination and integration of India into the British-centred world economy since the late eighteenth century significantly increased the demand for money through the enclosures of common land and forests, the commercialisation of agriculture, the payment of land taxes exclusively in cash, and a complete lack of government support, all of which were experienced unevenly amongst the subaltern population. Notably, chronic indebtedness was not only a result of this political economy of plunder but also a condition upon which the super-exploitation of indentured labourers on export-oriented plantations rested.

Figure 13: Overview of Regimes of Re/Productive Finance in Modern India

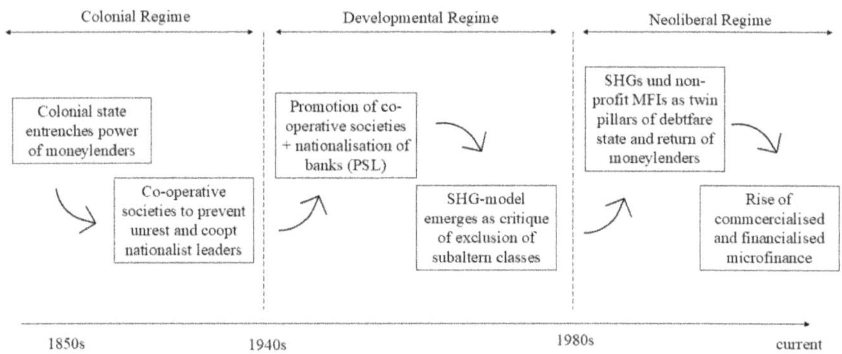

Source: own illustration.

The colonial political economy was not only based on plunder but also on the indirect racialised extinction in the form of devastating famines, which killed tens of millions of Indians during British rule. These and the entrenched subsistence crisis facilitated by the moneylender-state nexus called forth numerous powerful peasant insurgencies, which, towards the end of the nineteenth century, became increasingly organised by an emerging nationalist movement calling for independence. The introduction of credit cooperatives was a critical policy in pacifying unrest and coopting leaders of the nationalist movement. Still, despite impressive outreach within the early twentieth century, it never managed to replace the entrenched power of moneylenders and proved insufficient to contain the ascending anti-colonial mass movement. But, although the imperial regime of re/productive finance would be replaced in independent India, the new Congress-led government had to grapple with the colonial legacy.

The emergence of a developmental regime of re/productive finance paralleled the post-independence era. This era is significant for contemporary debates because it shows how the state has been the main driver for financial inclusion, substantially increasing the means for accessing credit in rural areas through the proliferation of credit cooperatives and, later, the nationalisation of banks, including quotas for lending to agriculture, small and medium enterprises. The state-directed political economy increased economic growth, built a diversified industrial base, and enhanced agricultural output and productivity, eventually achieving food self-sufficiency and overcoming the worst forms of famines that had marked the colonial era. Yet, from the perspective of subaltern classes, this era of social banking was highly ambiguous. It never challenged the roots of their subsistence crisis: the unequal land ownership and associated class inequalities, decent working conditions, employment opportunities beyond the agrarian economy, and a lack of social provisioning. Therefore, the significant extension of public rural credit through cooperatives and public banks largely benefitted the landlords, wealthy farmers and parts of the middle peasantry, leaving the mass of small and marginal peasants as well as landless labourers at the mercy of the landed classes, including moneylenders, and state bureaucrats.

The ambitious programmes for subsidised targeted credit for these excluded sections since the late 1970s already foreshadowed the critical contradiction of governing access to credit for subaltern classes. The scheme focussed almost exclusively on providing working capital for income-generating assets in the hope that the targeted populations could improve their livelihoods through business activities. As such, it resembled the logic of microfinance interventions and particularly the discourse of the entrepreneurial spirits of the poor. However, without permanent employment or social security, and within the context of entrenched class inequalities in the agrarian economy, subsidised public loans would simply add another source of reproductive debts to the household economy. Ultimately, these loans would fuse with the chronic indebtedness of subaltern classes with landlords, middlemen or other moneylenders, without providing the means for challenging their domination and exploitation. Meanwhile, numerous civil society organisations, backed by Western development agencies, proliferated and facilitated self-help groups of women, saving and borrowing small sums from each other. Notably, in contrast to the state-led approach to governing access to credit, these institutions recognised the relevance of reproductive debts for managing the subsistence crisis. However, rather than strategically organising and challenging the roots of this crisis, they focussed primarily on providing an alternative means for reproductive debt vis-à-vis the moneylenders, paving the way for the rise of microfinance.

The rise of commercialised and financialised microfinance in the neoliberal era since the 1990s has been the primary focus of most critical political economy literature. The regime analysis adds to this literature in many crucial ways. It demonstrates how this rise was contingent upon the state-backed infrastructure of the

SHG-BLP. The latter provided the organisation of millions of groups across the subcontinent and the public legitimacy on which the profit-driven model could rise. As a result, the NGO model of SHGs was incorporated by both the state and market, together producing the twin pillars of India's debtfare state. More importantly, corporate MFIs consciously emulated the SHG model's most tremendous success, providing reproductive debts for basic needs, education, health care or home improvement. In other words, they would financialise the subsistence gap by turning the problem-solving approach of NGOs into a vast market and attractive asset class. Significantly, the analysis of the neoliberal regime highlights how this strategy is not only a response to a pre-existing problem. Instead, the uneven jobless growth model of the neoliberal era and its focus on privatisation, liberalisation and financialisation creates the conditions in which reproductive debts emerge as a necessary survival mechanism for subaltern-working class households.

In contrast to the experiences of core capitalist countries, the financialisation of social reproduction in contemporary India is not linked to the retrenchment of the welfare state. The continuous rise of Naxalite peasant insurgencies, which challenged the power of land classes and the post-colonial state through guerrilla warfare and dominated a significant share of the Indian territory in the 2000s, has been a crucial background for the introduction of numerous welfare schemes on primary education, healthcare, public employment in rural areas, and food security. However, as shown in the case of health care, these welfare services perfectly integrate with market-based reproductive debt and fail to protect subaltern classes from chronic indebtedness.

This brings us to one of the most important findings of the regime analysis. The systemic view on re/productive finance puts into focus the persistence and entanglement of various debt relations in the same household economy (see Figure 13). The predatory nature of commercial microfinance in India does not primarily lie in substantially higher interest rates or fees for loan products. Instead, it is based on the chronic indebtedness of these populations throughout the life cycle without providing any means to challenge their domination and oppression as precarious labourers. Thus, to fully grasp the predatory aspects, one must broaden the view beyond the limited operations of MFIs. From the perspective of subaltern working-class households, microfinance debts provide yet another source which intersects with other debt relations (SHGs, moneylenders, etc.) and produces complex forms of dependency and exploitation. Operating at a rather high level of abstraction, Part III has primarily focussed on the general characteristics of subaltern indebtedness over the past two centuries. Yet, the following analysis of contemporary migrant workers in Bengaluru will further elaborate on these dynamics, by zooming into the contemporary neoliberal regime of re/productive finance.

Finally, the systemic view of re/productive finance highlights that India's subaltern working class is not only characterised by varying degrees of freedom and coercion concerning their labour and by combining various modes of work into the household economy (van der Linden 2014) but also how multiple debt relations are crucial in mediating and manifesting these fractured lives. In this sense, understanding money as "bonds of all bonds" and a "universal agent of separation" (Marx 1988, 138) remains a powerful metaphor for understanding the chasm between the benevolent rhetoric and structural violence of financial inclusion. The outlined history demonstrates how various forms of indebtedness are a critical mechanism of surplus appropriation and class oppression, which underpins and reinforces the exploitation of labour in the production process or the formal subsumption of small farmers and petty commodity producers under capital. In this process, the productivity of financial capital also rests on the accumulation of gendered and racialised fragmentations and segmentations that run through the social body and the working class.

Reversely, this systemic view of these three modern regimes also emphasises how reproductive debts are a crucial entry point for understanding class struggle in broader terms. The peasant insurgencies under colonial rule and in the post-colonial era are intimately related to the roots of the subsistence crisis of subaltern classes and the role oppressive debt relations play in managing the former. Moreover, these struggles have been central to institutional changes within each of these regimes, as is witnessed by the introduction of credit cooperatives under British rule in the early twentieth century, the IRDP as a publicly subsidised lending scheme in the 1980s, or the scaling of welfare programmes for subaltern classes in the 2000s. As such, thinking of class struggle systematically from the perspective of reproductive debt might offer exciting insights for vitalising contemporary struggles. This is an issue we will further discuss in the conclusion.

Part IV: Beyond India's Silicon Valley: Precarious Migrant Workers and Re/Productive Finance in Bengaluru

"The large urban underserved want more than loans. Like all of us, they too want a place to keep their hard-earned savings, they want health and life insurance, pensions and retirement plans, financial support to expand micro enterprises, loans to put children through English-medium schools. In short: a full-service financial institution to fuel their dreams."
–*Janalakshmi Financial Services (2018)*

"Debt and indebtedness generate entrapments that not only scar individual lives but also mark the human condition as one of imbalance: between aspiration and realization, between creditor and debtor, between desire and desperation, and between life and death."
–*A. R. Vasavi (2014)*

Chapter 13
Migrant Workers Between Expropriation, Exploitation, and Exclusion

In 2017, when I embarked on this research project, Bengaluru[1] led the City Momentum Index (CMI) list before Ho Chi Minh City, Silicon Valley, and Shanghai. The index ranks the most dynamic cities of the world in terms of city GDP, population growth, foreign direct investment (FDI), and commercial real estate dynamics related to changes in construction, rents, and investment volumes. According to the authors, the CMI aims to "[...] alert[ing] the market to signals of change and to highlight the defining features which are enabling cities to successfully compete in a new economic landscape" (JLL 2017). As such, Bengaluru is heading a broader trend in India and many other parts of the world. Cities are engines of economic growth (Mitra and Mehta 2011), and in recent decades, Bengaluru has been "remapped as a territory for accumulation of economic power" (Nair 2005, 345). Rapid urbanisation is a hallmark of many regions in the global South. However, according to the World Economic Forum, "India's urban development is among the most important – the country's urban population is forecasted to almost double from 2014 to 2050 (World Economic Forum 2015). Likewise, the McKinsey Global Institute (MGI) had high hopes for "India's urban awakening". In 2010, the researchers estimated that India's cities could generate 70 per cent of net new jobs created by 2030, produce more than 70 per cent of Indian GDP, and drive a nearly fourfold increase in per capita incomes across the nation (Sankhe et al. 2010). Undoubtedly, Bengaluru has mastered the game of global cities; it has become an attractive investment destination and a nodal point in the global financial flows of the finance-dominated service economy (Goldman 2010; Nair 2005).

Also called India's Silicon Valley due to the density of information technology firms, these references paint a modern success story. Indeed, the South Indian metropolis has come a long way: Upon independence, the city's population was

1 In 2007, the state government of Karnataka decided to rename Bangalore as Bengaluru, affirming the dominant language in the state (Kannada) and confronting the colonial heritage of English naming of cities.

less than 750,000. By 1990, Bengaluru had already grown to around four million. And in 2017, more than eleven million people lived in the city (Roy et al. 2018). Yet, the glittering appearance and spectacular growth of the metropolis is riddled with cracks. In the niches between apartment complexes and office buildings, metro lines and highways, construction sites and factories, the city consists of about 2,000 scattered slums, a tenfold increase in the past four decades, which provide a home to roughly a third of the city's population (Roy et al. 2018). The overwhelming majority of this slum population are low-caste, Dalit and Adivasi migrant workers from Karnataka, neighbouring states and, increasingly, from across poverty-ridden districts in other parts of the country.[2] They usually reside in comparatively small settlements with about 50 and 200 tents, shacks and other makeshift homes (see Picture 3).[3] Many of these slum dwellers build and sustain the city as construction or domestic workers, vegetable cart sellers, waste pickers, security guards, or auto drivers, yet they remain in the city's shadows (RoyChowdhury 2021).

To be sure, the existence of stark inequalities in close physical proximity is certainly no exception in the rise of global cities in past decades, as Mike Davis has shown in his seminal work *Planet of Slums* (Davis 2006). However, it provides an important and arguably neglected research context for studying microfinance and financial inclusion. After all, some of the largest MFIs in India, like Janalakshmi and Ujjivan, have started their business in the slums of Bengaluru (see Chapter 11). So, what can an investigation of precarious migrant labourers in the metropolis possibly tell us about the rise of microfinance and the contradictions of financial inclusion? I suggest that engaging with the "city of shadows" (RoyChowdhury 2021) may illuminate our understanding of the opaque workings of commercial microfinance in at least one central way. It can explain the massive demand for credit amongst subaltern working-class households as a result of uneven capitalist development. Rather than just needing credit because they belong to the category of unbanked or urban poor, expropriation, super-exploitation, and exclusion of migrant labourers figure prominently in shaping the demand for reproductive debt. Thus, focussing on the rural-urban continuum within the neoliberal regime of re/productive finance helps to understand how commercial microfinance fills a particular niche within an existing ecosystem of multiple creditor institutions, and what limits it is confronted with.

---

2 According to official numbers, there are slightly more men (54 %) than women (46%) residing in notified slums, and more than half of the inhabitants are from the ST/SC category (KSDB 2013).

3 Only about a third of these settlements are notified because many have just recently been constructed or only remain for a short period. At the same time, those labour migrants and civil society organisations faced difficulties in registering them with the Karnataka Slum Development Board (CSA_1, Pos. 16).

Picture 3: Makeshift Settlement of Migrant Workers in Krishnarajapura, 2019

Source: private archive.

This part draws on the method of a "singular form" of incorporated comparison (McMichael 1990, 389), to understand the shattered story of migrant workers through specific spatial configurations within the neoliberal regime of re/productive finance. It focuses on three crucial aspects, drawing on the particular experience of construction, domestic and garment workers. Making a broader argument of how reproductive debts are lived through by a significant share of India's contemporary subaltern working class, and how this relates to the expansion of commercial microfinance. Together, these three groups comprise roughly 1.5 million workers in Bengaluru. Focussing on a specific set of workers in each section is primarily a strategic move that helps balance an analysis of general features experienced by almost all migrant labourers, while also highlighting the specificities different workers face in the labour process. In other words, it tries to account for the diversity of fractured lives while upholding the claim that there is a shared experience amongst different migrant workers. As such, this chapter seeks to give subaltern indebtedness "a body, a voice, and a territory" (Cavallero and Gago 2021, 4).

This chapter investigates the structural drivers of labour migration, emphasising how migrant workers are torn between expropriation, exploitation, and exclusion. It introduces the notion of a debt-distress cycle, substantiating how demand for credit is rooted in a chronic subsistence crisis. Chapter 14 engages with how reproductive debts are lived through. It emphasises how caring for reproductive debts and juggling different sources and types of credit(ors) is an underappreciated, necessary work that mostly women engage in. Chapter 15 discusses the background story and afterlives of a short-lived but decisive strike of garment workers. This case illuminates the potential convergence of labour and debt struggles, providing valuable insights into how migrant workers struggle against the neoliberal regime of re/productive finance. Together, these three moments describe the structural violence of reproductive debts in contemporary India summarised in Chapter 16.

The Underbelly of India's Urbanisation

It is hardly surprising that the rise of the construction industry parallels "India's urban awakening" (Sankhe et al. 2010). The sector has become the country's second-largest employer, only behind agriculture. It currently employs around 51 million people and accounts for 9 per cent of the nation's GDP (Invest India 2023). According to estimates, there are over 100,000 construction companies, of which 250 are major corporations, and nearly 400,000 contractors and sub-contractors of whom the entire industry relies on (Deccan Herald 2012). Construction workers are predominantly rural-urban migrants from ST/SC/OBC categories who toil in the city as daily wage labourers.[4] Cyclical migration patterns and the informal nature of work make it hard to survey the sector. But there are likely some 1.5 million construction workers in Karnataka, of whom at least one-fourth are in Bengaluru (RoyChowdhury 2021, 110). The relevance of the industry for migrant workers can hardly be overestimated, as a long-standing civil society activist emphasised in one of the interviews:

> "Our recent experience is that migrants are coming. 90% of them are working in construction and construction-related activities. Because Bangalore is supposed to be the most dynamic construction happening in Asia. [...]. Second thing is that construction is today better paid than other sectors. For the skilled labourers, but also for unskilled labours." (CSA_1, Pos. 34)

On average, wages for unskilled labour in construction are significantly higher than those in agriculture, and employment is comparatively steadier, explaining why masses of effectively landless labourers turn to seasonal migration as primary livelihood (Pattenden 2016, 78; Srivastava 2018, 117). In this sense, labour migration can be a form of economic mobility for impoverished rural masses, including maintaining rural households through remittances. However, many studies have also pointed to the contradiction that even comparatively higher wage levels in urban areas may be below minimum wages, and chronic indebtedness may still shape

4 For an overview of construction workers in India, see Srivastava (2018).

their livelihoods, especially for the lower ranks of migrant workers (Breman 2019; Mansoor and O'Neill 2021; Mosse et al. 2002; RoyChowdhury 2021; Srivastava and Sutradhar 2016).

In this context, the overall segmentation and fragmentation of construction workers along gender, skills, or region are critical to the sourcing strategies of contractors and sub-contractors to maintain a cheap, flexible, and docile workforce (Parry 2014; Pattenden 2018; Srivastava 2022). For instance, all interviewees confirmed a significant gender wage gap, with women earning only two-thirds or sometimes even half of what their male counterparts get for the same work. Importantly, this gendered gap is also visible concerning the average monthly workdays. As a female construction worker from a slum in Kodigahalli remarked: "We would like to work more, but often we only get a job for three days a week. We can't plan because the contractor simply calls and then we have to spur" (HH_Cluster_5, Pos. 20). Women worker's position on the construction site is ambiguous. While contractors and employers understand them as "more docile and less likely to skip work, drink or cause trouble on site, they were also perceived as less efficient" (Bowers 2019, 30), devaluing their labour based on prevailing gender norms. This gendered devaluation continues with women's seemingly natural responsibility of unpaid reproductive labour at the worksite and beyond (HH_Cluster_5, Pos. 55–60).

A time-use survey amongst 100 female Adivasi construction workers found that, on average, women workers spent 17 hours a day performing both paid and unpaid work across construction sites, their living spaces, and accessing basic facilities in the city (Jayaram, Jain, and Sugathan 2019, 90). This would entail burdensome physical work with walking at least 10 kilometres, lifting and carrying more than 5,000 kg daily, and climbing around 480 steps, often on uneven terrain or shaky platforms – with little time to rest and additional burdens of unpaid care work on the construction site. Moreover, women usually wake up at 4 a.m. to perform household work like cooking, cleaning, and washing before leaving for work and continue this work straight after returning from the construction site (Jayaram, Jain, and Sugathan 2019, 91).

In addition to the physical and emotional double burden of paid construction and unpaid reproductive work, women in the construction industry point to the omnipresent reality of sexualised violence as part of their labour subordination, from the labour stands to the bus rides and construction sites (Bowers 2019, 31; Parry 2014). And the chronic lack of primary health care, including antenatal maternal services, leads to "unattended deliveries at the workplace, miscarriages, and reproductive health issues" (Jayaram, Jain, and Sugathan 2019, 95). Thus, female construction workers experience the full scale of precarity, a mix of fundamental uncertainty and insecurity regarding wages, employment, and bodily integrity.[5]

Given the harsh and exploitative realities in the construction industry, one might wonder why there is such a mass of migrant labourers. Most of the interviewed construction workers in Bengaluru come from dry-belt areas in Northern Karnataka and Andhra Pradesh or distant regions affected by high poverty, including Bihar, Jharkhand and Odisha. In all these cases, rural distress drives migration. A 16-year-old boy who had migrated from a drought-prone region in Andhra Pradesh summarised his despair as follows: "How can we go back? There are no jobs, nothing. Here at least sometimes jobs are available, we can earn some income" (HH_Cluster_6, Pos. 46). In shedding light on the background conditions of labour migration, the following sections attempt to show how exploitation of migrant workers is intimately connected to a variety of processes of expropriation and exclusion, and how the cumulation of these dynamics explains their chronic indebtedness.

Slow Violence and a Debt for Life

A woman from Gulbarga[6] who had recently migrated to Bengaluru and settled in a small hut on the outskirts of the metropolitan area explained how continuous droughts and heavy rainfalls have adversely impacted their subsistence farming, leading to cumulative debts of more than Rs. 100,000 with moneylenders, neighbours and family. Eventually, she and her husband searched for an income in the city in the booming construction industry. "We only came here to be able to repay the loans. We don't want to stay but return home after two or three years of labour" (HH_Cluster_2, Pos. 23). The "promise of the metropolis", as Janaki Nair (2005) has famously called it, remains a powerful imaginary for large parts of the rural population. Although the biographies of migrant labourers are diverse and unique in many regards, it wouldn't be exaggerated to claim that the collision between agrarian distress and urban promise drives a massive and arguably growing flow of people into the global city.

Most biographic interviews with relatively recent construction workers reveal a remarkably similar pattern: Recurring droughts, floods, adverse agrarian conditions, and bleak prospects of making a living otherwise in dry-belt areas

5 There are, of course, also other dimensions of insecurity which have not been mentioned here, including the inadequate equipment and hazardous working conditions at construction sites, with frequent accidents where workers literally risk their lives in the process of building the city (Pandey 2019).

6 Gulbarga is a city and district in Northern Karnataka which has been renamed Kalaburagi in 2016. I use the old name because interviewees from the region have consistently referred to it as Gulbarga.

like in Northern Karnataka (Gulbarga, Raichur, Yagdir) or the neighbouring state of Andhra Pradesh (Kurnool, Nandyal) had forced particularly low-caste, Dalit and Adivasi families and communities to search for a livelihood in Bengaluru (HH_Cluster_3; HH_Cluster_4). Other studies have also established this relationship (Pattenden 2016; RoyChowdhury 2021; Sridhar, Reddy, and Srinath 2013). Such distress-driven migration is grounded in a political ecology of inequality and the slow violence associated with the progressing climate change. And both processes are intimately bound up with the 'original sin' of producing debts for life. After all, debts accumulating due to unviable cultivation and the sheer impossibility of safeguarding social reproduction in rural areas are a significant reason that drives masses of workers to the booming construction industry (Krishna, Sriram, and Prakash 2014; Pattenden 2018).

Building on the extensive research on the agrarian crisis and distress-driven migration, the following highlights the constant, creeping, and cumulating threats that underpin the structural subsistence crisis of subaltern working-class households across the rural-urban spectrum. Rather than displacements through development projects or urban infrastructure, a topic we will engage with later, the agrarian crisis involves a more subtle and indirect form of dispossession, which, following Rob Nixon, can be called 'slow violence'. It "occurs gradually and out of sight, a violence of delayed destruction that is dispersed across time and space, an attritional violence that is typically not viewed as violence at all" (Nixon 2011, 2). Slow violence proceeds incremental and cumulative with abysmal effects that may stretch unevenly over space and time. Nonetheless, it is neither random nor without cause. As will be argued here, it is rooted in a political ecology of inequality in which capital and the state figure prominently, and urbanisation plays a key role.

As discussed in previous chapters, India's agrarian crisis is marked by a polarisation between a few capitalist farmers with large landholdings and commercially viable production, and a mass of petty commodity producers who struggle to sustain themselves through cultivation (Basole and Basu 2011b; Rupakula 2016). In recent decades, the average farm size in the agricultural sectors has shrunk to 1.13 hectares, and about 80 per cent of farming households consist of marginal and small farmers who struggle to make ends meet (Dandekar 2016; Naidu and Ossome 2016). Nonetheless, agriculture remains the largest employer in the country, and most of the rural population depends on it despite being effectively landless.

Lack of reliable irrigation threatens the subsistence of a significant share, especially in regions like the central Deccan, where rainfall is low and erratic. In this sense, the cumulating water crisis is a prism in which the relations between agrarian distress and urban development, public and private financing, and upper- and lower-caste/class domination refracts. While canals and tanks play a minor role in most parts of the country, the relevance of tube wells has considerably expanded since the Green Revolution (see Chapter 10).[7] Mediated by rural class and caste inequalities, this expansion is linked to groundwater's uneven appropriation and privatisation. The neoliberal reforms of the 1990s downscaled public financing of irrigation initiatives, and "the response to drought in conditions of high-risk commercial agriculture has been private borrowing to create new or deeper borewells" (Taylor 2011, 496). Between 1996 and 2014, the number of tube wells in Karnataka dry belts increased by a staggering 365 per cent, resulting in the deterioration of dry agricultural practices, which are less productive commercially but ecologically more viable (Vasavi 2020, 7).

Moreover, the uneven appropriation and use of water in the state are also shaped by urbanisation. Goldman and Narayan (2019) have identified three nested "hydrosocial regimes" which have marked the state's trajectory. Historically, Bengaluru has been sustained by the creation of a wetland environment of numerous water-holding facilities (kere/lakes, irrigation tanks, reservoirs, ponds), or what they call a "catchment-based regime". With the expansion of the city and public industries since the mid-twentieth century, the state of Karnataka increasingly relied on loans from the World Bank to finance an infrastructure that would provide piped water from the Cauvery River (100 kilometres from the city) to meet the demand of industries and wealthy households. This second "hydraulic regime" prioritised Bengaluru over the rest of Karnataka and, in the city, the upper- and middle-class neighbourhoods (Goldman and Narayan 2019, 102). Since the neoliberal turn in the early 1990s, both land and water have increasingly turned into speculative financial assets, leading to the rise of private water markets and competition over the appropriation of groundwater, deepening the existing inequalities in access to and distribution of safe drinking water (Goldman and Narayan 2019, 104f.).

The uneven appropriation of groundwater is closely interrelated with the subsistence crisis of subaltern classes. According to the NITI Aayog, the apex public policy think-tank of the Government of India, 600 million Indians face acute water stress, about 200,000 people die every year due to inadequate access to safe water, three-quarters of Indian households do not have drinking water on-premise, and 21 megacities, including Bengaluru, are likely to run out of groundwater in coming years (NITI Aayog 2018). Within a few decades, the erstwhile 'city of tanks' (*Kalyanagara*) had on its paths to a global city, turned into "a place where lakes represent valuable unused real estate capture and conversion to apartments and malls, or abandoned cesspools of sewage and solid waste" (Nagendra 2016, 174).

In this context, household debt has become a double-edged sword that seemingly liberates small and marginal farmers while simultaneously pushing many of them into even more distress. A farmer on the city's outskirts, whom I interviewed in

7 Shortly after independence, there were about 5 million tube wells. By 2019, the number had more than doubled to about 12 million (Vasavi 2020, 7).

the first phase of my field research, reported how he had taken on several loans from the cooperative society and local bank to deepen his borewell and address the water shortage compromising his cultivation. Within a decade, these loans allowed him to deepen the borewell by more than 1,000 feet, from 1350 to 2500 feet (HH_Cluster_1, Pos.16). While this strategy may work for individual cases and in the short run, it produces a problematic trend. About half of Bengaluru's water supply comes from groundwater, but the extraction is not formally monitored or regulated. There are about 105,000 registered private bore wells, but probably another 200,000 unregistered ones (Goldman and Narayan 2019, 105). The cumulative debt-based deepening of bore wells thus leads to the deterioration of groundwater levels, further intensifying the water crisis. This process intensifies rural inequalities both in terms of access to water and adverse effects of lacking irrigation because the smaller share of wealthy rural households has more means to decide the race for groundwater for them. In recent years, the overdrawing of groundwater, that is, withdrawal vs. recharge, stands at a staggering 378 per cent, according to some estimates (Goldman and Narayan 2019, 105). Similar trends appear in rural areas of Karnataka, where groundwater levels deteriorate at the expense of small and marginal farmers, reflecting unequal power relationships regarding control over land, water, and credit (Taylor 2013; Vasavi 2020). Moreover, the class- and caste-based marginality of farming households is rooted in the small size of land ownership and "the marginal political and social position they occupy in the immediate and larger political economies of the nation" (Vasavi 2014, 24).

Although migration may be an exit strategy from rural distress, possibly relieving the agrarian subsistence crisis through sending remittances from construction and other precarious wage labour, it is hardly an exit from the political ecology of inequality. Migrant labourers who reside in scattered slums or overcrowded colonies are most prone to the cumulating water crisis. Lack of access to safe drinking water and poor sanitation in these areas is an omnipresent and well-documented problem (Krishna 2013; Nagendra 2016, 71ff.; RoyChowdhury 2021, 108ff.). Consequently, water-borne diseases and respective effects like diarrhoea are recurrent phenomena. In cases of dehydration and exhaustion, treatment in the hospital may be necessary. Such treatment is not complicated, but it results in a financial burden that these households struggle with.[8] Borrowing money for such additional (health) expenditure is a regular case that construction and other migrant workers have described in interviews (HH_Cluster_5, Pos.63; HH_Cluster_6, Pos. 13–16).[9]

8 It is important to notice that the most vulnerable to dehydration are babies and young children.

9 On average, the relative health expenditure of slum dwellers in Bengaluru is more than double the one that other urban households have (Roy et al. 2018).

Disease and death associated with access to unsafe water usually occur gradually and out of sight, attesting to the significance of slow violence (Bowers 2019, 25). Yet, at times this violence also becomes publicly visible. In late 2017, around 1,500 construction workers left a makeshift colony provided by their employer after several cholera cases had erupted due to unhygienic conditions in the colony, with two dozen patients admitted to the hospital and two workers succumbing to the fatal illness (Alva 2018). Notably, the slow violence of the water crisis is gendered (Nagendra 2016, 84). Women, who are usually responsible for fetching water, preparing meals, cleaning clothes, or washing children, are at the frontline of dealing with the impossibility of safeguarding household members' social reproduction without risking fatal consequences. They are also adversely affected by a lack of privacy and sanitation, often getting up before sunset to wash or defecate in the open and being forced to clean menstrual cloth in highly unsanitary water bodies (Bowers 2019; Jayaram, Jain, and Sugathan 2019).

The line between slow violence and dispossession is thin and goes beyond the water crisis. According to the ecologist Harini Nagendra, about half of Bengaluru's slums are at risk of flooding, a third are affected by garbage, and many have insufficient protection from heat (Nagendra 2016, 79ff.). All these factors contribute to the precarity of construction and other migrant workers, understood as a toxic mix of fundamental uncertainty and insecurity. This precarity is visible at the worksite but stretches far beyond, including all sites of social reproduction. One of the field sites located close to Seetarampalya Lake in Whitefields (East Bengaluru) demonstrates this accurately. The lake is well maintained, with fencing, trees and other plants. There are even benches that invite you to linger. The tank is surrounded by expensive apartment complexes and office buildings of transnational IT corporations like SAP, Dell, Hewlett Packard, Huawei and several others. The site is satirically idyllic, with ducks swimming on the lake, a rare sight for Bengaluru's dried-up or heavily polluted tanks. At first glance, the place is representative of India's Silicon Valley. Yet, a closer look exposes the proximity between wealth and poverty. An older, dried-out tank bed stretches into the scenery at the margins of the well-maintained lake, in between luxury apartment complexes and office buildings. It hosts between 40 and 50 makeshift huts with migrant workers from Mantralaya in Andhra Pradesh who have settled here recently due to the agrarian crisis.

On the one hand, they describe their location as favourable to seek work as cleaners in office complexes or washing dishes in adjunct restaurants serving India's emerging middle-class professionals. On the other hand, the location is prone to recurrent floods and associated devastations during heavy rainfalls, literally pulling out the rug from under the migrant worker's feet (HH_Cluster_6, Pos. 55–58). Consequently, their place of residence is marked by both the promise of the metropolis in the context of the agrarian crisis and the sheer impossibility of subaltern working-class households to escape the fatal consequences of the political ecology of inequality.

Dispossession in the Name of Development

The slow violence associated with the agrarian crisis, uneven development and progressing climate change bear witness to the gradual and dispersed violence of displacement that forces masses of small and marginal farmers to secure their household reproduction through circular migration. But processes of dispossession that underpin labour migration can also be more more evident and spectacular. India's growth miracle since the neoliberal turn in the 1990s has been fuelled by the polarisation between a few large metropolitan areas and impoverished pockets, exacerbating the political ecology of inequality (Shrivastava and Kothari 2012, 230ff.). Significantly, the neoliberal era has witnessed a surge in corporate and market-driven "dispossessions without development" (Levien 2018) for the sake of appropriating natural resources, turning agricultural land into real estate, building large-scale energy infrastructure, and developing Special Economic Zones (SEZ) to attract foreign investment (Ahuja and Ganguly 2007; D'Costa and Chakraborty 2017; Roy 2023).[10]

For instance, the South Korean Pohang Iron and Steel Company (POSCO) envisaged building an integrated steel plant in the eastern state of Odisha in the mid-2000s. The project would have been India's largest FDI, comprising 12 billion USD. According to the corporate's plans, more than 20,000 people from eight villages would have been displaced from the steel plant and port area alone, and about 50,000 people were going to be affected by environmental destruction, loss of livelihoods or otherwise (Shah 2019, 42). After close to 12 years of resistance, local communities and civil society organizations managed to halt the plans that would have destroyed their vibrant local economy and use of commons (Padhi and Patana 2017; Shah 2019). However, in those cases where resistance is not successful and (indigenous) communities are separated from their ancestral land and their means of subsistence, people are likely to migrate in search of alternative livelihoods. Particularly, indigenous communities living in the resource-rich forest and mountain regions in the North and East of India are displaced in the name of development, continuing the legacy of colonial enclosures since the late eighteenth century

10 These trends are not exceptional for most former colonies. There are several thousand ongoing socio-ecological conflicts around land, water, and common resources across the globe where local communities fight against the corporate-led and state-backed appropriation of commons (Temper et al. 2018). However, India is certainly amongst the global hot spots of these struggles (Temper, del Bene, and Martinez-Alier 2015). For a comparative discussion of land grabs and urbanisation in the global South, see Zoomers et al. (2017).

(Parashar 2019; Roy 2023). Speaking about the reasons for Adivasis to migrate to Bengaluru, an NGO worker remarked:

> "In the forest areas, tribals have become more or less evicted. Forests cannot sustain their lives. Many things are planted for timber, tea, and the like. And they are fenced out and pushed out. Many of them are migrating as construction workers, road workers, or any other domestic workers when they are women." (CSA_4, Pos. 54)

In such cases, the protection of nature through forest reserves, national parks, elephant corridors or tiger reserves turns into a vital means of "accumulation by conservation" (Büscher and Fletcher 2015), threatening primarily the livelihoods of indigenous and other communities that sustain their subsistence from forest produce, and forcing them to migrate in search for alternative livelihoods (CSA_4, Pos. 55).

Case studies of the aftermath of dispossession through Special Economic Zones (SEZs) and similar development projects have documented how these processes intensify existing socio-economic inequalities and function as a catalyst for indebtedness with moneylenders through loss of the means of subsistence, inadequate or inexistent compensations and adverse incorporation as precarious wage labourers, especially amongst Adivasis and Dalits (Agarwal 2021; Agarwal and Levien 2020). In other words, while the slow violence of the agrarian crisis leads to cumulating indebtedness, creeping displacement, and eventual labour migration as a last resort to secure subsistence, the spectacular but by no means less common forms of development-induced displacements increase the likelihood of indebtedness through the immediate loss of the means of subsistence and the adverse incorporation into precarious wage work, for example, in the booming construction industry.

In other cases, collateralising land to access credit becomes a powerful lever for dispossession. One of the migrant labourers I interviewed in Bengaluru had reported how he had taken a loan of Rs. 150,000 from a commercial bank to turn cultivation to cash crops (cotton) and another Rs. 30,000 from an MFI to finance the medical treatment of his wife, who had diabetes. He used the five acres of land in the surroundings of Mysuru as collateral, and after a crop failure, he left the land with his brothers to come to Bengaluru as a daily wage labourer. His average earning in the city was Rs. 9,000 per month. Although the bank had not yet expropriated him, he expressed a constant fear of not being able to service the two loans and losing the land eventually (HH_Cluster_3, Pos. 21). These dynamics point to the multi-causal connections between dispossession and indebtedness, which is also known from many other regions in the global South.[11]

---

11 Similar dynamics concerning the connection between land expropriation and indebtedness can also be witnessed in other contexts, like South Africa, Chile and Cambodia (Ar-

The enclosures of common land and resources are by no means limited to rural areas far off the metropolis. As Michael Goldman (2010, 2020) has demonstrated, land acquisition and dispossessions at the fringes of Bengaluru have increasingly taken a speculative turn with rapidly rising real estate prices and a complex web of public, parastatal and private institutions invested in the debt-financed development of "the next world city". While some peri-urban farmers may benefit from rising land prices through land brokerage, leasing or selling land, the distribution of rewards and upward mobility remains highly uneven and are overshadowed by caste- and class inequalities (Rajeev and Scherrer 2021; Schwind and Altrock 2023; Upadhya and Rathod 2021). Notably, contemporary urban planning in Bengaluru around highways, metro lines, office parks, residential areas, and SEZs is aligned with the imperatives of capitalist growth, with little regard for the subsistence prospects of subaltern working-class households (Rajesh Bhattacharya and Sanyal 2011; Goldman 2010; Nair 2014).[12]

Even though processes of dispossession can be the primary reason for migrants to settle and search for livelihoods in the city, their new habitat is not necessarily an escape. Many interviewees have emphasised how they are constantly threatened by displacement since settling in the city (HH_Cluster_6, Pos. 29; HH_Cluster_5, Pos. 60). Because Bengaluru is characterised by scattered and comparatively small slums with often only a few shacks, displacing slums for the sake of real estate development or extending urban infrastructure is relatively convenient for state bodies and private corporations. For instance, one of the smaller slums I researched in Kodigahalli (North Bengaluru) houses almost exclusively construction workers. About 200 people had settled in a small niche between the railroad, a high-rise office building and a novel apartment complex just a few months before (see Picture 4). However, this place was not their first destination in the metropolis. Previously, they had camped less than a kilometre away but were displaced without much notice or compensation due to the building of yet another apartment complex. Since they had neither a land title nor were they registered with the KSDB, their insecure residency has never been officially recognised (HH_Cluster_5, Pos. 61).

boleda 2015a; Bond 2013; Green and Bylander 2021). In Cambodia, which has arguably turned into the most dynamic microfinance markets in the world in recent years, over-indebted peasants also increasingly resort of work as precarious migrant labourers in construction (Natarajan, Brickell, and Parsons 2021).

12 For instance, the Bengaluru-Mysuru Infrastructure Corridor (BMIC), a privately built and operated 119-kilometres tolled expressway, connecting the two cities, is likely to have displaced around 200,000 people in the adjunct villages (Goldman 2010, 11).

Picture 4: Makeshift Settlement of Construction Workers in Kodigahalli; 2019

Source: private archive.

But even for the notified slums, the politics of "speculative urbanism" (Goldman 2010) may be detrimental. As an NGO working with slum dwellers describes it, the tendency is to relocate slum dwellers to the periphery of the city where land prices are lower, while the "land broker state" (Levien 2018) may benefit from escalating real estate prices:

> "Another thing is that when slums need to be developed a lot of time land rights are a major issue. Because they are being shifted to very far away. And in the city real estate goes up, so they are shifting slums to 30–40 kilometres away. That approach we are also not very happy with. Because the slum dweller's livelihoods usually is around the slum, whether they are domestic workers, or construction workers, or auto rickshaw driver, whatever jobs they are doing. [...]" (CSA_1, Pos. 21)

Logically, the effects of distant relocations have detrimental consequences for migrant workers' livelihood. Starting anew in an entirely different part of the city or commuting long distances to their old worksites further drains their limited time and financial resources.[13]

13 This processes of displacement and relocation are marked by a double standard. Whereas the building of high-rise apartments, office parks or shopping malls, which primarily address

The constant threat of dispossession in various forms is entangled with the uneven development of rapid urbanisation. Financial imperatives of debt-fuelled development and market-oriented urban planning contribute to converting land and water into speculative assets, exacerbating the subsistence crisis of the masses (Goldman 2020; Ranganathan 2021). In this context, the dominant rationale of "marketized improvement [...] seeks to impart values of financial responsibility on informal subjects, while also serving to justify the state's long-standing failure to invest in affordable housing and services, while also producing forms of social and spatial difference" (Ranganathan 2018, 16). Consequently, the financial risks and obligations to access decent housing, safe drinking water, health care facilities or education for children are offloaded to super-exploited migrant workers, who essentially build and maintain the city. Still, in many cases, they cannot afford these services from their meagre wages – forcing them to take on debts from various creditors. In other words, the exclusion of migrant labourers from accessing (urban) commons and public infrastructure forces them into market-based social reproduction. Dispossession thereby also forms a vital background conditions upon which financial inclusion, primarily understood as widened access to credit, emerges as a sensible development intervention. Having no means of subsistence or valuable assets, dispossession dynamics also lower the respective workers' credit rating (Breman 2019, 242). These problems become even more virulent by excluding migrant workers from welfare schemes.

Exclusionary Welfare & Market-Based Social Reproduction

The previous section has demonstrated how the speculative nature of urbanisation, in which land and water are increasingly treated as assets, excludes migrant workers from access to common land and water, increasing their market-mediated reproduction. Likewise, many migrant workers remain excluded from public social security schemes. While government programmes may be accessible on paper, multiple obstacles are linked to migrant labourers' precarious livelihoods that prevent them from benefiting from such schemes. For instance, access to medical, sickness, maternity, disablement, dependants benefits, funeral expenses, disability and death insurance or basic pension through the Employee's Provident Fund (EPF) and the Employees State Insurance (ESI) requires 240 days of continuous work, which is the rare

upper-caste/class households, is justified in public discourse by the necessity of urban development, migrant labourer' settlements in dried-out tank beds or next to water bodies are frequently framed as "illegal encroachers" or "unclean, petty criminals" (Ranganathan 2021; Upadhya and Rao 2022).

exception of daily wage labourers.[14] And specific schemes for construction workers, like the Building and Other Construction Workers Act (B&OCWA), are famous for ineffective implementation (Pattenden 2016, 81; Srivastava 2018, 127).

Furthermore, urban land valuation is intimately connected to construction workers' insecure residence/housing and exclusion from government schemes. With escalating real estate prices, rents are increasing, even in basic makeshift settlements. While (migrant) workers in notified slums would pay between Rs. 2000 – and Rs. 4,000 rent per month, excluding water and electricity (CSA_4, Pos. 44–46), recent migrant workers tend to erect temporary accommodation from stones, bulky waste, blue plastic and tin sheet. Even for staying in these, they must pay between Rs 400 and Rs. 500 per month to the private landlord who claims the land their own, excluding additional expenses for accessing water or electricity from neighbouring households (HH_Cluster_6, Pos. 20). In the latter cases they don't get formal tenancy because landowners are speculating on appropriating financial gains once the slum becomes notified (see also Upadhya and Rao 2022). As discussed in the previous section, insecure tenancy creates a constant threat of being displaced. But it also affects their ability to access public social security schemes adversely:

> "Because in this process, what happens sometimes, what we have experienced in the slums, the real owner doesn't allow other people to get their entitlement, like ration card or Aadhaar card on that address. Because then he has to share the land, if the land is notified. So they will take the whole family living on a piece of land, and that will be divided between all the residents. That's why they will say you are only tenants, you can stay here, but you cannot get registered." (CSA_1, Pos. 30–32)

However, the ration or Aadhaar card acts as necessary address proof. It entitles the holder to access all relevant government schemes, including subsidised food grains through the public distribution system (PDS), old age, disability and widow's pensions, getting Bangalore Water Supply and Sewerage Board (BWSSB) water connection, admitting children to government schools, accessing governmental hospitals, and participating in slum development programmes (see also RoyChowdhury 2021, 109ff.).

Exclusion from welfare programmes exacerbates migrant worker's market dependency. This becomes particularly evident when looking at the PDS, the world's largest food security scheme, granting about 800 million people in India access to subsidised food grains. All interviewed households indicated that food and water were their single biggest expenditure. On average, slum households in Bengaluru spend around 56 per cent of their income on food and water, while another 7 per

---

14 See section 5.3.2 on Garmen Worker's Safety Nets for a detailed discussion of the relevance of EPF/ESI.

cent is spent on housing and health care (Roy et al. 2018). In this context, access to PDS is arguably the single most crucial welfare scheme for households who struggle to make ends meet. Since the National Food Security Act (NFSA) of 2013, priority households receive 5 kg of foodgrain at subsidised prices (rice: Rs. 3/wheat: Rs. 2/millet: Rs. 1), and the poorest households (Antyodaya) are entitled to 35 kg foodgrains per month. At the prevailing market rate of about Rs. 60 per kilogrammes of rice in Bengaluru in 2019 (HH_Cluster_5, Pos. 26–29; HH_Cluster_6, Pos. 67), the poorest households, if barred from access due to their insecure residency, would lose out on a public subsidy of basic foodgrains of roughly Rs. 2000 per month. Thus, access to the PDS amounts to something between 10 and 20 per cent of their monthly household income.

Against this backdrop, access to public social security may have a similar relevance to securing unsteady employment from the perspective of the social reproduction of precarious migrant workers. Therefore, the organisation of informal workers and collective action of parts of the subaltern working class has increasingly turned towards the state rather than towards employers in recent decades (Agarwala 2013). In this regard, the role of NGOs in filling the welfare gap and helping slum dwellers access basic amenities and public schemes has been pivotal, both from their self-understanding as well as from the perspective of migrant workers who reside in slums (CSA_1, Pos. 3; CSA_4, Pos. 36; CSA_6, Pos. 44; HH_Cluster_5, Pos. 26; HH_Cluster_6, Pos. 66). A comparative study of various slums in Bengaluru finds that households in those areas with sustained (social-work-oriented) NGO presence had on average much better access to basic amenities, including water and sanitation facilities, child care (Angandwadi), PDS and voter ID cards (RoyChowdhury 2021, 113f.).

SHGs frequently play a significant role in organising and mobilising slum dwellers for collective action. However, even if these initiatives successfully reclaim public infrastructure, the prospects of breaking the dependency on market-based social reproduction are limited and local groups end up torn between state and market capture (see Chapter 11). Against this backdrop, the following section suggests that reproductive debts are both a condition and a result of the interlocking dynamics of (super-)exploitation, expropriation, and exclusion. Acknowledging this entrenched debt-distress cycle is essential to broaden the research on financial inclusion and to engage with political strategies that confront the root causes of migrant workers' subsistence crisis.

The Debt-Distress Cycle of Re/Productive Finance

Many of the above-discussed aspects, that is, the gendered exploitation of construction workers, the linkages between the cumulating agrarian crisis and distress-driven migration, the dispossession in the name of development, and the exclusion of migrant labourers from public infrastructure and welfare schemes are well documented by diverse bodies of research. Yet, these dynamics are hardly recognised in studies on microfinance and financial inclusion (Kar 2018; Karim 2011; Mader 2015; Roy 2010). Bringing these seemingly background conditions to the fore, I suggest that the interlocking dynamics of expropriation, exploitation, and exclusion explain the massive demand for microcredits amongst those at the bottom of the pyramid. As such, they are essential to understanding how and why microfinance could proliferate so rapidly in India.

Figure 14: The Debt-Distress Cycle of Re/Productive Finance

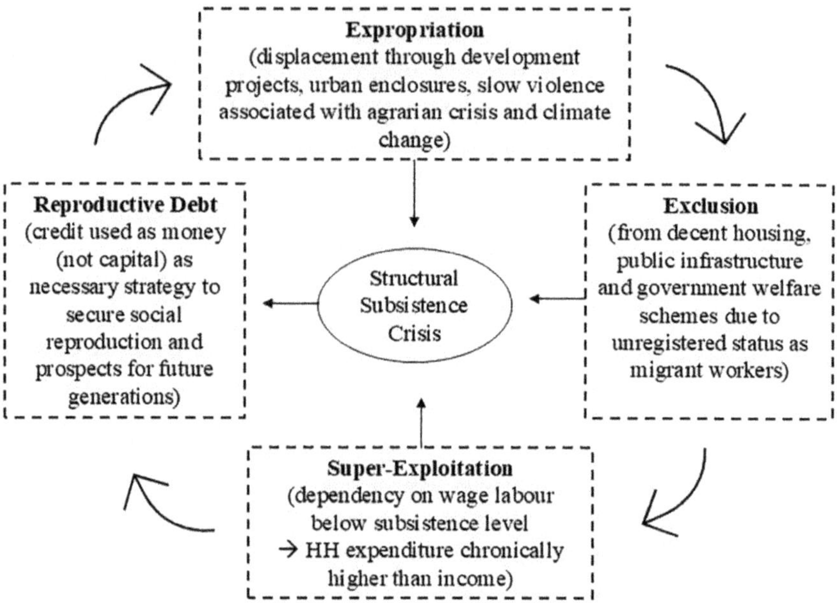

Source: own illustration.

Figure 14 illustrates how the three exes (expropriation, exclusion, exploitation) cumulate to intensify a chronic subsistence crisis amongst subaltern working-class households through increased market-dependent social reproduction. The separation from sufficient means of subsistence and the exclusion from public social security forces masses of rural-urban migrants to sell their labour power daily through a highly exploitative contracting system, which in most cases results in monthly incomes insufficient to meet necessary expenses. In such a context, reproductive debts emerge or consolidate as an essential survival strategy. The visualisation is consciously designed as a circle to show how enmeshed these dynamics are. Rather than a linear process with a clear beginning and end, the cycle demonstrates multiple potential entry points and reverse causality flows. For instance, dispossession from land may result from (reproductive) debts, as discussed in the section's opening. Likewise, reproductive debts can further intensify the chronic subsistence crisis it seeks to manage, as will be discussed in the following chapters.

Notably, the debt-distress cycle of migrant workers' livelihoods suggests a *systemic* relation that underpins the contemporary neoliberal regime. In this regard, it may be a vicious circle for many migrant workers. Based on more than 50 years of field research on India's transforming working class, Jan Breman seconds the relevance of the nexus between distress-driven labour migration, chronic indebtedness and vulnerability to super-exploitation. Initially, labour migration might be envisioned as temporary or circular, but in many cases, migrant workers are trapped in a seemingly endless cycle of dispossession, debt and immiseration:

> "These footloose labourers hang around the city's outskirts because indebtedness at home forces them to migrate in search of work. They try to sell their labour power in order to pay back the money borrowed from big farmers or traders and needed to afford life-cycle events (mainly marriage) or housebuilding or to cope with adversities such as illness, disability and old age in the family. These debts can run up to one lakh (100,000) rupees, a liability that is a heavy burden because of the extremely high rate of interest – which may lead to the doubling of the debt for the least credit-worthy ones within a year. Failure to comply with payment of regular instalments is a slippery slope that ends in complete bankruptcy. It comes as no surprise that such mishaps result in breaking away from the village and moving the whole household on a more permanent footing to the illegal camp at the city's periphery." (Breman 2019, 228)

Although their informal work is associated with high fluctuation, hardly any command over the labour process and a change in working sites, many migrant workers are tied to their contractors or employers for years. Debt relations, for example, through advance payments, play a significant role in dominating and exploiting cheap labour (Breman 2019, 184; Srivastava 2018, 122). This mode of subordination has striking similarities with the traditional bonded labour system, which has sustained rural economies across India for centuries through personal patronage and super-exploitation of labouring classes along caste-based lines. In trying to grasp the continuities and changes, including the increased relevance of market- and money-mediated relationships of unfree labour in contemporary India, agrarian and labour scholars thus speak of "neo-bondage" (Breman, Guérin, and Prakash 2009). Of course, indebtedness does not per se define unfree labour. But if debt relationships significantly restrict (migrant) workers' freedom, wages and bargaining power, they may turn into bonded labourers (Guérin 2013, 411).[15]

Understanding the debt-distress cycle as a systemic pattern allows us to account for multiple debts of precarious migrant workers, including relationships of dependency and exploitation with rural moneylenders, urban employers, microfinance institutions, and others. Ultimately, all these reproductive debts are associated with household strategies that seek to safeguard the social reproduction of subaltern working classes (van der Linden 2023, 111). The following section will engage with the intricate workings of juggling debts to understand how these strategies play out.

15 Ironically, this debt bondage to middlemen who might place them hundreds of kilometres far away from their native place to get them working at various construction sites can be understood "as a protective safety net for the labourers who otherwise has to resort to the upper caste moneylenders in the village and take loans at usurious interest rates" (Chauhan 2022, 96f.). For a similar discussion around microfinance indebtedness and unfree labour in Cambodia, see Natarajan, Brickell, and Parsons (2021).

Chapter 14
Caring for Debts...for Life

The previous chapter highlighted the debt-distress cycle that underpins migrant labourers' demand for credit, drawing on the experiences of construction workers. If the latter is an invisible workforce in the "city of shadows" (RoyChowdhury 2021), another segment of India's fragmented working class is even less accounted for. An estimated 400,000 domestic workers are reproducing life and labour in the city daily (Menon 2020). This part engages with the invisible, essential, and devalued nature of domestic work as an entry point to highlight how the proliferation of commercial microfinance is underpinned by the complex work of caring for debts. It highlights the contradictions of the formal/informal binary of the financial inclusion discourse, discussing the relational rationalities of indebtedness. Ultimately, this investigation allows us to understand the inherently exploitative dimensions of reproductive debts, in which corporate MFIs play an ever more critical role.

Invisible, Essential, Devalued: The Nature of Domestic Work

The invisibility of domestic workers in India is manifested in many ways. For instance, there are no reasonable estimates for the share of reproductive labour in urban areas as part of the GDP, and the accounting of domestic workers in official statistics remains patchy (Neetha and Palriwala 2011). According to the National Sample Survey (NSS) from 2011–12, roughly 4.13 million, overwhelmingly women, worked in the households of others (Joseph, Natrajan, and Lobo 2019, 100). In the first decade of the new millennium, the number of private homes with employed persons increased fourfold across the country (Neetha 2019, 35). This boom must be understood in the context of jobless growth, rapid urbanisation, and a relative decline in men's contribution to household income through the casualisation of wage work in the informal economy (Basole and Basu 2011a; Neetha and Palriwala 2011). Frequently, the wives of construction workers in Bengaluru and other megacities complement the household income through paid domestic work in different private homes.

The growth of domestic workers in India's megacities is attributed mainly to the increase in live-out and part-time workers.[1] Given the predominance of Brahmanism, it is hardly surprising that this labour is considered polluted and thus attributed to those at the margins of the caste-based social structure – namely Dalits and Adivasis (Wadhawan 2013). Although there are no official figures, all interviewed civil society organisations involved with domestic workers in Bengaluru confirmed that most of this workforce comes from Dalit communities. Their work is considered non-skilled and usually not even recognised as work. Yet, it is labour-intensive and operates under considerable time pressure, including managing multiple tasks in many different households during a workday. Domestic workers are frequently expected to support childcare, assist in cooking, or perform other chores as subsidiary tasks, although these never form part of the negotiation.

Since private homes are not officially recognised as a worksite, domestic workers are often not considered workers by the state and their employers. Most labour laws and social security benefits do not apply to them, and arguably, their working conditions are amongst the most informalised among India's working class (Joseph, Lobo, and Natrajan 2018; Neetha and Palriwala 2011). Notably, the degree of personal dependency from employers, from recruitment to bargaining for wages to negotiating for leave, bonus, or advances[2], is much higher than for construction, garment, or other informal sector workers. This can be partly explained by the history of domestic work, which emerged from feudal patronage relationships informed by caste hierarchies. Despite a significant change towards market-mediation of domestic work and official changes to an employer-employee relationship, these feudal hierarchies continue to undergird contemporary working conditions:

> "It is still the feudal notion of that work. Most of the workers are part of the Dalit community. Because the Dalit community used to work on the lands, they were landless labourers, therefore the whole emergence of this sector emerged from that. Domestic work was seen as cleaning work. Therefore, it is all the more devalued. Because in the caste hierarchy of our society, we have the notion of high/low and purity/pollution and mental/physical division of labour. Once this is in the psyche of society, anything you do for work – for example, Dalits clean the toilets in domestic work. Women clean the toilets, but they are not allowed to use them.

1 Other important sections of domestic workers include cooks, nannies, and live-in domestic workers. However, overall and especially in urban areas, the share of housemaids is by far the largest (Neetha and Palriwala 2011, 102).

2 The exploitation through placement agencies is similar to the construction sector, e.g. no transparent terms of employment, collection of salary from employer, fraudulent brokerage expenses, travel costs, boarding, and so on (Neetha and Palriwala 2011). However, it is further aggravated through endemic gender-based violence, and, in the case of live-in workers, cases of human trafficking (CSA_6, Pos.24).

> They do the most menial of the tasks, but they are not allowed to enter the Pooja room or the kitchen. Even for kitchen work, they will employ the upper-caste domestic workers, for the cleaning work they will employ Dalits." (CSA_6, Pos. 4)

As is evident from the quote, the exploitation of domestic workers is organised around Brahmanical hierarchies, which fragment the precarious working class, their tasks, valuation and social recognition along caste-based lines. While cooking has increasingly become a status symbol for middle-class urban households, these domestic workers are on-trend, recruited from within the caste order, and in comparison, better paid. On the other hand, cleaning remains a polluted task for the outcastes (Dalits), which results in the lowest valuation and treatment of this segment of domestic workers (CSA_4, Pos. 59–60). These multiple relations of oppression allow for fragmenting the precarious workforce and for keeping labour cheap and flexible: "Part-time is very scattered, very flexible, maids work in ten houses, some women work 15 houses per day because she must earn Rs. 15,000 [per month]" (CSA_6, Pos. 24).

In addition to the general pattern of caste-based and gendered class exploitation, the concrete working conditions reinforce personal dependency and the devaluation of work. In contrast to a construction site or factory, where you meet and interact with co-workers, domestic workers are usually employed on an individual basis in a household, where the work (including its surveillance and abuse) takes place in a private space:

> "In the informal economy workers are so scattered, and domestic workers are the last end of the unorganised sector. [...] They work in different households, different homes, different employers, they have no tools of production. In the whole sector of the work history, they are not considered as a productive workforce, and they don't think of themselves as a productive workforce because the sector is like that. It's a very personalized, individualized type of work where I will go and work for an individual employer. If that individual employer is nice to me, he's nice." (CSA_6, Pos. 3; see also CSA_4, Pos. 30)

These circumstances create a favourable climate for infringing on worker and human rights beyond law enforcement through the denial of wages, virtual incarceration in the employer's home, refusal of leave because of payments made by the employer to an agency, and sexual harassment and gender-based violence (Neetha and Palriwala 2011, 111).

In recent years, the increased market mediation of domestic work has meant that tasks and hours are more clearly defined and related to specific monetary wages. Moreover, the employing households in the city are not necessarily only upper caste as compared to rural areas (CSA_4, Pos. 31; CSA_6, Pos. 7). However, personal dependencies between employers and employees remain key due to the intimate nature of the work, the specificity of this labour market, and its relative exclusion from state social security. During the lockdown amidst the COVID-19 pandemic in 2020, most domestic workers in Bengaluru were told not to come to work; the vast majority did not receive any salary for April and about half of the workers above the age of 50 lost their jobs (Menon 2020). The structural violence underpinning the exploitation of paid care work is particularly pronounced amongst upper-class/caste households. In Kormangla, at the centre of Bengaluru, the National Games Village (NGV) comprises more than 3,000 apartments for bank officials, judges, army officers and other top-level government civil servants. Just opposite the site, a large slum stretches into the city, and provides a cheap labour force that maintains these apartments. Referring to current labour struggles and complaints at this site, an NGO worker involved in organising maids said:

> "Some of the worst culprits are in the judicial apartment block. And all the judges think they are above law. There is no leave facility, no bonus. Even police officers and IAS officers behave like that. You come to private apartments, you may find a few who treat their workers well, but none of them think that giving them weekly off is necessary for a domestic worker [...] Often they will ask them work for one hour and then they make them work for two hours. Therefore, the effective wage is low. [...] So that kind of conflict arises with domestic workers." (CSA_4, Pos. 34)

In this regard, domestic workers are not only the most vulnerable amongst Bengaluru's precarious migrant labourers. They are also torn between a limited and specified contractual relationship and personal dependency, producing a peculiar relationship of exploitation and an ambiguous class position (Joseph, Natrajan, and Lobo 2019, 106).

Moreover, the working conditions also pose a severe challenge for organising the workforce and even for workers to understand themselves as workers, not servants or a subordinate part of the employer's patriarchal family. Yet, the rise of apartment complexes and gated communities in urban areas has led to a proto worksite, where apartment gates transform into factory gates, opening new opportunities for organising labour and addressing employers collectively (Joseph, Natrajan, and Lobo 2019, 107). Although the overall share of organised labour has been historically low and currently comprises not more than several thousand out of more than 400,000 workers (CSA_1; CSA_4; CSA_6), numerous trade unions of domestic workers (facilitated mainly by NGOs) emerged in Bengaluru in the past decade. Presently, there are about ten small and medium-sized unions, which can be classified into three major categories: First, conventional NGOs, which focus on the welfare rights of domestic workers. Second, traditional trade unions are affiliated with a political party and mostly lobby for state schemes/welfare concerning domestic workers. Third, labour

NGOs operate through rank-and-file organising and as community-based organisations, fighting for a living wage, a weekly off, and an annual monetary bonus around festival season (Joseph, Natrajan, and Lobo 2019).

All three core demands are intimately related to the question of indebtedness. Endemically low real wages due to specific working conditions based on gender and caste, no time off and no emergency funds or bonus payments exacerbate the subsistence crisis of this segment of India's working class, and produce a tendency where women workers must resort to reproductive debt. The intimate personal dependency that persists despite the market mediation, monetisation, and standardisation of domestic work is specific to domestic workers in Bengaluru. As a result, domestic workers frequently "depend on the employer for loans, assistance in times of emergency, and other help" (Neetha and Palriwala 2011, 107). In this sense, the case of domestic workers is interesting to investigate the promise and limitations of commercial microfinance.

Relational Rationalities of Indebtedness

The predominant discourse on financial inclusion suggests that the poor lack access to credit because they don't have bank accounts. Usually, this financial service gap is attributed to the physical distance between financial institutions and a lack of education (esp. financial literacy). Hence, policies encouraging door-to-door banking, fostering digital financial services, and organising financial literacy workshops are presented as significant game-changers in tackling the root causes of financial exclusion. Much of this rationality follows the script of the tale of the rational economic man (*homo oeconomicus*) that has dominated modern economic common sense since the eighteenth century. Accordingly, economic subjects voluntarily enter exchange relations and decide freely about the goods and services offered in markets. Feminist scholars have long criticised how such a perspective conceals the actual real-world constraints that economic agents face and renders the class-based, racialised and gendered power inequalities that inform the involuntary participation in market relations invisible (Grapard 1995; Hanappi-Egger 2014; Hooper 2000).

The bottom line of this narrow thinking is that if provided the opportunity, people experiencing poverty would eventually make more rational decisions and opt for formal financial institutions with lower interest rates compared to those of informal creditors. However, the interviews with migrant workers in Bengaluru suggest a different story of financial exclusion. Asked about what keeps them from having a bank account and whether they would perceive this as an opportunity, two women in a temporary settlement in Kodigahalli (Northern Bangalore) who had been recently displaced through the construction of a multi-story residential building responded: "Why should we have a bank account if we cannot save anything?" (HH_Cluster_5,

Pos. 67). This incisive statement summarises the nearly unanimous response from all interviewed precarious migrant workers who had no bank account or who had not taken a loan from a commercial financial institution.[3] Awareness of the possibility was never an issue, contradicting the standard financial inclusion narrative. Instead, women consciously decided not to take a loan *for good reasons*. Or they decided to take loans from different sources *for good reasons* (see also CSA_7, Pos. 10).

So, while voluntary exclusion from formal banking is almost always linked to a lack of income through decent work or social security schemes, access to informal credit may be more attractive even in the case of higher interest rates. Perhaps even more importantly, from the perspective of borrowers, access to credit is not primarily a choice between formal and informal institutions. Multiple forms and types of credit that converge in the household economy may be a necessary and rational reproductive strategy of subaltern working-classes (van der Linden 2023, 111). This section seeks to understand the rise and limits of commercial microfinance amongst migrant workers by moving beyond the dichotomy of formal/informal credit and rational/irrational household decision-making. In doing so, it highlights the relationality of rationality.

The notion of relational rationality challenges the conventional understanding that questions around desirable loans are primarily about interest rates or quantitative assessment related to cheap/expensive credit. Based on my empirical fieldwork, I propose a multi-layered understanding of relational rationality across four dimensions, including social barriers of accessibility, the flexibility of loan size, freedom to use loans and conditions of repayment schedules. These four criteria are justified as follows. First, I maintain that the abstract formal/informal divide or financial literacy does not primarily determine the accessibility of credit. Instead, it is a matter of *social* distance between borrowers and customers and *social* obligations and dependencies that emerge from the specific debt relations. Second, a flexible loan size is pivotal for precarious migrant workers because the needs of credit range from regular expenses for private education for children to small lump sums for house repair to major emergency expenses for surgery. Third, the freedom to use the loans for various purposes is closely linked to the second dimension. It highlights that far from the idealised image of income-generating loans, most borrowers take out loans for different reproductive needs. Finally, a repayment schedule considering the actual cash flow of respective households, sensitive to the erratic livelihoods of workers (irregular incomes, emergency expenditure, vulnerability to crises), is arguably more important than the abstract interest rate.

---

3 This perspective is also supported by the World Bank's Global Findex Database. The most prominent reason for not having a bank account, i.e. being financially excluded, is that those people didn't have sufficient money to engage in such financial services (Demirgüc-Kunt et al. 2018).

Against this backdrop, we can assess the success and limits of microfinance as part of a broader ecosystem. Figures 15 visualises these four criteria for different creditor institutions, explaining the advantages and challenges of each from the perspective of precarious migrant workers in Bengaluru.

Figure 15: Visualisation of Loan (Dis-)Advantages by Source

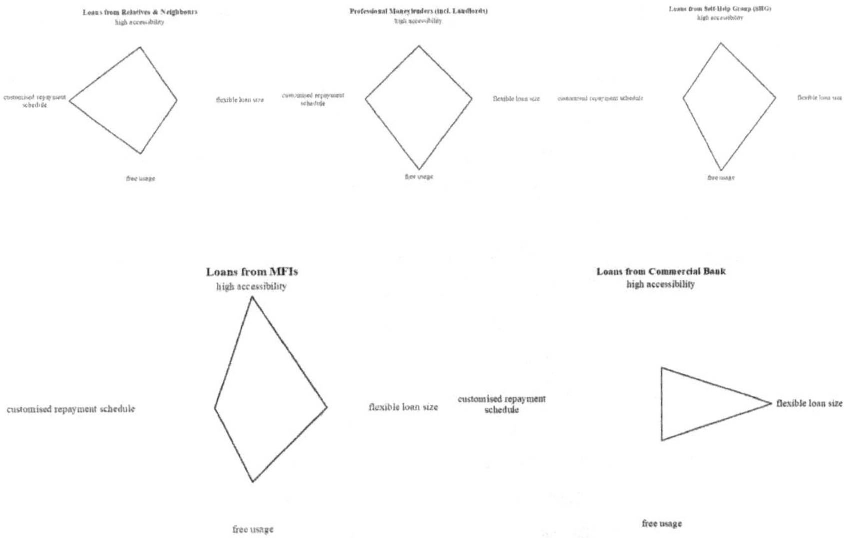

Source: own illustration based on fieldwork. The scales are deliberately not quantified because the assessment emerged from qualitative research (interviews) and primarily serves the purpose of visualising the tendencies associated with each creditor.

The relational rationality of access goes both ways. It encompasses the relationship between creditors and debtors, particularly the social interaction necessary for debts to emerge, persist and possibly disappear again. While commercial banks in India have been traditionally exclusive to many segments of the precarious working class despite bank nationalisation and priority sector lending (see Chapter 10), accessing credit from known persons in one's immediate surroundings, be it neighbours and relatives or landlords and employers, is comparatively easy. As an RBI official explains the persistence of moneylenders: "It's easy. They are from the communities. You will have 24/7 availability, and in cases of emergencies, these sources are always accessible" (RBI_2, Pos. 37). However, beyond the availability, accessibility is also mediated by the social obligations and potential dependencies that emerge from the creditor-debtor-relationship. Borrowing from local moneylenders, landlords, or employers may provide financially favourable conditions compared to commercial banks or MFIs. Still, such debts "are inscribed into a series of rights and obligations requiring multiple forms of compensation" (Guérin 2014, 45), including work obligations.

MFIs have carved out a distinct space in between this divide. As an official from the Reserve Bank of India put it, microfinance has been successful because they are a hybrid organisation "at the border between formal and informal sectors" (RBI_1, Pos. 63). They are mimicking the informal moneylenders in the sense of actively approaching borrowers, building strong social ties through regular group meetings and field staff or intermediate NGOs who know and regularly engage with these women as proxy-creditors (Kar 2018). Yet, the obligations for the collateral-free microloans imply the gendered work of caring for debts by engaging in group meetings, monitoring peers, and reporting to field officers. They do not come for free but are associated with offloading risks and responsibilities, creating multiple entrapments of women borrowers (Rankin 2002; Weber 2014; Wichterich 2017).

The relational rationality of loan usage and loan size refer to the multiple dimensions of household expenditure in relation to the subsistence crisis. I would argue that a critical reason for the popularity of SHGs and the persistence of moneylenders lies precisely in the fact that loans from these sources can be used for anything – whether it is seasonal home-repairs, steady expenditure for (private) education, or bigger lump-sums in cases of weddings or health emergencies. Commercial banks are thus less attractive not only because of the social distance described through low accessibility but also because they hardly provide for the actual needs of precarious workers, holding on to the fantasy that loans are or have been primarily used for productive investment (be in agriculture or small-scale business). For example, no commercial bank would lend Rs. 100,000 for a surgery without thoroughly checking the customer's credit rating and asking for collateral – which most of the urban working class do not have.

Once again, the success of MFIs can be explained by their business strategy to carve out a space in this context. While almost all MFIs started out with income-generating loans, usually without paying much attention to the actual use as long as repayments flowed in regularly, today, the credit portfolio offers a wide range of opportunities for reproductive finance, including loans for housing, education, emergencies, water purification and sanitation that is sensitive to people's life cycle (Kazim 2018; Mahajan 2005). Moreover, credit products are designed as an upward cascade, offering ever higher debt contracts upon repayment, as a manger from Janalakshmi Financial Services describes:

> "We look at the customers lifecycle to match and build our own products. The way we look at this, we start with a group loan, it was Rs. 10,000 to begin with. Then it went up to Rs. 15,000, later Rs. 20,000 and Rs. 25,000. With the RBI coming with guidelines post Andhra crisis, there are two MFIs who can lend up to Rs. 60,000 to

the same customers. So they take the first loan, 15 month or 18 month, two years, then they come back and take the second for Rs. 40,000 or Rs. 50,000. What happens is, it's like a kid trying to crawl and he will hold the parents hand and tries walking. And after some time, he or she will say no, you don't support me, I'll walk myself. Right? That's how we expect the kids to be. We expect the same behaviour with our customer" (MFI_3, Pos. 13)

The paternalistic tone, comparing grown-up women with kids, resonates with colonial discourses that still underpin development thinking, policy, and practice. What is striking is that the purported aim of the business model (empowering people to "walk themselves") is contradicted by the reality that social mobility through debt is considerably constrained by numerous factors beyond access to and use of credit. The cascade approach reveals that continued indebtedness, facilitated through different purposes and sizes of loans, is the primary objective of this business strategy. This dynamic points to another contradiction of the commercial microfinance model. While there is considerable scope to start with small sums (Rs. 10,000) and increase the amounts upon repayment, this strategy cannot continue indefinitely. As an industry insider explains:

> "That is also why MFIs are successful today. Because they are lending small amounts. Highest is about Rs. 30,000 – average is Rs. 25,000. And why is that people return? The only reason they are returning is because they expect a larger next round. That's the only reason people are returning. So if the government says it will lend Rs. 5 lakh under MUDRA – why should I return Rs. 5 lakh? Or Rs. 10 lakh even worse. Why should I return Rs. 5 lakh. If I borrow such an amount, I can live quite happily for three years or four years. Then comes elections and loan waivers. So why should I pay? It is the small loans that works." (CSA_7, Pos. 66–74)

If, as was argued throughout this research, reproductive debt serves as a survival buffer in the presence of a chronic subsistence crisis of India's precarious working class, and microfinance offers a unique creditor institution to acquire such debts, it is essential to highlight that there are inherent limits to this business model. Perhaps the most important is the impossibility of increasing loan sums indefinitely without risking mass delinquency. Importantly, this is not only an economic problem but also a political one, especially if excessive lending becomes politicised and state-sanctioned loan waivers risk creditor operations.

Finally, the relational rationality of repayment is perhaps the most complex dimension, interlocking with the points discussed above. When asked why moneylenders persist despite the rapid rise of microfinance, a long-standing sector expert explains that the relevance of social proximity mentioned above and the customisation of repayment are pivotal. Rather than fixing an interest rate and insisting on exact payment on time, moneylenders usually calculate repayment based on the actual cash flow of their clients: "Because they pay daily they don't feel that it's a burden to pay Rs. 100 or Rs. 150 per day. It's not a problem, whereas spending Rs. 2,000 at one point in time would be rather difficult" (CSA_9, Pos. 15). This point is also valid for landlords and employers. In contrast to MFIs or commercial banks, the former usually prioritise sustained personal dependency over the abstract value of money and narrow profit calculations.

Borrowers from professional moneylenders, landlords or employers cannot become insolvent. However, the higher flexibility in terms of repayment does not imply a less violent or power-laden relationship. While the customisation of repayment schedules allows for greater flexibility on their behalf, it may also keep them trapped in an endless cycle of debt repayment, which has been discussed in the literature as "neo-bondage" (Breman 2019; Guérin 2013). In such cases, migration or suicide/death becomes the only exit option from debt bondage. This phenomenon has marked the contemporary neoliberal regime of re/productive finance, especially in agrarian settings, where at least 300,000 indebted farmers committed suicide between 1995 and 2012 (Nagaraj et al. 2014).

The dimension of repayment schedules exposes one of the central contradictions of commercial microfinance in India. If there were a single most important criterion defining their loan product, it would be that loans are standardised in terms of tenure and size (CSA_7, Pos. 27; CSA_11, Pos. 35). This standardisation allows MFIs to operate in accordance with the rhythms of financial markets, including borrowing capital, raising equity through stock markets, and securitising their loan portfolio. Yet, the livelihoods of their customer base are marked by fundamental insecurity. The constant threat of delinquency haunts MFIs' profitability and sustainability, so peer-pressure, tight monitoring and aggressive repayment methods are endemic to the business model. The non-flexible repayment schedule is the Achilles heel of MFIs, especially in times of crisis (see Chapter 11). MFIs know that "the worst affected [by these crises] would be the ones we serve, we deal with" (MFI_3, Pos. 11). To prevent mass default and a collapse of the industry, many MFIs may temporarily compromise on strict repayment during crises like Demonetisation and the COVID-19 pandemic. However, maintaining their profit-driven business model requires resorting to coercive recovery practices and extracting revenue at the expense of debtor's livelihoods, who increasingly draw on informal credit to remain solvent (Guérin et al. 2021, 2022). This raises the question of how we can make sense of the exploitative dimensions of reproductive debts.

Exploitative Dimensions of Reproductive Debt

In the dominant discourse of financial inclusion, formal credit is usually associated with empowerment, working capital, and social participation, whereas informal lending is described as an usurious relationship. The previous section cautions against stylised imaginaries of the formal and the informal. Drawing on the distinction between money, credit and capital from Chapter 5, this section highlights the similarities and differences between various debt relations and explores the dynamics of exploitation through financial means in more detail.

There is a fundamental difference between credit used as capital and credit used as money. In the former case, borrowed money is invested, for example, in business activities, hoping that this investment generates revenue, allowing the borrower to repay the loan and keep a profit for themselves. Thus, the borrower becomes a functioning capitalist, even on a small scale. This strategy has many barriers, including small loan sums, intensive competition pushing prices down, saturation of local markets, lack of market linkages or capacities, etc. However, this type of loan theoretically allows dreaming of some poor entrepreneurs emerging from poverty with the help of access to credit. This differs from reproductive debts, where credit is primarily expended as money to purchase goods and commodified services like food, housing, or health care. In these cases, the money is not invested in the entrepreneurial sense and does not generate revenue directly. It is fictitious capital in the first and basic understanding of the term (see Chapter 5).

Even if part of the microloan is invested, as the previous chapter has argued, in a context where more than half of the country's adult population is apprehensive about not having enough money for monthly expenses, old age, education, and medical costs, it is hardly surprising that borrowing primarily serves reproductive purposes. A woman from Mantralaya in Andhra Pradesh, who had settled in Whitefield (East Bengaluru) a few years back and had to take a loan to pay her husband's appendix operation, summarises their dilemma as follows: "Whatever we earn is hardly enough for food, then how are we supposed to cope with hospital bills?" (HH_Cluster_6, Pos. 68). MFIs are very aware of the actual needs of their customer base, which is primarily credit used as money (not capital):

> "Predominantly they [borrowers] live in slums. There's no fixed cash flow coming in. They have to live on their daily wages kind of jobs. They have to do odd jobs. They don't have sufficient money to leave and see their family. [...] If they are living in a slum, the hygienic conditions are very bad, water supply, electricity and stuff like that is lacking. Obviously, they need money. And that's where we come in, we play that role." (MFI_3, Pos. 11)

This statement from a manager of Janalakshmi Financial Services (now Jana SFB) shows how borrowing credit as money (not capital) is part of the business strategy of one of the largest MFIs in the country. The pressure for regular and high repayment is further enforced through the second dimension of fictitious capital. The microloans in the books of Janalakshmi and other corporate MFIs are repackaged and sold off to investors through securitisation to finance the expansion of borrowing. So, while the fictitious capital turns money seemingly effortlessly into more money ($M\text{-}M^{(+)}$), this process appears as inverse capital from the perspective of indebted women. Money is borrowed to pay for goods or commodified services. Although this investment does not generate any revenue, more money must be paid back through fees and interest. Building on Marx's famous formulation of capital, we can understand this process from the borrower's perspective through the general formula $M - C - M^{(-)}$.

At first glance, the general formula of inverse capital appears to make little sense. Since the money value is necessarily a quantitative metric, this form of circulation is like a bottomless pit. How can those migrant workers sustain a seemingly continuous drain of money? While the rhetoric of the entrepreneurial poor continues to dominate public appearance, the business model of MFIs is premised on other flows of revenue:

> "NBFCs are basically women-town-based. That's where it's easier to handle. 80% or even 90% of them are working. They are maids, they are service people, they are this and that, they need some money. So, their recovery is not from the loan investment. How much are they lending? Rs 15,000, maybe Rs 20,000? What can you do with that? Highest loan is Rs 30,000. So, they need this money to overcome some short-term credit needs, which is fine. But they don't invest in assets. And their recovery doesn't come from investment. It comes from regular work. There are five maids in our flats. They return the loans from their salaries. They will get about Rs 15,000 per month salary, and they will return from that." (CSA_7, Pos. 16)

If reproductive debts are primarily paid from wage income, the proliferation of profit-driven financial services adds another layer to the exploitation of migrant workers in the concrete labour process, taking the form of what Lapavitsas (2009) calls "financial expropriation". Notably, the rise of MFIs does not necessarily replace other creditor institutions but rather complements them:

> "So their source of money is their salary. The old system of moneylending has changed. In fact, we used to have this pawning of things, gold pawning. The other thing that has happened in a big way is microfinance institutions have come with a very aggressive growth. In fact, they are very aggressive and very bureaucratic. It's a lot of money being eaten as interest and so on. They cut their throughts, literally for the women, to pay back all this. They juggle it like that." (CSA_6, Pos. 41)

Against this backdrop, the distinction between formal (non-exploitative) and informal (exploitative) becomes questionable, if not irrelevant. Rather, different creditors engage in various exploitation patterns: Debts with moneylenders, landlords and employers usually imply domination through personal dependency and enrichment. In these cases, borrowing is generally more directly linked to the subordination of labour. In contrast, debts through SHG-BLP and MFIs are more alienated and based on objective domination (*sachliche Herrschaft*), although personal relations are crucial to the group-lending model. In the latter cases, financial expropriation runs parallel to the exploitation in the labour process. Yet, both scenarios feed on the same dynamics: Since effectively landless labour migrants usually do not have any valuable possessions, like land or gold, they must pawn their future labour capacities, forcing them to take on even the most precarious types of jobs, just to stay solvent and survive through debt. In this sense, the proliferation of access to reproductive debts generates future obligations in abstract monetary terms, which are intimately bound up with facilitating and disciplining cheap labour in the present (Breman 2019; Cavallero and Gago 2021; Natarajan et al. 2021).

Proponents of microfinance highlight that, on average, MFIs offer cheaper interest rates than moneylenders, making them less exploitative. This is an important argument, and it can explain the attractiveness of MFIs to a certain extent. However, as the previous sections have shown, there are multiple related rationalities of indebtedness and creditor institutions do not necessarily compete but complement one another. Put differently, subaltern working-class households are not only characterised by multiple income sources and types of labour pooled into the household economy. The fractured lives of Bengaluru's migrant workers are also marked by a variety of different types and sources of reproductive debts that converge. The contradictory formula of inverse capital, $M\text{-}C\text{-}M^{(-)}$, can be partly explained through the process of financial expropriation. But it is also sustained through the gendered work of caring for debts. After all, microloans do not magically (dis-)appear in the lives of poor people. As discussed in Chapter 6, if debts are not cared for, they quickly become non-performing loans.

When we explore how debts are cared for, we can also understand why and how microfinance in South Asia is gendered. The general answer to this riddle lies in Muhammad Yunus' 'discovery' that microfinance can be a profitable business case, even without collateral, *if* loans are given to women who, as a group, vouch for each other. When asked why they are almost exclusively targeting women, the CEO of a microfinance organisation based in Bengaluru gives the following explanation:

> "See, there are a couple of reasons. One is they are more creditworthy. And if I want to go through a type of group-lending mechanisms it's comfortable to do it with women because they are more coercive in nature, and we're able to do the lending comfortably. And if we look at the main anchor of the family [...] They have a central point in finance. They ensure that things are going well in the family and all." (MFI_5, Pos. 7)

The first part of the quote reinstates the continued relevance of Yunus's discovery, revealing how microfinance banks go on and reinforce gendered roles of women as docile, devotional, and naturally caring for their families and peers for the sake of profit (thus allowing MFIs to "lending comfortably"). While women's better repayment rates may appear as a result of their "nature", as suggested by the quote above, it is, in fact, the result of their work in caring for debts – going to regular group meetings, supporting and disciplining other group members, and finding additional sources of income, including further debts with other creditors, to ensure repayment. Significantly, women are described as "anchors of the family" and "centre point in finance". This point is, however, not linked to some idealised imaginary of women's empowerment through access to credit. Rather, their central role is justified by "ensuring that things are going well", and, from the perspective of profitable lending, this includes primarily ensuring that debts are serviced on time.

In explaining how domestic workers in Bengaluru manage to pay back loans despite their meagre and irregular incomes, one trade union leader said, "[t]hey juggle it like that" (CSA_6, Pos. 41). Another NGO representative involved with organising Dalit domestic workers, qualifies this juggling as follows: "They usually have three or four different sources of loans. They are juggling between loans. Taking from here and paying there." (CSA_4, Pos. 51). Juggling with debts highlights how domestic workers simultaneously engage with multiple creditors and how in this process, they are working through the relative (dis-)advantages and constraints in relation to one another:

> "It [debt] has become so part of their daily life. They don't blink an eyelid paying 5 or 10 per cent interest. We calculate how much we should pay per annum. They are so used to daily and monthly interest that its almost normal. You cannot survive without it. And they can't afford to fight any moneylender because they know they need them. In fact, they are very happy that Ujjivan and all these others have come up. I mean, not happy, but it's another source in emergencies and if they don't have work for a few days or month. And also when someone in the family is sick, or for schools. [...] They are constantly indebted. And only when it reaches extreme things, they try something new and they set up something. Loans accumulate very high, and then they repay Rs. 5,000 – 6,000 interest per month. Many get trapped into that, only servicing interest. The principal remains." (CSA_4, Pos. 53)

This statement reaffirms the internal relationship of multiple debts that cuts through the formal-informal divide and renders the latter as an analytical category irrelevant. In practice, juggling debts point to the potential symbiosis between local moneylenders and commercial MFIs, challenging the claim that microfinance allows women to free themselves from "the clutches of the moneylender" (Rajan 2005). Some MFI experts and sector insiders support this view, claiming that "[a]ll that we can possibly say is that we have created one more level of for these people to borrow. And therefore, their ability to borrow might be at better terms." (CSA_11, Pos. 35).

In the presence of a chronic subsistence crisis, the demand for money is so high that competition between creditors is not necessarily constrained (CSA_8, Pos. 12; CSA_10, Pos. 25; RBI_1, Pos.60). In this context, juggling with debt explains how different types of loans in terms of multiple sources, free usage and variegated repayment schedules are fused into one and the same household economy, cancelling each other out or reinforcing one another:

> "It is common for microloans to first be used to repay old debts. Microcredit can be used to pay off financially expensive debts. This is often the case with loans from door-to-door lenders, whose incomparable advantage is their availability and convenience—they come to individuals' homes and require no material guarantee—but in return they are rather expensive. Microcredit can also be used to repay debts that are socially degrading or which threaten a family's reputation. Social relations of caste, kinship, and gender play a key role here. As indicated above, substituting one debt with another is only partial and provisional. When it comes to repaying microcredit, insofar as it only very rarely generates new revenues, the most common option is to reborrow else-where. Households are thus entangled in endless debts." (Guérin 2014, 44)

The potential symbiosis between multiple creditors should not be misread as automatic institutional complementary. Rather, juggling debts exposes the offloading of work, responsibility and risk, producing constant tensions between different logics, trade-offs, and conflicting interests that women borrowers have to work through on a day-to-day basis (Guérin 2014, 48–49). In this sense, juggling debts is an unappreciated though necessary form of care work.

However, there is no guarantee that juggling debt always works. Caring for debts may be an essential aspect of understanding inverse capital, but it has inherent limits, which also expose the limits of the financialisation of daily life:

> "What I'm critical of is this consumption increasing, and this is something that is emerging from our studies, indebtedness is increasing. If you borrow from one person Rs 10,000 or Rs 15,000 that may be fine. But if you borrow from four-five people Rs. 45,000 or Rs 50,000 then it is a major trouble, because their income is not increasing. So they are living of loans. You may be a maid. You earning Rs 15,000 or 20,000 per month. But your indebtedness is increasing." (CSA_7, Pos. 18)

Advertisements frequently gloss over the harsh reality of constantly being on the brink of over-indebtedness. While MFIs claim to provide "a full-service financial institution to fuel their dreams" (Janalakshmi Financial Services 2018), the reality looks more mundane when talking to the staff:

> "Those women who work as a housemaid or sweepers, or vegetable sellers at the roadside in the evening, we ask them, "did you study?" and they all say, "no, Sir, we're uneducated, we studied second class or first class of fourth standard, then my family got me married, there are kids now". When we ask them "What do you want for your kids?" they will all answer that education is important. I think that's the ambition. When we ask them which medium they go to schools, is it mother tongue or English medium, and they will say we'll put them in English medium school, not in government schools. This is the ambition you can see. And they want their children to be engineers and doctors. This is exactly the same ambitions you see in the middle class or upper middle class." (MFI_3, Pos. 15)

Domestic and other precarious wage workers are toiling under adverse conditions, but they have the aspiration of a decent life for their children. This has also been a consistent topic in the focused narrative interviews. Arguably, this is even more enforced by the bleak long-term effects of social mobility that precarious wage workers face. In studying the inter-generational occupational changes amongst slum dwellers in Bengaluru, Krishna (2013) finds that children from construction workers and maids, amongst other precarious wage workers, have hardly experienced upward mobility in the past.

This is the point where we come full circle. The rapid expansion of microfinance is based on a pervasive subsistence crisis of India's subaltern working-class, and, as shown for the case of migrant workers, it is fuelled by the aspiration that debts for life contribute not only to the present survival of respective households but also to a more decent life for the next generation. Since these expenditures do not create direct revenue, repayment of reproductive debt is ensured through the entwined process of financial expropriation (deduction of wages in the present and pawning of future labour capacities) and caring for debts by, for example, juggling different sources and types of loans. Against this backdrop, A. R. Vasavi's description of entrapments through indebtedness "between aspiration and realization, between creditor and debtor, between desire and desperation, and between life and death" (Vasavi 2014, 33) captures the fundamental contradictions of contemporary financial inclusion accurately. Rather than passively accepting their subordination and exploitation marked by chronic indebtedness, juggling debts can be understood as a strategic means at the individual level to navigate these contradictions.

Significantly, these personal struggles can become related to broader social struggles. For instance, the fight of domestic workers in Bengaluru for an annual monetary bonus (rather than perks in kind) is entwined with the omnipresent reality of outstanding loans (Joseph, Lobo, and Natrajan 2018, 42). With this in mind, the following section will explore the relationship between labour and debt struggles more thoroughly, drawing on the case of garment workers. Moreover, it will explore further strategies to ensure repayment that add to the processes of financial expropriation and juggling with debts.

Chapter 15
The Convergence of Labour and Debt Struggles

On 19 April 2016, the Karnataka Government imposed Section 144 of the Criminal Procedure Code, prohibiting the assembly of more than ten people in an area. The hasty and drastic decision was a reaction to one of the largest worker's protests that Bengaluru had seen in years and an expression of how government officials and police were taken by surprise by the massive demonstrations. More than 120,000 people – mostly female garment workers – had taken on the street since the day before, shutting down major roadways and blocking industrial areas all over the megacity. Neither officials nor unions had predicted anything like this and had difficulties making sense of what had happened: The 'flash strikes', as the newspapers referred to the unfolding events, seemed to have no leaders; they were not orchestrated or announced by unions or civil society organisations, and perhaps most remarkable, women workers headed these powerful protests.

The massive wave of local resistance was sparked by the announcement of the NDA government a few weeks earlier to reform the Employees Provident Fund (EPF), one of the largest social security schemes in the world (in terms of clientele), mainly covering public sector and industrial workers in India. According to the scheme, a share of salaried workers' income must be invested in the fund and is matched by a compulsory contribution on the side of employers, while ¾ of EPF corpus derives from worker's income and only ¼ from the employer's contribution. If certain conditions are met, like being unemployed for two months or reaching the age of retirement, workers can access the full amount, including interest accrued in the meantime. In 2018, roughly US$ 160 billion was under the management of the Employees' Provident Fund Organisation (EPFO), which comes under the Indian Ministry of Labour and Employment. Like in many other economies around the globe, corporate lobbyists and neoliberal policymakers had pushed for the financialisation of the pension scheme for years, allowing the substantial amount of assets under management to be invested in the share market.[1] The NDA government aggressively pushed

1 For global trends of the financialisation of pension schemes, see e.g. Bonizzi et al. (2021) and Braun (2022).

for this trend after coming to power in 2014. In the financial year of 2015 – 2016, the Ministry of Labour and Employment allowed the EPFO to invest between 5 and 15 per cent of its incremental corpus in equities. Hence, in 2015 Rs. 5,000 crores (roughly one billion US dollars) were placed in stocks through Exchange Traded Funds (ETF), which gradually increased in the following years.

Chitra Ramkrishna, CEO of the National Stock Exchange, was clearly excited about the shift: "EPFO's entry in stock markets will unlock savings into nation building. [...] It will certainly deepen the financial market in India." (The Economic Times 2015). However, the benefits of these investments in "nation-building" were distributed somewhat unevenly. Since government guarantees do not back the provident fund, losses result in reduced employee returns. By early 2020, the EPFO had invested more than Rs. 100,000 crores (roughly 75 billion US dollars) in the stock market but suffered losses of 8.29 per cent of the invested amount (Ray 2020). Moreover, employees did not only bear the losses of financial speculation. Restrictions on employees' access to the fund accompanied the creeping financialisation of India's pension scheme. To prevent workers from accessing the money before retirement age, Finance Minister Arun Jaitley proposed adding 60 per cent of the EPF corpus upon withdrawal to employees' taxable income and raising the retirement age from 55 years to 58 years. Even more critical for precarious workers, however, the plan was to withhold the employers' share in cases of unemployment. According to the proposal circulated in early 2016, employees would be allowed to withdraw only their portion of the EPF (incl. interest) after two months of unemployment, depriving workers of almost one-quarter of the whole EPF corpus, namely the employer's contribution. Workers and unions referred to this as 'single PF'. Moreover, women would be granted the money in cases of marriage, pregnancy, or childbirth *only* if they had signed an affidavit that they would not take up future employment (PUCL-K and WSS 2019, 17).

The EPF reform plans were undoubtedly an assault on workers' rights, and they sparked criticism and protests nationwide. Yet, neither politicians nor others had expected that the changes would spark such fierce and concentrated resistance as was visible in Bengaluru in mid-April 2016. When garment factory management informed workers about the changes and those who left the job received only their contribution to the EPF, word spread quickly amongst the workforces. On April 16, 2016, a local newspaper report warned garment workers they would lose out on their PF money if they had not withdrawn it by the end of the month, and two days later, workers went on strike. The protests were sudden and eruptive, and the police resorted to violent repression of the strike (CSA_5, Pos. 37). Nonetheless, after only two days of intensive strike action, carried mainly by women workers, the central government backed down on their reform plans.

The two-day strike was historic, and it left many observers baffled. Why did Bengaluru's garment workers, of whom the vast majority is not organised in unions, so determinedly resist reform proposals on a pension scheme? This section claims that the answer is closely related to migrant workers' contemporary crisis of social reproduction and the relevance of reproductive debt. To make this argument plausible, we will first engage with the role of (gendered) exploitation in Bengaluru's garment industry and explore how it is linked to workers' crisis of social reproduction before unravelling the role of reproductive debt and the EPF as garment workers' safety net. Finally, some observations on the intensification of the crisis of social reproduction after the strike in April 2016 will be outlined. While the previous parts of the chapter explored how the interlocking dynamics of expropriation, exploitation, and exclusion shape the demand for reproductive credit amongst migrant workers, how these debts signify diverse forms of financial expropriation, and how these debts are lived through by juggling different types and sources of loans, the final part of the incorporated comparison highlights the conflictual nature of reproductive debts, foreshadowing how labour and debt struggles may converge.

Gendered Exploitation in Garment Supply Chains

In the context of the emerging economic power of former colonies and the demand for a New International Economic Order (NIEO) in the 1960s and 1970s, the US, Canada and the EU thought to protect their garment industries from competition through a quota system that limited garment and textile imports from elsewhere, the so-called Multifibre Arrangement (MFA). With the liberalisation of global trade and the rise of the World Trade Organisation (WTO) in the 1990s, this protective measure was successively phased-out. As a result, global garment exports soared, increasing by 60 per cent between 2004 and 2011, with India becoming a significant hub for export-oriented production (Mani 2013). Before the COVID-19 pandemic, India's textile and clothing industry employed roughly 45 million (migrant) workers. It was valued at US$ 200 billion, contributing about 13 per cent of its industrial production and 12 per cent of export earnings (Majumdar, Shaw, and Sinha 2020). The rapid growth of the export-oriented output also spurred the expansion of particularly vibrant clusters around Delhi, Mumbai, Bengaluru and Tiruppur/Coimbatore. In Bengaluru, hundreds of production units mushroomed over the growing city, concentrating primarily in Boomanahalli, Mysore Road, and the Peenya industrial area. Since the early 2000s, the number of industrial (export-oriented) units and employed workers in Bengaluru has multiplied, turning the southern city into a hotspot of India's ready-made garment (RMG) industry, accounting for about 60 per cent of national garment exports (López 2021).

The rapid growth of Bengaluru's RMG industry was facilitated by intensifying exploitation with doubling production targets, increased surveillance, and aggressive anti-union rhetoric. A civil society activist and analyst of the sector recalls the significance and brutality of changing working conditions in Bengaluru's garment factories as follows:

> "The production targets increased enormously. If you talk to workers who were working in the 80s or early 90s, you would hear they were much more relaxed. They had to make 30 – 35 pieces per hour, and then you had some time to take a short nap, you had time to talk to your co-workers. That time was also not the time of the electric sowing machines. It used to be manual. They had more time, they had a much calmer work environment. After 1995, they saw this whole thing changing, screaming, yelling, and getting the production targets achieved. [...] Right now, it's about 80 – 120 pieces per hour. For every piece, every product they have a time machine. They see how many pieces could be made in few seconds, and that's how a production target is set [...] But what you don't consider is toilet breaks, water breaks, a break to just get up and stretch. And also, you don't measure – can you make the same production for the whole day, not recognising that the first hour or maybe first two hours are more productive as compared to the last hour of the day? The pressure remains the same throughout the day." (CSA_3, Pos. 4 – Pos. 6)

Unions and civil society organisations estimate that there were between 1,000 and 1,200 factories all over the city in 2018, employing more than 400,000 workers. Because many of them are small production units with less than 100 workers, they don't appear in official statistics and are not officially regulated under the Industrial Dispute Act, 1947.[2] While almost all workers in Bengaluru's garment industry are migrants, many unions and NGOs have observed a shift in migration patterns. During the 1990s and 2000s, most were intra-state migrants from Hassan, Chitradurga, Dharwad, Gulbarga, Hubli and other places in Karnataka. For about ten years, the number of migrants from distant states, especially from the East and Northeast India (Odisha, Jharkhand, Assam, etc.), has massively increased, with migrants travelling several thousand kilometres to toil in the booming sector (CSA_5, Pos. 48–53).

Most workers in Bengaluru's garment industry earn not more than the stipulated minimum wage, which has been heavily criticised by unions and civil society organisations for keeping labourers below the actual line of poverty (Mani, Mathew, and Bhattacharya 2018; RoyChowdhury 2015, 85). A 2012 survey amongst local garment workers suggested that average monthly wages were between Rs. 3,500 for unskilled workers (helper, ironer, checker) and Rs. 4,500 for tailors (GATWU 2012). The average monthly expenses, on the other hand, were more than twice as high as the

2 According to official figures, there are 766 factories with 282,000 workers in Bangalore.

regular average income, creating a considerable income-expenditure mismatch (see Table 5).[3]

Table 5: Average Monthly Expenses of Factory Garment Workers in Bengaluru, 2012

Category	Average monthly expense (Rs.)	Percent of total
Food	3855.22	41 %
Housing	2081.67	22 %
Utilities	400.97	4 %
Transport	767.42	8 %
Education	436.25	5 %
Health care	476.41	5 %
Others	1344.19	14 %
Total	9362.34	100 %

Source: GATWU (2012).

The average household expenses are, of course, subject to change over time, just as the payment of wages. In 2017 and 2019, the average wages had increased nominally, reaching between Rs. 7,000 – 8,000 per month and Rs. 9,000 – 10,000 per month, respectively (Anner and Dutta 2019; Mohan 2017).[4] However, the cost of housing (rent) has substantially increased in the context of rapid urbanisation, rising land prices and competition for space. Moreover, the trend of costly English private medium schools has also captured the urban poor as one of the main strategies to improve the livelihood chances of their children. Reflecting on these changes, a civil society activist reports the bleak prospects for worker's real incomes:

> "During Demonetisation, I had a series of meetings with workers. They get paid something like Rs. 7,000–8,000/month, out of which Rs. 4,000 goes immediately out for rent, which you pay in cash. Another Rs. 1,000 for school fees. If you have a medical emergency, you have to pay another Rs. 500 monthly. You need to pay

3 While women workers are not in all cases the only earners in the household, the majority of them are the principal breadwinner in their respective household.

4 Taking 2012 as baseline year, the Indian Consumer Price Index (CPI) increased from 100 in 2012 to 138.8 in 2018. Assuming a constant expenditure pattern, the households surveyed in 2012 would have total monthly expenses of roughly Rs. 13,000, indicating a modest increase in real wages. However, it is likely that rising house and food prices impact precarious worker's expenses disproportionately.

> the local doctor, and medication, and provisions for your house. They usually just have Rs. 500–600 left for other expenses. So, unless their salary increases dramatically, there is not much change possible. What they are cutting down is purchases because they don't have free cash. In the last six to seven years, there has been no substantial increase in wages. The wages, the daily wages adjustment and things like that have been very minimal. In fact, the real wage seems to be decreasing. Even though there are these small changes in your salary [...] it doesn't change your purchasing power." (CSA_2, Pos. 18)

Local unions and civil society organisations estimated a minimum monthly living wage in Bengaluru at least Rs. 18,000 (CSA_3, Pos. 43). The Asia Floor Wage Campaign (AFWC) even suggested a living wage of Rs. 23,588 in 2018 to cover support for all family members, basic nutritional needs, and other basic needs, including housing, healthcare, education, and some basic savings (AFWC 2018). In any case, the actual salaries of garment workers are grossly insufficient to meet their subsistence needs, even though many are primary breadwinners for their families. Wages below subsistence levels signify the super-exploitation of workers in global value chains, benefitting transnational capital and fuelling inequality (Gilbert 2022; Selwyn 2019; Suwandi 2019).

But cheap labour does not just exist. It is no natural disposition of particular peoples or regions, no matter how much mainstream economics seeks to naturalise it by claiming the universality of competitive advantage. Especially in labour surplus economies, it comes into existence by fragmenting and segmenting the labouring classes, for example, along gendered and racialised lines, disciplining a sense of inferiority, if necessary, through violence, and naturalising such assumptions of inequality in common sense (see Chapter 7). As Alessandra Mezzadri claims, cheap labour must be "manufactured, no less than T-shirts or jeans", and in this process, it can "bank on multiple socio-economic divides and inequalities" (Mezzadri 2017, 18), especially in contexts like India with significant regional disparities and massive reserve armies of labour.

Without a doubt, gendered hierarchies and violence are crucial to understanding the dismal working conditions in Bengaluru's RMG industry. While more than 90 per cent of the workforce are migrant women, almost all management and supervisory staff in the factories are men (CSA_2, Pos. 30). All interviewed unions, civil society organisations and academics observing the garment industry have emphasised how gendered violence is endemic to the industry and an essential part of disciplining the workforce and extracting surplus labour from women. According to a long-standing analyst of the garment sector, sexualised violence at the workplace has become normalised by many women workers because it is an ordinary, ever-present reality of their daily lives:

> "The stereotyping that is there in the family and the Indian culture of women being subservient is mirrored almost exactly at the factory. You have 85–90% workers, cutters, cleaners, packers, tailors. Almost all of them would be women in Bangalore. I'm not saying that the sector is like that in other places. [...] You are used to sexual harassment at home, you are used to sexual harassment on your journey from your home to the factory, so you normalise a lot sexual harassment in the factory, too. The tendency is towards that. These are all first-generation workers. These are not workers who come from a factory culture or who know factory issues or labour laws. Most of them would be semi-literate women, first-generation workers in a factory, with little to no exposure to labour rights, forget human rights" (CSA_2, Pos. 30)

These findings also resonate with other studies that have stressed how gendered discrimination, and patriarchal oppression cannot be understood solely in cultural terms and by focusing narrowly on the family/community as the unit of analysis. For example, Kavita Krishnan (2018) emphasises how familial regimes of gendered surveillance and extraction of women's labour must be understood in relation to one another (see also AFWC 2018; Bhattacharjee 2019; Wichterich 2019). The tight surveillance of women workers, through monitoring of toilet and canteen visits, constant threats of humiliation through verbal aggression or corporeal punishment, and public shaming are "used to discipline, demoralise and control the entire body of workers, not just the individual worker targeted". Moreover, such "[r]egimes of surveillance, sexualised abuse, sexual harassment and public humiliation are integral to the production process and used to keep the women workers insecure by pressuring them to meet impossible production targets" (Krishnan 2018, 81).

Furthermore, the fact that predominantly women are employed in the booming industry potentially challenges the gendered division of labour within the household economy, especially if male household members cannot find steady work. Even if garment workers are primary breadwinners, out of their homes for 12 hours a day or more, patriarchal norms still assign the burden of unpaid reproductive work (like cooking, cleaning and other household work) to them. In such a context, women workers are not only exposed to sexualised violence in factories but also to potentially increasing domestic violence:

> "More and more women take on the responsibility of being breadwinner. Men will not get employment very easily. There has been very unstable employment. Women who are domestic workers or garment workers they are going there, sticking around and continuing their work. Construction work is sporadic: three days you have work, three days you don't have. So, there's a lowering of the male role and status. And an increase of the responsibility and role of women. That itself has led to women not fulfilling effectively and efficiently their household chores, which they are supposed to do. While they are doing this, they are also

> expected to do this. You know, they go for garment sector work until 5.30, they make them work until 6, and by 7/7.30 they reach home. And nothing is cooked. They have to cook, they have to look after children – all that is blamed on the women. That is one major thing that is coming across. And women want to save their money, accounted for in their hands. [...]As soon as you come back, you rush into some kind of other work. And that becomes a major conflict. In that sense, violence is there. Earlier, they were doing their role, the old structure was maintained, and the violence was not as constant. Now, there are more and more conflicts." (CSA_4, Pos. 67)

Beyond the grim reality of gendered violence and exploitation, the gendered nature of social reproductive work also affects the prospects for organising labour. While the central unions, usually affiliated with political parties, do not play a significant role in Bengaluru, the three biggest unions organizing garment workers, the Garment and Textile Workers Union (GATWU), the Garment Labour Union (GLU), and Karnataka Textile Worker Union (KTWU) together organise not more than 15,000 workers – a tiny fraction of the large and growing workforce of more than 400,000. While interlocking aspects of super-exploitation through excessive production targets and disciplining through harassment and union busting are important barriers to challenging existing labour control regimes (Dutta 2021; López 2021), it is essential to highlight that the question of collective organisation is gendered. The division between social reproduction and production figures prominently as obstacles to unionisation, as becomes clear from the following quote:

> "[...] when you look at these women, they are not just doing jobs in the factory, they have additional responsibilities at home. The factory timings are between 9am and 5.30pm. They have to go back home immediately, to cook, take care of the children, feed their children, clean the house, wash their cloths and utensils. They are so occupied from the time they get home, from 6pm to 10–10.30pm, that they don't even get time for themselves. On the way they have to purchase, if they require things for their home, same is true for groceries. Since they have both work at home and in the factories, they do not have – unlike a bus driver – he would go to work, come back in the evening, sit and have tea or coffee and watch television, and have plenty of time for himself. Unlike men, women do not have time to sit in the union office for a meeting. It's very difficult for them to go to union meetings, or to participate in campaigns for one or two days – that's impossible. And this is also the major obstacle in organising these workers. In all the efforts, supporting these women does not stop at the workplace. They would require emotional, mental, and other support in terms of what's happening in their families. Their husband is ill-treating them, there's physical abuse at home." (CSA_3, Pos. 31)

Despite many obstacles and generally low levels of unionisation, organising labour happens beyond the company's premises, for example, at factory gate meetings or in residential neighbourhoods. Compared to construction and domestic work, garment workers seem much better organised. Arguably, higher levels of unionisation also impact workers' effective access to social security schemes, a theme we will further explore in the following section.

Reproductive Debt and Garment Workers' Safety Net(s)

The poor working conditions do not allow workers to improve their living standards, which, in many cases where workers care for a household of four or five, is below the subsistence level. Even if they work in the industry for 20 or 30 years, their livelihoods hardly improve (CSA_3, Pos. 16). According to the interviewed industry experts, the garment sector in Bengaluru has experienced a decline in real wages and a lack of economic empowerment in past years, given the surge in prices for housing, food, and other essentials (CSA_2, Pos. 18; see also RoyChowdhury 2018, 58). In this context, reproductive debt becomes an omnipresent reality and a necessary strategy for managing their precarity. A long-standing observer of Bengaluru's garment industry notes: "All the time, these workers have loans outstanding. I don't think you won't find anyone who has not taken a loan in this sector" (CSA_3, Pos. 55). A GATWU study from 2012 found that wages were insufficient to meet essential household expenditure, and 76 per cent of the interviewed workers were indebted with loan amounts totalling between Rs. 50,000 and Rs 100,000, i.e. the burden of debt being as high as an average *annual* household income in the sector (GATWU 2012). Another study suggests that when women workers leave the garment factories in their 30s, they hardly have any savings, and most have accumulated debts ranging from Rs. 50,000 to Rs. 500,000 (Mezzadri and Majumder 2020, 18). In most cases, the demand for loans is driven by reproductive needs, while entrepreneurial investments are irrelevant. Moreover, loans taken by the urban working poor are often related to the agrarian crisis discussed at the beginning of the chapter:

> "Many take it for education, marriage in the family, advance for housing, festivals at the native place, no rain at home, and relatives at native place won't have anything to dig borewell, to build a house at native place. Like this, they take many loans. [...] They take loans amount for more than one lakh and repay them. [...] Initially, they take 10,000, then after paying that they get 20,000, and then 30,000 etc. As per repayment, they get more money. When there are 2–4 persons at home, they all take loans and repay them." (CSA_5, Pos. 115–118)

These observations spark a question that runs through the whole chapter: If migrant workers earn wages below subsistence and accumulate debt over time, how can they still repay their loans? Or, put differently, why don't more chronically indebted workers default?

Based on my empirical fieldwork, I would claim that the repayment of loans by women garment workers is guaranteed primarily through six interlocked strategies. The first, the sale of assets like land, gold and jewellery, was briefly explored in chapter 13, in the context of the slow violence of the agrarian crisis. The second, financial expropriation through deduction of wages and pawning future labour capacities, was discussed in the previous chapter. Likewise, the third strategy, juggling different sources and types of debt to stay solvent while living through indebtedness, was also touched upon. Therefore, this section will focus on the three remaining strategies. A fourth strategy is lengthening the workday, i.e., working on piece-rate jobs after working full-time in the factory or engaging in additional domestic work to augment meagre incomes. This point expands the notion of financial expropriation. Wages below the subsistence level force these full-time factory workers to work extra shifts to make ends meet:

> "Many of them depend on their salary [to repay loans]. [...] In some places like Mysore Road, in the early morning, before going to work, they go to domestic work, some stitch cloths at home after finishing factory work. Some go to bathe the child. Some go to cook or make chapatis in the houses. Some go to market and buy flowers and they string them and send them with their children to sell in the morning. It's not just one work. They do several other jobs. Not just to repay the loan but these days rents of houses are high, cost of living is high. Wages are not enough. It's difficult to live, so they work extra. [...] People do minor works like washing utensils, placing Rangoli at the door etc." (CSA_5, Pos. 121–125)

These extra shifts also demonstrate the intimate connections between the productive/reproductive and formal/informal, which are often analysed separately but are just two sides of the same coin.

A fifth means, arguably the most drastic measure, is to cut on essential household expenditures. Most of the household income is usually spent on food and rent. But since rent is fixed and hardly negotiable, reducing food intake becomes an important measure with potentially drastic health consequences in times of severe income-expenditure-mismatches. This point will be further explored in the following section when discussing garment workers' livelihoods during major crises in recent years. Reducing expenditure may also be related to working longer hours. Usually, garment workers have 14 days of leave annually. The factories offer workers a bonus of 500 rupees per month if they decide not to take leave. Taking leave for migrant workers is almost always synonymous with travelling to their native places, possibly seeing their kids and other relatives. However, the travel is expensive and usually, children and other relatives expect gifts from the homecoming workers (CSA_3, Pos. 60). Hence, not travelling home for a festival season or other occasion may reduce expenditures and possibly also enhance their meagre incomes through the paid bonus, although the psychological burden of such a strategy may be tremendous.

A sixth and final strategy that distinguishes garment from domestic and many other precarious migrant workers is accessing existing social security schemes, most notably the Employees Provident Fund (EPF) or gratuity. If workers are employed for five consecutive years, they are entitled to compensation that depends, amongst other things, on their basic salary. Therefore, many workers try to work at a factory for five years before leaving the job and taking up another one. However, there are many obstacles to working in the same factory for five consecutive years, and the turnover is extremely high due to intolerable working conditions, constant verbal or physical harassment, and pregnancy/maternal leave:

> "Let's say most of the workforce is in the age group between 20 and 30 in this industry. On average, a woman would have at least two children, and that means at least two breaks in her career. She won't work for a year or so. Then again, she comes back to work when the child is one year old or so. Or if it's really an emergency, she will leave the child in the village and come back. Again, she'll work for two or three years, and then she will receive again. In ten years, there are many cases of abortions because of the heat in the industry, high-pressure jobs, and stress. Let's say that happens. They get gratitude's after five years. It is 75 days of salaries into the basic salary. If here salary is Rs 300/day, than 300*75 is what she would get [Rs. 22,500]. For the worker, this is quite a big amount. But they tend to lose out on that. When the factories don't have to pay that, it's a benefit for the factory." (CSA_3, Pos. 42)

The turn to younger and more vulnerable migrant workers – unfamiliar with the local context, without many bonds of solidarity and housed in hostels – has also benefitted factories strategically employing women workers for only a few years, certainly below five years, to retain social contributions (Mezzadri 2017, 90). In cases of medical emergencies, garment workers can access treatment through ESI. However, in many cases, they would instead go to a private clinic after work for practical reasons:

> "The reason is that if they go to the ESI they have to take leave from work. The ESI centres are open from 10am till 5pm. It's not helping the workers in any way. The worker has to take a half-day leave if the child is sick, with normal fever, diarrhoea – so the worker thinks, "oh I have to take leave from work, and that's difficult, so let me take the child to a private physician to just get some medicines and then sends them back. But in case there is a major illness, like the worker's husband

> having kidney stones, then they go to the ESI hospital, they get the check-up, they get scans and everything done" (CSA_3, Pos. 36)

Apart from the ESI and gratuity, the EPF is garment workers' most critical social security scheme. Rather than a savings mechanism for retirement, the provident fund constitutes the single most vital tool to access emergency funds and lump sums necessary for housing, healthcare emergencies, education, marriages, and the like. The fundamental role the PF plays in managing garment workers' crisis of social reproduction also explains the fierce resistance against the NDA government's reform plans announced in March 2016:

> "But for a lot of workers, that's the only savings they have. And when they have to shift the house, or there's a medical emergency, or if children are admitted to school, and there's a lump sum that has to be paid – these three are the cases that workers have mentioned in the context of PF. When they said that this can become a rule in March 2016, it was a huge and almost instant fear, and a major reason for people to protest was the high level of insecurity, because that's one thing that all workers depended on. In many cases, like sexual harassment or other types of labour rights violations, workers may choose to leave the company and search for a new one. So if you quit, you can close your account and withdraw that money. And then you get a new PF in the new company" (CSA_2, Pos. 27)

In short, accessing their PF is a central reproductive finance strategy for garment workers. Since their work lives are marked by constant insecurity, super-exploitation and various forms of violence, fluctuation may express a form of silent resistance and a necessary coping mechanism that allows withdrawing the PF as an emergency buffer of last resort: "For workers, this provident fund is so important in cases of emergencies that they don't mind leaving, withdrawing the money and joining in again later." (CSA_3, Pos. 57; see also Pos. 50 – 51).

Accessing the PF is closely related to juggling debts. Reflecting on the coercive practices of MFIs, a trade union secretary suggests one must understand the PF as a mechanism that allows workers to repay loans, as a financial safety net in case of over-indebtedness:

> "Many workers take many loans from Jan..... Janalakshmi, Ujjivan, Dhanlaxmi. These MFIs go only to the areas of garment workers. They go to the houses. They insist on punctual repayment on weekly-monthly basis. Even if someone has dead there, they don't listen. Repayment should be done. That type of system they have. If not paid, they fine the group. If one borrower has not paid, all have to collectively make the payment. MFIs do good business like this. Many workers go to them. Sometimes workers take a loan for high interest from house owners, neighbors, relatives and known etc. They seek loan by narrating their problems.

> When the loan amount is high, they resign the job, take the PF and repay and take up [a new] job." (CSA_5, Pos. 103–107)

The quote powerfully illustrates the relational rationalities of debt, comprising how different sources of credit also imply different types of rationality and degrees of alienation, for example, insisting on repayment upon the death of a family member versus narrating one's problems to the creditors. Ultimately, however, all these different types of creditor-debtor relationships are constitutive to the household's survival. In contrast to many precarious migrant workers in the urban informal economy, Bengaluru's garment workers have a substantial financial safety net with the EPF, which is worth fighting for.

Against this background, the massive protests in mid-April 2016 are not as surprising as many suggested. The importance of PF as a reproductive finance strategy for garment workers cannot be overestimated. Reflecting on the significance of women garment workers in these strikes, a union leader suggests the fierce resistance must be understood as part of highly precarious working conditions, including low salaries, exposure to various forms of violence, high turnover in the industry, and multiple burdens connected to social reproduction:

> "The question was, why only garment workers went on strike and no other workers. The answer is the garment workers get very low salary. The life of garment workers is such that, they work for five years in one place, then they resign and take the PF and gratuity. They would have done many commitments; they fulfil all these and then again join the new job. In such a situation, how can they wait for 58 years of age to get the PF money? This is the anger which prompted them to strike." (CSA_5, Pos. 39)

As was argued before, living through reproductive debt requires juggling loans, including different temporalities and obligations associated with various types and sources of credit. In this context, the EPF becomes a vital collateral for garment workers. After all, accessing the fund establishes garment workers' creditworthiness vis-à-vis different lenders.[5] Menon and Sundar (2019, 11) describe the EPF as "a condition of social reproduction [for garment workers], both by enabling periodic rest and recovery from the harsh discipline of the factories for the workers themselves and by enabling their children's education or wedding expense".

The case of the 2016 strike against the amendment of the provident fund is intriguing because it shows how labour and debt struggles may converge in a broad

5 In contrast to what Lavinas (2018) and Torkelson (2021) discuss as collateralisation of social security in Brazil and South Africa, where profit-driven financial institutions draw on regular welfare receipts as the poor's collateral, the case of the EPF implies a more indirect form of collaterlisation, in which lump sums can be withdrawn at critical conjunctures.

sense. While primarily directed against state policy, protecting social security benefits the labour movement had fought for in the past, this protest was launched as a wildcat strike. As such, it was not organised or orchestrated by trade unions, political parties, or civil society organisations, although the latter's involvement in the sector seemed to have played an essential role in the comparatively better organisation of this segment of migrant workers. This brief episode points to the significance of reproductive finance as a necessary and widespread means to manage a structural subsistence crisis and as a potential lever for collective action.

Clearly, this defensive struggle cannot be simply turned into an offensive one. However, the investigation of migrant garment workers in Bengaluru may provide a glimpse at how India's subaltern working classes can challenge the neoliberal regime of re/productive finance. A close inspection of women workers' every day (work) not only reveals the contradictions of capital and care as fought through indebtedness. They also demonstrate the multiplicity of their struggles as (informal) labourers, challenging the idea of docile and disposable third-world factory women and, ultimately, resisting and challenging the embodied experience of capitalist, patriarchal and caste-based oppression – all lived through at the same time (Dutta 2021; Menon and Sundar 2019; RoyChowdhury 2015).

The Intensification of An Existential Crisis of Social Reproduction

In light of the garment workers' fierce resistance against the corporate agenda of the NDA government, the Demonetisation in November 2016 almost appears like a revenge against the class struggle from below. In times of economic shocks and crises, corporations tend to pass on uncertainties and losses to their workforce:

> "With the demonetisation there were a lot of issues which became bigger for the migrant workers. Because you already have no support system. The last two or three years, one of the major challenges for workers, one, a lot of workers have been laid out of work, formally and informally, they have been told to not come to work for a few days, and that continues now. Earlier you had your work pay and you had overtime that was maybe not paid for, forced labour, there were some changes in the labour practices to get workers to add one hour to their working time each day. They tried different strategies to ensure that the minimum wage would go down, and that they could maximize the work time. But right now, it's reversed, they try to force workers on leave for a couple of days, because they don't have enough work to give to them on a daily basis." (CSA_2, Pos. 12)

These layoffs, in turn, increase the debt-distress cycle, pressuring workers to constantly search for alternative employment and manage (temporal) income gaps through indebtedness. As was mentioned before, food and rent are the most significant elements of expenditure for most precarious migrant workers. While the latter is hardly negotiable, households tend to reduce food intake during severe income-expenditure mismatches to ensure repayment. Recalling a survey in which garment workers were asked what they would cut on in case they did not have money, one of the interviewees confirms this assessment: "And some 59 per cent said it would be food. At the beginning of the month, they would buy some nice things to eat, and towards the end of the month it would just be rice and watery tomatoes gravy." (CSA_3, Pos. 29).

Such strategies are no singular event and are certainly not confined to Bengaluru. More recently, the COVID-19 pandemic significantly affected global supply chains, including garment exports, and apparel brands and retailers cancelled US$ 40 billion worth of orders (Anner 2022; Majumdar, Shaw, and Sinha 2020). As usual in crises, the workers at the bottom were at the receiving end of the unfolding misery. In Bengaluru, at least 65 factories closed, depriving more than 10,000 workers of a regular income. Many factories stopped providing transport, forcing migrant workers to resign or threatening workers that if they didn't leave, they would not get access to their dues (Joesph 2021). In addition, most garment factories refused to pay their workers the increased legal minimum wages, leading to an estimated US$ 58 million in wage theft for approximately 400,000 garment workers across Karnataka (Kelly 2021).[6] The forced resignations and withholding of wages intensified the social reproduction crisis that garment workers faced even before the pandemic. Since many garment workers are primary or important supplementary earners, these processes significantly reduced household income, pushing families further into distress and debt.

According to a study from the Alternative Law Forum (ALF) and the Garment Textile Workers' Union (GATWU), 47 per cent of the interviewed workers in Bengaluru said their household incomes had reduced between 30 – 50 per cent during the pandemic, and one in four reported of losses of total household income of more than 50 per cent. The vast majority did not have any savings to rely on, while half of the interviewed workers had outstanding loans and interest payments they hoped to serve with their wages. The already high burden of rent accumulated during unemployment. Devi, a former garment worker in her early 40s, said: "We haven't been able to meet our commitments after losing our job. We have migrated here, and we have had to take loans to survive" (Devi in Shivanand and Prathiba 2021, 29). With few options left to reduce their household expenditure, 80 per cent of the surveyed

6 Pressure from workers, trade unions and civil society organisations and a successful lawsuit reached that most companies commenced payments in early February 2022. However, worker's lacked this income during the most critical phase of the COVID-19 pandemic in 2020 and 2021.

families of garment workers had to reduce their food intake significantly, especially cutting on vegetables, meat, fruits, snacks and beverages like tea and coffee (including milk), and slashing meals to only one or two per day (CSA_2, Pos. 14, see also Kelly 2021). The female garment workers were now hungry, heavily indebted, and without steady income – but still shouldering the responsibility to take care of their families somehow. This episode vividly demonstrates the violence of reproductive debts, which is by no means limited to garment workers.

When Prime Minister Narendra Modi announced a nationwide 'Janata Curfew' [literally people's curfew] in March 2020, hundreds of thousands of migrant workers were laid off, stranded, and walking home for hundreds of kilometres. Drawing on surveys with roughly 10,000 of these migrant workers in the first month after the curfew had been in effect, the Stranded Workers Action Network (SWAN) published a report stating that 72 per cent said their rations would finish in two days, 78 per cent had less than Rs. 300 with them, 82 per cent had not received allocations from the government. Hardly any of these workers received any cash relief from the government (SWAN 2020). Once more, the necessity of reproductive debts became apparent. The same report claimed that almost 90 per cent of the workers had taken a loan for rations or other essentials, with most borrowing between Rs. 2,000 and 5,000 (48%) and almost one-third borrowing more than Rs. 5,000. Likewise, *The State of Work Report 2021* claims that poverty has significantly increased during the pandemic, with an increase of 230 million individuals falling below the national minimum wage (APU 2021, 116ff.). More than 90 per cent of the 2,800 respondents of a survey, of whom the majority were casual women workers predominantly Dalit, Adivasi or low caste, reported that their households had suffered a reduction in food intake due to the lockdown, and most reported increased burdens of unpaid care work related to preparing food, cleaning, washing and emotional care. Moreover, in April/May 2020, households were on average indebted with twice their pre-lockdown monthly income, while for the bottom income quarter, indebtedness signified almost four times their monthly wages, in most cases to meet food, health and other daily expenditures (see Table 6).

Non- or underpayment of wages, reduced food intake, increased burdens of unpaid reproductive work, exclusion from essential (public) services, and distress-driven indebtedness are like a red thread that runs through many cross-state studies on precarious migrant workers during the lockdown (Azeez et al. 2021; Foley and Piper 2021; Mookerjee et al. 2021; Narayan 2021).

Table 6: Income-Debt Ratios of Migrant Workers During the COVID-19 Pandemic

	Overall	**Bottom 25%**	**Second 25%**	**Third 25%**	**Top25%**
Median Income in February 2020 (Rs.)	8,500	4,000	7,000	10,000	18,000
Loan Amount (Rs.)	18,000	12,000	15,000	20,000	30,000
Ratio	2.1	3.8	2.10	2	1.4

Source: APU (2021, 126).

What is perhaps distinct for garment workers in Bengaluru is the relevance of the EPF as paramount financial safety net during and after the lockdown in 2020: "Women said they resigned because they wanted to withdraw accumulated PF and gratuity to pay for children's school fees or weddings or to pay off debts built up during the lockdown, or because they did not have child-care since schools and Anganwadis [child care] were not functioning" (Shivanand and Prathiba 2021, 13). This quote reaffirms how the intensified crisis of social reproduction through, for example, closed childcare forces women to take on debt. Far from the shiny images of entrepreneurial women lifting their families out of poverty through access to credit, the latter becomes a necessary survival strategy that reinforces the distress it seeks to relieve.

By looking at three distinct moments in the lives of migrant workers, this chapter aimed to shed light on the workings of the neoliberal regime of re/productive finance beyond the shiny image of India's Silicon Valley. It was argued that the interlocking dynamics of expropriation, super-exploitation, and exclusion drive the demand for reproductive debts, entrapping migrant workers in a debt-distress cycle. This dynamic implies various forms of financial expropriation linked to the subordination of labour under (financial) capital. Caring for reproductive debts, for instance, by juggling different sources and types of credit, becomes an important survival strategy predominantly female household members engage in. In this context, the rise of commercial microfinance must be understood as filling a particular niche within an existing ecosystem of creditors. Rather than replacing other debt relations, it intersects with them, producing ambiguous and potentially devastating consequences, particularly in times of crisis. In concluding this part, the following chapter summarises the key insights, emphasising the structural violence associated with reproductive debts.

Chapter 16
Synopsis: The Structural Violence of Re/Productive Finance in Bengaluru

In Chapter 2, we discussed how the international development agenda of financial inclusion leveraged the financial systems approach, expanding the realm of financial accumulation to the working poor across the globe. Widened access to credit provided by profit-oriented financial institutions is portrayed as a promising strategy to reunite finance-led economic growth with social inclusion and poverty reduction. It becomes legitimised through extending *financial opportunities* to individuals/households at the bottom of the pyramid rather than focusing on redistribution of land ownership, existing wealth, or the promotion of decent work and access to commons. In this sense, expanding access to credit for so-called underserved segments of society resonates with one of the most pertinent myths in development cooperation: helping people to help themselves. The allegory of teaching men (and increasingly women) to fish is undoubtedly one of the deepest-rooted rationales of international development interventions since about the 1970s. An industry insider who has worked around questions of microfinance and financial inclusion in India for nearly five decades reflects on this trope as follows:

> "When I was young, we used to say the problem in India is – in fact, my father said this – you don't give a fish to eat. But you teach people to fish. If you give them a fish, they are dependent on you; teach them to fish, and they can sustain themselves. But after coming back to India and going to the rural areas, I discovered, even after teaching to fish, they can't breach... Because there are so many obstacles, caste is there, politics is there, and then they reach the river the fish is already taken by someone – it's a power system. You have to break it." (CSA_7, Pos. 43)

This statement exposes the ahistorical and power-blind logic underpinning such development thinking. Significantly, it raises the question of what constitutes the power system that needs to be dismantled. From the perspective of a non-profit NGO engaged with microfinance, challenging the caste-dominated and gendered power of cooperative societies and public sector banks becomes a vital task and fostering SHGs appears as a sensible solution. While theoretically, there is merit in such an approach, practically, this strategy remains ambiguous and has proved prone to state and market capture (see Chapter 11). The analyses of precarious migrant workers in this chapter extend the understanding of the power system by scrutinising how precarious migrant workers live through debts and how this exposes the promises, limitations, and contradictions of contemporary microfinance.

Figure 16: The Structural Violence of Reproductive Debt

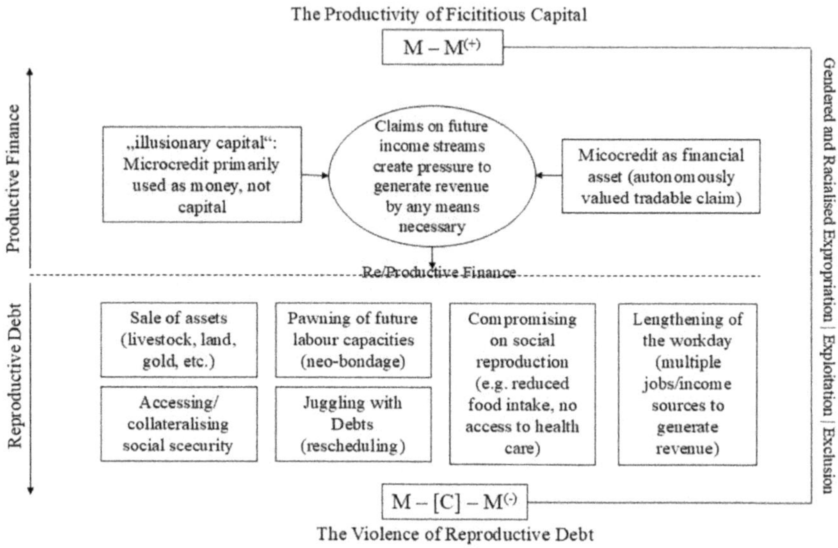

Source: own illustration.

By investigating the livelihoods of migrant workers in Bengaluru through three interconnected moments linked to construction, domestic and garment workers, this chapter, substantiated the claim that reproductive debt, that is, loans to secure the survival of household/family members, and the prospects of future generations, emerge against the background of a chronic subsistence crisis which is characterised by a structural imbalance between households' incomes and necessary expenditures. This subsistence crisis, in turn, must be understood in the context of exclusion from state social security and access to commons, the super-exploitation of informal sector workers, and the ever-present shadows of expropriation, be it in the form of displacement through development projects, urban enclosures or slow violence associated with the agrarian crisis and climate change. All these were understood as gendered and racialised processes that increase the likelihood of chronic proletarian indebtedness and are thus associated with the peculiar relationship between the productivity and structural violence of fictitious capital (see Figure 16).

The notion of inverse capital ($M - C - M^{(-)}$) challenges the myth of entrepreneurial credit. It emphasises that, from the perspective of subaltern working-class households, money is being borrowed primarily to access commodified goods and services and not for business activities. It must be repaid at a higher value, although its usage usually has no investment returns that directly generate revenue. Therefore, this process entails a contradictory drain of wealth, which underpins the productivity of financial accumulation in the form of fictitious capital. Moreover, this relationship is overdetermined by the structural violence associated with the interlocking processes of expropriation, super-exploitation, and exclusion, which drive the demand for credit as money, not capital.

In previous chapters, I have discussed six interlocking mechanisms that explain how the shadow sides of financial accumulation in the case of reproductive debts work. These include the sale of assets (land, livestock, gold, etc.) associated most prominently with the slow violence of agrarian crisis and climate change; the pawning of future labour capacities, facilitating and disciplining cheap labour; the juggling with different types of debt, including the social obligations attached; the lengthening of the effective workday through additional income sources and work associated with caring for debts; compromising social reproduction, like reduced food intake, especially for women, or withholding from healthcare; and the collateralisation of social security as discussed in the case of the EPF. Although not all six dimensions are always equally relevant for all households, they are all part of the systemic debt-distress cycle of re/productive finance (see Figure 14). As such, they also expose the ordinary structural violence of money in concrete contexts, challenging the claim of financial inclusion as inherently democratising and humanising the expansion of financial capitalism.

As mentioned at the beginning of the chapter, the illustration of three critical aspects of the structural violence of reproductive debts draws on the experiences of a specific set of workers while simultaneously highlighting these as part of a shared, shattered story. For instance, the household interviews revealed a frequent connection between husbands working in construction and their wives working as domestic workers. The specific arguments for each of these analytical sections thus often describe the lived reality of two different people in the *same* household. Moreover, work in the construction or garment sector is physically only possible for a limited time due to over-exhaustion, frequent accidents, and recruiting policies of contractors/firms. Therefore, many of these workers leave the construction/garment industry in their late 30s or 40s to become domestic workers or search for an income in the informal economy (CSA_6, Pos.20; see also Mezzadri and Majumder 2020). Finally, the struggle around the EPF may be specific to garment workers. Still, labour struggles around access to social security schemes – whether waged on the state's terrain or against employers – can be equally found for domestic and construction workers. And, just as in the case of garment workers, these struggles are intimately related to questions of indebtedness (see e.g. Joseph, Lobo, and Natrajan 2018). In this sense, the findings from previous chapters resonate with the livelihoods of most precarious (migrant) labourers in the informal economy, including those beyond the empirical focus, like auto drivers, waste pickers, security guards, and many more.

The structural violence of reproductive debts adds another layer to the dynamics of class exploitation, subordination and domination in contemporary India. Though distinct, it is deeply interwoven with other forms of violence that trap subaltern working-class households in a marginalised position. This violence may not always produce lethal consequences, but there are many instances where it does: remember the epidemic of farmer's suicides or how compromising on food intake, especially during a crisis, is linked to malnutrition, chronic illness, and lower life expectancy. Almost always, this structural violence is connected to the vulnerable position of precarious labourers:

> "When we talk of domestic workers, we don't have a workplace. Therefore, we don't have these other amenities which are supposed to be there under the Factory's Act, like a restroom, a childcare centre. We in the slums fight for Anganwadis [child care], in an area where there are no Anganwadis. This is in 4th block in Jayanagar area, in a posh area, where the slum is. In that slum there was no amenities. So, this lady, [name], has gone to work in the apartments and it was vacation time. So normally they [the workers] lock their children when there's no one else, no other children to play with. This was a small house with just a small window there. And these two children were inside, and they got suffocated. Because it was dark, they lit a fire with newspaper, and they didn't die in the fire but got suffocated because there was no way of escaping. In that one hour where she went to work and came back, she found the children dead. Now, who should provide for her compensation? Who is to take responsibility? This is because of the lack of the creshes that should have taken care of these children." (CSA_6, Pos. 46)

The tragic case of a mother who worked as a domestic worker and her children draws our attention to the politics of exclusion – from public childcare, a living wage, and decent housing. While these issues may seem disconnected from the question of financial inclusion, the analysis employed in this chapter has argued for a broader framing through the notion of re/productive finance, in which proliferating indebtedness is studied, problematised, and challenged *in relation* to precisely such seemingly disconnected and simultaneously occurring processes of inclusion and exclusion. After all, the poor housing conditions of the masses of migrant labourers, who live in the shadows but maintain the city, is a direct result of class- and caste-based urban planning and financialised urbanisation, where land has turned into a speculative asset (Goldman 2020; Ranganathan 2021). The circuits of fictitious capital associated with investments in real estate and urban infrastructure are entwined with the constant threat of dispossession and the denial of a decent life, as was discussed at the beginning of the chapter.

Highlighting the structural violence of re/productive finance is a necessary corrective against the widely held assumption that increased access to credit will magically improve the livelihoods of the (urban) poor. If anything, the investigation of migrant labourers in Bengaluru has demonstrated how uneven capitalist development has increased the demand for credit as a means to secure market-dependent social reproduction and class oppression in the present. Challenging the exploitative nature of microfinance can thus not be limited to reforming or regulating the sector. Against this background, the following chapter will summarise the main findings of this research and discuss the political implications thereof.

Concluding Remarks: The History and Afterlives of Unpayable Debts

> „It would be nice to end with a rosy image of the future of social science [and society]. But a social science worth having must be at times grim, documenting the pain of worldwide transformations"
> – *Raewyn Connell* (2007)

> "Instead of defending a notion of intellectual turf, the point of scholarly debate should be to extend the horizon of historical imagination"
> – *Susan Buck-Morss (2009)*

The proliferation of commercial credit and other financial services targeting the working poor is portrayed as a panacea for sustainable development and poverty alleviation by governments, development banks, NGOs, and financial institutions worldwide. Ostensibly, providing access to credit helps these populations to generate income and manage risks. Critiques have contested this view, suggesting that poverty finance has primarily turned into another market in which financial capital exploits poor households through predatory lending. This book contributes to the latter perspective by investigating the chasm between benevolent rhetoric and structural violence of contemporary financial inclusion. It sought to understand why and how microfinance has expanded rapidly in India in recent decades. The research extends the explanatory power of the critical political economy literature in three significant ways.

First, it provides a novel theoretical framework called regimes of re/productive finance to reframe the study and understanding of microfinance and financial inclusion as contemporary modes of gendered and racialised class oppression and exploitation (Part II). Second, applying this framework, this research embeds the rise of microfinance and financial inclusion into a broader history of the modern world economy, including the formative phase of European colonialism (Part III). Third, it proposed to understand the success of microfinance by uncovering the broader political, economic and social dynamics that shape the demand for credit, including borrowers' livelihoods as precarious labourers and the chronic subsistence crisis they experience (Part IV). As such, this research investigated how the rise of microfinance was contingent upon the fractured lives of India's unbanked population and how shifting modes of indebtedness further produce fractures within the social body, the labouring classes, and individual lives. This chapter summarises the key arguments of the book with a specific focus on answering the main research question, outlining significant contributions, and reflecting on the limitations. Finally, I will briefly discuss the political implications of these findings.

Microfinance and the Financialisation of Development Policy

In Part I, we reviewed the rise and transformation of microfinance as an increasingly prominent international development agenda. It was argued that within the broader shifts of the neoliberal counter-revolution, crushing the ambitions of postcolonial states for a New International Economic Order, disciplining indebted states in the global South through structural adjustment, and providing ever more room for manoeuvres for global finance and transnational capital, experiments with microcredits in the 1970s and 1980s were enthusiastically endorsed by DFIs, Western development agencies, NGOs, and neoliberal governments. Once some of these initiatives, like Grameen Bank in Bangladesh or PRODEM/Banco Sol in Bolivia, had demonstrated that borrowing microloans to the working poor (women) without collateral can be a profitable business case, the World Bank and other DFIs, corporate philanthropy, and established financial institutions pushed for scaling poverty finance as a market-driven panacea for poverty alleviation and women empowerment.

Since the global financial crisis, development discourse has moved on to a broadened notion of financial inclusion, including other financial services beyond credit. Yet, microfinance remains the backbone of the financial inclusion agenda. The latter has contributed to building broad institutional public-private alliances, like GPFI or AFI, that endorse the financial systems approach, aligning the operations of borrowing to the working poor with the rhythms of financial markets. This rather recent shift resonates with the broader trend towards market-based finance in the era of sustainable development, in which all kinds of interventions, programmes, and institutions become indexed against their bankability. Proponents of this agenda portray the proliferation of commercialised and financialised microfinance as a win-win situation. The working poor receive access to financial means, which allows for coping better with risks. At the same time, microfinance is a profitable market for (institutional) investors who foster growth and benefit from the extracted revenue.

This set of arguments focuses on how Development has been increasingly thought through the prism of financial markets and how the connections between global finance capital and local development interventions become ever more entangled. These political, economic, and ideological dynamics provide important insights into the rise of microfinance. However, they are already well-researched and have received considerable attention in the global political economy and development studies literature. Understanding microfinance as a powerful new development agenda is necessary but insufficient for a sophisticated explanation of the rise of microfinance. If employed exclusively, it produces a problematic top-down narrative in which microfinance enters the lives of the working poor as a global neoliberal project, rendering invisible the pre-history and parallel modes of financial domination and expropriation. In other words, this narrative cannot account for the fractured lives that the governance of access to credit produces and upon which profitable financial accumulation rests. Therefore, this research has focused on shedding light on these two underappreciated dimensions. To do so, it developed a novel theoretical framework which can be considered as the first major contribution to the literature.

Theorising Fractured Lives

To investigate the fractured lives and shattered story of India's unbanked population, I engaged with the method of "incorporating comparison" (McMichael 1990, 2000) and regime analysis in critical political economy. Notably, I developed the approach of regimes of re/productive finance to investigate microfinance's rise as part of a broader history of the modern world economy, and the positioning of subaltern classes (Part II). This approach allowed to periodise distinct phases of the (global) political economy, governance of access to credit and subaltern indebtedness, highlighting that together they constitute a fragmented whole. I followed Marx's methodological suggestion to understand the immediate appearance of social phenomena, i.e. the lack of money and demand for credit amongst the working poor, as a result of social and historical presuppositions. These presuppositions were traced theoretically, historically, and empirically through the regime analysis to understand and criticise this immediate appearance (demand for credit) as something different: the domination and exploitation of subaltern classes through multiple forms of indebtedness.

In developing an appropriate theoretical substance for the notion of regimes of re/productive finance, I combined three conceptual bodies of critical political economy: First, I engaged with a re-reading of Marx's understanding of money, finance, and power in capitalism to offer a more differentiated perspective on the power relations that underpin indebtedness than what contemporary credit theories of money can offer (Chapter 5). Second, I expanded this view through social reproduction feminism, particularly the notion of financialisation of social reproduction to account for the relevance of reproductive debt in mediating between the productive and reproductive economy (Chapter 6). Finally, in broadening the analysis of finance capitalism beyond the neoliberal era, I drew on the burgeoning literature on racial (finance) capitalism to highlight how the gendered and racialised fragmentation and segmentation of labouring classes is central to the dynamics of (financial) capital accumulation (Chapter 7). Ultimately, the combination of these three strands of critical theory aimed at contributing to the project of "Marx's open-ended critique" (Foster 2018). Instead of reiterating all major theoretical arguments, the following is confined to three central contributions.

First, in contrast to credit theories of money, which have become particularly prominent in IPE in recent years, I argued that Marx's understanding of monetary credit allows for a more nuanced analysis of the dynamics of subaltern indebtedness. The former highlights that money is credit, and the power of money is primarily confined to commercial banks creating money out of thin air by issuing credit. As a result, credit theories of money tend to focus rather narrowly on the creditor-debtor relationship, isolating the study of finance from the broader political economy, including labour relations and conditions of social reproduction. Instead, Marx develops a multifaceted approach to understanding money as a divisive and coercive mode of socialisation and a distinct societal relation of oppression. The power of money as a general equivalent of value is contingent upon the commodification of space, which turns money into a means of existence and a condition for life. The abstraction, alienation, and objectification of value in the money form conceal how our lives are mediated and reproduced by other people's labour and how uneven class relations of oppression and exploitation characterise this process. This perspective provided a fruitful vantage point from which the conditions and dynamics of subaltern indebtedness could be investigated.

Against this backdrop, Marx's notion of secondary exploitation and contemporary forms of "financial expropriation" (Lapavitsas 2009) add another layer to the exploitation and domination of working-class households. Importantly, the discussion of interest-bearing and fictitious capital helped to understand the distinction between credit employed as working capital and credit used as money that is spent but does not create direct revenue, such as reproductive debt. This first dimension of fictitious capital is the common ground between financial institutions offering household debt and older forms of usurer's capital, i.e. moneylenders. However, the former generally imply alienated debts in which debt contracts are less personalised and, through securitisation, can be turned into tradable assets sold to investors. Rather than consecutive, both forms and types of predatory lending to working-class households can converge to produce multiple forms of financial expropriation by different creditors. As such, these arguments provide a power-sensitive approach to studying money and finance and understanding the workings of microfinance and financial inclusion in the present.

Second, social reproduction feminism helped to clarify the separation between production and social reproduction as an ambiguous condition of capitalist development. Although the production of life and labour is central to the latter's existence, it is constantly devalued and taken for granted. The notion of re/productive finance highlights how household debt cuts through binary separations and how money mediates this contradictory relationship. This perspective can also help to revisit current debates on the positioning of subaltern classes. Many critical scholars have suggested that poverty finance is essentially a way of governing a growing surplus population, that is, a share of the global proletariat that cannot be usefully employed by capital and yet lacks the means of subsistence to live otherwise (Haiven 2020; Sanyal 2007; Soederberg 2015). For instance, Kalyan Sanyal (2007) has claimed that a substantial share of India's subaltern class lives in the 'need economy', struggling to make ends meet rather than the 'accumulation economy' and that this chasm between non-capital and capital characterises the specific constitution and dynamic of post-colonial capitalism. However, the analysis of precarious migrant workers in Bengaluru shows how they are a relevant, cheap, and flexible labour force that underpins the gendered and racialised dynamics of contemporary capital accumulation. From the perspective of social reproduction feminism, the distinction between the need and accumulation economy and capital and non-capital can be resolved by highlighting how they are part of a unitary system. As was argued, reproductive debt mediates between the productive and reproductive economy. As such, the governance of a surplus population through poverty finance is not a one-way road. Rather, the proliferation of market-based poverty finance draws on the chronic crisis of social reproduction amongst subaltern classes while entrenching their subordinate position in the (global) political economy, ultimately creating favourable conditions for their super-exploitation and expropriation upon which dynamic capital accumulation rests.

Finally, this book contributed to the burgeoning literature of racial capitalism by proposing to study race and caste as comparable though distinct relations of oppression which allow for the fragmentation and segmentation of the labouring classes and facilitate their exploitation, expropriation, exclusion, and – at times – extinction. This differentiation is necessary for overcoming a certain US-centrism in contemporary debates and to counter the dominant narrative that caste is primarily a cultural specificity and pre-modern inheritance of the Indian subcontinent with little relevance for understanding the workings of contemporary (financial) capital accumulation. Moreover, I engaged with the notion of racial finance capitalism to argue that the current dynamics of financialisation work through the production, exploitation, and accumulation of racialised differences that run through the social body and the working class. Notably, the predatory aspects of financial inclusion are rooted in ignoring, entrenching, and profiting from racialised exclusions, the depreciation of labour(ers), and the uneven distribution of risk. Together, these three strands of theory allow us to understand the chronic indebtedness of subaltern working-class households as a gendered and racialised process of exploitation and domination. This rich theoretical framework underpinning the notion of regimes of re/productive finance was applied historically and empirically.

Three Regimes of Re/Productive Finance

To investigate the fractured lives of subaltern indebtedness in India, I proposed to study history backwards, tracing the evolution of modern regimes of re/productive finance (Part III). The guiding assumption was that substantial parts of India's subaltern working class have historically experienced a chronic subsistence crisis managed through indebtedness vis-à-vis different creditors. The analysis of modern regimes of re/productive finance discussed the continuities and changes in governing access to credit in relation to the broader (global) political economy, particularly the accumulation regimes, the associated social stratification and positioning of subaltern classes, and the crisis of social reproduction experienced amongst the latter. This regime analysis deepened our understanding of the rise of microfinance in several ways.

To begin with, the analysis of the contemporary neoliberal regime expanded the arguments of microfinance as a powerful development agenda. It showed that the neoliberal restructuring of the entire political economy enabled the rise of commercialised and financialised microfinance (Chapter 11). Beginning in the early 1990s, these shifts introduced a new highly uneven jobless growth model in which the urban and rural upper classes gain the bulk of produced wealth, while the mass of small and marginal farmers, landless agricultural labourers, and precarious urban workers face a severe subsistence crisis. Despite pooling incomes from cultivation, animal husbandry, wage labour, and business activities into the household economy, between two-thirds and three-quarters of the rural population experience a significant subsistence gap, with expenditures increasing monthly incomes. In this context, microfinance expanded rapidly by offering reproductive debt, that is, small-ticket loans used for food, housing, health care, home improvement, and other aspects related to social reproduction.

Importantly, the rise of microfinance was facilitated by what I have called India's debtfare state. At a time when priority sector lending through public banks was diluted and the provisioning of rural credit retrenched, both central and state governments scaled women's self-help groups (SHGs) as a primary vehicle for rural development. They also decentralised welfare provisioning and widened access to credit through the bank linkage programme (SHG-BLP). Though distributed unevenly across the country, SHGs currently affect more than 140 million families, turning the programme into the single largest microfinance scheme in the world. Meanwhile, profit-oriented NGOs, foundations, and financial institutions have grown on the back of this publicly subsidised group-lending infrastructure, expanding exponentially in the 2000s. This rise was primarily driven by few corporate MFIs with tight connections to mainstream banking and institutional investors, consciously financialising the subsistence gap of subaltern working-class households. This new generation of corporate MFIs openly surpassed the narrow focus on income-generating loans and embraced the relevance of reproductive debt by providing loans for housing, health emergencies, education, sanitation, and other basic needs, including a focus on precarious urban workers.

Notably, the demand for such credit is exacerbated by the neoliberal political economy, as was shown in the case of the privatisation and financialisation of India's healthcare sector. The bulk of health expenditure in India comes from households in the form of out-of-pocket spending (OOPS), and those households experiencing a chronic subsistence gap as well as irregular incomes are hardest hit by sudden expenditures for medical treatment. Newer welfare programmes, like the national health insurance for informal sector workers, fail to address this issue because they only cover in-patient care and thereby tend to subsidise the private health industry. Against this backdrop, borrowing money for health expenses, including from corporate MFIs, turns into a necessary survival strategy. Therefore, I have characterised the neoliberal regime as one of market-based reproductive debt. While these arguments uncover the immediate conditions and channels through which microfinance expanded in the neoliberal era, the regime analysis explicitly set out to dig deeper.

The roots of this pervasive subsistence crisis and its management through monetary debts have been essentially shaped by British rule since the late eighteenth century. The colonial regime rested on an imperial political economy of plunder, which subordinated the subcontinent's wealth to the British-dominated world market. Essentially, this process entailed the violent enclosures of forests and common land, the (forced) commercialisation and export-orientation of agrarian production, and the reformation of land tax and the judicial system. These have crucially perpetuated caste-based class inequalities and driven monetised debt relations, in which most peasants and other parts of the rural population, were chronically indebted with diverse moneylenders, including traders, landlords, and wealthy farmers. I have referred to this constellation as the moneylender-state nexus to highlight that British colonial rule exacerbated the power of moneylenders through land taxation, amongst other policies, and thereby increased the need for money. At the same time, the colonial administration refrained from regulating moneylending or escalating land transfers based on indebtedness while backing creditors if they had a written debt record.

This investigation is particularly relevant to the contemporary financial inclusion discourse. The rise of informal moneylenders was facilitated by British rule, including land taxation, legal backing of creditors, and the absence of regulation (Chapter 9). This analysis challenges the deep-seated formal/informal divide in which the former is associated with modern, cheap, and inclusive financial institutions, while the latter is presented as backward and usurious, keeping people from benefitting from economic growth. Moreover, India's modern banking system was entirely dominated by European joint-stock companies, facilitating the massive drain of wealth and consciously excluding almost the entire Indian population from access to bank credit. Hence, India's vast unbanked population and its dependency on so-called informal moneylenders are a colonial legacy rooted in a modern imperial political economy of plunder.

The post-independence developmental regime has grappled with this legacy with mixed success (Chapter 10). Within only three decades, it extended the role of the state and public enterprise, facilitated economic growth and industrialisation, and overcame the worst forms of colonial famines that killed tens of millions under British rule. It considerably expanded rural credit through credit cooperatives and, later, through the nationalisation of major commercial banks, prescribing quotas for borrowing to agriculture, small and medium enterprises, and licensing bank branches in favour of rural areas. At the same time, it confronted neither the power of landed classes nor big Indian business effectively. Overall, land reforms only had a marginal effect on the skewed distribution of land ownership and associated class inequalities. As a result, the decentralised credit cooperatives essentially enabled dominant rural classes to accumulate private wealth and power while exploiting the small and marginal peasantry through forwarding credit with exorbitant interest rates and labour obligations attached.

The expansion of public banking followed the new agricultural policy (Green Revolution) adopting high-input commercialised cultivation and primarily addressed wealthy farmers and parts of the middle peasantry. This focus only began to change in the late 1970s, when the government used the public banking system to distribute targeted and subsidised loans for small and marginal farmers, artisans, and other poor households through the Integrated Rural Development Programme (IRDP). The basic idea resembled other microcredit experiments: Households below a certain income threshold received access to small loans to purchase assets, like milk animals or a sewing machine, which would eventually allow them to generate further income. Yet, since agrarian inequalities were still not addressed, there were hardly livelihood opportunities for the rural masses beyond precarious wage labour and petty commodity production. Moreover, the state invested little in the social provisioning of basic needs for subaltern classes (housing, sanitation, health, education). Consequently, most of these loans never reached their targets and aims. Instead, they fed into the household economy, including repaying pervasive reproductive debts with moneylenders.

Towards the end of the developmental regime, a new wave of civil society organisations increasingly fostered decentralised women's savings and credit groups, primarily focussing on the subaltern classes the credit cooperatives and public banks had poorly served. International donor agencies, government bodies, and profit-oriented financial institutions quickly endorsed these initiatives. Therefore, I have described the emergence of SHGs as one torn between state and market capture, laying the ground for the rapid expansion of commercialised and financialised MFIs.

Most importantly, the analysis of modern regimes of re/productive finance in India uncovered the continuities and changes in governing subaltern indebtedness through the "multiple form of incorporating comparison" (McMichael 1990). The general assumption that subaltern indebtedness is rooted in a chronic subsistence crisis and signifies a specific form of class oppression and exploitation was substantiated. However, the form, extent, and effects of this crisis have always been contingent upon the broader political economy, the fragmented and segmented class structure, and how access to credit is governed through all of this. As such, this analysis does not simply describe three distinct configurations of a colonial regime (ca. 1820 – 1940), a developmental regime (1940 – 1990), and a neoliberal regime (1990 – present). The formative creditor institutions of each phase, the power of moneylenders, credit cooperatives, commercial banks, SHGs, and MFIs converge in the present and constitute an ecosystem of creditor institutions with different relevance for subaltern classes (Chapter 12). Notably, class domination and exploitation work through these institutions. In this sense, market-driven financial inclusion can be understood as the latest incarnation of modern debt regimes subordinating a cheap, fragmented labour force under capital. This theme was further explored in the analysis of migrant workers in Bengaluru.

Precarious Migrant Workers and The Structural Violence of Reproductive Debt

Part IV deepened our understanding of the neoliberal regime of re/productive finance by investigating precarious migrant workers' livelihoods in Bengaluru, thereby giving subaltern indebtedness "a body, a voice, and a territory" (Cavallero and Gago 2021, 4). It departed from most contemporary analyses of financial inclusion by focusing primarily on the seeming background conditions of microfinance borrowers, highlighting their situatedness within the broader political economy. This singular form of incorporated comparison concentrated on three key moments. It built on the experiences of construction, domestic, and garment workers to understand the demand for reproductive debt, how (women) workers engage in various strategies to manage chronic indebtedness, and how they struggle against these conditions. Three main findings stand out from this analysis.

First, these chapters substantiated empirically how the interlocking gendered and racialised processes of expropriation, exclusion, and exploitation cumulate to intensify a chronic subsistence crisis amongst subaltern working-class households through increased market-dependent social reproduction. Instead of taking a lack of money amongst the working poor for granted, I highlighted how the slow violence associated with the agrarian crisis and escalating climate change makes cultivation for smallholders increasingly unviable, exacerbates rural inequalities, and keeps the subaltern classes chronically indebted with moneylenders, landlords, and wealthy peasants. Moreover, the displacement through large-scale development projects (including mining, dams, SEZs, etc.) is associated with loss of livelihood, especially for tribal communities and others who depend on forests and other common resources. In this context, seasonal, circular, or permanent migration to Bengaluru and other cities becomes a household strategy to safeguard social reproduction and repay old debts.

All these variegated processes facilitate a cheap and flexible labour force that works, for example, as daily wage labourers in construction, part-time and live-out domestic workers, or garment workers in export-oriented factories. Most of these workers are super-exploited in the sense that they receive wages below the subsistence level, even though this income forms the primary subsistence of these households. In other words, their monthly expenditures for food and water, rent, health care, education, and other essentials are structurally higher than their incomes. The exclusion from public provisioning of decent housing, public infrastructure, and access to welfare schemes further exacerbates this problem. Even though the latter formally exist, there are multiple barriers to getting subsidised food grains or other services due to their unregistered status as migrant workers.

Against this backdrop, reproductive debt, loans used primarily for the social reproduction of households, become an essential livelihood strategy for migrant workers, who, through debt, can access safe drinking water, health treatment, decent housing, education for their children or social functions (marriages, funerals). These dynamics were understood as a systematic debt-distress cycle because they describe a regular pattern that shapes the livelihoods of most rural-urban migrant workers (Chapter 13). However, the relative importance of different dimensions of the debt-distress cycle may differ across households. Moreover, the cyclical nature of these interlocking dynamics points towards continuous and changing forms of these categories. For instance, the constant threat of urban enclosures, driven by financialised land speculation, further exacerbates the fundamental uncertainty and insecurity that mark migrant worker's livelihoods and pushes them further into super-exploitation, exclusion, and indebtedness.

Second, the analysis challenged the narrow understanding of rational household decision-making that underpins the dominant financial inclusion discourse (Chapter 14). Instead of simply focusing on cheap/expensive debt, measured by interest rates, I proposed to understand the relational rationalities of household strategies as one informed by the social barriers of accessibility, the flexibility of loan size, freedom to use loans and conditions of repayment schedules. This analysis highlighted that creditors have different strengths and weaknesses, with variegated conditions and obligations attached. It was argued that MFIs have carved out a distinct niche within the ecosystem of creditors, mimicking the moneylenders and SHGs in terms of accessibility and free usage of loans, including for reproductive purposes, while aligning borrowing with the broader circuits of (global) financial capital. Rather than providing the initial working capital to start an enterprise, MFI's business model is strategically centred around the working poor's lifecycle, offering credit as an upward cascade for those who manage repayments. The focus on women's joint-liability groups allows them to offload a part of the disciplining work and ensure the profitability of lending. Importantly, MFIs do not provide an exclusive alternative to other creditors. This is where we come to a third central insight that engages with the structural violence of contemporary microfinance.

The pervasiveness of reproductive debt creates a puzzle: If loans are not used for business activities, how can migrant workers repay them? Or, put differently, where does the revenue that sustains profit-driven poverty finance come from? Answering this question is central to understanding the success of commercialised and financialised microfinance in terms of growing loan portfolios and the growing interest of institutional investors. I discuss six interlocking mechanisms that can explain this puzzle and reveal the structural violence of reproductive debt (Chapter 16). The first is the sale of assets, like livestock, land, and gold, and is usually associated with increased agrarian inequalities and the moneylender's business model. Likewise, the second dimension, pawning future labour capacities through forms of labour attachment and debt bondage, is a frequent mechanism. As shown in the contracting system of migrant workers, this dynamic is not confined to rural areas. Chronic indebtedness facilitates a cheap and disciplined labour force in agriculture, industries, and services.

The third dimension relates to the relational rationalities of debt. Caring for these debts, that is, juggling different sources and types of loans, repayment schedules, and obligations attached, is a critical work through which women sustain the solvency of households while living through debts. This work builds on regular group meetings of SHGs and JLGs but extends beyond. The fourth and perhaps most drastic measure is compromising on the social reproduction of household members through reduced food intake or withholding from seeking medical treatment, instead using household income to service debts and acquiring new debts to maintain survival. This is particularly visible in times of severe crisis, like Demonetisation or the COVID-19 pandemic. The fifth dimension is lengthening the workday by engaging in other jobs beyond their primary occupation to augment the household income, for example, through petty commodity production or part-time services.

Finally, accessing social security and welfare services is another critical dimension that allows precarious migrant workers to manage reproductive debts. This was demonstrated through the case of Bengaluru's garment workers' flash strike in 2016 for maintaining the Employees' Provident Fund (EPF). The latter primarily serves as a savings scheme for pensions. Instead, precarious garment workers access the EPF as an emergency fund to pay for lump sums related to reproductive needs, including the repayment of reproductive debt.

In sum, this research demonstrated how microfinance is not just a popular contemporary development policy but the latest incarnation of a class-based mode of dominating and exploiting subaltern classes on the Indian subcontinent through gendered and racialised indebtedness. The predatory nature of commercialised and financialised microfinance is thus not primarily rooted in exorbitant interest rates but in enfolding subaltern classes in permanent debt relations through cascading loans. Importantly, repayment is not premised primarily on business activities but on diverse forms of financial expropriation, including the deduction of wages below subsistence level, using different types and sources of debt to stay solvent, and other strategies outlined above. These violent dynamics are a common ground for predatory lending from moneylenders and MFIs. While the former is usually sustained by personal relationships of dependency and exploitation, the latter implies a more abstract domination, dependency and exploitation. Turning regular repayments into a tradable asset class through the securitisation of microcredit loan portfolios has increased the pressure to generate revenue by any means necessary. As such, the financialisation of microfinance has facilitated the expansion of contemporary microfinance by banking on a pervasive subsistence gap. However, this success is contingent upon the multifaceted structural violence of reproductive debt. There are limits to this business model because uncollateralised loans cannot be extended indefinitely without risking delinquency, and strict repayment schedules are necessary to work in accordance with the rhythms of banking and financial markets. Yet, considering the broader ecosystem of creditors, these limits are contingent upon the ability of households to acquire other forms of debt and obligations.

Looking Ahead: The Future of Unpayable Debts

In the epigraph, Susan Buck-Morss claims that "the point of scholarly debate should be to extend the horizon of historical imagination" (Buck-Morss 2009, 14). In this sense, the present analysis might modestly contribute to the radical rethinking of microfinance and financial inclusion. There is little reason to believe that regulating commercial microfinance changes the predatory nature of poverty finance. As shown in Chapter 11, curbing interest rates, limiting the number of creditors for each household, or prescribing a quota for income-generating loans neither limits the expansion of financialised microcredit nor challenges the pervasive crisis of social reproduction amongst subaltern classes. Of course, such measures have effects on individual households. But the structural violence of financialised microfinance is not exclusively, or even primarily, rooted in exorbitant interest rates and excessive borrowing of singular institutions. Instead, it becomes visible in the culmination of various types and forms of debt. The alienated, securitised debt of MFIs intersects with other types of indebtedness, deepens the vulnerability to various processes or expropriation, and facilitates the disciplining of a cheap labour force super-exploited in casualised wage work without offering any means to escape this subordinate position. In other words, it banks on and produces fractured lives.

The analysis of regimes of re/productive finance in modern India has shown how these multiple fractures that run through the social body, households, and individual lives are not only mediated by debt relations. These fractures can also turn into a powerful lever for collective mobilisation and fighting back against various modes of oppression. The analysis of the garment worker's strike in Bengaluru in 2016 hinted at the convergence of labour and debt struggles. This theme raises crucial questions about organising and mobilising a fragmented and segmented working class. Twentieth-century trade union strategies have focussed primarily on formal sector wage workers. For instance, 97 per cent of trade union membership in India is in the formal sector, although it employs only 35 million out of 460 million workers (George and Sinha 2017). Non-governmental organisations with diverse political affiliations, strategies, and ambitions have increasingly filled this gap since the 1980s, producing ambiguous outcomes.

The SHG model can be viewed as a novel form of organising the mass of informal sector workers both in rural and urban areas. This strategy has been discussed as ambiguous, torn between state and market capture because many organisations that facilitate SHGs view their work as apolitical development intervention helping the poor and depending on financial resources from donor agencies or the state. Thus, in most cases, the organisation of women's groups primarily fulfils the function of a supplementary to government welfare and has laid the foundations for the profitable expansion of commercial microfinance. However, there are also instances where political organisations consciously draw on these small-scale solidarity women's groups to organise a fragmented working class, fight neoliberal austerity policies, or challenge employers for decent work while remaining sensitive to patriarchal, caste-based, and racial oppression.

For example, the All-India Democratic Women's Association (AIDWA), the women's wing of the Communist Party of India (Marxist), organises more than 10 million labourers, with a substantial basis amongst the Dalit and Adivasi population. It has consciously used the SHG model and the facilitation of savings and credit groups in many rural and urban areas as a means for politicising broader issues, like basic social provisioning, public employment, equal and minimum wages, land and housing rights (Biju and Kumar 2013; Chari-Wagh 2015). Likewise, some of the NGOs engaged with precarious migrant workers in urban agglomerations have moved from focusing their work on advocacy and access to government welfare to organising workers in labour struggles vis-à-vis both the state and employers (Joseph, Natrajan, and Lobo 2019; RoyChowdhury 2021). These experiences do not yet challenge the roots of modern regimes of re/productive finance, and they may be limited to the dynamics of solving problems for marginalised sections of society without challenging the broader relations of power and oppression. However, they might articulate with more radical approaches, like the continuous peasant insurgencies or recent mass mobilisations of peasants against the further corporatisation of Indian agriculture.

The status quo of market-based reproductive debt will likely continue if the uneven distribution of land ownership, the absence of livelihood opportunities beyond precarious subsistence, petty commodity production and wage labour, and the exclusion from commons, including provisioning of social infrastructure, persist. Challenging this entrenched constellation requires bridging the manifold fragmentations that run through the social body and the working class through broad-based mobilisation. In this context, the women's SHGs might provide a fertile ground for struggling against the tyranny of unpayable debts if linked to broader coalitions of left parties, social movements, trade unions, and civil society organisations interested in overcoming the neoliberal regime of re/productive finance. Studying history backwards is crucial for such endeavours. After all, the radical imagination is not only about envisioning the future differently. It is equally about "radical remembering" (Haiven 2014), understanding how the world has become what it is now by acknowledging this history as a lived experience and as a result of collective labour and class struggles thought broadly. Neither money's coercive and divisive mode of socialisation as second nature nor reproductive debts exist naturally or eternally. They are the result of specific social and historical processes and, as such, can be overcome.

These insights are also relevant beyond the Indian context. The financialisation of social reproduction and the violence of predatory lending to working-class households are essential features of contemporary capitalism. In recent years, the structural violence of chronic indebtedness has become a central theme for social movements and powerful political mobilisations across the world. In the neoliberal era, the class struggle from above pushes for the individualisation and externalisation of risks and responsibilities through credit and other financial services under the banner of democratising finance, exploiting working-class households financially *and* in the labour process. The class struggle from below is often limited to fighting for better working conditions and pay or equal rights to access public services on the terrain of the state. However, the pervasiveness of chronic indebtedness amongst the global working poor might provide a more creative and radical approach to politicising these "unpayable debts from above" (Haiven 2020).

The oppressive nature of chronic indebtedness may be challenged by strategically inverting this relationship and claiming "unpayable debts from below" (Haiven 2020). For instance, the 2020 International Feminist Strike in Argentina has mobilised the masses against neoliberal austerity and pervasive household debt under the slogan "the debt is owed to us" (Cavallero and Gago 2021). Women were not demanding the right to work or become financially or otherwise included. Instead, they highlighted how their labour has been the cornerstone of producing wealth for centuries and how capitalist classes *owe them* (Cavallero and Gago 2021; Federici 2018). This relates to the broader shift in perspective that social reproduction feminism has called for. Moreover, it resonates with the critique of racial (finance) capitalism, which works through the production, exploitation, and accumulation of differences in the social body and the global proletariat. Debt struggles may thus prove a powerful form of contemporary class struggle, "turning of the tables on the powerful to insist that the oppressed and exploited are owed a debt that, importantly, cannot be repaid in the currency, value paradigm, or legal apparatus of the powerful" (Haiven 2020, 50). These unpayable debts can only be settled by dismantling those social relations and institutions of oppression and exploitation that create, maintain, and impose dependency on reproductive debt. In this sense, remembering the modern history of regimes of re/productive finance and the contemporary structural violence of reproductive debt in India might contribute to expanding the historical horizon towards a future of unpayable debts from below worth living and fighting for.

Bibliography

Abraham, Neha. 2019. "Over 80% Indians Now Have Bank Accounts. How Many Are Actually Using Them?" *Scroll.in*. https://scroll.in/article/923798/over-80-now-indians-have-bank-accounts-how-many-are-actually-using-them [last access: 27.09.2023].

Acharya, Amitav. 2022. "Race and Racism in the Founding of the Modern World Order." *International Affairs* 98(1): 23–43.

AFI. 2018. *AFI Annual Report 2018. Making Financial Services More Accessible to the World's Unbanked*. https://www.afi-global.org/sites/default/files/publications/2019-06/AFI_AR18_AW_digital.pdf [last access: 27.09.2023].

African Development Bank et al. 2015. *From Billions to Trillions: Transforming Development Finance*. Concept Paper for the Development Committee. https://documents1.worldbank.org/curated/en/602761467999349576/pdf/98023-BR-SecM2015-0233-IDA-SecM2015-0147-IFC-SecM2015-0105-MIGA-SecM2015-0061-Box391499B-OUO-9.pdf [last access: 27.09.2023].

AFWC. 2018. *Gender Based Violence in the GAP Garment Supply Chain*. https://asia.floorwage.org/wp-content/uploads/2022/01/GBV-Gap-May-2018.pdf. [last access: 27.09.2023].

Agarwal, Samantha. 2021. "Indebted by Dispossession: The Long-Term Impacts of a Special Economic Zone on Caste Inequality in Rural Telangana." *Journal of Agrarian Change* 21(3): 459–84.

Agarwal, Samantha, and Michael Levien. 2020. "Dalits and Dispossession: A Comparison." *Journal of Contemporary Asia* 50(5): 696–722.

Agarwala, Rina. 2013. *Informal Labour, Formal Politics, and Dignified Discontent in India*. Delhi: Cambridge University Press.

Ahuja, Pratul, and Rajat Ganguly. 2007. "The Fire within: Naxalite Insurgency Violence in India." *Small Wars and Insurgencies* 18(2): 249–74.

Aitken, Rob. 2015. *Fringe Finance. Crossing and Contesting the Borders of Global Capital*. New York: Routledge.

Alami, Ilias, Adam D. Dixon, and Emma Mawdsley. 2021. "State Capitalism and the New Global D/Development Regime." *Antipode* 53(5): 1294–1318.

Alami, Ilias, and Vincent Guermond. 2022. "The Color of Money at the Financial Frontier." *Review of International Political Economy*, 30(3): 1073–1097.

Altvater, Elmar. 1997. "Financial Crises on the Threshold of the 21st Century." *Social Register*, 33: 48–74.

Alva, Niharika. 2018. "Workers Quit Colony after Cholera Scare." *Times of India*. https://timesofindia.indiatimes.com/city/bengaluru/workers-quit-colony-after-cholera-scare/articleshow/62320449.cms [last access: 27.09.2023].

Ambedkar, Bhimrao R. 1917. "Castes in India: Their Mechanisms, Genesis and Development." *Indian Antiquary* XLI. http://www.columbia.edu/itc/mealac/pritchett/00ambedkar/txt_ambedkar_castes.html. [last access: 27.09.2023].

Ambedkar, Bhimrao R. 2014. *Annihilation of Caste. The Annotated Critical Edition*. New Delhi: Narayana Press.

Anand, Ishan, and Anjana Thampi. 2016. "Recent Trends in Wealth Inequality in India." *Economic and Political Weekly* 51(50): 59–67.

Anderson, Clare. 2009. "Convicts and Coolies: Rethinking Indentured Labour in the Nineteenth Century." *Slavery and Abolition* 30(1): 93–109.

Anievas, Alexander, and Kerem Nişancıoğlu. 2015. *How the West Came to Rule. The Geopolitical Origins of Capitalism*. London: Pluto Press.

Anner, Mark. 2015. "Labor Control Regimes and Worker Resistance in Global Supply Chains." *Labor History* 56(3): 292–307.

Anner, Mark. 2022. "Power Relations in Global Supply Chains and the Unequal Distribution of Costs during Crises: Abandoning Garment Suppliers and Workers during the COVID-19 Pandemic." *International Labour Review* 161(1): 59–82.

Anner, Mark, and Madhumita Dutta. 2019. *Sourcing Dynamics, Worker's Rights, and Inequality in Garment Supply Chains*. https://ler.la.psu.edu/wp-content/uploads/sites/4/2021/11/CGWR-Garment-Sourcing-and-Workers-Rights-in-India-Nov.-15-2019.pdf [last access: 27.09.2023].

Ansari, Shaukat. 2022. "Cash Transfers, International Finance and Neoliberal Debt Relations: The Case of Post-Apartheid South Africa." *Development and Change* 53(3): 551–75.

APU. 2021. "State of Working India 2021." https://cse.azimpremjiuniversity.edu.in/state-of-working-india/ [last access: 27.09.2023].

Arboleda, Martín. 2015a. "Financialization, Totality and Planetary Urbanization in the Chilean Andes." *Geoforum* 67: 4–13.

Arboleda, Martín. 2015b. "On the Alienated Violence of Money: Finance Capital, Value, and the Making of Monstrous Territories." *New Geographies* 09: 95–101.

Archer, Margaret S. et al., eds. 1998. *Critical Realism. Essential Readings*. London, New York: Routledge.

Archer, Margaret S. 1995. *Realist Social Theory. The Morphogenetic Approach*. Cambridge: Cambridge University Press.

Armendáriz, Beatriz, and Jonathan Morduch. 2010. *The Economics of Microfinance*. Cambridge: MIT Press.

Armendáriz, Beatriz, and Nigel Roome. 2006. "Gender Empowerment in Micro Finance." In *Microfinance. Emerging Trends and Challenges*, ed. Suresh Sundaresan. Cheltenham: Edward Elgar, 108–22.

Arnold, David. 1979. "Looting, Grain Riots and Government Policy in South India 1918." *Past & Present* 84: 111–45.

Arrighi, Giovanni. 2010. *The Long Twentieth Century. Money, Power and the Origins of Our Time*. London and New York: Verso.

Arruzza, Cinzia. 2016. "Functionalist, Determinist, Reductionist: Social Reproduction Feminism and Its Critics." *Science & Society* 80(1): 9–30.

Azeez, Abdul E P, Dandub Palzor Negi, Asha Rani, and Senthil Kumar A P. 2021. "The Impact of COVID-19 on Migrant Women Workers in India." *Eurasian Geography and Economics* 62(1): 93–112.

Bag, Kheya, and Susan Watkins. 2021. "Structures of Oppression: Querying Analogies of Race and Caste." *New Left Review* 132: 55–82.

Bagchi, Amiya Kumar. 1982. *The Political Economy of Underdevelopment*. Cambridge: Cambridge University Press.

Bagchi, Amiya Kumar. 1985. "Anglo-Indian Banking in British India: From the Paper Pound to the Gold Standard." *The Journal of Imperial and Commonwealth History* 13(3): 93–108.

Bagchi, Amiya Kumar. 1987. *The Presidency Banks and the Indian Economy. 1876–1914*. Calcutta: Oxford University Press.

Bagchi, Amiya Kumar. 1992. "Land Tax, Property Rights and Peasant Insecurity in Colonial India." *The Journal of Peasant Studies* 20(1): 1–49.

Bagchi, Amiya Kumar. 2008. *Perilous Passage: Mankind and the Global Ascendancy of Capital*. Lanham: Rowman & Littlefield Publishers.

Bagchi, Amiya Kumar. 2010. *Colonialism and Indian Economy*. New Delhi: Oxford University Press.

Bakker, Isabella. 2007. "Social Reproduction and the Constitution of a Gendered Political Economy." *New Political Economy* 12(4): 541–56.

Bakker, Isabella, and Stephen Gill. 2003. "Ontology, Method, and Hypotheses." In *Power, Production and Social Reproduction*, eds. Isabella Bakker and Stephen Gill. Basingstoke: Palgrave Macmillan, 17–41.

Balibar, Etienne. 1991a. "Is There Neo-Racism?" In *Race, Nation, Class. Ambiguous Identities*, eds. Etienne Balibar and Immanuel Wallerstein. London & New York: Verso, 17–28.

Balibar, Etienne. 1991b. "Racism and Nationalism." In *Race, Nation, Class. Ambiguous Identities*, eds. Etienne Balibar and Immannuel Wallerstein. London & New York: Verso, 37–67.

Banaji, Jairus. 1977. "Capitalist Domination And The Small Peasantry: The Deccan Districts In The Late Nineteenth Century." *Economic & Political Weekly* 12(33/34): 277–332.

Banaji, Jairus. 2010. *Theory as History. Essays on Modes of Production and Exploitation*. Leiden and Boston: Brill.

Banaji, Jairus. 2013. "Seasons of Self-Delusion: Opium, Capitalism and the Financial Markets." *Historical Materialism* 21(2): 3–19.

Banaji, Jairus. 2020. *A Brief History of Commercial Capitalism*. Chicago: Haymarket Books.

Banerjee, Abhijit, Esther Duflo, Rachel Glennerster, and Cynthia Kinnan. 2009. "The Miracle of Microfinance? Evidence from a Randomized Evaluation." *American Economic Journal: Applied Economics* 7(1): 22–53.

Bannerjee, Abhijit and Esther Duflo. 2011. *Poor Economics. Rethinking Poverty & the Ways to End It*. Noida: Random House India.

Banerjee, Supurna, and Nandini Ghosh, eds. 2018. *Caste and Gender in Contemporary India: Power, Privilege and Politics*. London: Routledge.

Bannerji, Himani. 2020. *The Ideological Condition. Selected Essays on History, Race and Gender*. Leiden and Boston: Brill.

Basole, Amit, and Deepankar Basu. 2011a. "Relations of Production and Modes of Surplus Extraction in India: Part I – Agriculture." *Economic and Political Weekly* 46(14): 41–58.

Basole, Amit, and Deepankar Basu. 2011b. "Relations of Production and Modes of Surplus Extraction in India: Part II – 'Informal' Industry." *Economic and Political Weekly* 46(15): 63–79.

Basu, Deepankar, Debarshi Das, and Kartik Misra. 2016. "Farmer Suicides in India: Trends across Major States, 1995–2011." *Economic and Political Weekly* 51(21): 61–65.

Bateman, Milford. 2010. *Why Doesn't Microfinance Work? The Destructive Rise of Local Neoliberalism*. London and New York: ZedBooks.

Bateman, Milford. 2019. "Impacts of the Microcredit Model. Does Theory Reflect Actual Reality?" In *The Rise and Fall of Global Microcredit. Development, Debt and Disillusion*, eds. Milford Bateman, Stephanie Blankenburg, Richard Kozuk-Wright. Abingdon, New York: Routledge, 42–68.

Bateman, Milford, Stephanie Blankenburg, and Richard Kozul-Wright, eds. 2019. *The Rise and Fall of Global Microcredit. Development, Debt and Disillusion*. Abingdon, New York: Routledge.

Bateman, Milford and Ha-Joon Chang. 2012. "Microfinance and the Illusion of Development: From Hubris to Nemesis in Thirty Years." *World Economic Review* 1: 13–36.

Bauer, Rolf. 2019. *The Peasant Production of Opium in Nineteenth-Century India*. Leiden: Brill.

Bayliss, Kate, Mary Robertson, and Ben Fine, eds. 2018. *Material Cultures of Financialization*. London: Routledge.

Bayliss, Kate and Elisa Van Waeyenberge. 2018. "Unpacking the Public Private Partnership Revival." *Journal of Development Studies* 54(4): 577–93.

Bayly, C A. 1985. "State and Economy in India over Seven Hundred Years." *The Economic History Review* 38(4): 583–96.

Beckert, Sven. 2014. *Empire of Cotton. A New History of Global Capitalism*. London: Penguin.

Behal, Rana P., and Marcel van der Linden, eds. 2007. *Coolies, Capital and Colonialism*. Cambridge: Cambridge University Press.

Belfrage, Claes, and Felix Hauf. 2017. "The Gentle Art of Retroduction: Critical Realism, Cultural Political Economy and Critical Grounded Theory." *Organization Studies* 38(2): 251–71.

Bennholdt-Thomsen, Veronika, and Maria Mies. 1999. *The Subsistence Perspective: Beyond the Globalized Economy*. London and New York: ZedBooks.

Berman, Peter, Rajeev Ahuja, and Laveesh Bhandari. 2010. "The Impoverishing Effect of Healthcare Payments in India: New Methodology and Findings." *Economic and Political Weekly* 45(16): 65–71.

Bernards, Nick. 2018. *The Global Governance of Precarity. Primitive Accumulation and the Politics of Irregular Work*. London/New York: Routledge.

Bernards, Nick. 2021. "Poverty Finance and the Durable Contradictions of Colonial Capitalism: Placing 'Financial Inclusion' in the Long Run in Ghana." *Geoforum* 123(April): 89–98.

Bernards, Nick. 2022. *A Critical History of Poverty Finance: Colonial Roots and Neoliberal Failures*. London: Pluto Press.

Bernards, Nick, and Susanne Soederberg. 2021. "Relative Surplus Populations and the Crises of Contemporary Capitalism: Reviving, Revisiting, Recasting." *Geoforum* 126: 412–19.

Bernstein, Henry. 2010. *Class Dynamics of Agrarian Change*. Nova Scotia: Fernwood Publishing.

Bezanson, Kate, and Meg Luxton, eds. 2006. *Social Reproduction: Feminist Political Economy Challenges Neo-Liberalism*. Quebec: McGill-Queen's University Press.

Bhabha, Homi K. 1994. *The Location of Culture*. London and New York: Routledge.

Bhambra, Gurminder K. 2014. *Connected Sociologies. Theories for a Global Age*. London, New Delhi, New York, Sydney: Bloomsbury.

Bhaskar, Roy. 2008. *A Realist Theory of Science*. London: Routledge.

Bhatt, Ela R. 1998. "Doosri Azadi. SEWA's Perspectives on Early Years of Independence." *Economic & Political Weekly*: 33(17): 25–27.

Bhattacharjee, Shikha Silliman. 2019. "Fast Fashion, Production Targets, and Gender-Based Violence in Asian Garment Supply Chains." In *Labor, Global Supply*

Chains, and the Garment Industry in South Asia, ed. Sanchita Banerjee Saxena. London: Routledge.

Bhattacharya, Rajesh, and Kalyan Sanyal. 2011. "Bypassing the Squalor: New Towns, Immaterial Labour and Exclusion in Post-Colonial Urbanisation." *Economic & Political Weekly* 46(31): 41–48.

Bhattacharya, Ruchira. 2015. "Estimating Poverty Including Social Expenditure: Adequacy and Implications of New Official Methods in the Context of Urban India." *Agrarian South: Journal of Political Economy* 4(3): 394–432.

Bhattacharya, Tithi. 2017a. "How Not to Skip Class: Social Reproduction of Labor and the Global Working Class." In *Social Reproduction Theory. Remapping Class, Recentering Oppression*, London: Pluto Press, 68–93.

Bhattacharya, Tithi, ed. 2017b. *Social Reproduction Theory. Remapping Class, Recentering Oppression*. London: Pluto Press.

Bhattacharyya, Gargi. 2018. *Rethinking Racial Capitalism. Questions of Reproduction and Survival*. London: Rowman & Littlefield International.

Bhende, M. J. 1986. "Credit Markets in Rural South India." *Economic and Political Weekly* 21(38/39): A119–24.

Bieler, Andreas, and Adam David Morton. 2018. *Global Capitalism, Global War, Global Crisis*. Cambridge: Cambridge University Press.

Biju, B. L., and K. G. Abhilash Kumar. 2013. "Class Feminism: The Kudumbashree Agitation in Kerala." *Economic and Political Weekly* 48(9): 22–26.

Birla, Ritu. 2009. *Stages of Capital. Law, Culture and Market Governance in Late Colonial India*. Durham and London: Duke University Press.

Biswas, Arindam. 2016. "Development in Practice Insight on the Evolution and Distinction of Inclusive Growth." *Development in Practice* 26(4): 503–16.

Blackburn, Robin. 2006. "Finance and the Fourth Dimension." *New Left Review* 39: 39–70.

Blaikie, Norman, and Jan Priest. 2017. *Social Research. Paradigms in Action*. Cambridge: Polity Press.

Bohrer, Ashley J. 2019. *Marxism and Intersectionality. Race, Gender, Class and Sexuality under Contemporary Capitalism*. Bielefeld: transcript.

Bonacich, Edna, Sabrina Alimahomed, and Jake B Wilson. 2008. "The Racialization of Global Labor." *American Behavioral Scientist*, 52(3): 342–55.

Bond, Patrick. 2013. "Debt, Uneven Development and Capitalist Crisis in South Africa: From Moody's Macroeconomic Monitoring to Marikana Microfinance Mashonisas." *Third World Quarterly* 34(4): 569–92.

Bond, Patrick, Milford Bateman, Lena Lavinas, and Erin Torkelson. 2023. "Incoming World Bank President Ajay Banga's Predatory-Finance Background Threatens Even More Prolific Bank Poverty-Creation." CADTM, 12. April. https://www.cadtm.org/Incoming-World-Bank-President-Ajay-Banga-s-predatory-finance-background [last access: 27.09.2023].

Bonizzi, Bruno, Jennifer Churchill, and Diego Guevara. 2021. "Variegated Financialization and Pension Fund Asset Demand: The Case of Colombia and Perú." *Socio-Economic Review* 19(2): 789–815.

Bose, Sugata. 1994. "The Peasantry in Debt: The Working and Rupture of Systems of Rural Credit Creation." In *Credit, Markets and the Agrarian Economy of Colonia*, New Delhi: Oxford University Press, 248–300.

Bose, Sugata. 2019. "A History of the Indian Economy in Asian and Global Contexts, 1810s-2010s." In *Emerging States and Economies. Their Origins, Drivers, and Challenges Ahead*, eds. Takashi Shiraishi and Tetsushi Sonobe. Berlin, Heidelberg: SpringerOpen, 139–52.

Bowers, Rebecca. 2019. "Navigating the City and the Workplace: Migrant Female Construction Workers and Urban (Im)Mobilities." *Global Labour Journal* 10(1): 19–36.

Boyer, Robert. 2005. "From Shareholder Value to CEO Power: The Paradox of the 1990s." *Competition & Change* 9(1): 7–47.

Bracking, Sarah. 1999. "Structural Adjustment: Why It Wasn't Necessary & Why It Did Work." *Review of African Political Economy* 80: 207–26.

Brand, Ulrich. 2016. "'Transformation' as a New Critical Orthodoxy: The Strategic Use of the Term Transformation Does Not Prevent Multiple Crises." *GAIA – Ecological Perspectives for Science and Society* 25(1): 23–27.

Braun, Benjamin. 2022. "Fueling Financialization: The Economic Consequences of Funded Pensions." *New Labor Forum* 31(1): 70–79.

Braverman, Avishay, and J. Luid Guasch. 1986. "Rural Credit Markets and Institutions In Developing Countries: Lessons for Policy Analysis from Practice and Modern Theory." *World Development* 14(10/11): 1253–67.

Breda, Stefano. 2021. "Der marxsche und vormarxsche Begriff des fiktiven Kapitals. Zur Entstehungsgeschichte einer begrifflichen Konfusion." In *Auf Den Schultern von Marx.*, eds. Thomas Sablowski, Alex Demirovic, Katharina Pühl, and Ingar Solty. Münster: Westfälisches Dampfboot, 109–23.

Breman, Jan. 1974. *Patronage and Exploitation. Changing Agrarian Relations in South Gujarat, India*. Berkely, Los Angeles, London: University of California Press.

Breman, Jan. 2010. *Outcast Labour in Asia. Circulation and Informalization of the Workforce at the Bottom of the Economy*. New Delhi: Oxford University Press.

Breman, Jan. 2019. *Capitalism, Inequality and Labour in India*. Cambridge: Cambridge University Press.

Breman, Jan, Isabelle Guérin, and Aseem Prakash, eds. 2009. *India's Unfree Workforce: Of Bondage Old and New*. New Delhi: Oxford University Press.

Breman, Jan, and Marcel van der Linden. 2014. "Informalizing the Economy: The Return of the Social Question at a Global Level." *Development and Change* 45(5): 920–40.

Bruck, Nicholas. 1998. "The Role of Development Banks in the Twenty-First Century." *Journal of Emerging Markets* 3: 39–67.

Brunhoff, Suzanne de, and Duncan K. Foley. 2006. "Karl Marx's Theory of Money and Credit." In *A Handbook of Alternative Monetary Economics*, eds. Philip Arestis and Malcom Sawyer. Cheltenham: Edward Elgar, 188–204.

Bryan, Dick, Randy Martin, and Mike Rafferty. 2009. "Financialization and Marx: Giving Labor and Capital a Financial Makeover." *Review of Radical Political Economics* 41(4): 458–72.

Bryan, Dick, Michael Rafferty, and Chris Jefferis. 2015. "Risk and Value: Finance, Labor, and Production." *South Atlantic Quarterly* 114(2): 307–29.

Buck-Morss, Susan. 2009. *Hegel, Haiti and Universal History*. Pittsburgh: University of Pittsburgh Press.

Buroway, Michael. 1985. *The Politics of Production. Factory Regimes Under Capitalism and Socialism*. London: Verso.

Büscher, Bram, and Robert Fletcher. 2015. "Accumulation by Conservation." *New Political Economy* 20(2): 273–98.

Calomiris, Charles W, and Charles P Himmelberg. 1994. "Directed Credit Programs for Agriculture and Industry. Arguments from Theory and Fact". *World Bank Economic Review*, 7(1): 113–138.

Camfield, David. 2016. "Elements of a Historical-Materialist Theory of Racism." *Historical Materialism* 24(1): 31–70.

Cammack, Paul. 2012. "Developmental Liberalism: The G20, the Crisis, and the Rise of Global Developmental Liberalism." *Third World Quarterly* 33(1): 1–16.

Casolo, Jennifer, and Sapana Doshi. 2013. "Domesticated Dispossessions? Towards a Transnational Feminist Geopolitics of Development." *Geopolitics* 18(4): 800–834.

Cavallero, Lucí, and Verónica Gago. 2021. *A Feminist Reading of Debt*. London: Pluto Press.

CGAP. 2022. *How Much International Funding Is Going to Support Financial Inclusion in South Asia*. https://www.cgap.org/sites/default/files/datasets/2022_01_CGAP_Funder_Survey_Regional_Snapshot_SoAsia.pdf [last access: 27.09.2023].

Chakrabarty, Dipesh. 2000. *Provincializing Europe. Postcolonial Thought and Historical Difference*. Princeton and Oxford: Princeton University Press.

Chakravarthi, Indira, Bijoya Roy, Indranil Mukhophaya, and Susana Barria. 2017. "Healthcare Industry in India." *Economic & Political Weekly* 52(45): 50–56.

Chakravarti, Uma. 2005. "Reconceptualizing Gender: Phule, Brahmanism, and Brahmanical Patriarchy." In *Gender & Caste*, ed. Anupama Rao. London & New York: Zed Books.

Chakravarti, Uma. 2019. "Caste: An Autobiographical Journey." In *Caste and Gender in Contemporary India: Power, Privilege and Politics*, eds. Supurna Banerjee and Nandini Ghosh. London & New York: Routledge.

Chakravartty, Paula, and Denise Ferreira da Silva. 2012. "Accumulation, Dispossession, and Debt: The Racial Logic of Global Capitalism – An Introduction." *American Quarterly* 64(3): 361–85.

Chakravarty, Sukhamoy. 1987. *Development Planning. The Indian Experience*. Oxford: Clarendon Press.

Chakravorty, Sanjoy. 2019. *The Truth About Us: The Politics of Information from Manu to Modi*. New Delhi: Hachette Books.

Chandavarkar, A.G. 1983. "Money and Credit (1858 – 1947)." In *The Cambridge Economic History of India. Volume 2: C.1757 – c.1970*, eds. Dharma Kumar and Meghnad Desai. Cambridge: Cambridge University Press, 762–803.

Chandra, Uday. 2014. "The Maoist Movement in Contemporary India." *Social Movement Studies* 13(3): 414–19.

Chandrasekhar, C.P. 2007. "Credit Risk and Bank Fragility in the New Financial Environment." In *Capture and Exclude: Developing Economies and the Poor in Global Finance*, eds. Amiya Kumar Bagchi and Gary A. Dymski. New Delhi: Tulika Books, 195–215.

Chandrasekhar, C.P., and Jayati Ghosh. 2002. *The Market That Failed. Neoliberal Economic Reforms in India*. New Delhi: LeftWord Books.

Chandrasekhar, C.P. and Jayati Ghosh. 2017. "The Financialization of Finance? Demonetization and the Dubious Push to Cashlessness in India." *Development and Change* 49 (2): 420 – 436.

Chari-Wagh, Anurekha. 2015. "The Transformational Potential of Microfinance: Two Case Studies." In *Microfinance in India. Approaches, Outcomes, Challenges*, ed. Tara S. Nair. London, New York, New Delhi: Routledge, 69–86.

Chatterjee, Partha. 2002. "Development Planning and the Indian State." In *Politics and the Indian State*, ed. Zoya Hasan. New Delhi: SAGE Publications.

Chauhan, Komal. 2022. "Why Do Dalits Migrate? A Case Study of Neo-Bondage in Western Uttar Pradesh." *Contemporary Voice of Dalit* 14(1): 95–102.

Chavan, Pallavi. 2005. "How 'Inclusive' Are Banks under Financial Liberalisation?" *Economic and Political Weekly* 40(43): 4647–49.

Chavan, Pallavi. 2017. "Public Banks and Financial Intermediation in India: The Phases of Nationalization, Liberalization and Inclusion." In *Public Banks in the Age of Financialization. A Comparative Perspective*, ed. Christoph Scherrer. Cheltenham: Edward Elgar, 116–35.

Cheesman, David. 1982. "The Omnipresent Bania:' Rural Moneylenders in Nineteenth-Century Sind." *Modern Asian Studies* 16(3): 445–62.

Chibber, Vivek. 2006. *Locked in Place. State-Building and Late Industrialisation in India*. Princeton and Oxford: Princeton University Press.

Citi. 2017. *Banking on 2030: Citi & the Sustainable Development Goals*. https://www.citigroup.com/citi/about/citizenship/download/Banking-on-2030-Citi-and-the-SDGs-Report.pdf?ieNocache=124 [last access: 27.09.2023].

Clarke, Simon. 1988. *Keynesianism, Monetarism and the Crisis of the State*. Aldershot: Edward Elgar.

Clarke, Simon. 2003. "The Rationality and Irrationality of Money." *Value and the World Economy Today: Production, Finance and Globalization*, eds. Richard Westra, Alan Zuege. Cham: Palgrave Macmillan: 25–39.

Cleaver, Harry M. 1972. "The Contradictions of the Green Revolution." *The American Economic Review* 62(1): 177–186.

Collier, Paul, and David Dollar. 2002. *Globalization, Growth and Poverty. Building an Inclusive World Economy*. Washington, D.C. and Oxford: World Bank and Oxford University Press.

Collins, Daryl, Jonathan Morduch, Stuart Rutherford, and Orlanda Ruthven. 2009. *Portfolios of the Poor. How the World's Poor Live on $2 a Day*. Princeton and Oxford: Princeton University Press.

Connell, Raewyn. 2007. *Southern Theory. The Global Dynamics of Knowledge in Social Science*. Cambridge: Polity Press.

Convergences. 2011. *Microfinance Barometer 2011*. http://www.convergences.org/wp-content/uploads/2017/05/Barometre-Microfinance-2011-UK_web.pdf [last access: 27.09.2023].

Convergences. 2018. *Microfinane Barometer 2018. Microfinance and Profitabilities*. http://www.convergences.org/wp-content/uploads/2018/09/BMF_2018_EN_VFINALE.pdf [last access: 27.09.2023].

Cooper, Melinda, and Angela Mitropoulos. 2009. "The Household Frontier." *ephemera. theory & politics in organization* 9(4): 363–68.

Corbridge, Stuart, and Alpa Shah. 2013. "Introduction: The Underbelly of the Indian Boom." *Economy and Society* 42(3): 335–47.

Corbridge, Stuart, and Manoj Srivastava. 2013. "Mapping the Social Order by Fund Flows: The Political Geography of Employment Assurance Schemes in India." *Economy and Society* 42(3): 455–79.

Cowan, L Gray. 1985. "Divestment, Privatization and Development." *The Washington Quarterly* 8(4): 47–56.

Cox, Robert. 1981. "Social Forces, States and World Orders: Beyond International Relations Theory." *Millenium: Journal of International Studies* 10(2): 126–55.

Crouch, Colin. 2009. "Privatised Keynesianism: An Unacknowledged Policy Regime." *The British Journal of Politics and International Relations* 11: 382–99.

Cull, Robert, and Jonathan Morduch. 2018. "Microfinance and Economic Development." In *Handbook of Finance and Development*, eds. Thorsten Beck and Ross Levine. Cheltenham: Edward Elgar, 550–72.

D'Costa, Anthony P., and Achin Chakraborty, eds. 2017. *The Land Question in India. State, Dispossession, and Capitalist Transition*. Oxford: Oxford University Press.

Dalla Costa, Mariarosa. 1996. "Capitalism and Reproduction." *Capitalism Nature Socialism* 7(4): 111–21.

Damodaran, Vinita. 2002. "Gender, Forests and Famine in 19th-Century Chotanagpur, India." *Indian Journal of Gender Studies* 9(2): 133–63.

Dandekar, Ajay. 2016. "India's Agriculture and Farmer Suicides: An Anatomy of a Crisis." *India International Centre Quarterly* 43(2): 48–55.

Dantwala, M. L. 1952. "Agricultural Credit in India-The Missing Link." *Pacific Affairs* 25(4): 349.

Das, Kartick. 2010. "Naxalbari to Today's Maoists: Uprisings and Implications." *The Indian Journal of Political Science* 71(2): 492–95.

Davis, Angela Y. 1982. *Women, Race & Class*. London: The Women's Press.

Davis, Mike. 2006. *Planet of Slums*. London: Verso.

Davis, Mike. 2011. *Late Victorian Holocausts. El Nino Famines and the Making of the Third World*. London and New York: Verso.

Deccan Herald. 2012. "Construction Industry Nation's Second Largest Employer." https://www.deccanherald.com/content/222581/construction-industry-nations-second-largest.html [last access: 27.09.2023].

Demirgüc-Kunt, Asli et al. 2018. *The Global Findex Database 2017. Measuring Financial Inclusion and the Fintech Revolution*. Washington, D.C.: World Bank.

Demirgüc-Kunt, Asli, Leora Klapper, and Dorothe Singer. 2018. "Household Finance and Economic Development." In *Handbook of Finance and Development*, eds. Thorsten Beck and Ross Levine. Cheltenham: Edward Elgar, 534–49.

Desan, Christine A. 2014. *Making Money: Coin, Currency, and the Coming of Capitalism*. Oxford: Oxford University Press.

Deshpande, Ashwini. 2018. *The Grammar of Caste: Economic Discrimination in Contemporary India*. Oxford: Oxford University Press.

Dhanagare, D. N. 1988. "The Green Revolution and Social Inequalities in Rural India." *Critical Asian Studies* 20(2): 2–13.

Dirks, Nicholas B. 2001. *Castes of Mind. Colonialism and the Making of Modern India*. Princeton: Princeton University Press.

Dirlik, Arif. 1999. "Is There History after Eurocentrism?: Globalism, Postcolonialism, and the Disavowal of History." *Cultural Critique* 42: 1–34.

Dörre, Klaus. 2009. "Die neue Landnahme. Dynamiken und Grenzen des Finanzmarktkapitalismus." In *Soziologie Kapitalismus Kritik. Eine Debatte*, ed. Hartmut Rosa, Dörre, Klaus; Lessenich, Stephan. Berlin: Suhrkamp.

Dörre, Klaus. 2012. "Landnahme, Das Wachstumsdilemma und die 'Achsen der Ungleichheit.'" *Berliner Journal für Soziologie* 22(101–128).

Dreze, Jean. 1990. "Poverty in India and the IRDP." *Economic And Political Weekly* 25(39).

Dreze, Jean, and Reetika Khera. 2017. "Recent Social Security Initiatives in India." *World Development* 98: 555–72.

Duggal, Ravi, and Nitin Jadhav. 2018. "User Charges Onslaught On." *Economic and Political Weekly* 53(4): 23–25.

Durand, Céderic. 2017. *Fictitious Capital. How Finance Appropriates Our Future*. New York and London: Verso.

Dutt, Romesh. 2001. *The Economic History of India in the Victorian Age. From the Accession of Queen Victoria in 1837 to The Commencement of the Twentieth Century*. London: Routledge.

Dutta, Madhumita. 2021. “Becoming ‘Active Labour Protestors’: Women Workers Organizing in India’s Garment Export Factories.” *Globalizations* 18(8): 1420–35.

Duvendack, Maren et al. 2011. *What Is the Evidence of the Impact of Microfinance on the Well-Being of Poor People?* London: EPPI-Centre, Social Science Research Unit, Institute of Education, University of London. https://ueaeprints.uea.ac.uk/id/eprint/35466/3/Microfinance2011Duvendackreport.pdf [last access: 27.09.2023].

Duvendack, Maren. 2015. “Revisiting the Impact of SEWA Bank.” In *Microfinance in India. Approaches, Outcomes, Challenges*, ed. Tara S. Nair. London, New York, New Delhi: Routledge, 180–90.

Duvendack, Maren, and Philip Mader. 2020. “Impact of Financial Inclusion in Low- and Middle-Income Countries: A Systematic Review of Reviews.” *Journal of Economic Surveys* 34(3): 594–629.

Dymski, Gary, Jesus Hernandez, and Lisa Mohanty. 2013. “Race, Gender, Power, and the US Subprime Mortgage and Foreclosure Crisis: A Meso Analysis.” *Feminist Economics* 19(2).

Ehrbeck, Tilman, Mark Pickens, and Michael Tarazi. 2012. *Financially Inclusive Ecosystems: The Roles of Government Today*. https://www.cgap.org/sites/default/files/Focus-Note-Financially-Inclusive-Ecosystems-The-Roles-of-Government-Today-Feb-2012.pdf [last access: 27.09.2023].

Eich, Stefan. 2022. *The Currency of Politics. The Political Theory of Money from Aristotle to Keynes*. Princeton: Princeton University Press.

Elsner, Carsten, Manuel Neumann, Franziska Müller, and Simone Claar. 2022. “Room for Money or Manoeuvre? How Green Financialization and de-Risking Shape Zambia’s Renewable Energy Transition.” *Canadian Journal of Development Studies* 43(2): 276–95.

Elson, Diane. 2015. “The Value Theory of Labour.” In *Value. The Representation of Labour in Capitalism*, ed. Diane Elson. London, New York: Verso, 115–80.

Escobar, Arturo. 1995. *Encountering Development. The Making and Unmaking of the Third World*. Princeton: Princeton University Press.

Escobar, Arturo. 1999. “The Invention of Development.” *Current History* 98: 382–86.

Esteva, Gustavo. 2010. “Development.” In *The Development Dictionary. A Guide to Knowledge as Power*, ed. Wolfgang Sachs. London, New York: ZedBooks, 1–23.

Everett, Jana, and Mira Savara. 1984. “Bank Loans to the Poor in Bombay: Do Women Benefit?” *Signs: Journal of Women in Culture and Society* 10(2): 272–90.

Fanconi, Peter, and Patrick Scheurle. 2017. *Small Money – Big Impact. Fighting Poverty with Microfinance*. Hoboken: Wiley.

Federici, Silvia 2004. *Caliban and the Witch. Women, Body and Primitive Accumulation*. New York: Autonomedia.

Federici, Silvia. 2012. *Revolution at Point Zero. Housework, Reproduction, and Feminist Struggle*. Oakland: PM Press.

Federici, Silvia. 2014a. "The Reproduction of Labour Power in the Global Economy and the Unfinished Feminist Revolution." In *Workers and Labour in A Globalised Capitalism. Contemporary Themes and Theoretical Issues*, ed. Maurizio Atzeni. Basingstoke: Palgrave Macmillan, 85–110.

Federici, Silvia. 2014b. "From Commoning to Debt: Financialization, Microcredit, and the Changing Architecture of Capital Accumulation." *South Atlantic Quarterly* 113(2): 231–44.

Federici, Silvia. 2018. "Women, Money and Debt: Notes for a Feminist Reappropriation Movement." *Australian Feminist Studies* 33(96): 178–86.

Federici, Silvia. 2020. *Beyond the Periphery of the Skin. Rethinking, Remaking, and Reclaiming the Body in Contemporary Capitalism*. Oakland: PM Press.

Fekete, Liz. 2001. "The Emergence of Xeno-Racism." *Race & Class* 43(2): 23–40.

Ferguson, Susan. 2020. *Women and Work. Feminism, Labour and Social Reproduction*. London: Pluto Press.

Fernandez, Aloysius Prakash. 2018. *The Myrada Experience. 50 Years of Learning Through Promoting Social Entrepreneurship and Institutions of the Poor*. Bengaluru: Myrada.

Finch, Gavin, David Koncieniweski, Sinduja Rangarajan, and Christopher Cannon. 2022. "Big Money Backs Tiny Loans That Lead to Debt, Despair and Even Suicide." *Bloomberg*. https://www.bloomberg.com/graphics/2022-microfinance-banks-profit-off-developing-world/ [last access: 27.09.2023].

Flick, Uwe. 2022. *Doing Interview Research. The Essential How to Guide*. London: Sage.

Flores, Gabriela, Jaya Krishnakumar, Owen O'Donnell, and Eddy van Doorslaer. 2008. "Coping with Health-Care Costs: Implications for the Measurement of Catastrophic Expenditures and Poverty." *Health Economics* 17(1): 1393–1412.

Foley, Laura, and Nicola Piper. 2021. "Returning Home Empty Handed: Examining How COVID-19 Exacerbates the Non-Payment of Temporary Migrant Workers' Wages." *Global Social Policy* 21(3): 468–89.

Foster, John Bellamy. 2018. "Marx's Open-Ended Critique." *Monthly Review* 70(1): 1–16.

Fraser, Nancy. 2014a. "Behind Marx 's 'Hidden Abode'. For an Expanded Conception of Capitalism." *New Left Review* 86: 55–72.

Fraser, Nancy. 2014b. "Can Society Be Commodities All the Way Down? Post-Polanyian Reflections on Capitalist Crisis." *Economy and Society* 43(4): 541–58.

Fraser, Nancy. 2016. "Contradictions of Capital and Care." *New Left Review* 100: 99–117.

Fraser, Nancy. 2017. "Crisis of Care? On the Social-Reproductive Contradictions of Contemporary Capitalism." In *Social Reproduction Theory. Remapping Class, Recentering Oppression*, ed. Thiti Bhattacharya. London: Pluto Press, 21–36.

Fraser, Nancy. 2018. "From Exploitation to Expropriation. Historic Geographies of Racialized Capitalism." *Economic Geography* 94(1): 1–17.

Fuji, Lee Ann. 2018. *Interviewing in Social Science Research. A Relational Approach*. London: Routledge.

Gabor, Daniela. 2018. "Goodbye (Chinese) Shadow Banking, Hello Market-Based Finance." *Development and Change* 49(2): 394–419.

Gabor, Daniela. 2021. "The Wall Street Consensus." *Development and Change* 52(3): 429–59.

Gabor, Daniela, and Sally Brooks. 2016. "The Digital Revolution in Financial Inclusion: International Development in the Fintech Era." *New Political Economy* 22(4): 423–36.

Gago, Verónica. 2018. "Is There a War 'on' the Body of Women? Finance, Territory, and Violence." *Viewpoint Magazine*. https://viewpointmag.com/2018/03/07/war-body-women-finance-territory-violence/ [last access: 27.09.2023].

Gallas, Alexander. 2023. "Beyond Methodological Fordism. The Case for Incorporated Comparison." In *The Handbook on Critical Political Economy and Public Policy*, eds. Ana Garcia, Joscha Wullweber, and Christoph Scherrer. Cheltenham: Edward Elgar, 127–43.

Garikipati, Supriya. 2013. "Microcredit and Women's Empowerment: Have We Been Looking at the Wrong Indicators?" *Oxford Development Studies* 41: 37–41.

GATWU. 2012. "Wage Survey of Garments Sector in Bangalore." 10(February). https://gatwu.files.wordpress.com/2013/10/wage-survey-of-garments-sector-in-bangalorefeb-march-2012.pdf [last access: 27.09.2023].

George, Sobin, and Shalini Sinha. 2017. "Labourscape and Labour Space in Post-Liberalised India." In *Redfined Labour Spaces: Organising Workers in Post Liberalized India*, eds. Sobin George and Shalini Sinha. New Delhi: Routledge, 17–43.

George, Susan. 1990. *A Fate Worse than Debt. A Radical New Analysis of the Third World Debt Crisis*. London: Penguin Books.

Getachew, Adom. 2019. *Worldmaking after Empire. The Rise and Fall of Self-Determination*. Princeton and Oxford: Princeton University Press.

Ghosh, Jayathi. 2015. "Macroeconomic Processes and Economic Inequality in India." In *Combating Inequality. The Global North and South*, eds. Alex Gallas, Hansjörg Herr, Frank Hoffer, and Christoph Scherrer. London, New York: Routledge.

Ghosh, Saibal, and D. Vinod. 2017. "What Constrains Financial Inclusion for Women? Evidence from Indian Micro Data." *World Development* 92: 60–81.

Ghosh, Soumitra. 2018. "Publicly Financed Health Insurance Schemes." *Economic and Political Weekly* 53(23): 16–18.

Gidla, Sujatha, and Alan Horn. 2021. "Caste, Race, and Class." *New Left Review* 68(1): 151–56.

Gilbert, Chris. 2022. "Super-Exploitation from the Perspective of the Global Working Class." *Science & Society* 86(3): 439–48.

Gilmore, Ruth Wilson. 2007. *Golden Gulag: Prisons, Surplus, Crisis, and Opposition in Globalizing California*. Berkely, Los Angeles, London: University of California Press.

Go, Julian. 2020. "Three Tensions in the Theory of Racial Capitalism." *Sociological Theory* 39(1): 38–47.

Goldman, Michael. 2005. *Imperial Nature. The World Bank and Struggles for Social Justice in the Age of Globalization*. New Haven and London: Yale University Press.

Goldman, Michael. 2010. "Speculative Urbanism and the Making of the Next World City." *International Journal of Urban and Regional Research* 35(3): 555–81.

Goldman, Michael. 2020. "Dispossession by Financialization: The End(s) of Rurality in the Making of a Speculative Land Market." *Journal of Peasant Studies* 47(6): 1251–77.

Goldman, Michael, and Devika Narayan. 2019. "Water Crisis through the Analytic of Urban Transformation: An Analysis of Bangalore's Hydrosocial Regimes." *Water International* 44(2): 95–114.

Goswami, Manu. 1998. "From Swadeshi to Swaraj: Nation, Economy, Territory in Colonial South Asia, 1870 to 1907." *Comparative Studies in Society and History* 40(4): 609–36.

Gough, Kathleen. 1976. "Indian Peasant Uprisings." *Critical Asian Studies* 8(3): 2–18.

Grapard, Ulla. 1995. "Robinson Crusoe: The Quintessential Economic Man?" *Feminist Economics* 1(1): 33–52.

von Grebmer, Klaus et al. 2018. *Global Hunger Index. Forced Migration and Hunger*. Dublin/Bonn. https://www.globalhungerindex.org/pdf/en/2018.pdf [last access: 27.09.2023].

von Grebmer, Klaus et al. 2021. *Global Hunger Index. Hunger and Food Systems in Conflict Settings*. https://www.globalhungerindex.org/pdf/en/2021.pdf [last access: 27.09.2023].

Green, Marcus. 2011. "Rethinking the Subaltern and the Question of Censorship in Gramsci's Prison Notebooks." *Postcolonial Studies* 14(4): 387–404.

Gronbach, Lena Sophia. 2023. "Social Cash Transfers in Sub-Saharan Africa: Financialization, Digitization and Financial Inclusion." In *Financializations of Development. Global Games and Local Experiments*, eds. Éve Chiapello, Anita Engels, and Eduardo Goncalves Gresse. London: Routledge.

Grosfoguel, Ramón. 2007. "The Epistemic Decolonial Turn: Beyond Political-Economy Paradigms." *Cultural Studies* 21(2–3): 211–23.

Gruffydd Jones, Branwen. 2012. "Method of Political Economy." In *The Edward Elgar Companion to Marxist Economics*, eds. Ben Fine, Alfredo Saad-Filho, Macro Boffo. Cheltenham: Edward Elgar, 220–226.

Gruffydd Jones, Branwen. 2013. "Slavery, Finance and International Political Economy. Postcolonial Reflections." In *Postcolonial Theory and International Relations*, London: Routledge, 49–69.

Guérin, Isabelle. 2013. "Bonded Labour, Agrarian Changes and Capitalism: Emerging Patterns in South India." *Journal of Agrarian Change* 13(3): 405–23.

Guérin, Isabelle. 2014. "Juggling with Debt, Social Ties, and Values: The Everyday Use of Microcredit in Rural South India." *Current Anthropology* 55: 40–50.

Guérin, Isabelle. 2015. "Microfinance and the Dynamics of Financial Vulnerability." In *Microfinance in India. Approaches, Outcomes, Challenges*, ed. Tara S. Nair. London, New York, New Delhi: Routledge, 114–41.

Guérin, Isabelle. 2021. "COVID-19 and the Unequalizing Infrastructures of Financial Inclusion in Tamil Nadu." *Development and Change* 52(4): 927–51.

Guérin, Isabelle. 2022. "Surviving Debt and Survival Debt in Times of Lockdown." *Economic & Political Weekly* 57(1): 9.

Guérin, Isabelle, Bert D Espallier, and G Venkatasubramanian. 2015. "The Social Regulation of Markets: Why Microcredit Fails to Promote Jobs in Rural South India." *Development and Change* 46(6): 1277–1301.

Guérin, Isabelle, Santhosh Kumar, and Isabelle Agier. 2013. "Women' s Empowerment: Power to Act or Power over Other Women? Lessons from Indian Microfinance." *Oxford Journal of Development* 41(1): 76–94.

Guérin, Isabelle, Marc Labie, and Jean-Michel Servet, eds. 2015. *The Crises of Microcredit*. London: ZedBooks.

Guermond, Vincent. 2020. "Marketisation as Financialisation in the Making? The Construction of Remittance Markets in Senegal." *Geoforum* 117: 234–45.

Guha, Ranajit. 1999. *Elementary Aspects of Peasant Insurgency in Colonial India*. Durham and London: Duke University Press.

Gupta, Akhil. 1998. *Postcolonial Developments. Agriculture in the Making of Modern India*. Durham, London: Duke University Press.

Gupta, Indrani, and Samik Chowdhury. 2014. "Public Financing for Health Coverage in India Who Spends, Who Benefits and at What Cost?" *Economic and Political Weekly* 49(35): 59–63.

Guttmann, Robert. 2016. *Finance-Led Capitalism. Shadow Banking, Re-Regulation, and the Future of Global Markets*. Basingstoke: Palgrave Macmillan.

Habib, Irfan. 1964. "Usury in Medieval India." *Comparative Studies in Society and History* 6(4): 393–419.

Habib, Irfan. 1975. "Colonization of the Indian Economy, 1757–1900." *Social Scientist* 3(8): 23–53.

Haiven, Max. 2014. *Crisis of Imagination, Crisis of Power. Capitalism, Creativity and the Commons*. London & New York: ZedBooks.

Haiven, Max. 2017. "The Uses of Financial Literacy: Financialization, the Radical Imagination, and the Unpayable Debts of Settler Colonialism." *Cultural Politics* 13(3): 348–69.

Haiven, Max. 2020. *Revenge Capitalism. The Ghosts of Empire, the Demons of Capital and the Settling of Unpayable Debts*. London: Pluto Press.

Hall, Stuart. 1986. "Gramsci's Relevance for the of Race and Ethnicity." *Journal of Communication Inquiry* 10(2): 5–27.

Hall, Stuart. 1996. "Race, Articulations, and Societies Structured in Dominance." *Black British Cultural Studies: A Reader*: 16–60.

Hall, Stuart. 2003. "Marx's Notes on Method: A "Reading" of the "1857 Introduction." *Cultural Studies* 17(2): 113–149.

Hall, Stuart. 2017. *The Fateful Triangle. Race, Ethnicity, Nation*. Cambridge, MA and London: Harvard University Press.

Hall, Stuart. 2021. *Selected Writing on Race and Difference*. eds. Paul Gilroy and Ruth Wilson-Gilmore. Duke University Press.

Hamid, Naved. 1982. "Dispossession and Differentiation of the Peasantry in the Punjab during Colonial Rule." *The Journal of Peasant Studies* 10(1): 52–72.

Hanappi-Egger, Edeltraud. 2014. "Homo Oeconomicus and 'His' Impact on Gendered Societies." In *Sage Handbook of Feminist Theory*, eds. Mary Evans et al. London: SAGE, 397–412.

Hansen, Jan C., and Jürgen Osterhammel. 2013. *Decolonization. A Short History*. Princeton and Oxford: Princeton University Press.

Hardiman, David. 1996. "Usury, Dearth and Famine in Western India." *Past & Present* 152: 113–56.

Harris-White, Barbara, and Nandini Gooptu. 2001. "Mapping India's World of Unorganized Labour." *Socialist Register* 37: 89–118.

Harris, John. 2001. *Depoliticizing Development. The World Bank and Social Capital*. New Delhi: LeftWord Books.

Harriss-White, Barbara, Wendy Olsen, Penny Vera-Sanso, and V. Suresh. 2013. "Multiple Shocks and Slum Household Economies in South India." *Economy and Society* 42(3): 398–429.

Harriss, John. 2005. "Middle-Class Activism and Poor People's Politics: An Exploration of Civil Society in Chennai." *LSE Working Paper* 44(5). https://www.files.ethz.ch/isn/137958/WP72.pdf [last access: 27.09.2023].

Hart, Gillian. 2006. "Denaturalizing Dispossession: Critical Ethnography in the Age of Resurgent Imperialism." *Antipode* 38(5): 977–1004.

Hart, Gillian. 2010. "D/Developments after the Meltdown." *Antipode* 41: 117–41.

Hart, Gillian. 2016. "Relational Comparison Revisited: Marxist Postcolonial Geographies in Practice." *Progress in Human Geography* 42(3): 371–94.

Harvard Business Review. 2021. "CEO Series: Mastercard's Ajay Banga on Promoting Financial Inclusion." https://hbr.org/podcast/2021/05/ceo-series-mastercards-ajay-banga-on-promoting-financial-inclusion [last access: 27.09.2023].

Harvey, David. 1998. "The Body as Accumulation Strategy." *Environment and Planning D: Society and Space* 16: 401–21.

Harvey, David. 2003. *The New Imperialism*. Oxford: Oxford University Press.

Harvey, David. 2005. *A Brief History of Neoliberalism*. Oxford: Oxford University Press.

Harvey, David. 2006. *The Limits Capital*. London and New York: Verso.

Harvey, David. 2010. *The Enigma of Capital: And the Crises of Capitalism*. Oxford, New York: Oxford University Press.

Harvey, David. 2011. "Roepke Lectures in Economic Geography – Crises, Geographic Disruptions and the Uneven Development of Political Response." *Economic Geography* 87(1): 1–22.

Harvey, David. 2014. *Seventeen Contradictions and the End of Capitalism*. London: Profile Books.

Hein, Christoph, and Patrick Bernau. 2011. "Arme Bauern in Der Schuldenfalle." *Frankfurter Allgemeine*. https://www.faz.net/aktuell/wirtschaft/wirtschaftspolitik/mikrokredite-arme-bauern-in-der-schuldenfalle-1582856.html [last access: 27.09.2023].

Heinrich, Michael. 1994. "Abstrakte Arbeit." In *Historisch-Kritisches Wörterbuch des Marxismus*, ed. Wolfgang Fritz Haug. Berlin: Argument, 55–63.

Heinrich, Michael. 2001. "Monetäre Werttheorie. Geld und Krise bei Marx." *Prokla. Zeitschrift für kritische Sozialwissenschaft* 123(2): 1–30.

Heinrich, Michael. 2020. *Die Wissenschaft vom Wert. Die Marxsche Kritik der Politischen Ökonomie zwischen wissenschaftlicher Revolution und klassischer Tradition*. Münster: Westfälisches Dampfboot.

Helleiner, Eric. 1994. *States and the Reemergence of Global Finance. From Bretton Woods to the 1990s*. Ithaca: Cornell University Press.

Hembruff, Jesse, and Susanne Soederberg. 2015. "Debtfarism and the Violence of Financial Inclusion: The Case of the Payday Lending Industry." *Forum for Social Economics 48(1)*: 49–68.

Henley, David. 2010. "Microfinacne in Indonesia. Evolution and Revolution, 1900 – 2000." In *Southeast Asia's Credit Revolution: From Moneylenders to Microfinance*, eds. Aditya Goenka and David Henley. London and New York: Routledge.

Hennessy, Rosemary. 2017. "Feminism & Materialism: Keeping Capital in Focus." In *Material Turn: Feministische Perspektiven auf Materialität und Materialismus*, eds. Chrstine Löw, Katharina Volk, Imke Leicht, and Nadja Meisterhans. Opladen, Berlin, Toronto: Barbara Budrich, 95–116.

Hensman, Rohini. 2011. "Revisiting the Domestic-Labour Debate: An Indian Perspective." *Historical Materialism* 19(3): 3–28.

Hermes, Niels, and Robert Lensink. 2011. "Microfinance: Its Impact, Outreach, and Sustainability." *World Development* 39(6): 875–81.

Hickel, Jason. 2016. "The True Extent of Global Poverty and Hunger: Questioning the Good News Narrative of the Millennium Development Goals." *Third World Quarterly* 37(5): 749–67.

Hinchy, Jessica. 2014. "Obscenity, Moral Contagion and Masculinity: Hijras in Public Space in Colonial North India." *Asian Studies Review* 38(2): 274–94.

Hooper, Charlotte. 2000. "Disembodiment, Embodiment and the Construction of Hegemonic Masculinity." In *Political Economy, Power and the Body. Global Perspectives*, ed. Gillian Young. Houndmills, Basingstoke: Macmillan Press, 31–51.

Hoskyns, Catherine, and Shirin M. Rai. 2007. "Recasting the Global Political Economy: Counting Women's Unpaid Work." *New Political Economy* 12(3): 297–317.

Hulme, David, and Paul Mosley. 1996. *Finance Against Poverty, Volume 1*. London and New York: Routledge.

Hund, Wulf D. 2010. "Negative Societalisation. Racism and the Constitution of Race." In *Wages of Whiteness & Racist Symbolic Capital*, eds. Wulf D. Hund, Jeremy Krikler, and David Roediger. Berlin: Lit Verlag, 57–96.

Hunter, Benjamin M., and Susan F. Murray. 2019. "Deconstructing the Financialization of Healthcare." *Development and Change* 50(5): 1263–87.

Ince, Onur Ulas. 2022. "Deprovincializing Racial Capitalism: John Crawfurd and Settler Colonialism in India." *American Political Science Review* 116(1): 144–60.

Ingham, Geoffrey. 2004. *The Nature of Money*. Cambridge: Polity Press.

Invest India. 2023. "Construction." https://www.investindia.gov.in/sector/construction [last access: 27.09.2023].

Iqbal, Iftekhar. 2017. "Cooperative Credit in Colonial Bengal: An Exploration in Development and Decline, 1905–1947." *Indian Economic and Social History Review* 54(2): 221–37.

Islam, Asadul, and Pushkar Maitra. 2012. "Health Shocks and Consumption Smoothing in Rural Households: Does Microcredit Have a Role to Play?" *Journal of Development Economics* 97(2): 232–43.

Islam, M. Mufakharul. 1995. "The Punjab Land Alienation Act and the Professional Moneylenders." *Modern Asian Studies* 29(2): 271–91.

Issar, Siddhant. 2021. "Listening to Black Lives Matter: Racial Capitalism and the Critique of Neoliberalism." *Contemporary Political Theory* 20: 48–71.

Ivanova, Maria N. 2020. "Marx's Theory of Money: A Reappraisal in the Light of Unconventional Monetary Policy." *Review of Radical Political Economics* 52(1): 137–51.

Jafri, Juvaria. 2019. "When Billions Meet Trillions: Impact Investing and Shadow Banking in Pakistan." *Review of International Political Economy* 26(3): 520–44.

Janalakshmi Financial Services. 2018. "Our Operating Model." http://www.janalakshmi.com/who-we-are#operating-model [last access: 19.03.2018].

Janda, Karel, and Barbora Svárovksá. 2010. "Investing into Microfinance." *Journal of Business Economics and Management* 11(3): 483–510.

Jayaram, Nivedita, Priyanka Jain, and Sangeeth Sujatha Sugathan. 2019. "No City for Migrant Women: Construction Workers' Experiences of Exclusion from Urban Governance and Discrimination in Labour Markets in Ahmedabad." *Gender and Development* 27(1): 85–104.

Jenkins, Destin, and Justin Leroy. 2021. "Introduction: The Old History of Capitalism." In *Histories of Racial Capitalism*, eds. Destin Jenkins and Justin Leroy. New York: Columbia University Press.

Jessop, Bob. 2013. "Credit Money, Fiat Money and Currency Pyramids: Reflections on the Financial Crisis and Sovereign Debt." In *Financial Crises and the Nature of Capitalist Money*, eds. G. Harcout and J. Pixley. Basingstoke and New York: Palgrave Macmillan.

Jessop, Bob. 2015. "Hard Cash, Easy Credit, Fictitious Capital: Critical Reflections on Money as a Fetishised Social Relation." *Finance and Society* 1(1): 20–37.

JLL. 2017. *Which Cities Are Changing Fastest? City Momentum Index 2017*. http://www.jll.com/research/189/jll-city-momentum-index-2017 [last access: 27.09.2023].

Jodhka, Surinder S. 2002. "Nation and Village: Images of Rural India in Gandhi, Nehru and Ambedkar." *Economic and Political Weekly* 37(32): 3343–53.

Joesph, Krupa. 2021. "Garment Workers Forced to Resign En Masse, Says Report." *Deccan Herald*. https://www.deccanherald.com/metrolife/metrolife-cityscape/garment-workers-forced-to-resign-en-masse-says-report-968440.html [last access: 27.09.2023].

Johnson, Doug, and Sushmita Meka. 2010. *Access to Finance in Andhra Pradesh*. Chennai. https://www.findevgateway.org/sites/default/files/publications/files/mfg-en-paper-access-to-finance-in-andhra-pradesh-2010.pdf [last access: 27.09.2023].

Johnson, Susan. 2009. "Microfinance Is Dead! Long Live Microfinance! Critical Reflections on Two Decades of Microfinance Policy and Practice." *Enterprise, Development & Microfinance* 20(4): 291–303.

Joseph, Rajesh, Roshni Lobo, and Balmurli Natrajan. 2018. "Between 'Baksheesh' and 'Bonus': Precarity, Class, and Collective Action among Domestic Workers in Bengaluru." *Economic and Political Weekly* 53(45): 38–45.

Joseph, Rajesh, Balmurli Natrajan, and Roshni Lobo. 2019. "Domestic Workers and the Challenges of Collectivization: Labor NGOs, Neighborhoods, Apartment Complexes." *Decision* 46(2): 99–109.

Joshi, Deepali Pant. 2006. *Social Banking. Promise. Performance, and Potential*. New Delhi: Foundations Books.

Kabeer, Naila. 2001. "Conflicts Over Credit: Re-Evaluating the Empowerment Potential of Loans to Women in Rural Bangladesh." *World Development* 29(1): 63–84.

Kabeer, Naila, and Helzi Noponen. 2005. Imp-Act *Social and Economic Impacts of PRADAN's Self Help Group Microfinance and Livelihoods Promotion Program. Analysis from Jharkand, India.* https://www.findevgateway.org/sites/default/files/publications/files/mfg-en-case-study-social-and-economic-impacts-of-pradans-self-help-group-microfinance-and-livelihoods-promotion-program-analysis-from-jharkhand-india-2005.pdf [last access: 27.09.2023]

Kamenov, Nikolay. 2019. "Imperial Cooperative Experiments and Global Market Capitalism, c.1900-c.1960." *Journal of Global History* 14(2): 219–37.

Kannabiran, Vasanth, and Kaplana Kannabiran. 2005. "Caste and Gender: Understanding Dynamics of Power and Violence." In *Gender &Caste*, ed. Anupama Rao. London and New York: ZedBooks, 249–60.

Kannan, K. P. 2017. "India's Labour Question Is Also a Social Question: Inequalizing Growth and Increasing Social Equality under Neoliberal Economic Regimes." *Journal of Social and Economic Development2* 19(2): 263–82.

Kannan, K. P. and Jan Breman, eds. 2013. *The Long Road to Social Security. Assessing the Implementation of Social Security Initiatives for the Working Poor in India.* Oxford: Oxford University Press.

Kannan, K. P. and G Raveendra. 2009. "Growth sans Employment: A Quarter Century of Jobless Growth in India's Organised Manufacturing." *Economic & Political Weekly* 44(10): 80–91.

Kapur, Devesh, and Prakirti Nangia. 2015. "Social Protection in India: A Welfare State sans Public Goods?" *India Review* 14(1): 73–90.

Kar, Sohini. 2018. *Financializing Poverty: Labor and Risk in Indian Microfinance.* Stanford: Stanford University Press.

Karaagac, Esra Alkim. 2020. "The Financialization of Everyday Life: Caring for Debts." *Geography Compass* 14(11): 1–15.

Karat, Brinda. 2017. "Legacy of the Russian Revolution Is Still Relevant Today." *Peoples Democracy* 16(46). https://peoplesdemocracy.in/2017/1112_pd/legacy-russian-revolution-still-relevant-today [last access: 27.09.2023].

Karim, Lamia. 2011. *Microfinance and Its Discontents. Women in Debt in Bangladesh.* Minneapolis: University of Minnesota Press.

Katz, Cindi. 2001. "Vagabond Capitalism and the Necessity of Social Reproduction." *Antipode* 33(4): 709–28.

Kaur, Amrajit. 2011. "Indian Ocean Crossings: Indian Labor Migration and Settlement in Southeast Asia, 1870 to 1940." In *Connecting Seas and Connected Ocean Rims. Indian, Atlantic, And Pacific Oceans and China Seas Migrations from the 1830s to the 1930s*, eds. Donna R. Gabaccia and Dirk Hoerder. London and Boston: Brill, 134–68.

Kazim, Amy. 2018. "Indian Microfinance Gives Birth to Smaller Banking Model." *Financial Times.* https://www.ft.com/content/0b3dd4ce-8077-11e8-af48-190d103e32a4 [last access: 27.09.2023].

Keating, Christine, Claire Rasmussen, and Pooja Rishi. 2010. "The Rationality of Empowerement: Microcredit, Accumulation by Disposession, and the Gendered Economy." *Signs* 36(1): 153–76.

Kelly, Annie. 2021. "'Worst Fashion Wage Theft': Workers Go Hungry as Indian Suppliers to Top UK Brands Refuse to Pay Minimum Wage." *The Guardian2*. https://www.theguardian.com/global-development/2021/dec/16/worst-fashion-wage-theft-workers-go-hungry-as-indian-suppliers-to-top-uk-brands-refuse-to-pay-minimum-wage [last access: 27.09.2023].

Kentikelenis, Alexander E., Thomas H. Stubbs, and Lawrence P. King. 2016. "IMF Conditionality and Development Policy Space, 1985–2014." *Review of International Political Economy* 23(4): 543–82.

Kerswell, Timothy, and Surendra Pratap. 2017. "Labour Imperialism in India: The Case of SEWA." *Geoforum* 85: 20–22.

Khan, Mishal. 2021. "The Indebted among the Free." In *Histories of Racial Capitalism*, eds. Destin Jenkins and Justin Leroy. New York: Columbia University Press.

Kish, Zenia, and Justin Leroy. 2015. "Bonded Life: Technologies of Racial Finance from Slave Insurance to Philanthrocapital." *Cultural Studies* 29(5–6): 630–51.

Klein, Naomi. 2007. *The Shock Doctrine. The Rise of Disaster Capitalism*. New York: Metropolitan Books.

Kohli, Atul. 2004. *State-Directed Development. Political Power and Industrialization in the Global Periphery*. Cambridge: Cambridge University Press.

Komlosy, Andrea. 2018. *Work. The Last 1,000 Years*. London: Verso.

KPMG. 2018. *Microfinance — Going Digital While Retaining the Humane Touch*. https://assets.kpmg.com/content/dam/kpmg/in/pdf/2018/12/microfinance-digital-fintech-collaboration.pdf [last access: 27.09.2023].

Krishna, Anirudh. 2013. "Stuck in Place: Investigating Social Mobility in 14 Bangalore Slums." *Journal of Development Studies* 49(7): 1010–28.

Krishna, Anirudh, M S Sriram, and Purnima Prakash. 2014. "Slum Types and Adaptation Strategies: Identifying Policy-Relevant Differences in Bangalore." *Environment and Urbanization* 26(2): 568–85.

Krishna, Sankaran. 2015. "A Postcolonial Racial/Spatial Order. Gandhi, Ambedkar, and the Construction of the International." In *Race and Racism in International Relations. Confronting the Global Colour Line*, eds. Alexander Anievas, Nivi Manchanda, and Robbie Shilliam. Abindgon, New York: Routledge, 139–56.

Krishnan, Kavita. 2018. "Gendered Discipline in Globalising India." *Feminist Review* 119(1): 72–88. https://doi.org/10.1057/s41305-018-0119-6.

KSDB. 2013. "Details of Declared Slums in Bangalore City." https://ksdb.karnataka.gov.in/page/Slums/Abstract+Details+Of+Slums/en [last access: 20.08.2019]

Kudaisya, Medha. 2014. "The Promise of Partnership: Indian Business, the State, and the Bombay Plan of 1944." *Business History Review* 88(1): 97–131.

Kulkarni, Lalitagauri. 2017. "Financial Efficiency versus Social Outreach of Indian Microfinance Institutions: Mission Drift or Character Shift." *Journal of Social and Economic Change* 19(2): 323–40.

Kumar, Ravinder. 1965. "The Deccan Riots of 1875." *The Journal of Asian Studies* 24(4): 613–35.

Kumar, Thangellapali Vijay. 2018. *Colonial Land Tax and Property Rights. The Agrarian Conditions in Andhra Under the British Rule: 1858–1900*. Abingdon, New York: Routledge.

Kundnani, Arun. 2021. "The Racial Constitution of Neoliberalism." *Race and Class* 63(1): 51–69.

Kundnani, Arun. 2023: *What is Antiracism? And why it means Anticapitalism*. London, New York: Verso.

Kuntz, Aaron M. 2012. "The Politics of Space in Qualitative Research." In *New Approaches to Qualitative Research. Wisdom and Uncertainty*, eds. Maggi Savin-Baden and Claire Howell Major. London: Routledge, 145–53.

Kuri, Pravat Kumar, and Arindam Laha. 2011. "Financial Inclusion and Human Development in India: An Inter-State Analysis." *Indian Journal of Human Development* 5(1): 61–77.

Kurian, N J. 1987. "IRDP: How Relevant Is It?" *Economic and Political Weekly* 22(52): A161–76.

Ladejinsky, Wolf. 1970. "Ironies of India's Green Revolution." *Foreign Affairs* 48(4): 758–68.

Langley, Paul. 2020. "Assets and Assetization in Financialized Capitalism." *Review of International Political Economy* 28(2): 382–93.

Lapavitsas, Costas. 2003. *Social Foundations of Markets, Money and Credit*. London and New York: Routledge.

Lapavitsas, Costas. 2009. "Financialised Capitalism: Crisis and Financial Expropriation." *Historical Materialism* 17(2): 114–48.

Lapavitsas, Costas. 2014. *Profiting without Producing: How Finance Exploits Us All*. London: Verso.

Laslett, B., and J. Brenner. 1989. "Gender and Social Reproduction: Historical Perspectives." *Annual Review of Sociology* 15: 381–404.

Latimer, Amanda. 2021. "Super-Exploitation, the Race to the Bottom, and the Missing International." In *The Palgrave Encyclopedia of Imperialism and Anti-Imperialism*, Cham: Palgrave Macmillan, 2546–61.

Lavinas, Lena. 2018. "The Collateralization of Social Policy under Financialized Capitalism." *Development and Change* 49(2).

Lavoie, Marc. 2020. *Post-Keynesian Monetary Theory. Selected Essays*. Cheltenham: Edward Elgar.

Lazarus, Neil. 2011. "What Postcolonial Theory Doesn't Say." *Race and Class* 53(1): 3–27.

Lazonick, William, and Mary O'Sullivan. 2000. "Maximizing Shareholder Value: A New Ideology for Corporate Governance." *Economy and Society* 29(1): 13–35.

Lazzarato, Maurizio. 2009. "Neoliberalism in Action. Inequality, Insecurity and the Reconstitution of the Social." *Theory, Culture & Society* 26(6): 109–33.

Lazzarato, Maurizio. 2012. *The Making of the Indebted Man*. Los Angeles: Semiotext(e).

Lazzarato, Maurizio. 2015. *Governing by Debt*. South Pasadena: Semiotext(e).

LeBaron, Genevieve. 2010. "The Political Economy of the Household: Neoliberal Restructuring, Enclosures, and Daily Life." *Review of International Political Economy* 17(5): 889–912.

Ledgerwood, Joanna, Julie Earne, and Candace Nelson, eds. 2013. *The New Microfinance Handbook. A Financial Market System Perspective*. Washington, D.C.: World Bank.

Ledgerwood, Joanna, and Alan Gibson. 2013. "The Evolving Financial Landscape." In *The New Microfinance Handbook. A Financial Market System Perspective*, eds. Joanna Ledgerwood, Julie Earne, and Candace Nelson. Washington, D.C.: World Bank, 15–48.

Lerche, Jens, and Alpa Shah. 2018. "Conjugated Oppression within Contemporary Capitalism: Class, Caste, Tribe and Agrarian Change in India." *Journal of Peasant Studies* 45(5–6): 927–49.

Levenson, Zachary, and Marcel Paret. 2022. "The Three Dialectics of Racial Capitalism: From South Africa to the U.S. and Back Again." *Du Bois Review: Social Science Research on Race*, 20(2): 333–351.

Levien, Michael. 2012. "The Land Question: Special Economic Zones and the Political Economy of Dispossession in India." *Journal of Peasant Studies* 39(3–4): 933–69.

Levien, Michael. 2018. *Dispossession without Development. Land Grabs in Neoliberal India*. New York: Oxford University Press.

van der Linden, Marcel. 2014. "Who Is the Working Class? Wage Earners and Other Labourers." In *Workers and Labour in A Glablised Capitalism. Cotemporary Themes and Theoretical Issues*, ed. Maurizio Atzeni. New York: Palgrave Macmillan, 70–84.

van der Lindien, Marcel. 2023. *The World Wide Web of Work*. London: UCL Press.

Linebaugh, Peter, and Markus Rediker. 2000. *The Many-Headed Hydra*. Boston: Beacon Press.

Lockwood, David. 2012. "Was the Bombay Plan a Capitalist Plot?" *Studies in History* 28(1): 99–116.

Lopatta, K, and M Tchikov. 2015. "Do Microfinance Institutions Fulfil Their Promise? Evidence from Cross-Country Data." *Applied Economics*, 48(18): 1655–1677.

López, Tatiana. 2021. "A Practice Ontology Approach to Labor Control Regimes in GPNs: Connecting 'Sites of Labor Control' in the Bangalore Export Garment Cluster." *Environment and Planning A* 53(5): 1012–30.

Lowe, Lisa. 2015. *The Intimacies of Four Continents*. Durham and London: Duke University Press.

Luxemburg, Rosa. 2003. *The Accumulation of Capital*. London, New York: Routledge.

Luxton, Meg. 2006. "Feminist Political Economy in Canada and the Politics of Social Reproduction." In *Social Reproduction. Feminist Political Economy Challenges Neo-Liberalism*, eds. Kate Bezanson and Meg Luxton. Montreal & Kingston, London, Chicago: McGill-Queen's University Press, 11–44.

Luxton, Meg. 2018. "The Production of Life Itself: Gender, Social Reproduction and IPE." In *International Political Economy of Gender*, Cheltenham and Northampton: Edward Elgar, 37–49.

Lysandrou, Photis. 2016. "The Colonization of the Future: An Alternative View of Financialization and Its Portents." *Journal of Post Keynesian Economics* 39(4): 444–72.

Macaulay, Thomas. 1965. *Macauly's Essays. Selected and Introduced by Hugh Trevor-Roper*. ed. Hugh Trevor-Roper. London and Glasgow: Collins Clear-Type Press.

Mader, Philip. 2011. "Attempting the Production of Public Goods through Microfinance: The Case of Water and Sanitation." *Journal of Infrastructure Development* 3(2): 153–70.

Mader, Philip. 2013. "False Histories: Microfinance and Its Non-Lineage of German Cooperative Banking." In *Governance across Borders: Transnational Fields and Transversal Themes*, Berlin: epubli, 268–71.

Mader, Philip. 2015. *The Political Economy of Microfinance. Financializing Poverty*. Basingstoke: Palgrave Macmillan.

Mader, Philip. 2016. "Card Crusaders, Cash Infidels and the Holy Grails of Digital Financial Inclusion." *BEHEMOTH. A Journal on Civilisation* 9(2): 50–81.

Mader, Philip. 2018. "Contesting Financial Inclusion." *Development and Change* 49(2): 461–483.

Mader, Philip, and Sophia Sabrow. 2015. "All Myth and Ceremony? Examining the Causes and Logic of the Mission Shift in Microfinance from Microenterprise Credit to Financial Inclusion." *Forum for Social Economics* 44: 1–27.

Mahadeva, M. 2011. "Poverty of Access to Financial Services and Its Alleviation: Some Lessons to India from the United Kingdom." *Journal of Asian Public Policy* 4(2): 187–200.

Mahajan, Vijay. 2005. "From Microcredit to Livelihood Finance." *Economic and Political Weekly* 40(41): 4416–19.

Majumdar, Abhijit, Mahesh Shaw, and Sanjib Kumar Sinha. 2020. "COVID-19 Debunks the Myth of Socially Sustainable Supply Chain: A Case of the Clothing Industry in South Asian Countries." *Sustainable Production and Consumption* 24: 150–55.

Mani, Mohan. 2013. *"Ready Made" – Garments in India: Producing Cheap Commodities in the Global South, for the Global North*. New Delhi. https://www.rosalux.de/fileadmin/rls_uploads/pdfs/sonst_publikationen/Mohan_Mani_Zimmerwald_7thFeb2014.pdf [last access: 27.09.2023].

Mani, Mohan, Babu Mathew, and Dithhi Bhattacharya. 2018. *Critiquing the Statutory Minimum Wage. A Case of the Export Garment Sector in India*. Bangalore. https://mpp.nls.ac.in/wp-content/uploads/2019/02/Paper-5-Critiquing-the-Minimum-Wage.pdf [last access: 27.09.2023].

Manjapra, Kris. 2018. "Plantation Dispossessions. The Global Travel of Agricultural Racial Capitalism." In *American Capitalism. New Histories*, eds. Sven Beckert and Christine Desan. Columbia University Press, 361–388.

Manjapra, Kris. 2020. *Colonialism in Global Perspective*. Cambridge: Cambridge University Press.

Mankiw, N. Gregory. 2012. *Principles of Macroeconomics*. Mason: South-Western Cengage Learning.

Mann, Michael. 2011. "Migration—Re-Migration—Circulation: South Asian Kulis in the Indian Ocean and Beyond, 1840–1940." In *Connecting Seas and Connected Ocean Rims. Indian, Atlantic, And Pacific Oceans and China Seas Migrations from the 1830s to the 1930s*, eds. Donna R. Gabaccia and Dirk Hoerder. London and Boston: Brill, 108–33.

Mansoor, Kashif, and Donal O'Neill. 2021. "Minimum Wage Compliance and Household Welfare: An Analysis of over 1500 Minimum Wages in India." *World Development* 147: 105653.

Markotoff, Kalyeena. 2023. "World Bank Chief Resigns after Climate Stance Misstep." *The Guardian*. https://www.theguardian.com/business/2023/feb/15/david-malpass-world-bank-president-steps-down [last access: 27.09.2023].

Martin, Randy. 2002. *Financialization of Daily Life*. Philadelphia: Temple University Press.

Marx, Karl. 1844a. "Comments of James Mill, Élements D'économie Politique." https://www.marxists.org/archive/marx/works/1844/james-mill/ [last access: 27.09.2023].

Marx, Karl. 1844b. "On the Jewish Question." https://www.marxists.org/archive/marx/works/1844/jewish-question/ [last access: 27.09.2023].

Marx, Karl . 1853a. "India." *New-York Daily Tribune*. https://www.marxists.org/archive/marx/works/1853/08/05.htm [last access: 27.09.2023].

Marx, Karl. 1853b. "The East India Company – Its History and Results." *New-York Daily Tribune*. https://www.marxists.org/archive/marx/works/1853/07/11.htm [last access: 27.09.2023].

Marx, Karl. 1937. *The Eighteenth Brumaire of Louis Bonaparte*. Moscow: Progress Publishers.

Marx, Karl. 1973. *Grundrisse. Foundations of the Critique of Political Economy*. London: Penguin Books.

Marx, Karl. 1976. *Capital. A Critique of Political Economy. Volume One*. London: Penguin Books.

Marx, Karl. 1981. *Capital. A Critique of Political Economy. Volume Three*. London: Penguin Books.

Marx, Karl. 1988. *Economic and Philosophical Manuscripts of 1844 and the Communist Manifesto*. New York: Prometheus Books.

Marx, Karl. 2012. “Ökonomische Manuskripte 1863–1867. Teil 2. Manuskript 1863/65 Zum 3. Buch Des ‘Kapital’.” In *Marx-Engels-Gesamtausgabe (MEGA)*, Berlin: Dietz.

Mastercard. 2023. “Our Mission.” https://www.mastercardcenter.org/about-us#our-mission [last access: 27.09.2023].

Mathur, Kuldeep. 1995. “Politics and Implementation of Integrated Rural Development Programme.” *Economic and Political Weekly* 30(41/42): 2703–8.

Mawdsley, Emma. 2018. “‘From Billions to Trillions’: Financing the SDGs in a World ‘beyond Aid.’” *Dialogues in Human Geography* 8(2): 191–95.

Mawdsley, Emma, and Jack Taggart. 2022. “Rethinking d/Development.” *Progress in Human Geography* 46(1): 3–20.

Mayaram, Shail. 2003. “Kings versus Bandits: Anti-Colonialism in a Bandit Narrative.” *Journal of the Royal Asiatic Society* 13(3): 315–38.

Mbembe, Achille. 2017. *Critique of Black Reason*. Durham and London: Duke University Press.

McGuire, John. 2005. “Exchange Banks, India and the World Economy: 1850–1914.” *Asian Studies Review* 29(2): 143–63.

McGuire, John. 2007. “The Imperial Impact on the Globalization of Indian Finance Prior to the First World War. The Role of the British Colonial Exchange Banks.” In *Capture and Exclude: Developing Economies and the Poor in Global Finance*, New Delhi: Tulika Books, 85–114.

McGuire, Paul B, and John D Conroy. 2000. “The Microfinance Phenomenon.” *Asia-Pacific Review* 7(1): 90–108.

McMichael, Philip. 1990. “Incorporating Comparison within a World-Historical Perspective: An Alternative Comparative Method.” *American Sociological Review* 55(3): 385.

McMichael, Philip. 2000. “World-Systems Analysis, Globalization, and Incorporated Comparison*.” *Journal of World-Systems Research* 6(3): 668–99.

McMichael, Philip. 2009. “A Food Regime Genealogy.” *Journal of Peasant Studies* 36(1): 139–69.

McMichael, Philip. 2017. *Development and Social Change. A Global Perspective*. Los Angels, London, New Delhi, Singapore, Washington DC: SAGE Publications.

McMichael, Philip. 2019. “Incorporating Comparison in Ontological Encounters.” *Revista História Comparada* 13(1): 209–37.

McNally, David. 2011a. *Global Slump: The Economics and Politics of Crisis and Resistance*. Oakland: PM Press.

McNally, David. 2011b. *Monsters of the Market. Zombies, Vampires and Global Capitalism*. Leiden and Boston: Brill.

McNally, David. 2015. "The Dialectics of Unity and Difference in the Constitution of Wage- Labour: On Internal Relations and Working- Class Formation." *Capital & Class* 39(1): 131–46.

McNally, David. 2020. *Blood and Money. War, Slavery, Finance, and Empire*. Chicago: Haymarket Books.

Melamed, Jodi. 2015. "Racial Capitalism." *Critical Ethnic Studies* 1(1): 76–85.

Menon, Gayatri A., and Aparna Sundar. 2019. "Uncovering a Politics of Livelihoods: Analysing Displacement and Contention in Contemporary India." *Globalizations* 16(2): 186–200.

Menon, Geeta. 2020. *The COVID-19 Pandemic and the Invisible Workers of the Household Economy*. https://cis-india.org/raw/files/dwru-bbgs-mku-covid19-invisible-household-workers-report [last access: 27.09.2023].

Menon, Nivedita. 2019. "Marxism, Feminism and Caste in Contemporary India." In *Racism after Apartheid. Challenges for Marxism and Anti-Marxism*, ed. Vishwas Satgar. Johannesburg: Wits Univerity Press.

Meyer, Marco. 2017. "The Right to Credit." *The Journal of Political Philosophy* 26(3): 304–26.

Mezzadri, Alessandra. 2017. *The Sweatshop Regime: Labouring Bodies, Exploitation, and Garments Made in India*. Cambridge: Cambridge University Press.

Mezzadri, Alessandra. 2019. "On the Value of Social Reproduction. Informal Labour, the Majority of the World and the Need for Inclusive Theories and Politics." *Radical Philosophy*: 33–41.

Mezzadri, Alessandra and Sanjita Majumder. 2020. "Towards a Feminist Political Economy of Time: Labour Circulation, Social Reproduction & the 'Afterlife' of Cheap Labour." *Review of International Political Economy* 29(6): 1804–1826.

Mies, Maria. 1986. *Patriarchy and Capital Accumulation on a World Scale*. London: Zed-Books.

Mies, Maria. 2012. *The Lace Makers of Narsapur. Indian Housewives Produce for the World Market*. Melbourne: Spinifex.

Mies, Maria. 2014. "Housewifisation – Globalisation – Subsistence-Perspective." In *Beyond Marx. Theorising Global Labour Relations of the Twenty-First Century*, eds. Marcel van der Linden and Karl-Heinz Roth. Leiden and Boston: Brill, 209–37.

Mignolo, Walter D. 2002. "The Geopolitics of Knowledge and the Colonial Difference." *South Atlantic Quarterly* 10(1).

Milonakis, Dimitris, and Ben Fine. 2009. *From Political Economy to Economics: Method, the Social and the Historical in the Evolution of Economic Theory*. Abingdon, New York: Routledge.

Mirowski, Philip, and Dieter Plehwe, eds. 2009. *The Road from Mont Pelerin. The Making of the Neoliberal Thought Collective*. Cambridge: Harvard University Press.

Mishra, Vivek, and Anirban Bhattacharya. 2017. "GDP Grows But Job Security Falls: Only 16% Indians Earn Regular Wage." *IndiaSpend*. http://archive.indiaspend.c

om/special-reports/gdp-grows-but-job-security-falls-only-16-indians-earn-regular-wage-99612 [last access: 27.09.2023].

Mitra, Arup, and Barjor Mehta. 2011. "Cities as the Engine of Growth: Evidence from India." *Journal of Urban Planning and Development* 137(2): 171–83.

Mohan, Rohini. 2017. "For Bengaluru's Garment Hub Workers, the Minimum Wage Is Actually the Maximum Wage." *Scroll.in*. https://scroll.in/article/834986/for-bengalurus-garment-hub-workers-the-minimum-wage-is-actually-the-maximum-wage [last access: 27.09.2023].

Montgomerie, Johnna. 2013. "America's Debt Safety-Net." *Public Administration* 91(4): 871–88.

Montgomerie, Johnna, ed. 2017. *Critical Methods in Political and Cultural Economy*. London: Routledge.

Montgomerie, Johnna and Daniela Tepe-Belfrage. 2017. "Caring for Debts: How the Household Economy Exposes the Limits of Financialisation." *Critical Sociology* 43(4–5): 653–68.

Mookerjee, Devalina et al. 2021. "A Culture-Centered Approach to Experiences of the Coronavirus Pandemic Lockdown Among Internal Migrants in India." *American Behavioral Scientist* 65(10): 1426–44.

Morduch, Jonathan. 1999. "The Microfinance Promise." *Journal of Economic Literature* 37(4): 1569–1614.

Mosley, Paul. 2001. "Microfinance and Poverty in Bolivia." *The Journal of Development Studies* 37(4): 101–32.

Mosse, David et al. 2002. "Brokered Livelihoods: Debt, Labour Migration and Development in Tribal Western India." *The Journal of Development Studies* 38(5): 59–88.

Mosse, David. 2018. "Caste and Development: Contemporary Perspectives on a Structure of Discrimination and Advantage." *World Development* 110: 422–36.

Mueller, Robin Alison. 2019. "Episodic Narrative Interview: Capturing Stories of Experience With a Methods Fusion." *International Journal of Qualitative Methods* 18: 1–11.

Mukherjee, Ramkrishna. 1999. "Caste in Itself, Caste and Class, or Caste in Class." *Economic & Political Weekly* 34(27): 1759–61.

Musthaq, Fathimath. 2021. "Development Finance or Financial Accumulation for Asset Managers?: The Perils of the Global Shadow Banking System in Developing Countries." *New Political Economy* 26(4): 554–73.

Nagaraj, K., P. Sainath, R. Rukmani, and R. Gopinath. 2014. "Farmer's Suicides in India: Magnitudes, Trends, and Spatial Patterns, 1997 -2012." *Review of Agrarian Studies*: 53–83.

Nagendra, Harini. 2016. *Nature in the City. Bengaluru in the Past, Present and Future*. New Delhi: Oxford University Press.

Naidu, Sirisha C, and Lyn Ossome. 2016. "Social Reproduction and the Agrarian Question of Women's Labour in India." *Agrarian South: Journal of Political Economy* 5(1): 50–76.

Nair, Janaki. 2005. *The Promise of the Metropolis. Bangalore's Twentieth Century*. New Delhi: Oxford University Press.

Nair, Janaki. 2014. "The City Is History: New Indian Urbanism and the Terrain of the Law." *South Asia Chronicle* 4: 165–99.

Nair, Tara S. 2015. "Vignettes in Transformation: Indian Microfinance Sicne the 1990s." In *Microfinance in India. Approaches, Outcomes, Challenges*, ed. Tara S. Nair. London, New York, New Delhi: Routledge, 1–41.

Nair, Tara S., and Rutwik J. Gandhe. 2015. "Issues and Challenges before Liberal Microfinance Cooperatives. A Case Study." In *Microfinance in India. Approaches, Outcomes, Challenges*, ed. Routledge. London, New York, New Delhi, 191–214.

Nambiar, Devaki et al. 2014. "Who Cares? Urban Health Care and Exclusion." In *India Exclusion Report*, http://www.indianet.nl/pdf/IndiaExclusionReport2013-2014.pdf [last access: 27.09.2023].

Narayan, Swati. 2021. "Time for Universal Public Distribution System: Food Mountains and Pandemic Hunger in India." *Indian Journal of Human Development* 15(3): 503–14.

Natarajan, Nithya et al. 2021. "Challenging the Financial Inclusion-Decent Work Nexus: Evidence from Cambodia's over-Indebted Internal Migrants." *Global Public Policy and Governance* 1(3): 361–81.

Natarajan, Nithya, Katherine Brickell, and Laurie Parsons. 2021. "Diffuse Drivers of Modern Slavery: From Microfinance to Unfree Labour in Cambodia." *Development and Change* 52(2): 241–64.

Nathan Green, W., and Maryann Bylander. 2021. "The Exclusionary Power of Microfinance: Over-Indebtedness and Land Dispossession in Cambodia." *Sociology of Development* 7(2): 202–29.

Natile, Serena. 2020. *The Exclusionary Politics of Digital Financial Inclusion. Mobile Money, Gendered Walls*. London: Routledge.

Natrajan, Balmurli. 2021. "Racialization and Ethnicization: Hindutva Hegemony and Caste." *Ethnic and Racial Studies* 45(2): 298–318.

Natrajan, Balmurli, and Paul Greenough. 2009. "Introduction." In *Against Stigma. Studies in Cast, Race and Justice since Durban*, Hyderabad: Orient Black Swan, 1–44.

Nayyar, Deepak. 2016. *Catch Up. Developing Countries in the World Economy*. Oxford: Oxford University Press.

Ndlovu-Gatsheni, Sabelo J. 2020. "The Cognitive Empire, Politics of Knowledge and African Intellectual Productions: Reflections on Struggles for Epistemic Freedom and Resurgence of Decolonisation in the Twenty-First Century." *Third World Quarterly* 42(5): 882–901.

Neelima, Kota. 2018. *Widows of Virdhaba. Making of Shadows*. New Delhi: Oxford University Press.

Neetha, N., and Rajni Palriwala. 2011. "The Absence of State Law: Domestic Workers in India." *Canadian Journal of Women and the Law* 23(1): 97–119.

Neetha, N. 2019. "Paid Domestic Work: Making Sense of the Jigsaw Puzzle." *Economic and Political Weekly* 48(43): 35–38.

Nelson, Anitra. 1999. *Marx's Concept of Money. God of Commodities*. London and New York: Routledge.

Nelson, Anitra. 2005. "Marx's Objections to Credit Theories of Money." In *Marx's Theory of Money. Modern Appraisals*, ed. Fred Moseley. Houndmills, Basingstoke, Hampshire: Palgrave Macmillan, 65–77.

Nigam, Aditya. 2019. "Hindutva, Caste and the 'National Unconcious.'" In *Racism after Apartheid. Challenges for Marxism and Anti-Marxism*, ed. Vishwas Satgar. Johannesburg: Wits Univerity Press.

Nigam, Sanjay. 1990. "Disciplining and Policing the 'Criminals by Birth', Part 1: The Making of a Colonial Stereotype— The Criminal Tribes and Castes of North India." *Indian Economic & Social History Review* 27(2): 131–64.

NITI Aayog. 2018. *Composite Water Management Index. A Tool of Water Management*. h ttp://www.niti.gov.in/writereaddata/files/document_publication/2018-05-18-Water-index-Report_vS6B.pdf%0Ahttp://dx.doi.org/10.1016/j.cirp.2016.06.00 1%0Ahttp://dx.doi.org/10.1016/j.powtec.2016.12.055%0Ahttps://doi.org/10.1016 /j.ijfatigue.2019.02.006%0Ahttp [last access: 27.09.2023].

Nixon, Rob. 2011. *Slow Violence and the Environmentalism of the Poor*. Cambridge, MA: Harvard University Press.

Nuruzzaman, Mohammed. 2007. "The World Bank, Health Policy Reforms and the Poor." *Journal of Contemporary Asia* 37(1): 59–72.

Ollman, Bertell. 2003. *Dance of the Dialectic: Steps in Marx's Method*. Urbana and Chicago: University of Illinois Press.

Ollman, Bertell. 2015. "Marxism and the Philosophy of Internal Relations, or How to Replace the Mysterious 'Paradox' with 'Contradictions' That Can Be Studied and Resolved." *Capital & Class* 39(1): 7–23.

Otero, María. 2000. "Bringing Development Back into Microfinance." *Journal of Microfinance* 1(1): 8–19.

Otero, María, and Elisabeth Ryhne, eds. 1994. *The New World of Microenterprise Finance. Building Healthy Financial Institutions for the Poor*. West Hartford: Kumarian Press.

Padhi, Ranjana, and Nigam Patana. 2017. "POSCO Exit. Pyrrhic Victory for the People's Movement." *Economic & Political Weekly* 52(41): 33–35.

Pailey, Robtel Neajai. 2021. "Race in/and Development." In *Critical Development Studies*,.

Pandey, Gyanendra. 2016. "Racialization of Subaltern Populations Across the Globe: The Politics of Difference." *The Review of Black Political Economy* 43(2): 87–99.

Pandey, Vika. 2019. "Behind India's Construction Boom: 'We Risk Our Lives to Build Your Homes.'" *BBC*. https://www.bbc.com/news/world-asia-india-46698626 [last access: 27.09.2023].

Parashar, Swati. 2019. "Colonial Legacies, Armed Revolts and State Violence: The Maoist Movement in India." *Third World Quarterly* 40(2): 337–54.

Parry, Jonathan. 2014. "Sex, Bricks and Mortar: Constructing Class in a Central Indian Steel Town." *Modern Asian Studies* 48(5): 1242–75.

Parthasarathi, P. 1998. "Rethinking Wages and Competitiveness in the Eighteenth Century: Britain and South India." *Past and Present* 158: 79–109.

Parthasarathi, Prasannan, and Giorgio Riello. 2014. "The Indian Ocean in the Long Eighteenth Century." *Eigteenth-Century Studies* 48(1): 1–19.

Parthasarthi, Prasannan. 2011. *Why Europe Grew Rich and Asia Did Not. Global Economic Divergence, 1600–1800*. New York: Cambridge University Press.

Patel, Amrit. 2016. "Financial Inclusion: Harnessing Poor Families' Potential for Development." 5(1): 15–22.

Patel, Raj. 2013. "The Long Green Revolution." *Journal of Peasant Studies* 40(1): 1–63.

Patel, Raj, and Jason W. Moore. 2017. *A History of the World in Seven Cheap Things. A Guide to Capitalism, Nature and the Future of the Planet*. Oakland: University of California Press.

Patnaik, Prabhat, and C.P Chandrasekhar. 1995. "Indian Economy under Structural Adjustment." *Economic & Political Weekly* 30(47): 3001–13.

Patnaik, Utsa. 1983. "On the Evolution of the Class of Agricultural Labourers in India." *Social Scientist* 11(7): 3.

Patnaik, Utsa. 1991. "The Journal of Peasant Food Availability and Famine: A Longer View." *The Journal of Peasant Studies* 19(1): 1–25.

Patnaik, Utsa. 2007. *The Republic of Hunger and Other Essays*. New Delhi: ThreeEssays Collective.

Patnaik, Utsa. 2017. "Revisiting the 'Drain', or Transfer from India to Britain in the Context of Global Diffusion of Capitalism." In *Agrarian and Other Histories: Essays for Binay Bhushan Chaudhuri*, New Delhi: Tulika Books.

Pattenden, Jonathan. 2010. "A Neoliberalisation of Civil Society? Self-Help Groups and the Labouring Class Poor in Rural South India." *Journal of Peasant Studies* 37(3): 485–512.

Pattenden, Jonathan. 2016. *Labour, State and Society in Rural India- A Class-Relational Approach*. Manchester: Manchester University Press.

Pattenden, Jonathan. 2018. "The Politics of Classes of Labour: Fragmentation, Reproduction Zones and Collective Action in Zones and Collective Action in Karnataka, India." *The Journal of Peasant Studies* 6150: 1039–59.

Perry, Keston K. 2021. "The New 'Bond-Age', Climate Crisis and the Case for Climate Reparations: Unpicking Old/New Colonialities of Finance for Development within the SDGs." *Geoforum* 126: 361–71.

Pettifor, Anne. 2017. *The Production of Money. How to Break the Power of Bankers*. London, New York: Verso.

Phillips, Nicola. 2017a. "Doing Research in the Shadows of the Global Political Economy." In *Critical Methods in Political and Cultural Economy*, ed. Johnna Montgomerie. London & New York: Routledge, 115–20.

Philips, Nicola. 2017b. "Power and Inequality in the Global Political Economy." *International Affairs* 93(2): 429–44.

Pistor, Katharina. 2019. *The Code of Capital. How the Law Creates Wealth and Inequality*. New Jersey: Princeton University Press.

Pitt, M M, and S R Khandker. 2002. "Credit Programmes for the Poor and Seasonality in Rural Bangladesh." *The Journal of Development Studies* 39(2): 1–24.

Pitt, Mark M., Shahidur R. Khandker, and Jennifer Cartwright. 2006. "Empowering Women with Micro Finance: Evidence from Bangladesh." *Economic Development and Cultural Change* 54(4): 791–831.

Pitt, Mark M, and Shahidur R Khandker. 1998. "The Impact of Group-Based Credit Programs on Poor Households in Bangladesh: Does the Gender of Participants Matter?" *Journal of Political Economy* 106(5): 958–96.

Politi, James. 2019. "No End to Poverty without Financial Inclusion, Says World Bank." *Financial Times*. https://www.ft.com/content/0fb60294-4b36-11e9-bde6-79eaea5acb64 [last access: 27.09.2023].

Pomeranz, Kenneth. 2000. *The Great Divergence. China, Europe, and the World Economy*. Princeton and Oxford: Princeton University Press.

Porteous, David. 2004. *Making Financial Markets Work for the Poor*. https://www.microfinancegateway.org/sites/default/files/mfg-en-paper-making-financial-markets-work-for-the-poor-oct-2004.pdf [last access: 27.09.2023].

Prahalad, C. K. 2005. *The Fortune at the Bottom of the Pyramid. Eradicating Poverty Through Profits*. Upper Saddle River: Wharton School Publishing.

Prashad, Vijay. 2012. *The Poorer Nations. A Possible History of the Global South*. London and New York: Verso.

Provost, Claire. 2012. "The Rise and Fall of Microfinance." *The Guardian*. https://www.theguardian.com/global-development/poverty-matters/2012/nov/21/rise-fall-microfinance [last access: 27.09.2023].

PUCL-K, and WSS. 2019. "A Fact-Finding Report on Garment Workers Protest". https://data-opencity.sgp1.cdn.digitaloceanspaces.com/Documents/Recent/PUCL-WSS_FF-on-April-2016-Strike_English.pdf *[last access: 27.09.2023]*.

Ragin, Charles C. 2014. *The Comparative Method. Moving Beyond Qualitative and Quantitative Strategies*. Oakland: The University of California Press.

Rajan, Raghuram G. 2005. *I Do What I Do. On Reform, Rhetoric and Resolve*. New Delhi: HarperCollins India.

Rajasekhar, D., R. Manjula, and Suchitra J.Y. 2017. "Can Microfinance Promote Livelihoods and Reduce Vulnerability Among Adivasis? A Study of Some NGO Interventions from Karnataka and Tamil Nadu." *Social Change* 47(1): 65–80.

Rajeev, Meenakshi, and Christoph Scherrer. 2021. "Smallholders' Challenges: Realizing Peri-Urban Opportunities in Bengaluru." *Sustainability* 13(18): 1–18.

Ralph, Michael, and Maya Singhal. 2019. "Racial Capitalism." *Theory and Society* 30(1): 270–90.

Ramanathan, S. 1991. "Rajasthan's Sorrow: Report of Workshop on Indira Gandhi Canal." *Economic & Political Weekly* 26(31/32): 1842–44.

Ramesh, Randeep. 2007. "'Credit Is a Basic Human Right.'" *The Guardian*. https://www.theguardian.com/world/2007/jan/05/outlook.development [last access: 27.09.2023].s

Ranganathan, Malini. 2018. "Rule by Difference: Empire, Liberalism, and the Legacies of Urban 'Improvement.'" *Environment and Planning A* 50(7): 1386–1406.

Ranganathan, Malini. 2019. "Empire's Infrastructures: Racial Finance Capitalism and Liberal Necropolitics." *Urban Geography* 41(4): 492–96.

Ranganathan, Malini. 2021. "Caste, Racialization, and the Making of Environmental Unfreedoms in Urban India." *Ethnic and Racial Studies*.

Rangarajan, Mahesh. 1994. "Imperial Agendas and India's Forests: The Early History of Indian Forestry, 1800–1878." *Indian Economic & Social History Review* 31(2): 147–67.

Rankin, Katharine N. 2013. "A Critical Geography of Poverty Finance." *Third World Quarterly* 34(4): 547–68.

Rankin, Katherine N. 2002. "Social Capital, Microfinance, and the Politics of Development." *Feminist Economics* 8(1): 1–24.

Rao, Anupama, ed. 2005. *Gender & Caste*. London & New York: Zed Books.

Rao, Smriti. 2021. "Beyond the Coronavirus: Understanding Crises of Social Reproduction." *Global Labour Journal* 12(1): 39–53.

Rao, Smriti, and Vamsi Vakulabharanam. 2019. "Migration, Crises, and Social Transformation in India Since the 1990s." *The Oxford Handbook of Migration Crises*. London & New York: Oxford University Press, 260–78.

Rath, Nilakantha. 1985. "Garibi Hatao: Can IRDP Do It?" *Economic and Political Weekly* 20(6): 238–46.

Ravallion, Martin. 2004. "Pro-Poor Growth: A Primer." *World Bank Policy Research Working Paper* No. 3242. https://openknowledge.worldbank.org/handle/10986/14116 [last access: 27.09.2023].

Ray, Debraj. 1998. *Development Economics*. Princeton, New Jersey: Princeton University Press.

Ray, Surya Sarathi. 2020. "Negative Returns: Panel Pulls up EPFO for Investing in Failing Markets." *Financial Express*. https://www.financialexpress.com/market/

negative-returns-panel-pulls-up-epfo-for-investing-in-falling-market/2111105 / [last access: 27.09.2023].

Reed, Adolph. 2013. "Marx, Race, and Neoliberalism." *New Labor Forum* 22(1): 49–57.

Reed, Larry et al. 2015. *Mapping Pathways out of Poverty. The State of the Microcredit Summit Campaign Report, 2015*. https://www.results.org/wp-content/uploads/SOCR 2015_English_Web.pdf [last access: 27.09.2023].

Reinhard, Wolfgang. 2017. *Die Unterwerfung der Welt. Globalgeschichte der europäischen Expansion 1415 – 2015*. Bonn: Bundeszentrale für politische Bildung.

Rhyne, Elisabeth, and María Otero. 2006. *Microfinance through the Next Decade: Visioning the Who, What, Where, When, and How*. Boston. https://www.microfinancegateway.orga/sites/default/files/mfg-en-paper-microfinance-through-the-next-decade-visioning-the-who-what-where-when-and-how-2006_0.pdf [last access: 27.09.2023].

Robert, Bruce L. 1970. "Agricultural Credit Cooperatives in Madras, 1893–1937." The Indian Economic and Social History Review 16(2): 163–184.

Roberts, Adrienne. 2015. "Gender, Financial Deepening and the Production of Embodied Finance: Towards a Critical Feminist Analysis." *Global Society* 29(1): 107–27.

Roberts, Adrienne. 2016. "Household Debt and the Financialization of Social Reproduction: Theorizing the UK Housing and Hunger Crises." In ed. Susanne Soederberg. Bingley: Emerald, 135–64.

Roberts, Adrienne, and Susanne Soederberg. 2014. "Politicizing Debt and Denaturalizing the 'New Normal.'" *Critical Sociology* 40(5): 657–68.

Robins, Nick. 2012. *The Corporation That Changed the World. How the East India Company Shaped the Modern Multinational*. London: Pluto Press.

Robinson, Cedric J. 2010. *Black Marxism. The Making of the Black Radical Tradition*. Dublin: Penguin Classics.

Robinson, Marguerite S. 2001. *The Microfinance Revolution. Sustainable Finance for the Poor*. Washington, D.C.: World Bank.

Roodman, David. 2012. "Microcredit Doesn't End Poverty, despite All the Hype." *The Washington Post*. https://www.washingtonpost.com/opinions/microcredit-doesnt-end-poverty-despite-all-the-hype/2012/01/20/gIQAtrfqzR_story.html?noredirect=on&utm_term=.fc63b444474c [last access: 27.09.2023].

Ross, Andrew. 2013. "Occupy, Debt, and the Wages of the Future: A Response to Guy Standing." *Public Culture* 25(1): 25–28.

Roy, Ananya. 2010. *Poverty Capital. Microfinance and the Making of Development*. New York: Routledge.

Roy, Animesh. 2023. "From Colonial to Neoliberal Regime: Understanding the Paradigms of Land Dispossession in India." *Journal of Land and Rural Studies* 11(1): 28–51.

Roy, Arundathi. 2014. "The Doctor and the Saint." In *Annihilation of Caste. The Annotated Critical Edition*, ed. S. Anand. New Delhi: Navayana Publishing.

Roy, Arundathi. 2017. *The Ministry of Utmost Happiness*. London: Penguin Books.

Roy, Debraj et al. 2018. "Survey-Based Socio-Economic Data from Slums in Bangalore, India." *Scientific Data* 5: 1–9. http://dx.doi.org/10.1038/sdata.2017.200.

Roy, Indrajit. 2023. "How Welfare Wins: Discursive Institutionalism, the Politics of the Poor, and the Expansion of Social Welfare in India during the Early 21st Century." *Policy and Society*, online first: https://doi.org/10.1093/polsoc/puad010.

Roy, Subir. 2018. *Ujjivan. Transforming with Technology*. New Delhi: Oxford University Press.

Roy, Tirthankar. 2005. Rethinking Economic Change in India: Labour and Livelihood *Rethinking Economic Change in India: Labour and Livelihood*. London and New York: Routledge.

RoyChowdhury, Supriya. 2015. *Bringing Class Back In. Informality in Bangalore*. Socialist Register 2015. Transforming Classes. Eds. Leo Panitch, Greg Albo. London: Merlin Press, 73–92.

RoyChowdhury, Supriya. 2018. "Welfare without Work or Wages A Contradiction?" *Economic and Political Weekly* 53(35): 53–60.

RoyChodhury, Supriya. 2021. *City of Shadows. Slums and Informal Work in Bangalore*. Cambridge: Cambridge University Press.

Rupakula, Ramanamurthy V. 2016. "Class Differentiation and the Crisis of Agrarian Petty Producers in India." *World Review of Political Economy* 7(1): 85–105.

Sa-Dhan. 2016. *The Bharat Microfinance Report 2016*. https://www.sa-dhan.net/wp-content/uploads/2023/05/BMR-2016_c.pdf [last access: 27.09.2023].

Saad-Filho, Alfredo. 1993. "A Review of Marx's Critique of John Gray's Monetary Analysis." *History of Political Economy* 25(1): 65–84.

Saad-Filho, Alfredo. 2010. *Growth , Poverty and Inequality: From Washington Consensus to Inclusive Growth*. https://www.un.org/esa/desa/papers/2010/wp100_2010.pdf [last access: 27.09.2023].

Sachs, J. D., and J. W. McArthur. 2005. "The Millennium Project: A Plan for Meeting the Millennium Development Goals." *Lancet* 365(9456): 347–53.

Sachs, Wolfgang, ed. 2010. *The Development Dictionary. A Guide to Knowledge as Power*. London, New York: ZedBooks.

Saikia, Arupjyoti. 2010. "The Moneylenders and Indebtedness." *Indian Historical Review* 37(1): 63–88.

Sankhe, Shirish et al. 2010. *India's Urban Awakening: Building Inclusive Cities, Sustaining Economic Growth*. https://www.mckinsey.com/featured-insights/urbanization/urban-awakening-in-india [last access: 27.09.2023].

Santiago-Valles, Kelvin. 2005. "Racially Subordinate Labour within Global Contexts: Robinson and Hopkins Re-Examed." *Race and Class* 47(2): 54–70.

Santos, Bouventura de Sousa. 2014. *Epistemologies of the South. Justice against Epistemicide*. London: Routledge.

Dos Santos, Paulo L. 2009. "On the Content of Banking in Contemporary Capitalism." *Historical Materialism* 17(2): 180–213.

Santos, Paulo L, and Ingrid Harvold Kvangraven. 2017. "Better than Cash , but Beware the Costs: Electronic Payments Systems and Financial Inclusion in Developing Economies." *Development and Change* 48(2): 205–27.

Sanyal, Kalyan. 2007. *Rethinking Capitalist Development. Primitive Accumulation, Governmentality & Post-Colonial Capitalism*. New Delhi: Routledge.

Sathi, Sreerekha. 2023. "How Do We Pay Back? Women Health Workers and the COVID-19 Pandemic in India." *Globalizations* 20(2): 292–303.

Sayer, Andrew. 1992. *Method in Social Science: A Realist Approach*. London and New York: Routledge.

Sayer, Andrew. 2000. *Realism and Social Science*. London: SAGE Publications.

Schwarz, Henry. 2010. *Constructing the Criminal Tribe in Colonial India. Acting like a Thief*. Malden: Wiley-Blackwell.

Schwind, Michael, and Uwe Altrock. 2023. "Negotiating Land in Rurban Bengaluru, South India." *Sustainability* 15(3): 1–17.

Scofield, Rupert. 2018. "It's Time To Act On Financial Inclusion For A Sustainable Future." *Forbes*. https://www.forbes.com/sites/forbesnonprofitcouncil/2018/05/14/its-time-to-act-on-financial-inclusion-for-a-sustainable-future/#346e0bd247f1 [last access: 27.09.2023].

Seamster, Louise. 2019. "Black Debt, White Debt." *Contexts* 18(1): 30–35.

Seccombe, Wally. 1974. "The Housewife and Her Labour under Capitalism." *New Left Review* January/Fe: 3–24.

Seibel, Hans Dieter, and Mayumi Ozaki. 2009. *Re-Structuring of State-Owned Financial Institutions. Lessons from Bank Rankyat Indonesia*. Mandaluyong City: Asian Development Bank.

Selwyn, Benjamin. 2017. *The Struggle for Development*. Cambridge: Polity Press.

Selwyn, Benjamin. 2019. "Poverty Chains and Global Capitalism." *Competition and Change* 23(1): 71–97.

Sen, Amartya. 1981. "Ingredients of Famine Analysis: Availability and Entitlements." *The Quarterly Journal of Economics* 96(3): 433–64.

Sen, Suhit K. 2016. "The Politics of Bank Nationalization in India." In *Accumulation in Post-Colonial Capitalism*, Singapore: Springer, 125–45.

Shah, Alpa, and Barbara Harriss-White. 2011. "Resurrecting Scholarship on Agrarian Transformations." *Economic and Political Weekly* XLVI(39): 13–18.

Shah, Alpa, and Jens Lerche. 2020. "Migration and the Invisible Economies of Care: Production, Social Reproduction and Seasonal Migrant Labour in India." *Transactions of the Institute of British Geographers* 45(4): 719–34.

Shah, Anil. 2019. "Luxemburg Meets Schumpeter: Understanding Contemporary Socio-Ecological Conflicts as Processes of Destructive Creation." *Journal für Entwicklungspolitik* 35(1): 41–64.

Shah, Mihir, Rangu Rao, and P. S.Vijay Shankar. 2007. "Rural Credit in 20th Century India: Overview of History and Perspectives." *Economic and Political Weekly* 42(15): 1351–64.

Shahrawat, Renu, and Krishna D. Rao. 2012. "Insured yet Vulnerable: Out-of-Pocket Payments and India's Poor." *Health Policy and Planning* 27(3): 213–21.

Sharma, Atul et al. 2020. "Out-of-Pocket Expenditure on Healthcare among the Urban Poor in India." *Economic & Political Weekly* 45(32 & 33): 49–55.

Sharma, Jayeeta. 2009. "Lazy Natives, Coolie Labour, and the Assam Tea Industry." *Modern Asian Studies* 43(6): 1287–1324.

Shiva, Vandana. 1993. *The Violence of the Green Revolution. Third World Agriculture, Ecology and Politics*. London: ZedBooks.

Shivanand, Swathi, and R Prathiba. 2021. *Forced Resignations, Stealthy Closures*. Research Report. Garment and Textile Workers' Union and Alternative Law Forum. https://media.business-humanrights.org/media/documents/English_GATWU_ALF_Forced-resignations1.pdf [last access: 27.09.2023].

Shrivastava, Aseem. 2016. "A-Meri-India: A Note from the Land of Frustrated Aspirants." *Economic & Political Weekly* 51(29): 75–78.

Shrivastava, Aseem, and Ashish Kothari. 2012. *Churning the Earth. The Making of Global India*. New Delhi: Penguin.

Silver, Beverly. 2014. "Theorising the Working Class in Twenty-First-Century Global Capitalism." In *Workers and Labour in A Glablised Capitalism. Contemporary Themes and Theoretical Issues*, ed. Maurizio Atzeni. London & New York: Palgrave Macmillan, 46–69.

Simmons, Colin. 1985. "'De-Industrialization', Industrialization and the Indian Economy, c.1850-1947." *Modern Asian Studies* 19(3): 593–622.

Simon, Jenny. 2021. "Verbriefung." *PERIPHERIE – Politik, Ökonomie, Kultur* 162–163: 324–27.

Sinclair, Hugh. 2012. "Confessions of a Microfinance Heretic. How Microlending Lost Its Way and Betrayed the Poor."

Singh, Naresh. 2008. "A Critical Review of Self-Help Group – Bank Linkage Programme of Micro-Finance in India Critical Review of The Self-Help Group-Bank Linkage." *Paradigm* 12(1): 50–56.

Singh, Nikhil Pal. 2016. "On Race, Violence, and So-Called Primitive Accumulation." *Social Text* 34(3): 27–50.

Sinha, Pankaj, and Nitin Navin. 2021. "Performance of Self-Help Groups in India." *Economic and Political Weekly* 56(5): 36–43.

Sinha, Shilpy. 2018. "Northern Arc Capital to Raise 1,000 Crore." *Economic Times of India*. https://economictimes.indiatimes.com/markets/stocks/news/n

orthern-arc-capital-to-raise-rs-1000-cr/articleshow/62994583.cms [last access: 27.09.2023].

Skeggs, Beverly. 2022. "Class." In *The SAGE Handbook of Marxism*, eds. Beverley Skeggs, Sara Farris, Alberto Toscano, and Svenja Bromberg. London: Sage, 191–211.

Sobhan, Rehman. 1979. "Politics of Food and Famine in Bangladesh." *Economic & Political Weekly* 14(48): 1973–80.

Soederberg, Susanne. 2005. "The Transnational Debt Architecture and and Punishment The Transnational Debt Architecture and Emerging Markets: The Politics of Paradoxes and Punishment." *Third World Quarterly* 26(6): 927–49.

Soederberg, Susanne. 2012. "The Mexican Debtfare State: Dispossession, Micro-Lending, and the Surplus Population." *Globalizations* 9(4): 561–75.

Soederberg, Susanne. 2013. "Universalising Financial Inclusion and the Securitisation of Development." *Third World Quarterly* 34(4): 593–612.

Soederberg, Susanne. 2015. *Debtfare States and Poverty Industry. Money, Discipline and the Surplus Population*. London: Routledge.

de Soto, Hernando. 2001. *The Mystery of Capital – Why It Works Only in the West*. London: Black Swan.

Sreerekha, M S. 2017. *State Without Honour. Women Workers in India's Anganwadis*. New Delhi: Oxford University Press.

Sridhar, Kala Seetharam, A. Venugopala Reddy, and Pavan Srinath. 2013. "Is It Push or Pull? Recent Evidence from Migration into Bangalore, India." *Journal of International Migration and Integration* 14(2): 287–306.

Sriram, Krupa, Kajol Tanaya Behera, Smita Premchandar, and Dipayan Pal. 2022. "Self-Help Groups: Beyond 3 Decades, Finding a Good Way Forward." In *Inclusive Finance India Report 2022*, ed. N.S. Vishwanathan. New Delhi: Access Development Services, 55–68.

Sriram, M.S. 2018. *Talking Financial Inclusion in Liberalised India. Conversations with Governors of Reserve Bank of India*. Abingdon, New York: Routledge.

Sriram, M. S. 2010. "Commercialisation of Microfinance in India: A Discussion of the Emperor ' s Apparel." *Economic and Political Weekly* xlv(24): 65–74.

Sririam, M. S. 2017. *Inclusive Finance India Report 2016*. New Delhi: SAGE. http://www.inclusivefinanceindia.org/uploads-inclusivefinance/publications/1002-1001-FILE.pdf [last access: 27.09.2023].

Sririam, M.S., and Rajesh S. Upadhyayula. 2004. "The Transformation of the Microfinance Sector in India. Experiences, Options, and Futures." *Journal of Microfinance* 6(2): 89–112.

Srivastava, Ravi. 2018. "Building India Brick by Brick: Labourers in the Construction Industry." *Indian Exclusion Report 2018*. Eds. Centre for Equity Studies. New Delhi: Left Word, 112–136.

Srivastava, Ravi. 2022. "Migration, Informality and the Growing Precarity of Work." *Social Change* 52(4): 449–66.

Srivastava, Ravi 2005. *Bonded Labour in India: Its Incidence and Pattterns*. https://www.ilo.org/wcmsp5/groups/public/---ed_norm/---declaration/documents/publication/wcms_081967.pdf [last access: 27.09.2023].

Srivastava, Ravi, and Rajib Sutradhar. 2016. "Labour Migration to the Construction Sector in India and Its Impact on Rural Poverty." *Indian Journal of Human Development* 10(1): 27–48.

Stein, Peer, Bikki Randhawa, and Nina Bilandzic. 2011. *Toward Universal Access. Addressing the Global Challenge of Financial Inclusion*. Washington, D.C.

Sundar, Nandini. 2011. "At War with Oneself: Constructing Naxalism as India's Biggest Security Threat." *India's Contemporary Security Challenges*: 1–23.

Sundararaman, T., Indranil Mukhopadhyay, and V. R. Muraleedharan. 2016. "No Respite for Public Health." *Economic and Political Weekly* 51(16): 39–42.

Suwandi, Intan. 2019. *Value Chains. The New Economic Imperialism*. New York: Monthly Review Press.

Swamy, Vighneswara. 2014. "Financial Inclusion, Gender Dimension, and Economic Impact on Poor Households." *World Development* 56: 1–15.

SWAN. 2020. *32 Days and Counting. COVID-19 Lockdown, Migrant Workers, and the Inadequacy of Welfare Measures in India*. http://strandedworkers.in/mdocs-posts/32-days-and-counting/ [last access: 27.09.2023].

Symbiotics, and CGAP. 2016. *Microfinance Funds. 10 Years of Research & Practice. A Review and Analysis of CGAP & Symbiotics' Microfinance Investment Vehicles Surveys*. http://symbioticsgroup.com/wp-content/uploads/2016/11/201612-Symbiotics_10yMIV_whitepaper.pdf [last access: 27.09.2023].

Taneja, Anjela, and Amitabha Sarkar. 2023. *First, Do No Harm. Examining the Impact of the IFC's Support to Private Healthcare in India*. Oxfam India. https://www.oxfamindia.org/knowledgehub/workingpaper/first-do-no-harm-examining-impact-ifcs-support-private-healthcare-india [last access: 27.09.2023].

Tankha, Ajay. 2012. *Banking on Self-Help Groups. Twenty Years On*. Los Angels, London, New Delhi, Singapore, Washington DC: SAGE Publications.

Taylor, Keeanga-Yamahtta. 2019. *Race for Profit. How Banks and the Real Estate Industry Undermined Black Homeownership*. Chapel Hill: The University of North Carolina Press.

Taylor, Marcus. 2005. "Opening the World Bank: International Organisations and the Contradictions of Global Capitalism." *Historical Materialism* 13(1): 153–70.

Taylor, Marcus. 2011. "'Freedom from Poverty Is Not for Free': Rural Development and the Microfinance Crisis in Andhra Pradesh, India." *Journal of Agrarian Change* 11(4): 484–504.

Taylor, Marcus. 2012. "The Antinomies of 'Financial Inclusion': Debt, Distress and the Workings of Indian Microfinance." *Journal of Agrarian Change* 12(4): 601–10.

Taylor, Marcus. 2013. "Liquid Debts: Credit, Groundwater and the Social Ecology of Agrarian Distress in Andhra Pradesh, India." *Third World Quarterly* 34(4): 691–709.

TED. 2021. "Financial Inclusion, the Digital Divide and the Future of Money, Whitney Pennington Rodgers Interviews Ajay Banga." https://www.youtube.com/watch?v=znwzw7kkmEo [last access: 27.09.2023].

Teltumbe, Anand. 2010. *The Persistence of Caste. The Kairlanji Murders & India's Hidden Apartheid*. London and New York: ZedBooks.

Teltumbe, Anand. 2018. *Republic of Caste. Thinking Equality in the Time of Neoliberal Hindutva*. New Delhi: Navayana Publishing.

Temper, Leah et al. 2018. "Ecological Distribution Conflicts as Forces for Sustainability: The Global Atlas of Environmental Justice." *Sustainability Science* 13(3): 573–84.

Temper, Leah, Daniela del Bene, and Joan Martinez-Alier. 2015. "Environmental Justice Atlas." www.ejatlas.org. [last access: 27.09.2023].

The Economic Times. 2015. "EPFO to Invest Nearly 5,000 Crore in Stocks in 2015–16." https://economictimes.indiatimes.com/industry/banking/finance/epfo-to-invest-nearly-rs-5000-crore-in-stocks-in-2015-16/articleshow/48375783.cms [last access: 27.09.2023].

The White House. 2023. "President Biden Announces U.S. Nomination of Ajay Banga to Lead World Bank." https://www.whitehouse.gov/briefing-room/statements-releases/2023/02/23/president-biden-announces-u-s-nomination-of-ajay-banga-to-lead-world-bank/ [last access: 27.09.2023].

Tilley, Lisa. 2020. "Extractive Investibility in Historical Colonial Perspective: The Emerging Market and Its Antecedents in Indonesia." *Review of International Political Economy* 28(5): 1099–1118.

Toissant, Eric. 2023. *The World Bank. A Critical History*. London: Pluto Press.

Tolzmann, Molly. 2022. *CGAP Funder Survey 202.0 Trends in International Funding for Financial Inclusion*. Washington. https://www.cgap.org/sites/default/files/publications/2022_01_Focus_Note_2020_Funder_Survey.pdf. [last access: 27.09.2023].

Torkelson, Erin. 2021. "Sophia's Choice: Debt, Social Welfare, and Racial Finance Capitalism." *Environment and Planning D: Society and Space* 39(1): 67–84.

Torri, Michelguglielmo. 1975. "Factional Politics and Economic Policy: The Case of India's Bank Nationalization." *Asian Survey* 15(12): 1077–96.

Toyama, Kentaro. 2011. "Lies, Hype and Profit: The Truth about Microfinance." *The Atlantic*. https://www.theatlantic.com/business/archive/2011/01/lies-hype-and-profit-the-truth-about-microfinance/70405/ [last access: 27.09.2023].

Unger, Corinna R. 2018. "The Decolonization of Development: Rural Development in India Before and After 1947." *Internationalism, Imperialism and the Formation of the Contemporary World*. Eds. Miguel Bandeira Jerónimo, José Pedro Monteiro. Cham: Palgrave Macmillan, 253–78.

United Nations. 2003. *Monterrey Consensus on Financing for Development*. https://www.un.org/esa/ffd/wp-content/uploads/2014/09/MonterreyConsensus.pdf [last access: 27.09.2023].

United Nations. 2006. *Building Inclusive Financial Sectors for Development*. New York: United Nations.

United Nations. 2015a. *Addis Ababa Action Agenda of the Third International Conference on Financing for Development*. New York.

United Nations. 2015b. Resolution *Transforming Our World: The 2030 Agenda for Sustainable Development*. https://www.un.org/ga/search/view_doc.asp?symbol=A/RES/70/1&Lang=E [last access: 27.09.2023].

Upadhya, Carol, and Deeksha M Rao. 2022. "Dispossession without Displacement: Producing Property through Slum Redevelopment in Bengaluru, India." *Environment and Planning A: Economy and Space* 55(2).

Upadhya, Carol, and Sachinkumar Rathod. 2021. "Caste at the City's Edge: Land Struggles in Peri-Urban Bengaluru." *South Asia Multidisciplinary Academic Journal* (26): 0–28.

Vaidyanathan, A. 2013. "Future of Cooperatives in India." *Economic and Political Weekly* 48(18): 30–34.

Vakulabharanam, Vamsi. 2010. "Does Class Matter? Class Structure and Worsening Inequality in India." *Economic and Political Weekly* 45(29): 67–76.

Varma, Nitin. 2017. *Coolies of Capitalism. Assam Tea and the Making of Coolie Labour*. Berlin and Boston: de Gruyter.

Vasavi, A. R. 2020. "The Tiger and the Tube Well: Malevolence in Rural India." *Critical Asian Studies* 52(3): 429–45.

Vasavi, A.R. 2009. "Suicides and the Making of India's Agrarian Distress." *South African Review of Sociology* 40(1): 94–108.

Vasavi, A R. 2014. "Debt and Its Social Entrapments." *WSQ: Women's Studies Quarterly* 42(1&2): 23–37.

Vasudevan, Ramaa. 2019. "Money, Power, and Capitalism: Marx's Theory of Money and the Contemporary State-Credit Standard." In *Karl Marx's Life, Ideas, and Influences. A Critical Examination on the Bicentenary*, eds. Shaibal Gupta, Marcello Musto, and Babak Amini. Palgrave Macmillan.

Venegas, Kristan M, and Adrian H. Huerta. 2012. "Urban Ethnography. Approaches, Perspectives and Challenges." In *New Approaches to Qualitative Research. Wisdom and Uncertainty*, London and New York: Routledge, 154–61.

Verghese, Ajay. 2016. "British Rule and Tribal Revolts in India: The Curious Case of Bastar." *Modern Asian Studies* 50(5): 1619–44.

Viola, Deborah, Qiuhu Shi, and Padmini Murthy. 2013. "Health Care for Women International Microfinance Safety Net: Back to Basics." *Health Care for Women International* 34(11): 1005–14.

Virdee, Satnam. 2019. “Racialized Capitalism: An Account of Its Contested Origins and Consolidation.” *Sociological Review* 67(1): 3–27.

Virdee, Satnam. 2023. “Racism and State Formation in the Age of Absolutism.” *Historical Materialism* 31(2): 104–35.

Vogel, Lise. 2013. *Marxism and the Oppression of Women. Toward a Unitary Theory*. Leiden and Boston: Brill.

Wade, Robert H. 2011. “Emerging World Order? From Multipolarity to Multilateralism in the G20 , the World Bank , and the IMF.” *Politics & Society* 39(3): 347–78.

Wadhawan, Neha. 2013. “Living in Domesti-City: Women and Migration for Domestic Work from Jharkhand.” *Economic and Political Weekly* 48(43): 47–54.

Walby, Sylvia. 2005. “Introduction: Comparative Gender Mainstreaming in a Global Era.” *International Feminist Journal of Politics* 7(4): 453–70.

Walia, Harsha. 2021. *Border and Rule. Global Migration, Capitalism, and the Rise of Racist Nationalism*. Chicago: Haymarket Books.

Wang, Jackie. 2018. *Caraceral Capitalism*. South Pasadena: semiotext(e).

Warner, H. William. 2020. “The Kabuliwalas: Afghan Moneylending and the Credit Cosmopolis of British India, c. 1880–1947.” *Indian Economic and Social History Review* 57(2): 171–98.

Washbrook, David. 1994. “The Commercialization of Agriculture in Colonial India: Production, Subsistence and Reproduction in the ‘Dry South’, c. 1870–1930.” *Modern Asian Studies* 28(1): 129–64.

Washbrook, David. 2007. “India in the Early Modern World Economy: Modes of Production, Reproduction and Exchange.” *Journal of Global History* 2(1): 87–111.

Weber, Heloise. 2014. “Global Politics of Microfinancing Poverty in Asia: The Case of Bangladesh Unpacked.” 38(4): 544–563.

Webster, Edward. 2011. “Organizing in the Informal Economy: Ela Bhatt and the Self-Employed Women’s Association of India.” *Labour, Capital and Society* 44(1): 98–125.

Werner, Richard A. 2014. “Can Banks Individually Create Money out of Nothing? – The Theories and the Empirical Evidence.” *International Review of Financial Analysis* 36(C): 1–19.

Wichterich, Christa. 2012. “The Other Financial Crisis: Growth and Crash of the Microfinance Sector in India.” *Development* 55(3): 406–12.

Wichterich, Christa. 2017. “Microcredits, Returns and Gender: Of Reliable Poor Women and Financial Inclusion in South Asia.” In *Work, Institutions and Sustainable Livelihoods*, , 275–301.

Wichterich, Christa. 2019. “Gender-Based Violence of Economic Globalisation in Contemporary India. An Intersectional Approach to Gender and Violence.” In *Gender and Violence in Historical and Contemporary Perspectives*, eds. Jyoti Atwal and Iris Flessenkämpfer. Routledge, 200–216.

Williams, Michelle. 2014. "Rethinking the Development State in the Twenty-First Century." In *The End of the Development State?*, ed. Michelle Williams. London and New York: Routledge, 1–29.

Wilson, Kalpana. 2012. *Race, Racism and Development. Interrogating History, Discourse and Practice*. London: ZedBooks.

World Bank. 2001. *World Development Report 2000/2001: Attacking Poverty*. Oxofrd: Oxford University Press.

World Bank. 2008. *Finance for All? Policies and Pitfalls in Expanding Access*. Washington, D.C.: The World Bank.

World Bank. 2011. "The National Rural Livelihoods Project." https://www.worldbank.org/en/news/feature/2011/07/05/the-national-rural-livelihoods-project [last access: 27.09.2023].

World Bank. 2014. *Global Financial Development Report: Financial Inclusion*. Washington, D.C.: The World Bank.

World Bank. 2017. *Maximizing Finance for Development: Leveraging the Private Sector for Growth and Sustainable Development*. https://www.devcommittee.org/content/dam/sites/devcommittee/doc/documents/mgr/DC2017-0009_Maximizing_8-19.pdf [last access: 27.09.2023].

World Bank. 2022. *World Development Report 2022. Financing for an Equity Recovery*. Washington, D.C.: The World Bank. https://www.worldbank.org/en/publication/wdr2022 [last access: 27.09.2023].

World Bank. 2024. *Pathways out of the Polycrisis. Poverty, Property, and Planet Report*. Washington, D.C. https://www.worldbank.org/en/publication/poverty-prosperity-and-planet [last access: 31.01.2025].

World Economic Forum. 2015. *The Future of Urban Development & Services: Urban Development Recommendations for the Government of India*. https://www3.weforum.org/docs/WEF_The_Future_of_Urban_Development_Services_report_2015.pdf [last access: 27.09.2023].

World Health Organization. 2022. *Global Spending on Health*. https://www.who.int/publications/i/item/9789240017788 [last access: 27.09.2023].

Wullweber, Joscha. 2019. "Money, State, Hegemony: A Political Ontology of Money." *New Political Science* 41(2): 313–28.

Yang, Anand A. 2007. "Bandits and Kings: Moral Authority and Resistance in Early Colonial India." *The Journal of Asian Studies* 66(4): 881–96.

Yengde, Suraj. 2019. *Caste Matters*. Haryana: Viking.

Young, Stephen. 2010a. "Gender, Mobility and the Financialisation of Development." *Geopolitics* 15(3): 606–27.

Young, Stephen. 2010b. "The 'Moral Hazards' of Microfinance: Restructuring Rural Credit in India." 42(1): 201–23.

Yunus, Muhammad. 2007. *Creating a World Without Poverty. Social Business and the Future of Capitalism*. New York: Public Affairs.

Yunus, Muhammad. 2010. *Building Social Business: The New Kind of Capitalism That Serves Humanity's Most Pressing Needs*. New York: Public Affairs.

Yunus, Muhammad. 2011. "Sacrificing Microcredit for Megaprofits." *New York Times*. https://www.nytimes.com/2011/01/15/opinion/15yunus.html?rref=collection%2Ftimestopic%2FMicrofinance [last access: 27.09.2023].

Yunus, Muhammad, and Alan Jolis. 1998. *Banker to the Poor. The Autobiography of Muhammad Yunus, Founder of the Grameen Bank*. London: Aurum Press.

Zeuske, Michael. 2017. "Coolies – Asiáticos and Chinos: Global Dimensions of Secondary Slavery." In *Bonded Labour. Global and Comparative Perspectives (18th – 21st Century)*, eds. Sabine Damir-Geilsdorf et al. Bielefeld: Transcript, 35–58.

Ziai, Aram. 2016. *Development Discourse and Global History. From Colonialism to the Sustainable Development Goals*. London & New York: Routledge.

Zoomers, Annelies et al. 2017. "The Rush for Land in an Urbanizing World: From Land Grabbing Toward Developing Safe, Resilient, and Sustainable Cities and Landscapes." *World Development* 92: 242–52.

Zulfiqar, Ghazal. 2017. "Does Microfinance Enhance Gender Equity in Access to Finance? Evidence from Pakistan." *Feminist Economics* 23(1): 160–85.

Appendix

List of Interviews

Household Interviews

HH_Cluster_1 (Area: Doddabalapura/Devanahalli, Bengaluru Rural District)

1. Cultivator, Grandrajpura, male, 08.02.2018.
2. Cultivator and agricultural labourer, Gandrajpura, male, 08.02.2018.
3. Cultivator (and animal husbandry), male, Sothenahalli, 08.02.2018.
4. Cultivator, male, Sothenahalli, 08.02.2018.
5. Cultivator and agricultural labourer, female, Sothenahalli, 08.02.2018.
6. Cultivator (and animal husbandry), male, Venkatapura, 08.02.2018.
7. Cultivator, male, Venkatapura, 08.02.2018.
8. Agricultural labourer, male, Bettenahalli, 09.02.2018.
9. Cultivator (and animal husbandry), female, Bettenahalli, 09.02.2018.
10. Cultivator (and animal husbandry), male, Bettenahalli, 09.02.2018.
11. Cultivator (and animal husbandry), male, 09.02.2018.
12. Construction worker, male, Bettahalsur, 09.02.2018.
13. Construction worker, male, Bettahalsur, 09.02.2018.
14. Shop owner, female, Bettahalsur, 09.02.2018.
15. Wage Labourer (Plummer), male, Bettahalsur, 09.02.2018.
16. Construction worker, female, Bettahalsur, 09.02.2018.
17. Animal husbandry and wage labourer, male, Venkatala, 09.02.2018.
18. Garment worker, female, Venkatala, 09.02.2018.
19. Wage Labourer (Carpenter), male, Venkatala, 09.02.2018.
20. Auto driver, male, Venkatala, 09.02.2018.

HH_Cluster_2 (Area: Hosakote, Bengaluru Rural District)

21. Auto driver, male, Poojena Agrahara, 14.02.2018.
22. Agricultural daily wage labourer, male, Poojena, Agrahara, 14.02.2018.
23. Cultivator and Animal Husbandry, female, Poojena, Agrahara, 14.02.2018.

24. Three Construction workers, male, Poojena, Agrahara,14.02.2018.
25. Domestic worker, female, Poojena, Agrahara, 14.02.2018.
26. Construction worker, female, Poojena Agrahara, 14.02.2018.
27. Agriculutral daily wage labourer, male, Poojena Agrahara, 14.02.2018.
28. Factory workers, male, Poojena Agrahara, 14.02.2018.
29. Cultivator, male, Poojena Agrahara, 14.02.2018.
30. Kiosk owner, female, Poojena Agrahara, 14.02.2018.

HH_Cluster_3 (Area: Nelamangla, Bengalurur Rural District)

31. Construction worker, female, Dasanapura, 04.03.2018.
32. Construction worker, female, Dasanapura, 04.03.2018.
33. Sanitation worker, male, Avalahalli, 04.03.2018.
34. Three agricultural daily wage labourers, men, Avalahalli, 04.03.2018.
35. Agricultural daily wage labourer, female, Avalahalli, 04.03.2018.
36. Factory worker, male, Malatahalli, 04.03.2018.
37. Two agricultural daily wage labourers, female, Malatahalli, 04.03.2018.
38. Factory worker, female, Malatahalli, 04.03.2018.

HH_Cluster_4 (Area: Yelahanka, Bengaluru Urban)

39. Agricultural daily wage labourer, female, Yelahanka, 05.03.2018.
40. Cultivators, female and male, Yelahanka, 05.03.2018.
41. Construction worker, female, Yelahanka, 05.03.2018.
42. Two construction workers, male and female, Yelahanka, 05.03.2018.
43. Agricultural daily wage labourer, Yelahanka, 05.03.2018.
44. Domestic worker, female, Yelahanka, 05.03.2018.
45. Kiosk owner, female, Yelahanka, 05.03.2018.
46. Brick kiln worker, female, Yelahanka, 05.03.2018.
47. Tailor, male, Sonnapanahalli, 05.03.2018.
48. Domestic worker, female, Sonnapanahalli, 05.03.2018.

HH_Cluster_5 (Area: Doddabommasandra/Kodigahalli, Bengaluru Urban)

49. Construction worker, female, Kodigahalli Moor, 06.03.2019.
50. Construction worker, female, Kodigahalli Moor, 06.03.2019.
51. Construction worker, male, Kodigahalli Moor, 06.03.2019.
52. Domestic worker, female, Kodigahalli Moor, 06.03.2019.
53. Construction worker, female, Kodigahalli Moor, 06.03.2019.

54. Domestic worker, female, Kodigahalli Moor, 06.03.2019.
55. Construction worker, female, Kodigahalli Moor, 06.03.2019.
56. Construction worker, female, Kodigahalli Moor, 06.03.2019.
57. Construction worker, female, Kodigahalli Moor, 06.03.2019.
58. Petty entrepreneur (knife whetting), Kodigahalli, 06.03.2019.
59. Construction worker, female, Kodigahalli, 06.03.2019.
60. Domestic worker, female, Kodigahalli, 06.03.2019.
61. Construction worker, female, Kodigahalli, 06.03.2019.

HH_Cluster_6 (Area: Krishnarajapura/Seetarampalya, Bengaluru Urban)

62. Construction worker, female, Krishnarajapuram, 13.03.2019.
63. Construction worker, female, Krishnarajapuram, 13.03.2019.
64. Domestic worker, female, Krishnarajapuram, 13.03.2019.
65. Construction worker, female, Krishnarajapuram, 13.03.2019.
66. Construction worker, female, Seetarampalya, 14.03.2019.
67. Construction worker, female, Seetarampalya, 14.03.2019.
68. Domestic worker, female, Seetarampalya, 14.03.2019.

Microfinance Institutions (MFIs)

1. Ujjivan SFB Branch Manager, male, Kodigahalli, 06.03.2019.
2. Ujjivan SFB Branch Manager, male, Whitefield, 07.03.2019.
3. Janalakshmi Financial Services/Jana SFB Headquarters, Manager, male, 02.03.2018.
4. NABFINS, Managing Director, male, 01.03.2018.
5. Samasta Microfinance, Managing Director, male, 20.02.2018.

Reserve Bank of India (RBI)

1. Economic and Policy Research Department, RBI Mumbai, female, 18.03.2019.
2. Financial Inclusion and Development Department, RBI Mumbai, female, 20.03.2019.
3. Monetary Policy Department, RBI Mumbai, male, 20.03.2019.
4. Financial Inclusion and Development Department, RBI Bengaluru, male, 11.03.2019.

5. Department of Non-Banking Supervision, RBI Bengaluru, male, 12.03.2019.

Civil Society Actors (CSA), including Academics

1. Association for Promoting Social Action (APSA), male, 28.03.2019.
2. NGO Consultant focused on Garment Workers, female, via Skype, 28.10.2019.
3. CIVIDEP India, female, 13.03.2019.
4. Foundation for Educational Innovations in Asia (FEDINA), female, 28.03.2019.
5. Garment Labour Union (GLU), female, 27.03.2019.
6. Domestic Workers Rights Union (DWRU), female, 27.03.2019.
7. Mysore Resettlement and Development Agency (MYRADA), male, 25.03.2019.
8. Professor working on microfinance, Institute for Social and Economic Change (ISEC), Bengaluru, male, 11.03.2019.
9. Professor working on informal sector workers, Institute for Social and Economic Change (ISEC), Bengaluru, female, 05.03.2019.
10. Economic Journalist, Business Standard, male, via Phone, 12.03.2019.
11. Professor working on microfinance, male, Indian Institute of Management (IIM), Bengaluru, via Skype, 12.04.2019.

Anil Shah (Dr. rer. pol.), born in 1989, is a lecturer in global political economy at the University of Kassel and a research associate at the chair for development and postcolonial studies. His PhD project emerged from a collaboration between the University of Kassel and the Institute for Social and Economic Change in Bengaluru, India.

GPSR Authorized Representative: Easy Access System Europe, Mustamäe tee 50, 10621 Tallinn, Estonia, gpsr.requests@easproject.com

www.ingramcontent.com/pod-product-compliance
Lightning Source LLC
Jackson TN
JSHW071108030126
96391JS00012B/414
* 9 7 8 3 8 3 7 6 8 0 6 4 5 *